U-BOAT
DESTROYE

U-BOATS DESTROYED

GERMAN SUBMARINE LOSSES IN THE WORLD WARS

Paul Kemp

ARMS & ARMOUR

ARMS & ARMOUR
An imprint of Cassell & Co
Wellington House, 125 Strand, London WC2R 0BB

First published 1997
This edition 1999

British Library Cataloguing-in-Publication data:
A catalogue record for this book is available from the British library

ISBN 1-85409-515-3

Distributed in the USA by Sterling Publishing Co. Inc.,
387 Park Avenue South, New York, NY 10016-8810

Edited and designed by Roger Chesneau/DAG Publications Ltd

Printed and bound in Great Britain by
MPG Books Ltd, Bodmin, Cornwall

Contents

Preface

'German U-boats are not sunk—they are destroyed!' is what Winston Churchill is alleged to have said to a midshipman in HMS *Prince of Wales*. The midshipman in question had the temerity to ask the Prime Minister whether a U-boat whose position was marked on the map had been sunk. Churchill's vehemence reflected his concern with the threat posed to Britain's survival by Germany's U-boats. In two World Wars they had sought, by attacking Britain's vital overseas trade, to starve the country into surrender.

A quarter of a century and a technological revolution separate the Armistice in 1918 and surrender in 1945, yet there are many similarities in the anti-submarine campaigns used in both world wars. In the early years of both wars, successful anti-submarine actions took place largely on the surface. The U-boat was either spotted on the surface or blown to the surface, engaged with gunfire or rammed and sunk. As technology developed, escorts acquired the capability to detect, attack and destroy a submerged submarine. Reports of such actions become highly technical documents, devoid of much human interest. The sure guarantee of a kill in such circumstances was the grim detritus floating on the water after a successful attack; 'I don't know what it is but the surgeon says it was human', was the comment made by the CO of sloop after wreckage had been recovered from the water. The cases of *UC49* sunk on 8 August 1918 and *U327* sunk on 27 February 1945 show how far anti-submarine techniques developed along parallel paths in both world wars. Both were detected by hydrophones or asdic and both were depth-charged to destruction while dived. The wrecks of both were subsequently plastered with more depth charges in order to break them open and release debris to the surface as confirmation that the boat was sunk.

In the First World War geography, the possession of the choke points (Dover Strait, Strait of Otranto, the UK–Shetlands–Norway gap), through which U-boats had to pass to reach their patrol areas, gave the *Entente* powers a huge advantage in sinking U-boats. By the end of the war the U-boats were being steadily and relentlessly blockaded in their bases by massive minelaying and the construction of fixed defences. Thus the U-boats, though not beaten, were controlled. In the Second World War it was a different matter. Even as Soviet armour gathered for the final attack on Berlin, the U-boats were poised to launch a new offensive from their Norwegian bases with new fast, deep-diving submarines to which the Allies possessed no reliable counter other than the deployment of anti-submarine forces on a massive scale. At the end of the war there were twenty-five U-boats in British coastal waters which were tying down 400 ships and 800 aircraft. These led the Official Historian to conclude that 'We never gained a firm and final mastery over the U-boats'. He was subsequently required to retract this conclusion in favour of something more optimistic in order that the newly re-armed *Bundeswehr* should be in no doubt over their defeat in 1945.

This book is a record of the 178 U-boats sunk in the First World War and the 784 sunk or destroyed in the Second World War. It does not include boats scuttled or damaged after the Armistice in 1918 or the surrender in 1945. Neither does it include peacetime accidents. Amassing data on these sinkings has been no easy task, and in no sense can some of this research be considered to be the last word on the subject. Studies in this field will continue and some U-boat losses for which there is little or no data will be revised.

The book is also a record of a casualty rate on a massive scale. German COs of the Flanders Flotilla painted eyes on their boats' bows to help guide them through the minefields, and with good reason—over 5,400 officers and men died in U-boats between 1914 and 1918, nearly 30 per cent of the total U-boat forces. This may be a trifling figure compared to the bloodletting on the Western Front, but it is a significant one none-theless. In the Second World War the figures are more startling: 27,491 officers and men were killed at sea—six times the casualty rate of the First World War. No other military or naval force suffered casualties on such as scale as did the *U-bootWaffe*. The names of all those for whom there is no grave but the sea are recorded on the U-boat memorial at Kiel.

I am deeply grateful to the individuals and institutions who have helped with the research for this book: Dick Boyle; Horst Bredow of the *U-boot Archiv*; Gus Britton of the Royal Navy Submarine Museum; Colin Bruce and Allison Duffield of the Department of Printed Books at the Imperial War Museum; the late Commander J. R. H. Bull RN; my long-suffering editor Roger Chesneau; David Gibbons and Tony Evans at DAG; the very helpful staff at Kent County Council Central Lending Library; David Lees; Lloyds Bank (for keeping their nerve); Jane Middleton, for allowing me access to her grandfather's unique Q-ship archive; the Naval Historical Branch; Guy Robbins of the National Maritime Museum; Vice-Admiral Sir John Roxburgh; the Public Record Office; and the US Navy Historical Center. A Gold Star goes to my daughter Sophie who demonstrated her newly acquired literacy skills by reading out a long list of U-boat numbers. Any errors in that direction can be laid firmly at her door. Lastly, as ever, I am deeply grateful to my wife Kitty, who has been tremendously supportive throughout the writing of this book.

Paul Kemp

1914

Note: U-boats of the Imperial and Royal Austro-Hungarian Navies are distinguished by having their designations in roman numerals.

U15	*Launched*	*Commissioned*
	18 Sept 1911	7 Jul 1912
Type	U13	
CO	*Kapitänleutnant* R. Pohle (lost)	
Date of loss	9 Aug 1914	
Location	North Sea, Fair Isle	
Cause	Ramming	
Casualties	23	
Survivors	None	
Salvaged	No	

Notes The cruiser HMS *Birmingham* sighted the submarine lying on the surface in thick fog. The submarine was stopped and the sounds of hammering from within indicated that some kind of extemporary maintenance was in progress. As the submarine got under way, *Birmingham* rammed her at full speed. Two large pieces of wreckage came to the surface but no survivors.

U13	*Launched*	*Commissioned*
	16 Dec 1910	25 Apr 1912
Type	U13	
CO	*Kapitänleutnant Graf* A. von Schweinitz (lost)	
Date of loss	12 August 1914	
Location	Heligoland Bight	
Cause	Mine (?)	
Casualties	23	
Survivors	None	
Salvaged	No	

Notes *U13* had left Heligoland on 6 August and was not heard from again. She may have been mined on the German defensive minefield in the Heligoland Bight or she may have been the victim of an accident arising from mechanical or drill failure.

U18	*Launched*	*Commissioned*
	25 Apr 1912	7 Nov 1912
Type	U17	
CO	*Kapitänleutnant* Heinrich von Hennig (survived)	
Date of loss	23 November 1914	
Location	Scapa Flow, Pentland Firth	
Cause	Ramming	
Casualties	1	
Survivors	22	
Salvaged	No	

Notes *U18* had tried to enter the base at Scapa Flow in the Orkney Islands. However, Hennig was not to know that the U-boat scare had driven the Grand Fleet away to a number of dispersed anchorages on the west coast of Scotland and Ireland, and that the great Flow was practically empty. He followed a steamer as far as the Hoxa Boom but, finding no targets, abandoned the attempt and headed south toward Cromarty. Shortly after midday *U18*'s periscope was sighted by a vigilant trawler and there was a general hue and cry. The trawler *Dorothy Grey* was able to ram the periscope, thus blinding the U-boat. *U18* began an hour of seesawing between the bottom and the surface, where she was rammed again, this time by the destroyer *Garry*. *U18* disappeared and went down to 250ft before her crew were able to bring her to the surface. Von Henning ordered the submarine to be scuttled and the survivors were taken off by the *Garry*. Compare this sinking with that of *UB116* (q.v.)—which was also sunk trying to enter Scapa Flow—as an illustration of how anti-submarine techniques changed over the next four years.

U11	*Launched*	*Commissioned*
	2 Apr 1910	21 Sept 1910
Type	U9	
CO	*Kapitänleutnant* F. von Suchodoletz (lost)	

Date of loss	c. 9 December 1914
Location	Belgian coast
Cause	Mine (?)
Casualties	29
Survivors	None
Salvaged	No

Notes Possibly mined just north of Zeebrugge. However, the possibility that the submarine was lost by accident arising from mechanical or drill failure cannot be ignored.

	Launched	*Commissioned*
U5	8 Jan 1910	2 July 1910
Type	U5	
CO	*Kapitänleutnant* J. Lemmer (lost)	
Date of loss	c. 18 December 1914	
Location	Belgian coast	
Cause	Mine	
Casualties	29	
Survivors	None	
Salvaged	Raised and broken up	

Notes Possibly mined just north of Zeebrugge. However the possibility that the submarine was lost by accident arising from mechanical or drill failure cannot be ignored.

1915

U31

	Launched	Commissioned
U31	7 Jan 1914	18 Sept 1914
Type	U31	
CO	*Oberleutnant zur See* Wachendorf (lost)	
Date of loss	January 1915	
Location	E coast of England	
Cause	?	
Casualties	31	
Survivors	None	
Salvaged	No	

Notes Possibly mined off the east coast of England. The rumour that she was found on the surface with her crew all dead inside is completely false. However the possibility that the submarine was lost by accident arising from mechanical or drill failure cannot be ignored.

U7

	Launched	Commissioned
U7	28 July 1910	18 July 1911
Type	U5	
CO	*Kapitänleutnant* Georg Koenig (lost)	
Date of loss	21 January 1915	
Location	Dutch coast	
Cause	Submarine attack	
Casualties	26	
Survivors	1	
Salvaged	No	

Notes The first submarine to be sunk by another of her own side. *U7* had inadvertently moved out of her patrol area into that occupied by *U22* (*Kapitänleutnant* Bruno Hoppe). In poor visibility *U22* sighted *U7* and offered one challenge, but when no reply was received assumed that the latter submarine was British, dived and fired one torpedo. It was only when the sole survivor was plucked from the oily water that the identity of the target was discovered.

U8

	Launched	Commissioned
U8	14 Mar 1911	18 Jun 1911
Type	U5	
CO	*Kapitänleutnant* Alfred Stoss (survived)	
Date of loss	4 March 1915	
Location	Strait of Dover	
Cause	Explosive sweep towed by destroyer	
Casualties	?	
Survivors	?	
Salvaged	No	

Notes *U8* was a victim of a newly laid indicator net barrage across the Strait of Dover. On 4 March she was passing westwards through the Strait when she ran into the nets. Her attempts to get clear attracted the attentions of the drifter *Robur*, which called up the destroyer patrol. The destroyer *Gurkha* lowered an explosive sweep and when the line snagged on an underwater obstruction the charge was fired. Every lamp in the U-boat was smashed, rivets were started in many places in the pressure hull and the boat began to take on water; the main switchboard caught fire and both motors broke down. Stoss ordered the submarine to the surface, where she was abandoned, though not before *Gurkha* and *Maori* had opened a hot fire on her. That evening Stoss and his officers were invited to dinner with British officers in the depot ship *Arrogant*, where they were asked, doubtless after the port had gone round the table once or twice, to sing the famous 'Hymn of Hate' against England. Such was the spirit of war in 1915!

U12

	Launched	Commissioned
U12	6 May 1910	25 Apr 1912
Type	U9	
CO	*Kapitänleutnant* Kratzsch (lost)	
Date of loss	10 March 1915	
Location	North Sea, off Fife Ness	

Cause	Ramming/gunfire
Casualties	20
Survivors	2 officers, 8 ratings
Salvaged	No

Notes *U12* had left Heligoland on 4 March to attack shipping off the east coast of England. On the morning of the 10th a trawler sighted a U-boat off Fife Ness and three destroyers were dispatched to the location. Within an hour they sighted a surfaced U-boat which promptly began to dive on being shelled. The destroyer *Ariel* managed ram the conning tower as the U-boat went down and at least one hit with a shell was scored on the conning tower. Kratzsch brought the boat back to the surface. She was hit again in the conning tower and Kratzsch was killed. The crew now set the scuttling charges and abandoned the submarine, but she sank so quickly that only ten men were picked up.

U29	*Launched*	*Commissioned*
	13 Oct 1913	1 Aug 1914
Type	U27	
CO	*Kapitänleutnant* Otto Weddigen	
Date of loss	10 March 1915	
Location	Pentland Firth, 58°20'N 00°57'E	
Cause	Ramming	
Casualties	32	
Survivors	None	
Salvaged	No	

Notes *U29* was on patrol in the waters between the tip of Scotland and the Orkney Islands when she encountered the entire British Grand Fleet at sea. Weddigen fired at the battleship HMS *Neptune* but missed and was evidently so engrossed in the attack that he was not aware of the battleship HMS *Dreadnought* approaching behind him. *Dreadnought* spotted the submarine's periscope and turned into to ram at full speed. The submarine was thrown to the surface before sinking and the number 'U-29' painted on her bow was clearly visible before she sank. Otto Weddigen had achieved fame while in command of *U9* when he torpedoed the British cruisers *Cressy*, *Hogue* and *Aboukir* on 22 September 1914.

U37	*Launched*	*Commissioned*
	25 Aug 1914	9 Dec 1914
Type	U31	
CO	*Kapitänleutnant* E. Wilke (lost)	
Date of loss	April 1915	
Location	E Strait of Dover	
Cause	?	
Casualties	32	
Survivors	None	
Salvaged	No	

Notes Possibly mined off Zeebrugge. However, the possibility that the submarine was lost by accident arising from mechanical or drill failure cannot be ignored.

UB3	*Launched*	*Commissioned*
	5 Mar 1915	14 Mar 1915
Type	UB1	
CO	*Oberleutnant zur See* S. Schmidt (lost)	
Date of loss	May 1915	
Location	Aegean	
Cause	?	
Casualties	14	
Survivors	None	
Salvaged	No	

Notes The first German U-boat to be lost in the Mediterranean. The possibility that *U37* was lost by accident as a result of drill or mechanical failure cannot be ruled out.

U14	*Launched*	*Commissioned*
	11 Jul 1913	25 Apr 1912
Type	U13	
CO	*Oberleutnant zur See* M. Hammerle (lost)	
Date of loss	5 June 1915	
Location	North Sea, off Peterhead,	
Cause	Gunfire	
Casualties	1	
Survivors	6 officers, 21 ratings	
Salvaged	No	

Notes *U14* approached the trawler *Oceanic II* off Peterhead with the intention of sinking her by gunfire. However, the Admiralty, alarmed at the depredations U-boats were making in the trawler fleet, were arming some of the trawlers for self-defence. *Oceanic II* returned fire and Hammerle tried to escape by diving. An error in the diving drill meant that the forward tanks were not flooded and *U14* remained above the surface as *Oceanic II*, now joined by another trawler, moved in. A succession of shells struck the bow and *U14* sank.

U40

	Launched	*Commissioned*
U40	22 Oct 1914	14 Feb 1915

Type U31
CO *Kapitänleutnant* Gerhard Furbringer (survived)
Date of loss 23 June 1915
Location North Sea, off Aberdeen
Cause Submarine attack
Casualties 29
Survivors 3
Salvaged No

Notes The continued assault on the fishing fleet by U-boats led the British to develop a yet more ingenious method to halt their activities. The Secretary to Vice-Admiral David Beatty, Paymaster Commander Frank Spicknernell, had the idea of using a decoy trawler to tow a submarine, the two vessels being connected by telephone cable. The trawler should act as a 'tethered goat' to attract the U-boat. When a U-boat was sighted, the trawler could inform the submarine by telephone and slip the tow at the critical moment.

When *U40* sighted the trawler *Taranaki* on the afternoon of 23 June, she had no reason to believe that the boat was anything but an easy victim. But submerged behind the trawler was the British submarine *C24* (Lt Taylor RN), who was being informed by an excited trawler skipper that there was a U-boat on the surface. It was at this moment that everything went wrong. When Taylor tried to slip the cable connecting him to the *Taranaki*, it would not release. Instead he ordered the *Taranaki* to let go her end and, despite being weighed down by several fathoms of cable (which must have made the task of maintaining the trim awkward), proceeded to work *C24* into an attacking position and fire one torpedo, which struck *U40* just below the conning tower. Furbringer and two of his officers were rescued. On being brought on board the *Taranaki*, Furbringer complained that he had been sunk by a 'dirty trick'.

UC2

	Launched	*Commissioned*
UC2	12 May 1915	17 May 1915

Type UC1
CO *Oberleutnant zur See* K. Mey (lost)
Date of loss 2 July 1915
Location North Sea, off Yarmouth
Cause Ramming/detonation of own mines
Casualties 15
Survivors None
Salvaged Yes: raised by the British but details of ultimate fate unknown

Notes On 2 July the steamer *Cottingham* struck an underwater object off Yarmouth. The position was dragged with nets and an obstruction found. That evening a heavy explosion took place, and when a diver was sent down the next morning he found the shattered hull of *UC2*. Damage to her hull suggested that she had been sunk by the explosion of one of her own mines which had detonated under her stern when laid. However, it is not clear whether she was dead on the bottom when struck by *Cottingham*. The explosion witnessed by the salvage teams was another of her mines, shaken about by the dragging of the net.

U23

	Launched	*Commissioned*
U23	12 Apr 1913	11 Sept 1913

Type U23
CO *Oberleutnant zur See* H. Schulthess (survived)
Date of loss 20 July 1915
Location North Sea, Fair Isle
Cause Submarine attack
Casualties 24
Survivors 4 officers, 6 ratings
Salvaged No

Notes Another success for the trawler/submarine combination. The trawler *Princess Louise* with *C27* in tow, sighted a submarine. Just as the skipper was taking the details, the telephone line broke. Undeterred, the submarine's CO slipped the tow and fired a torpedo, which missed. In an effort to gain time the *Princess Louise*'s crew pretended to abandon ship, but when this charade could not be maintained they raised the White Ensign and opened fire. Meanwhile *C27* had fired a second torpedo, which struck *U23* just aft of the conning tower.

U36	*Launched*	*Commissioned*
	6 Jun 1914	14 Nov 1914
Type	U31	
CO	*Kapitänleutnant* Ernst Graeff (survived)	
Date of loss	24 July 1915	
Location	Atlantic, off the Hebrides, 59°05'N 06°01'W	
Cause	Gunfire of decoy vessel	
Casualties	18	
Survivors	4 officers, 11 ratings	
Salvaged	No	

Notes The first sinking of a U-boat by a Q-ship or decoy vessel. These were merchant ships fitted with a concealed armament and with their holds packed with empty oil drums to give them additional buoyancy. The intention was to lure the unsuspecting U-boat to within range and then open fire. *U36* approached the tramp steamer *Prince Charles* and ordered her to heave-to. She then came to within 600yds of the ship and at this point the 'tramp' suddenly hoisted the White Ensign and opened a heavy and accurate fire on the submarine from her concealed armament. *U36* was at full buoyancy and needed three minutes to dive but, overwhelmed by the gunfire, she started to sink and was abandoned.

UXII	*Launched*	*Commissioned*
	14 Mar 1911	1 Aug 1914
Type	Holland type	
CO	*Linienschiffsleutnant* Egon Lerch (lost)	
Date of loss	8 August 1915	
Location	N Adriatic, 7.6m bearing 104° from lighthouse at Punta Sabbioni in Venetian lagoon	
Cause	Mine	
Casualties	13	
Survivors	None	
Salvaged	Raised and docked in Venice 3 January 1917 but subsequently broken up	

Notes *UXII* was damaged by the Italian destroyer *Rossolino Pilo* on 6 August while on patrol off Venice. On 8 August 1915 a heavy explosion was observed in a defensive minefield and divers sent down to investigate found the wreck of *UXII* with the stern blown off. The crew were buried with full honours in the cemetery on the island of San Michele.

UIII	*Launched*	*Commissioned*
	20 Aug 1908	24 Jan 1909
Type	Germania type: U3/4 group	
CO	*Linienschiffsleutnant* Karl Strnad (lost)	
Date of loss	13 August 1915	
Location	Mediterranean, Strait of Otranto, 41°N 18°15'E	
Cause	Ramming/gunfire	
Casualties	7	
Survivors	14	
Salvaged	No	

Notes *UIII* was rammed by the Italian armed merchant cruiser *Città di Catania* on 12 August and badly damaged, unable to dive. She was sighted by the French destroyer *Bisson* on 13 August and sunk by gunfire.

UB4	*Launched*	*Commissioned*
	23 Mar 1915	?
Type	UB1	
CO	*Oberleutnant zur See* C. Groos (lost)	
Date of loss	15 August 1915	
Location	North Sea, Yarmouth, 52°43'N 02°18'E	
Cause	Gunfire of decoy vessel	
Casualties	15	
Survivors	None	
Salvaged	No	

Notes *UB4* had stopped the fishing smack *Inverlyon* off the Smith's Knoll Spar Buoy. The trawler let the submarine come to within 30yds before opening fire. The first and third rounds exploded in the U-boat's conning tower and the submarine began to drift as if out of control. Four more shells struck the U-boat before she was seen to sink by the bow.

U27	*Launched*	*Commissioned*
	14 July 1913	12 Aug 1910
Type	U27	
CO	*Kapitänleutnant* Bernhard Wegener (lost)	
Date of loss	19 August 1915	
Location	Western Approaches, Isles of Scilly, 50°25'N 08°15'W	
Cause	Gunfire of decoy vessel	
Casualties	37 (see notes)	
Survivors	None	

Salvaged	No

Notes *U27* had stopped the steamer *Nicosian* and was about to sink her (with her cargo of mules destined for the British Army) and thus was unaware of the British Q-ship *Baralong* (Lt-Cdr Godfrey Herbert RN) approaching. *Baralong* kept *Nicosian* between herself and the submarine so that when the latter finally came into sight from behind *Nicosian*, the range was only 600yds. *Baralong* engaged and fired 34 rounds, which quickly disposed of the submarine. About a dozen survivors reached the *Nicosian*. Fearful that they would try to sink the ship, Herbert ordered *Baralong*'s Royal Marines to fire on them and a number were killed as they climbed up the falls. Four did manage to reach the ship and vanished inside. However, a boarding party sent over from *Baralong* tracked them down to the engine room, where they were shot. Whether the shooting of these men was carried out in cold blood or whether the Germans were caught trying to scuttle the *Nicosian* has never been determined. Wegener was shot in the water as he tried to swim to the *Nicosian*

The British placed an embargo on reporting the affair, but when some of *Nicosian*'s American passengers returned home, details reached the press. The German government was outraged and demanded that *Baralong*'s crew be tried for murder—which the British rejected. However, Herbert spent the rest of his life in fear of German revenge. On another note, the American government was concerned to know that *Baralong* had worn the Stars and Stripes during the approach. Some reports suggested that the flag had not been hauled down until after *Baralong* had engaged, and the US authorities demanded assurances that American colours would not be used as a *ruse de guerre* except under the proper rules.

	Launched	*Commissioned*
U26	16 Oct 1913	20 May 1914
Type	U23	
CO	*Kapitänleutnant* von Berckheim (lost)	
Date of loss	August/September 1915	
Location	Gulf of Finland	
Cause	?	
Casualties	30	
Survivors	None	
Salvaged	No	

Notes The possibility that *U26* was lost by accident as a result of drill or mechanical failure cannot be ruled out.

	Launched	*Commissioned*
U6	18 May 1910	12 Aug 1910
Type	U5	
CO	*Kapitänleutnant* Rheinhold Lepsius (survived)	
Date of loss	15 September 1915	
Location	Arctic, off Stavanger, 58°55'N 05°10'E	
Cause	Submarine attack	
Casualties	24	
Survivors	5	
Salvaged	No	

Notes *U6* was on the surface, running on her Korting heavy oil engines which gave off a considerable amount of smoke, condensing in the cold air into clouds of steam visible from some distance away. The smoke was spotted by the British submarine *E16* (Lt-Cdr E. Talbot DSO RN). Talbot fired both bow tubes from a range of just under 500yds on a 90° track angle and saw one torpedo hit just below the conning tower.

	Launched	*Commissioned*
U41	10 Oct 1914	1 Sept 1915
Type	U31	
CO	*Kapitänleutnant* K. Hansen (lost)	
Date of loss	24 September 1915	
Location	Western Approaches, Isles of Scilly, 49°10'N 07°20'W	
Cause	Gunfire of decoy vessel	
Casualties	35	
Survivors	2 officers	
Salvaged	No	

Notes *U41* was sinking the steamer *Urbino* off the Isles of Scilly when the *Baralong* hove in sight. Hansen was suspicious and dived, but when the new arrival raised American colours he surfaced and ordered *Baralong*'s 'master' to send his papers over in a boat. Although *U41*'s deck gun was manned, when *Baralong* opened fire the crew only managed to get one round away, which went wild. *U41* dived and Hansen hoped to escape under water, but the boat plunged to below 76m. All tanks were blown and she shot back to the surface, where she was abandoned. However, she sank so quickly that only two of her crew were able to escape.

UC9	*Launched*	*Commissioned*
	11 Jul 1915	15 Jul 1915
Type	UC1	
CO	*Oberleutnant zur See* P. Schurmann (lost)	
Date of loss	21 October 1915	
Location	Long Sands LightVessel, 51°47'N 01°37'E	
Cause	?	
Casualties	14	
Survivors	None	
Salvaged	No	

Notes *UC9* left Zeebrugge on 20 October to lay mines off the Long Sands LightVessel. While the exact circumstances of her fate are unknown, the possibility that she was blown up on her own mines is the most likely explanation for her fate, especially as the body of her engineer officer was later found off Long Sands. The mines laid by UC class submarines were held to their sinker by a water-soluble plug which dissolved, releasing the mine, after the minelaying submarine had moved away. In some cases the sinker dissolved too quickly, allowing the mine to rise so that it struck the submarine's bottom.

UC13	*Launched*	*Commissioned*
	May 1915	15 May 1915
Type	UC1	
CO	*Oberleutnant zur See* Kirchner	
Date of loss	29 November 1915	
Location	Black Sea	
Cause	Stranding	
Casualties	None	
Survivors	?	
Salvaged	No	

Notes *UC13* suffered a compass failure during a storm and went aground 55° east of the Bosporus.

1916

UC12

	Launched	Commissioned
UC12	29 Apr 1915	2 May 1915
Type	UC1	
CO	*Oberleutnant zur See* E. Frohner (lost)	
Date of loss	16 March 1915	
Location	Taranto, Italy, 40°27'N 17°11'E	
Cause	Explosion of own mines	
Casualties	15	
Survivors	None	
Salvaged	Yes	

Notes *UC12* was ordered to lay mines in the approaches toTaranto harbour. Germany was not yet at war with Italy, but this little inconvenience was avoided by placing the ship under nominal Austrian command (Italy having been at war with Austria-Hungary for some time) and placing an Austrian liaison officer on board. While *UC12* was laying her mines, one detonated prematurely, throwing up a column of water and alerting the harbour authorities. At the scene of the explosion bubbles, pieces of wreckage and human remains were observed coming to the surface. Divers were sent down and found the shattered hull. The Italians were more than interested to find that the vessel so assiduously mining their waters belonged to a country with which they were not at war and with which they had a military alliance! The incident did much to whip up anti-German feeling in Italy and pave the way for the Italian declaration of war on Germany.

U68

	Launched	Commissioned
U68	1 June 1916	17 Aug 1915
Type	UD	
CO	*Kapitänleutnant* L. Güntrel (lost)	
Date of loss	22 March 1916	
Location	SW of Ireland, 51°54'N 10°53'W	
Cause	Gunfire of decoy vessel	
Casualties	38	
Survivors	None	
Salvaged	No	

Notes *U68* encountered the Q-ship *Farnborough* disguised as a collier and fired one torpedo at her which missed. She then surfaced to put a shot across the *Farnborough*'s bows. While the ship's 'panic party' went over the side into a boat, *U68* closed to within 800yds and fired another shot which fell short. *Farnborough* then revealed her true colours, opening fire and, once *U68* had submerged, dropping two depth charges. *U68* came back to the surface and it could be seen that there was a large hole in her bow. *Farnborough* continued to fire, scoring several hits before *U68* sank, leaving oil and wooden wreckage on the surface.

UB26

	Launched	Commissioned
UB26	14 Dec 1915	7 Jan 1916
Type	UBII	
CO	*Oberleutnant zur See* W. Smiths (survived)	
Date of loss	5 April 1916	
Location	Le Havre Roads, 49°28'N 00°02'E	
Cause	Nets/patrols	
Casualties	None	
Survivors	21	
Salvaged	Yes	

Notes Intelligence—the source is uncertain—was received on 3 April that two U-boats were to be sent to operate off Le Havre. The harbour defences were alerted and, sure enough, a drifter collided with a U-boat's periscope. The submarine tried to escape by lying on the bottom but was depth-charged by the French destroyer *Trombe*. Nets were laid over the position which snared *UB26*'s propellers. In trying to free the submarine, Smiths resorted to some drastic manoeuvring, which caused the motors to overheat and catch fire. He had no option but to surface and scuttle the boat

Although Smiths had made an attempt to destroy all his confidential books and papers, the French sent down divers who were able to recover a mass of documentation from the wreck, including charts showing the location of German minefields and presumed British minefields in the Strait of Dover.

UB26 was raised by the French on 3 August 1916 and commissioned as *Roland Morillot* (named after a French submarine CO killed in the Adriatic); she paid off and was broken up in January 1925.

UB13	*Launched*	*Commissioned*
	8 Mar 1915	6 Apr 1915
Type	UB1	
CO	*Oberleutnant zur See* A. Metz (lost)	
Date of loss	24 April 1916	
Location	Belgian coast, 51°33'N 02°35'E	
Cause	Mine	
Casualties	17	
Survivors	None	
Salvaged	No	

Notes Possibly as a result of intelligence gleaned from the wreck of *UB26*, the British laid 1,565 mines to the north and north-west of Zeebrugge on 24 April. *UB13* had sailed for patrol on the evening of the 23rd, so it possible that she struck one of these newly laid mines. However the possibility that she was lost from accident cannot be ruled out.

UC5	*Launched*	*Commissioned*
	13 Jun 1915	19 Jun 1915
Type	UC1	
CO	*Oberleutnant zur See* Mohrbutter (survived)	
Date of loss	27 April 1916	
Location	North Sea, Shipwash Shoal, 51°59'N 01°38'E	
Cause	Stranding	
Casualties	None	
Survivors	15	
Salvaged	Yes	

Notes *UC5* grounded on the Shipwash Shoal and was left stranded by the retreating tide. While the crew destroyed charts and papers, Mohrbutter tried to radio Zeebrugge with news of his predicament. The message was also received by the British, and when the destroyer *Firedrake* appeared Mohrbutter ordered the submarine to be abandoned and tried to fire the scuttling charges. The charges failed to detonate and *UC5* was later raised and used for exhibition purposes in Britain to generate money for war loans.

UVI	*Launched*	*Completed*
	12 Jun 1909	1 Jul 1910
Type	Holland	
CO	*Linienschiffsleutnant* Hugo von Falkenhausen (survived)	
Date of loss	13 May 1916	
Location	Mediterranean, Strait of Otranto, 40°10'N	
Cause	Net barrage	
Casualties	None	
Survivors	15	
Salvaged	No	

Notes *UVI* was caught in a net towed by the drifters *Calistoga*, *Dulcie Dorry* and *Evening Star*. Unable to break free, von Falkenhausen surfaced and scuttled his submarine.

U74	*Launched*	*Commissioned*
	10 Aug 1915	24 Nov 1915
Type	UE	
CO	*Kapitänleutnant* E. Weisbach (lost)	
Date of loss	27 May 1916	
Location	Peterhead	
Cause	Gunfire	
Casualties	34	
Survivors	None	
Salvaged	No	

Notes *U74* had been ordered to lay a minefield off Rosyth as part of German plans for preliminary moves for a sortie by the High Seas Fleet (which would culminate in the Battle of Jutland). On the 27th four trawlers sighted *U74* off Peterhead using a sail (possibly as a disguise). She returned the trawlers' fire and tried to dive, but she must have been badly damaged for she returned to the surface again. The trawler *Kimberley* closed to almost point-blank range, firing continuously before *U74* sank.

UC3

	Launched	Commissioned
UC3	28 May 1915	1 June 1915
Type	UC1	
CO	*Oberleutnant zur See* G. Kreysern (lost)	
Date of loss	27 May 1916	
Location	N of Zeebrugge, 59°35'N 03°08'E	
Cause	Mine	
Casualties	18	
Survivors	None	
Salvaged	No	

Notes On 26 May the British laid another field of 750 mines north of Zeebrugge and patrolled it with seaplanes and destroyers. *UC3* had been ordered to sea with three other submarines to lay mines off Orfordness. She was sighted close to where the new mines had been laid by *UC1* but was not seen or heard from again. She may have been a victim of one of these newly laid mines, but the possibility exists that she was lost by accident resulting from mechanical or drill failure.

U10

	Launched	Commissioned
U10	24 Jan 1911	31 Aug 19111
Type	U3	
CO	*Kapitänleutnant* F. Stuhr (lost)	
Date of loss	June 1916	
Location	Gulf of Finland	
Cause	?	
Casualties	29	
Survivors	None	
Salvaged	No	

Notes *U10* may have been mined, but the possibility that she was lost by accident resulting from mechanical or drill failure must be considered.

UC7

	Launched	Commissioned
UC7	6 July 1915	9 July 1915
Type	UC1	
CO	*Oberleutnant zur See* G. Haag (lost)	
Date of loss	6 July 1916	
Location	English Channel, N of Zeebrugge, 51°22'N 01°35'E	
Cause	Mine	
Casualties	18	
Survivors	None	
Salvaged	No	

Notes *UC7* is presumed to have been mined in a newly laid British minefield between Thornton Bank and Zeebrugge. On 5 July she was sighted by *UB12* heading toward the position of this minefield. However, the possibility exists that she was lost by accident resulting from mechanical or drill failure.

U77

	Launched	Commissioned
U77	9 Jan 1916	10 Mar 1916
Type	UE	
CO	*Kapitänleutnant* E. Gunzel (lost)	
Date of loss	July 1916	
Location	N North Sea	
Cause	?	
Casualties	33	
Survivors	None	
Salvaged	No	

Notes *U77* left Heligoland on 5 July to lay mines off Kinnaid Head. Two days later the British found the mines and swept them, but nothing further was heard from *U77*. She may have been mined, but the possibility that she was lost by accident resulting from mechanical or drill failure must be considered.

U51

	Launched	Commissioned
U51	25 Nov 1915	24 Feb 1916
Type	Improved U41	
CO	*Kapitänleutnant* W. Rumpel (lost)	
Date of loss	14 July 1916	
Location	North Sea, Ems estuary	
Cause	Submarine attack	
Casualties	34	
Survivors	4	
Salvaged	No	

Notes *U51* was leaving the Ems estuary when she was attacked and sunk by the British submarine *H.5* (Lt H. 'Crom' Varley RN). Varley should not have been there at all: he had been 'bored' in his assigned patrol area and therefore had moved to what he regarded as a more fruitful location because he 'wanted to sink a U-boat'. He fired two torpedoes at *U51* and saw one hit just below the conning tower. Even though he was in the German Navy's 'back yard', Varley surfaced to search for survivors to take back to Britain as 'evidence', but he was forced to submerge by the gunfire of destroyers. *H.5* was then hunted for a number of hours before being able to get clear.

Inside *U51* eighteen survivors had gathered in the fore ends with the commanding officer. Since there were not enough escape sets to go around they appear to have resigned themselves to a slow death by carbon dioxide poisoning. Some four hours after the sinking, they decided to make an attempt to escape, but of the eighteen men in the fore ends only two reached the surface. Another three men trapped in the stern escaped, but one died on the way to the surface.

Varley's reception in Britain was less than overwhelming—he had, after all, violated his orders. Nevertheless he had sunk a U-boat. The Admiralty made him wait for a year before awarding him his DSO.

UB44	*Launched*	*Commissioned*
	20 Apr 1916	11 May 1916
Type	UBII	
CO	*Oberleutnant zur See* F. Wager (lost)	
Date of loss	August 1916	
Location	Aegean	
Cause	?	
Casualties	24	
Survivors	None	
Salvaged	No	

Notes *UB44* left Cattaro for Constantinople on 4 August and was not heard from again. She may have been sunk in an attack by the drifters *Quarrie*, *Knowe* and *Garrigil* on 4 August in 48°12'N 18°46'E but the evidence is inconclusive. The possibility that she was sunk by accident resulting from mechanical or drill failure must be considered.

UC10	*Launched*	*Commissioned*
	15 Jul 1915	17 Jul 1915
Type	UC1	
CO	*Oberleutnant* W. Albrecht (lost)	
Date of loss	21 August 1916	
Location	Strait of Dover, Schouwen Bank, 52°02'N 03°54'E	
Cause	Submarine attack	
Casualties	18	
Survivors	None	
Salvaged	No	

Notes *UC10* was homeward-bound, having laid mines off the Humber. Off the Schouwen Bank she was sighted by the British submarine *E54* which was on patrol there for that very purpose. *E54* fired two torpedoes, saw one hit and *UC10* vanished in a cloud of smoke.

UB7	*Launched*	*Commissioned*
	6 May 1915	?
Type	UB1	
CO	*Oberleutnant zur See* H. Lutjohann (lost)	
Date of loss	September 1916	
Location	Black Sea	
Cause	?	
Casualties	15	
Survivors	None	
Salvaged	No	

Notes Claims have been made that this boat was sunk in 44°30'N 33°15'E by a Russian aircraft, although there is no supporting evidence. *UB7* may have been mined, but the possibility that she was lost by accident arising from mechanical or drill failure must be considered.

UXVI	*Launched*	*Commissioned*
	28 Aug 1915	6 Oct 1915
Type	UB1	
CO	*Linienschiffsleutnant* Oerst von Zopa (lost)	
Date of loss	17 October 1916	
Location	Adriatic, off the Albanian coast	
Cause	Ramming (?)	
Casualties	11	
Survivors	2	
Salvaged	No	

Notes *UXVI* was rammed by the steamer *Bormida* after torpedoing the Italian destroyer *Nembo*, although an alternative version for her loss, quoted in the Austrian official history, is that she was destroyed by the explosion of *Nembo*'s depth charges, which had not been set to 'safe' before she sank.

U56	*Launched*	*Commissioned*
	18 Apr 1916	23 Jun 1916
Type	Improved U41	
CO	*Kapitänleutnant* H. Lorenz (lost)	
Date of loss	2 November 1916	
Location	Arctic, exact location unknown	
Cause	?	
Casualties	35	

Survivors	None
Salvaged	No

Notes *U56* had sunk the Norwegian steamer *Ivanhoe* on 2 November and had rescued the survivors, despite being shelled by four Russian trawlers. The next day Lorenz put the Norwegian crew ashore in Tana Fjord and then sailed, never to be heard from again. The submarine may have been mined, but the possibility that she was lost by accident arising from mechanical or drill failure must be considered.

U20

	Launched	*Commissioned*
	18 Dec 1912	5 Aug 1913
Type	U19	
CO	*Kapitänleutnant* Walther Schwieger (survived)	
Date of loss	4 November 1916	
Location	North Sea, W coast of Jutland peninsula, 56°33'N 08°08'E	
Cause	Stranding	
Casualties	None	
Survivors	35	
Salvaged	Wreck blown up *in situ* 5 November and finally demolished 1925	

Notes *U20*—which had torpedoed and sunk the *Lusitania* under Schweiger's command in April 1915—grounded in heavy fog and radioed for help. A force of four battleships, a battlecruiser and a half-flotilla of destroyers from the High Seas Fleet escorted the salvage vessels, but all salvage efforts were in vain. The wreck was blown up after the crew had been taken off. However, all the wireless traffic required to arrange the operation had been intercepted by the British and the submarine *J1* (Cdr Noel Laurence RN) had been sent to the area. On 5 November Laurence sighted the German ships on their way home and fired four torpedoes. Two struck and damaged the battleships *Grosser Kurfürst* and *Kronprinz Wilhelm*—the only occasion in history that two capital ships have been damaged by the same salvo.

UB45

	Launched	*Commissioned*
	12 May 1916	25 May 1916
Type	UBII	
CO	*Kapitänleutnant* K. Palis (lost)	
Date of loss	6 November 1916	
Location	Black Sea, Varna, 43°12'N 28°09'E	
Cause	Mine	
Casualties	?	
Survivors	5	
Salvaged	Raised and broken up in Bulgaria 1936	

Notes *UB45* was leaving the Black Sea port of Varna preceded by two minesweepers when she struck a newly laid deep mine and sank at once.

UC15

	Launched	*Commissioned*
	19 May 1915	28 Jun 1915
Type	UCI	
CO	*Oberleutnant zur See* B. Weller	
Date of loss	November 1916	
Location	Black Sea	
Cause	?	
Casualties	15	
Survivors	None	
Salvaged	No	

Notes *UC15* had been ordered to lay mines off Sulina at the mouth of the Danube and was not heard from again. She may have been mined, but the possibility that she was lost by accident arising from mechanical or drill failure must be considered.

UB19

	Launched	*Commissioned*
	2 Sept 1915	17 Dec 1915
Type	UBI	
CO	*Oberleutnant zur See* E. Niemeyer (survived)	
Date of loss	30 November 1916	
Location	English Channel, 50°00'N 02°48'W	
Cause	Gunfire of decoy vessel	
Casualties	8	
Survivors	16	
Salvaged	No	

Notes *UB19* encountered the decoy vessel *Penshurst* eight days after leaving Zeebrugge. She first fired a warning shot and then closed to read her victim's name. As he neared the vessel Niemeyer could see the 'crew' abandoning ship, but his suspicions were aroused by the fact that the vessel bore no name and was painted battleship grey. Just as he began to dive, *Penshurst* opened fire at a range of 250yds. *UB19* could not survive this onslaught.

	Launched	Commissioned
UC19	15 Mar 1916	22 Aug 1916
Type	UCII	
CO	*Oberleutnant zur See* A. Nitzsche (lost)	
Date of loss	6 December 1916	
Location	Western Approaches, off S coast of Ireland, 49°41'N 06°31'W	
Cause	Explosive sweep towed by destroyer	
Casualties	25	
Survivors	None	
Salvaged	No	

Notes *UC19*'s conning tower was sighted by the destroyer *Ariel*, which dropped a single depth charge and then lowered her explosive sweep and fired it at a depth of 30ft. Oil and wreckage came to the surface.

	Launched	Commissioned
UB46	31 May 1916	12 Jun 1916
Type	UBII	
CO	*Kapitänleutnant* C. Bauer (lost)	
Date of loss	7 December 1916	
Location	Black Sea, Bosporus, 41°26'N 28°35'E	
Cause	Mine	
Casualties	20	
Survivors	None	
Salvaged	No	

Notes On 6 December Bauer sighted a large Russian submarine north of the Bosporus and the next day, when only 300yds from the shore, *UB46* was mined—possibly on a mine laid by this submarine. Rough seas meant that none of *UB46*'s crew was rescued.

	Launched	Commissioned
UB29	31 Dec 1915	18 Jan 1916
Type	UBII	
CO	*Oberleutnant zur See* E. Platsch (lost)	
Date of loss	13 December 1916	
Location	English Channel, 59°09'N 01°46'E	
Cause	Depth charge	
Casualties	22	
Survivors	None	
Salvaged	No	

Notes *UB29* was sighted by the destroyer HMS *Landrail*, which dropped two depth charges. Two days later a large, spreading oil slick was sighted at the spot.

1917

UB37

	Launched	*Commissioned*
UB37	28 Dec 1915	17 May 1916

Type UBII
CO *Oberleutnant zur See* P. Günther (lost)
Date of loss 14 Janaury 1916
Location English Channel, 50°07'N 01°47'E
Cause Gunfire of decoy vessel
Casualties 21
Survivors None
Salvaged No

Notes The Q-ship *Penshurst*, masquerading as a tramp steamer, was stopped by a U-boat and immediately the'panic party' went over the side. The U-boat closed, evidently intending to finish off her victim with gunfire. When the range was less than 700yds the gunners who remained on board *Penshurst* opened fire. At least five hits were observed around the base of the conning tower before the U-boat sank stern first, her diving hastened by two depth charges dropped by *Penshurst*. No wreckage was brought up but a large oil slick spread over the surface.

U76

	Launched	*Commissioned*
U76	12 Mar 1916	11 May 1916

Type U71
CO *Kapitänleutnant* W. Bender (survived)
Date of loss 22 January 1917
Location North Cape, 71 00'N 23 00'E
Cause Foundered in bad weather
Casualties 1
Survivors 32
Salvaged Raised July 1971 and broken up

Notes *U76* sustained damage when rammed by an unknown Russian trawler on 21 January. The next day, in bad weather and off Hammerfest, her engines broke down and she began to founder. Distress flares were fired and the whole crew was taken off by a Norwegian fishing vessel. The crew were not interned as the Norwegian government ruled that the submarine had been lost as a result of an accident rather than the violence of the enemy.

UXXX

	Launched	*Commissioned*
UXXX	27 Dec 1916	17 Feb 1917

Type UBII
CO *Linienschiffsleutnant* Friedrich Fähndrich (lost)
Date of loss ?
Location Either Otranto Strait or area between Malta and Crete
Cause ?
Casualties 14
Survivors None
Salvaged No

Notes *UXXX* departed from Cattaro (Kotor) on 31 March 1917 for a patrol in the area between Malta and Crete. Nothing was heard from her after her departure and there are no indications in Allied records of any incidents which might account for her loss. It is therefore proposed to record that she was lost either as a result of an accident or a drifting mine.

UC46

	Launched	*Commissioned*
UC46	15 Jul 1916	15 Sept 1916

Type UCII
CO *Oberleutnant zur See* E. Moecke (lost)
Date of loss 8 February 1917
Location SE of Goodwin Sands, English Channel, 51°07'N 01°39'E
Cause Ramming
Casualties 23
Survivors None
Salvaged No

Notes *UC46* was returning to port via the English Channel and just after midnight on 8 February she surfaced to the east of the Goodwin Sands. Moecke may have been thinking of making the final part of the journey, when it would be high water, on the surface so that the mines would be at their maximum dip. *UC46* came to the surface in bright moonlight less than half a mile away from the destroyer HMS *Liberty*, which promptly rammed her.

	Launched	*Commissioned*
UC39	25 Jun 1916	29 Oct 1916

Type UCII
CO *Oberleutnant zur See* Otto Ehrentrant (lost)
Date of loss 8 February 1917
Location North Sea, Flamborough Head, 53°56'N 00°06'E
Cause Depth charge/gunfire
Casualties 7
Survivors 17 crew, 2 British PoWs
Salvaged No; wreck surveyed by divers June 1918

Notes *UC39* was sighted by the destroyer HMS *Thrasher* while she lay stopped on the surface, sinking the collier *Hornsey*. On sighting the destroyer the U-boat dived but *Thrasher* ran over the spot and dropped a single depth charge ahead of the swirl. Despite being dropped by eye with no sophisticated means of control, the depth charge did the trick for *UC39* was blown to the surface. The moment she reappeared *Thrasher* commenced a heavy and accurate fire which killed the first members of *UC39*'s crew as they emerged. In an act of bravery, a British prisoner-of-war on board the U-boat, the Master of the *Hannah Larsen*, jumped up to the bridge waving a white cloth which finally brought an end to the firing.

	Launched	*Commissioned*
U83	13 Jan 1916	6 Jun 1916

Type U81
CO *Kapitänleutnant* Bruno Hoppe (lost)
Date of loss 17 February 1917
Location SW of Ireland, 51°34'N 11°23'W
Cause Gunfire of decoy vessel
Casualties 36
Survivors None
Salvaged No

Notes *U83* stopped a steamer south-west of Ireland and Hoppe conducted a submerged assessment of his target. He fired one torpedo which exploded in the ship's engine room and immediately the crew were seen to abandon ship. In fact the 'innocent' ship was the Q-ship *Farnborough* (Capt Gordon Campbell RN). Hoppe was an experienced commanding officer and was taking no chances. He first inspected the panic party in their lifeboat: his periscope came so close to the lifeboat that one of the crew quipped, 'Don't speak so loud, he'll hear you!' He then circled *Farnborough* and passed so close that Campbell and those remaining on board could see the hull of the U-boat quite clearly under the water. Hoppe was evidently satisfied that the ship was harmless for he surfaced less than 100yds away on the target's beam. As he climbed up and out on to his bridge the last thing he saw was the White Ensign rising up the halyards and the sides falling away from the concealed gun mountings before the first of *Farnborough*'s shells decapitated him. As Hoppe's headless body fell back into the control room, *U83* was repeatedly hit by 12pdr and 6pdr shells: a total of 45 rounds were fired and nearly all of them hit. *U83* sank very quickly, leaving eight men struggling in the cold and oily water. Only two survived to be rescued by *Farnborough*.

Farnborough herself was in a poor state, with heavy flooding from the torpedo hit. Nevertheless, she eventually staggered into Berehaven, where she was beached. Campbell was awarded the Victoria Cross for this action while a total of two DSOs, three DSCs, ten DSMs and 24 Mentions in Despatches were also awarded. However, such was the secrecy surrounding Q-ship operations that Campbell's citation was not printed in the *Gazette* and thus he became known as the 'Mystery VC'.

Kapitänleutnant Bruno Hoppe had been the commanding officer of *U22* when she torpedoed and sank *U7* (q.v.) in error on 21 January 1915.

	Launched	*Commissioned*
UC18	4 Mar 1916	15 Aug 1916

Type UCII
CO *Oberleutnant zur See* W. Kiel (lost)

Date of loss	19 February 1917
Location	English Channel, 49°15'N 02°34'W
Cause	Gunfire of decoy vessel
Casualties	28
Survivors	None
Salvaged	No

Notes Kiel and his ship's company paid the price for carelessness. After stopping a steamer (the Q-ship *Lady Olive*) in the English Channel with a torpedo, he circled her on the surface and passed close under her quarter, evidently trying to get her name for his records before he sank her. The concealed gunners opened fire and within minutes *UC18* had sunk. However, on this occasion the damage suffered by the *Lady Olive* was such that she sank several hours later.

UC32

	Launched	*Commissioned*
	12 Aug 1916	13 Sept 1916
Type	UCII	
CO	*Oberleutnant zur See* H. Breyer (survived)	
Date of loss	23 February 1917	
Location	North Sea, off Sunderland, 54°55'N 01°20'W	
Cause	Explosion of own mines	
Casualties	19	
Survivors	3	
Salvaged	No; on 26 February divers surveyed the wreck and recovered, among other things, a torpedo	

Notes *UC32* was just beginning to lay her mines off Roker Pier Lighthouse when she blew up and sank. The plug holding the mine to the sinker on one of her mines must have dissolved far too quickly: the mine rose and exploded under her stern. An examination vessel subsequently found Breyer and two of his crew in the water.

UC43

	Launched	*Commissioned*
	5 Oct 1916	25 Oct 1916
Type	UCII	
CO	*Kapitänleutnant* E. Sebelin (lost)	
Date of loss	10 March 1917	
Location	Shetlands, N of Muckle Flugga, 60°57'N 01°11'W	
Cause	Submarine attack	
Casualties	26	
Survivors	None	
Salvaged	No	

Notes The British submarines *E49* and *G13* were on patrol to the north and east of the Shetlands to bar the northern route into the Atlantic used by U-boats. On 10 March *E49* signalled that she was returning to port on account of the bad weather; two days later she was lost after striking a mine laid by *UC43*. *G13*'s commanding officer (Lt-Cdr Bradshaw RN) remained at sea and at 1600 that afternoon sighted a submarine. Bradshaw dived, a demanding task in such bad weather, and the coxswain then had a very difficult job keeping the big submarine at periscope depth. In the huge seas Bradshaw could only get momentary glimpses of the submarine and for a while she was totally hidden in a snow squall. When it passed Bradshaw found that the U-boat had altered course away and *G13* had to go to full speed in order to catch up. Finally Bradshaw had to fire two torpedoes at the very long range of 3,000yds. Just as his navigator was reporting that the torpedoes had missed (by looking at his stopwatch) there was a cracking explosion. On looking through the periscope Bradshaw saw the U-boat's bows rise up into the air.

U85

	Launched	*Commissioned*
	22 Aug 1916	23 Oct 1916
Type	U81	
CO	*Kapitänleutnant* W. Petz (lost)	
Date of loss	12 March 1917	
Location	English Channel, Start Point, 50°02'N 04°13'W	
Cause	Gunfire of decoy vessel	
Casualties	38	
Survivors	None	
Salvaged	No	

Notes U86 attacked the Q-ship *Privet* and after firing one torpedo, which missed, came to the surface and opened fire with her gun. *Privet* replied and scored a number of hits on the U-boat which then dived. However, the damage caused by the Q-ship was considerable, for the submarine could seen broaching as if attempting to return to the surface before she sank stern first. *Privet* was beached, surveyed and later recommissioned.

UB6	*Launched*	*Commissioned*
	?	8 Apr 1915
Type	UB1	
CO	?	
Date of loss	12 March 1917	
Location	North Sea, Dutch coast, 51°53'N 03°58'E	
Cause	Stranded and subsequently interned	
Casualties	None	
Survivors	14	
Salvaged	Yes: refloated and taken to port of Hellevoetsluis	

Notes Stranded on the Dutch coast in fog, the boat and crew were interned by the Dutch from 13 March after their legal status had been sorted out. Since *UB6* was in sea-going condition when she took the ground, her crew could not expect to be treated as shipwrecked mariners. However, on 18 March she sank at Hellevoetsluis, probably due to lack of maintenance. She was raised and was ultimately ceded to France. She was broken up at Brest in 1921.

UC68	*Launched*	*Commissioned*
	12 Aug 1916	17 Dec 1916
Type	UCII	
CO	*Oberleutnant zur See* H. Degetau (lost)	
Date of loss	13 March 1917	
Location	English Channel, Start Point, 50°17'N 03°32'W	
Cause	Explosion of own mines	
Casualties	27	
Survivors	None	
Salvaged	No	

Notes *UC68* left Zeebrugge for her first patrol on 16 February. On 13 March a heavy underwater explosion was observed off Start Point, after which the British swept a number of German mines.

U22	*Launched*	*Commissioned*
	6 Mar 1913	25 Nov 1913
Type	U23	
CO	?	
Date of loss	6 April 1917	
Location	North Sea, Horns Reef	
Cause	Mine	
Casualties	?	
Survivors	Presumed all of the crew of 27	
Salvaged	Yes: she was refitted but only ever used for training purposes	

Notes The Germans had established an elaborate series of defensive minefields in the Heligoland Bight though which a number of safe passages had been made in order that ships or U-boats could exit to and return from the North Sea. Naturally the British took a great interest in finding these safe passages and, having located them, mining them. During the first three months of 1917 the Royal Navy laid over 4,000 mines in the Bight. In particular three minelayers had laid a field of 1,235 mines at the end of what the Germans knew as the Blue Route. On 6 April *U22*, returning through the Blue Route, reported that she had been mined aft and was sinking. Torpedo boats were dispatched and towed her back. Her stern had been totally destroyed.

UC30	*Launched*	*Commissioned*
	27 Jul 1916	22 Aug 1916
Type	UCII	
CO	*Oberleutnant zur See* H. Stenzler (lost)	
Date of loss	21 April 1917	
Location	North Sea, Horns Reef, 55°20'N 07°15'E	
Cause	Mine	
Casualties	27	
Survivors	None	
Salvaged	No	

Notes After *U22* had been damaged the Germans moved the safe passage known to them as the Blue Route further to the west. The British promptly laid over 1,500 mines around the exit of the new route. *UC30*, homeward-bound from patrol and still with her cargo of mines embarked, reported her position on 19 April but after that nothing further was heard from her. Bad weather prevented searches by Zeppelins or torpedo boats being organised. It is presumed that she was the victim of the new British fields, although the possibility of loss by accident arising from drill or mechanical failure cannot be excluded.

U81	*Launched*	*Commissioned*
	24 Jun 1916	22 Aug 1916
Type	U81	

CO	*Kapitänleutnant* R. Weisbach (survived)
Date of loss	1 May 1917
Location	W coast of Ireland, 51°25'N 13°05'W
Cause	Submarine attack
Casualties	24
Survivors	7
Salvaged	No

Notes The British submarine *E54* (Lt-Cdr R. H. Raikes RN), based at Queenstown for anti-U-boat operations west of Ireland, surprised *U81* in the act of sinking a merchant ship. Raikes dived just as the U-boat surfaced to finish off his victim. As *U81* passed under the steamer's stern to take her name, *E54* came round the bow and fired two torpedoes at a range of 400yds. As a humorous sequel to this sinking, the crew of the steamer had watched events from their lifeboat and were not at all sure who had torpedoed whom. When Raikes surfaced and approached them, the merchant seamen thought *E54* was a U-boat and began rowing for all they were worth! Raikes had to chase them for some time before he could establish his identity and persuade them to re-board their ship.

UC26

	Launched	*Commissioned*
	22 Jun 1916	18 Jul 1916
Type	UCII	
CO	*Oberleutnant zur See Graf* von Schmettow (lost)	
Date of loss	9 May 1917	
Location	Thames estuary, 51°03'N 01°40'E	
Cause	Rammed by destroyer	
Casualties	24	
Survivors	2	
Salvaged	No	

Notes *UC26* was returning to Zeebrugge having laid mines off Le Havre, Ouisterham and Cherbourg. At dawn on the 9th the submarine was off Calais, where she was sighted by the destroyer HMS *Milne*. Schmettow started to dive but was too slow. *UC26* was rammed squarely by *Milne* (which emerged from the encounter with a badly distorted stem and pieces of the U-boat's casing embedded in her forecastle) and then depth-charged by two other destroyers. Eight men managed to escape from her hull but *Milne* only managed to pick up two of them.

UC76

	Launched	*Commissioned*
	25 Nov 1916	17 Dec 1916
Type	UCII	
CO	?	
Date of loss	10 May 1917	
Location	North Sea, Heligoland, 54°10'N 07°54'E	
Cause	Explosion of own mines	
Casualties	15	
Survivors	11	
Salvaged	Raised the same day by the salvage vessel *Oberelbe*; repaired but used solely for training purposes from July 1918	

Notes *UC76* was lost while loading mines at Heligoland. One of the mines was not held by its retaining bolt and fell through the tube and exploded on the sea bed below the submarine. At the end of the war *UC76* was taken to Sweden, where she was interned at Karlskrona on 13 November 1918 by her crew, who evidently preferred a Swedish internment camp to a British prisoner-of-war camp. The boat was surrendered to the Royal Navy on 1 December 1918 and broken up at Briton Ferry in 1919–20.

U59

	Launched	*Commissioned*
	20 Jun 1916	7 Sept 1916
Type	U43	
CO	*Kapitänleutnant* von Firks (lost)	
Date of loss	14 May 1917	
Location	North Sea, Horns Reef, 55°33'N 07°15'E	
Cause	German mine	
Casualties	33	
Survivors	4	
Salvaged	No	

Notes In response to the British minelaying offensive in the Bight, the Germans laid another two fields near Horns Reef. On the evening of the 14th *U59* was being escorted out into the North Sea by three *Sperrbrecher*. In the bad weather the Germans were more to the north than they thought and *U59* was mined in one of the new German fields. Most of her crew were rescued but in the darkness and confusion the rescue ships strayed into the minefields and in the end only four of her crew survived.

UB39

	Launched	Commissioned
	29 Dec 1915	29 Apr 1916

Type UBII
CO *Oberleutnant zur See* H. von Kustner (lost)
Date of loss 14/15 May 1917
Location English Channel, 50°20'N 01°20'E
Cause Mine
Casualties 24
Survivors None
Salvaged No

Notes *UB39* disappeared in the English Channel. When she was formally reported overdue the commanding officer of *UB12* reported seeing an underwater explosion near the British 9A buoy. Since this was a reference point used by U-boats on passage through the Strait of Dover, it is presumed that *UB39* was mined near this point.

UV

	Launched	Commissioned
	10 Feb 1909	1 Apr 1910

Type Holland type
CO *Linienschiffsleutnant* Friedrich Schlosser (survived)
Date of loss 16 May 1917
Location Adriatic, Fasana Channel, 44°57'8"N 13°44'2"E
Cause Mine
Casualties 5
Survivors 15
Salvaged Raised 23 June 1917 but not returned to service; used as an instructional submarine for rest of the war

Notes *UV* was mined at a depth of 9.5m while conducting a torpedo firing exercise. Schlosser managed to bring the boat to 4.3m to allow eighteen officers and men to escape.

UC36

	Launched	Commissioned
	25 Jun 1916	3 Nov 1916

Type UCII
CO *Kapitänleutnant* G. Buch (lost)
Date of loss May 1917
Location English Channel
Cause ?
Casualties 27
Survivors None
Salvaged No

Notes *UC36* was ordered to lay mines off the Nab Light Vessel and the Needles and left Zeebrugge on 16 May. The mines she laid off the Nab were swept but no mines were ever found off the Needles. It is possible that she was lost as a result of the explosion of her own mines. However, the possibility that she was lost through accident arising from mechanical or drill failure cannot be ruled out.

UB36

	Launched	Commissioned
	15 Jan 1916	22 May 1916

Type UBII
CO *Oberleutnant zur See* von Keyserlinck (lost)
Date of loss 21 May 1917
Location Ushant, 48°42'N 05°14'W
Cause Ramming
Casualties 23
Survivors None
Salvaged No

Notes *UB36* had attacked a French convoy off Ushant and had sunk one steamer. Forty minutes later she fired at another steamer but missed. The track of her torpedo was seen by the Master of the steamer *Molière*, which swung out of line and rammed the U-boat, whose hull was clearly visible beneath the water. No wreckage other than large bubbles of air came to the surface.

UC24

	Launched	Commissioned
	4 Mar 1916	17 Aug 1916

Type UCII
CO *Kapitänleutnant* K. Willich (lost)
Date of loss 24 May 1917
Location Adriatic, off Bocche di Cattaro, 42°06'N 18°09'E
Cause Submarine attack
Casualties 24
Survivors 2
Salvaged No

Notes *UC24* was leaving the Austrian base of Cattaro in company with *UC74*. Patrolling off the entrance to the port was the French submarine *Circe* (*Lieutenant de Vaisseau* de Cambourg). A keen and dedicated officer, Cambourg took his submarine as close to the entrance of the landlocked harbour as he dared without risking running into the extensive defensive minefields (laid since the days of 1914–15 when French submarines had entered Cattaro with impunity) or being spotted by the extremely vigilant Austrian coast-watching service. His persistence was rewarded with the sight of the two U-boats coming straight towards him. *UC74* had increased speed and was pulling ahead so Cambourg fired two torpedoes from a range of 250yds and scored two hits on *UC24*.

UC29	*Launched* 15 Jul 1916	*Commissioned* 15 Aug 1916
Type	UCII	
CO	*Kapitänleutnant* Ernst Rosenow (lost)	
Date of loss	7 June 1917	
Location	S coast of Ireland, 51°50'N 11°50'W	
Cause	Gunfire of decoy vessel	
Casualties	23	
Survivors	1 officer, 1 rating	
Salvaged	No	

Notes Just after 0800 the decoy ship *Pargust* (Cdr Gordon Campbell VC DSO RN) was struck by a torpedo on her starboard side. The panic party went over the side with commendable realism. Lt Francis Hereford RNR played the part of 'Master' and went over the side in his best bowler hat clutching a stuffed parrot in a cage for added realism. The U-boat circled the ship, coming extremely close—sometimes as close as 50yds—while conducting a periscope reconnaissance, for nearly thirty minutes. Eventually the U-boat surfaced but then headed off after the lifeboats containing the panic party, evidently in order to interrogate the crew and take the Master as a prisoner. The panic party pulled back towards their ship with the U-boat following. As they did so there was a lot of laughter, clearly audible in *Pargust*, as the men realised that they were luring the U-boat to her destruction. Campbell was very worried lest this give the game away.

As the U-boat closed the 'stricken' merchant ship, men came up on to her casing and manned the gun. Campbell waited until the U-boat was 50yds away before opening fire with his gun armament as well as firing a torpedo (which missed). The U-boat stopped and began to list to port after a number of hits were observed. The engine room hatch was opened and several men came up on the after casing as if to surrender. *Pargust* ceased fire but Campbell ordered it to be resumed when it appeared that the U-boat was trying to get away. The men on the casing were swept off by a wave, and after a few well-directed salvos the U-boat blew up with a shattering explosion, *UC29* still having her mines loaded. Two survivors were picked up by the panic party. One, an officer, was brought on to *Pargust*'s bridge to be received by Campbell (now properly dressed as a Commander RN). He identified the boat as *UC29* before vomiting copiously over the chart table.

Pargust was taken in tow by the sloop *Crocus* and, screened by the sloop *Zinnia* and US destroyer *Cushing*, reached Queenstown the next day. In the usual course of events Campbell was asked to recommend officers and men of his ship's company for honours and awards in connection with the sinking of *UC29*. Campbell considered that the conduct of each and every one of his officers and men was in the highest traditions of the Service and that it would be invidious to single out an individual. Acting in accordance with Clause 13 of the Statutes of the Victoria Cross, HM King George V bestowed two VCs on the ship, to be awarded to an officer and a rating chosen by secret ballot of their peers. The two recipients were Lt Donald Stuart DSO RNR and Able Seaman William Williams DSM. Campbell received a Bar to his DSO and accelerated promotion to Captain. Other awards for the sinking of *UC29* totalled two DSOs, two DSCs, eight DSMs and eleven Mentions in Despatches.

UC66	*Launched* 15 Jul 1916	*Commissioned* 18 Nov 1916
Type	UCII	
CO	*Oberleutnant zur See* Herbert Pustkuchen (lost)	
Date of loss	12 June 1917	
Location	English Channel, off The Lizard, 49°45'N 05°10'W	
Cause	Depth charge	
Casualties	23	
Survivors	None	
Salvaged	No	

Notes In June 1917 the Royal Navy deployed a group of trawlers equipped with hydrophones to operate in the western Channel in response to increased U-boat activity in the area. *UC66* came to the surface less than a mile from the trawler *Sea King*. Either Pustkuchen thought the trawler an easy target or he was totally unaware of her presence. *Sea King* bore down on the U-boat, forcing her to dive, and dropped a depth charge right on top of the swirl. The explosion of the single charge was followed by six very violent underwater detonations which were probably caused by the U-boat's mines exploding.

While in command of *UB29* Pustkuchen had torpedoed and sunk the cross-Channel steamer *Sussex* on 24 March 1916. The steamer had been carrying passengers, including 25 Americans. The diplomatic reaction to the sinking was strong and casued the abandonment of the Germans' second campaign of unrestricted submarine warfare.

U99	*Launched* 27 Jan 1917	*Commissioned* 28 Mar 1917
Type	U81	
CO	*Kapitänleutnant* M. Elstester (lost)	
Date of loss	7 July 1917	
Location	North Sea, 58°00'N 03°05'E	
Cause	Submarine attack	
Casualties	40	
Survivors	None	
Salvaged	No	

Notes *U99* was operating between Norway and the Shetlands and had sunk the destroyer *Itchen* on 6 July 70 miles east of the Pentland Firth. The next day the British submarine *J2* sighted a submarine at a distance of between two and three miles, fired four torpedoes and observed one hit.

UC1	*Launched* 26 Apr 1915	*Commissioned* 7 May 1915
Type	UCI	
CO	*Oberleutnant zur See* Mildenstein (lost)	
Date of loss	19 July 1917	
Location	English Channel, off Nieuport	
Cause	Mine	
Casualties	17	
Survivors	None	
Salvaged	No	

Notes On 14 July 1917 the British acted to block the routes used by U-boats to and from the port of Zeebrugge by laying over 150 mines in the shoals off Nieuport. Four days later *UC1*, the first of the little UC-type minelayers, left for a minelay off Calais. She did not return and is presumed mined in one of these new fields.

UC61	*Launched* 11 Nov 1916	*Commissioned* 13 Dec 1916
Type	UCII	
CO	*Oberleutnant zur See* G. Gerth (survived)	
Date of loss	26 July 1917	
Location	English Channel, W of Boulogne, 50°53'N 53°00'E	
Cause	Stranding	
Survivors	26	
Casualties	None	
Salvaged	No	

Notes *UC61* grounded on the French coast close to Cap Gris Nez and could not be refloated. Gerth wrecked the boat before blowing her up. The crew were subsequently captured by a troop of Belgian cavalry who were resting nearby. Despite the scuttling and wrecking, the intelligence haul was immense. A periscope was recovered intact and turned over to the Royal Navy (the British were well aware that German priscopes were superior), together with charts showing German and British minefields.

Some French sources claim that *UC61* was carrying an officer who, when captured, was found to be in possession of a large amount of currency issued by the military authorities in the Calais/Boulogne area for use by British troops. It is suggested that this officer was a spy who was being landed by *UC61*. It is not mentioned in any British accounts, primary or secondary, and is at best an unlikely scenario: any putative spy would have made sure that compromising evidence would have been destroyed before he fell into enemy hands!

UB20	*Launched* 26 Sept 1915	*Commissioned* 10 Feb 1916
Type	UBII	
CO	*Oberleutnant zur See* H. Glimpf	
Date of loss	28 July 1917	
Location	Belgian coast, off Zeebrugge	
Cause	?	
Casualties	13	
Survivors	None	
Salvaged	No	

Notes *UB20* had put to sea on 28 July in order to conduct a series of diving trials so as to check repair work carried out during a recent maintenance period. The trials were expected to last no more than half a day but she failed to return. It is presumed that she fell victim to a mine but the possibility that she was lost by accident resulting from mechanical or drill failure—an especially likely cause given the nature of her voyage—cannot be ruled out.

UB27	*Launched*	*Commissioned*
	10 Feb 1916	23 Feb 1916
Type	UBII	
CO	*Oberleutnant zur See* von Stein (lost)	
Date of loss	29 July 1917	
Location	E coast of England, near Smith's Knoll Spar Buoy, 52°47'N 02°24'E	
Cause	Ramming/depth charge	
Casualties	22	
Survivors	None	
Salvaged	No	

Notes The old torpedo gunboat (a precursor of the destroyer) HMS *Halcyon* was on routine patrol off the Smith's Knoll Buoy when she sighted a periscope. She increased speed and turned towards and rammed the submarine before dropping two of the new 500lb depth charges as she passed over the spot. A lot of oil subsequently came to the surface. The position was later swept with bottom lines and a large obstruction was found lying on the sea bed. Divers were sent down but the visibility was so poor that they could not find the object.

U69	*Launched*	*Commissioned*
	24 Jun 1915	4 Sept 1915
Type	U66	
CO	*Oberleutnant zur See* Wilhelms (lost)	
Date of loss	July 1917	
Location	SW of Ireland	
Cause	?	
Casualties	40	
Survivors	None	
Salvaged	No	

Notes *U69* had left Emden on 9 July 1917 for operations in the Western Approaches south-west of Ireland. On 11 July she sent a routine signal reporting her presence south of Norway but nothing was heard from her thereafter. Intercepted British signals showed that *U69* was active in her operational area until 23 July.

No Allied or American claims exist for the loss of *U69*. She may have been the victim of a drifting mine, but the possibility that she was lost by accident arising from mechanical or drill failure cannot be ruled out.

UC44	*Launched*	*Commissioned*
	10 Oct 1916	4 Nov 1916
Type	UCII	
CO	*Kapitänleutnant* Kurt Tebbenjohanns (survived)	
Date of loss	4 August 1917	
Location	S coast of Ireland, off Waterford, 52°07'N 06°59W	
Cause	German mine	
Casualties	28	
Survivors	1	
Salvaged	Raised September 1917 and broken up	

Notes *UC44*'s loss was a result of some very adroit manipulation of radio intelligence by Rear-Admiral W. 'Blinker' Hall, the outstandingly successful Director of Naval Intelligence. Hall knew from intercepted German communications that the British code used when reporting that German minefields had been cleared had been either broken by the Germans or compromised through the cipher falling into enemy hands. Hall arranged with the CinC at Queenstown, Admiral Sir Lewis Bayley, that when the next German field was found it should be marked and reported in the usual fashion but left uncleared. Thus the mines laid off southern Ireland by *UC42* in June 1917 were found and reported but not swept. Accordingly, *UC44* was ordered to lay mines in the area where *UC42*'s had just been 'swept'. The result was predictable and *UC44* ran into the mines left by *UC42*. Tebbenjohanns made a remarkable one-man escape without any apparatus from the conning tower.

The wreck was beached off Waterford on 26 September. However, salvage officers had already recovered a good deal of information, including orders to U-boat commanders regarding how to transit the Strait of Dover.

U44

	Launched	*Commissioned*
	15 Oct 1914	7 May 1915

Type — U43
CO — *Kapitänleutnant* P. Wagenführ (lost)
Date of loss — 12 August 1917
Location — Off S coast of Norway, 58°51'N 04°20'E
Cause — Ramming
Casualties — 44
Survivors — None
Salvaged — No

Notes *U44* had had a frustrating patrol in the area west of St Kilda. There had been repeated encounters with Q-ships, the last of which, with the *Chagford* on 5 August, had resulted in a quick dive during which sea water had entered the battery. After a meeting with *U84* west of the Hebrides, Wagenführ decided to break off his patrol, but atmospheric conditions were so bad that it took nearly 24 hours before the *Reichsmarine*'s communications HQ at Nauen outside Berlin acknowledged his signal that he would be off Lyngvig at 0600 on the 13th to meet the escort through the minefields.

It was not only the *Reichsmarine* which listened to *U44*'s transmissions: her signals were also received and decoded by the Royal Navy, and the Third Light Cruiser Squadron, at sea off southern Norway on a routine sweep, were alerted. At 0600 on the 12th the destroyer HMS *Oracle*, one of the 3LCS screen, sighted a suspicious vessel on the horizon and closed to investigate. The vessel was *U44*, which was wearing an improvised sail as a disguise. Why Wagenführ remained on the surface for so long is open to conjecture. Possibily the encounter with the *Chagford* had damaged the battery so badly that his boat could not develop sufficient electric power to remain dived for any length of time and so had to proceed on the surface.

As *Oracle* closed the vessel her look-outs reported the tell-tale bow and stern of a U-boat, but the submarine dived before the destroyer could engage. However, less than ten minutes later the U-boat surfaced again, dived and resurfaced. Either *U44*'s LI could not maintain the trim or conditions in the boat were so bad that it was impossible for her to remain dived. After her second appearance on the surface she was rammed by *Oracle*. The destroyer reported that she cut clean through the U-boat's hull and then dropped a depth charge as her stern passed over the site. A substantial amount of oil and wreckage came to the surface, including cork insulation from inside the hull, some of which was recovered by *Oracle* as evidence.

UC72

	Launched	*Commissioned*
	12 Aug 1916	5 Dec 1916

Type — UCII
CO — *Oberleutnant zur See* E. Voigt (lost)
Date of loss — 20 August 1917
Location — Bay of Biscay, 46°08'N ??°48'W
Cause — Gunfire of decoy vessel
Casualties — 31
Survivors — None
Salvaged — No

Notes *UC72* had left Zeebrugge on 12 August for a minelaying operation off the French coast and then to pursue unrestricted submarine warfare in the Bay of Biscay. She survived an encounter with the decoy vessel *Penshurst* on 19 August but the next day encountered the decoy vessel *Acton*. *Acton*'s well-drilled panic party went over the side with commendable realism, leaving fires burning on board (carefully set and watched by the stay-behind party) to foster the impression that the ship was sinking. Voigt passed so close to *Acton* during his periscope reconnaissance that he actually collided with her. He was evidently satisfied so he gave the order to surface. The U-boat was overwhelmed by the decoy's gunfire and sank quickly. There were no survivors.

UC72 was the last U-boat to be sunk by a decoy vessel. As long as U-boats observed the prize rules and surfaced to interrogate their victims before sinking them, the decoy vessel retained validity as an anti-submarine weapon. However, as U-boat commanders became more cautious and as the Germans adopted unresricted submarine warfare, these vessels became less useful in their role.

UC41

	Launched	*Commissioned*
	3 Sept 1916	10 Nov 1916

Type — UCII
CO — *Oberleutnant zur See* H. Foerste (lost)
Date of loss — 21 August 1917
Location — Tay estuary, 56°25'N 02°35'E

Cause	Explosion of own mines/depth charge
Casualties	27
Survivors	None
Salvaged	No

Notes On 12 August the trawlers *Jacinth*, *Thomas Young* and *Chikara* were on routine patrol in the Tay estuary when a massive underwater explosion was reported. The trawlers made for the position and their hydrophones reported the sound of electric motors running. Depth charges were dropped over the position and oil and air bubbles came to the surface. Finally there was another massive underwater explosion which brought wreckage, including human remains, to the surface. Divers subsequently inspected the wreck and brought up a number of items, including the submarine's gun, which identified it as that of *UC41*.

UC41 was engaged in laying her mines in the Tay estuary and either sighted the trawlers through the periscope or picked up their engines on her hydrophone. Foerste must have decided to clear the area and have run on to one of his own mines, which accounted for the first explosion. The second explosion was most likely the rest of *UC41*'s mines exploding as a result of the depth charges being dropped.

	Launched	*Commissioned*
U50	31 Dec 1915	4 Jul 1916
Type	U43	
CO	*Kapitänleutnant* G. Berger (lost)	
Date of loss	End of August 1917	
Location	Terschelling, exact position unknown	
Cause	?	
Casualties	44	
Survivors	None	
Salvaged	No	

Notes *U50* had just left on patrol and had been escorted to the end of the Yellow Route, one of the safe routes through the German defensive minefields in the Heligoland Bight. She reported her position on 31 August and the *Beobachterdienst* placed her position as 55°15'N 4°10'E. However, nothing further was heard from her and there are no British claims which could account for her loss. At the end of September Berger's body was washed ashore in the North Frisian Islands. A post mortem examination indicated that he had been in the water for about a month.

It is most likely that *U50* was lost on new British minefields laid at the exits of the three swept passages used by U-boats. Nearly 2,000 mines were laid in these locations at the beginning of August. On 22 August the outward-bound *UB21* sighted the British minelayers heading home after completing their task of mining the end of the Yellow Route but chose not to report it. *U50*'s route took her across this newly laid field and thus a mine is the most likely cause for her loss. However, her loss by accident arising from drill or mechanical failure cannot be ruled out.

	Launched	*Commissioned*
U28	30 Aug 1913	26 Jun 1914
Type	U23	
CO	*Kapitänleutnant* G. Schmidt (lost)	
Date of loss	2 September 1917	
Location	Arctic, off North Cape, 72°34'N 27°56'E	
Cause	Explosion of steamer *Olive Branch*	
Casualties	39	
Survivors	None	
Salvaged	No	

Notes *U28* had torpedoed the *Olive Branch*, which had been sailing to Archangel loaded with ammunition. After the crew abandoned ship the submarine surfaced to finish her victim off with gunfire. The second shell caused the *Olive Branch*'s cargo to explode and *U28* was wrecked. Although some of *U28*'s crew survived the sinking, they were not rescued by the *Olive Branch*'s crew in their lifeboats.

This loss bears similarities to that of *U132* on 4 November 1942 (q.v.).

	Launched	*Commissioned*
U66	22 Apr 1915	23 Jul 1915
Type	U66	
CO	*Kapitänleutnant* G. Muhle (lost)	
Date of loss	September 1917	
Location	Dogger Bank, North Sea, exact location unknown	
Cause	?	
Casualties	40	
Survivors	None	
Salvaged	No	

Notes *U66* successfully made the passage out of the Heligoland Bight through the German defensive minefields and the British fields. Early on 3 September she reported her position near the Dogger Bank but nothing was heard from her thereafter. She may have been mined, but her loss may instead be attributable to an accident arising from mechanical or drill failure.

U88	*Launched*	*Commissioned*
	22 Jun 1915	23 Jul 1915
Type	U66	
CO	*Kapitänleutnant* Walther Schwieger (lost)	
Date of loss	5 September 1917	
Location	Terschelling, North Sea, exact location not recorded	
Cause	Mine	
Casualties	43	
Survivors	None	
Salvaged	No	

Notes *U88* was heading off the Bight into the North Sea behind *U54* (Heeseler) Both boats used the Yellow Route and began passing through the new British fields at the exit end, *U54* actually scraping a mine cable on her pressure hull. When *U54* was in position 54°09'N 04°47'E she reported two massive underwater explosions ten minutes apart. *U88* made no more transmissions, so it is presumed that she was mined in the British field.

While commanding officer of *U20* Schwieger had earned international opprobrium by torpedoing the Cunard liner *Lusitania* on 7 May 1915.

UC42	*Launched*	*Commissioned*
	21 Sept 1916	18 Nov 1916
Type	UCII	
CO	*Oberleutnant zur See* Müller (lost)	
Date of loss	10 September 1917	
Location	S of Ireland, off Cork, 51°44'N 08°12'W	
Cause	Explosion of own mines	
Casualties	27	
Survivors	None	
Salvaged	No; wreck surveyed by divers	

Notes *UC42* was destroyed by the explosion of one of her own mines while on a minelay off Cork. However, it was not until the end of October that an oil slick over the spot alerted the patrols, which plastered the area with depth charges. On 3 November a diver went down to investigate the wreck. He found the forward mine chute empty and the stern completely destroyed—a clear indication that the soluble plug on one of the submarine's mines had been more soluble than most and had released the mine right under her stern, with devastating results. More importantly, the diver found the forward and conning tower hatches open, as if the crew had tried to escape. No bodies were ever recovered at sea. Further salvage operations recovered a number of items from the wreck, including a periscope and a telephone buoy. Documents recovered from the wreck, including the control room log, showed the last entries to have been written on 10 September.

The Germans would have been unaware of *UC42*'s loss were it not for two American prisoners from the destroyer *Jacob Jones*, torpedoed by *U53* on 6 December. The Americans reported that divers had found and worked on the wreck of a minelaying submarine off Cork. It could only have been *UC42*. Ironically, she had been sunk not far from where her own mines had disposed of *UC44* (q.v.).

U49	*Launched*	*Commissioned*
	26 Nov 1915	31 May 1916
Type	U43	
CO	*Kapitänleutnant* R. Hartmann (lost)	
Date of loss	11 September 1917	
Location	Bay of Biscay, 46°17'N 14°42'W	
Cause	Ramming/gunfire	
Casualties	43	
Survivors	None	
Salvaged	No	

Notes *U49* had been ordered to cut a telephone cable in the North Sea west of the Dogger Bank. She reported that her cutting apparatus had broken down and that she was heading off into the Atlantic for Handelskrieg. Nothing further was heard from her. On 11 September the steamer *British Transport* exchanged gunfire with a surfaced U-boat. Later that night the tracks of two torpedoes were sighted coming in from ahead. Some adroit manoeuvring saved the *British Transport*, which then began to forge ahead at full speed. A little while later her look-outs sighted a phosphorescent track in the sea, at the end of which was a dark object resembling a submarine. The Instructions issued to British Masters for these situations were unequivocal: if in doubt, ram! The U-boat stopped and began to settle by the stern. As three men clambered out on to the casing calling for help, a shell from the *British Transport* exploded inside the U-boat's pressure hull. The U-boat sank quickly and in the darkness it was impossible to rescue any survivors.

U45

	Launched	*Commissioned*
	15 Apr 1915	9 Oct 1915
Type	U43	
CO	*Kapitänleutnant* R. Sittenfeld (lost)	
Date of loss	12 September 1917	
Location	W of Shetlands, 55°48'N 07°30'W	
Cause	Submarine attack	
Casualties	43	
Survivors	2	
Salvaged	No	

Notes *U45* was torpedoed by HM Submarine *D7*, which spotted her on the surface. *D7* fired one torpedo from her stern tube and observed a hit by the conning tower. Two survivors were rescued, one of whom was the radio operator.

UB32

	Launched	*Commissioned*
	4 Dec 1915	11 Apr 1916
Type	UBII	
CO	*Kapitänleutnant* Hans von Ditfurth (lost)	
Date of loss	22 September 1917	
Location	English Channel, Sunk Light Vessel, 51°45'N 02°05'W	
Cause	Air attack	
Casualties	23	
Survivors	None	
Salvaged	No	

Notes *UB32* was the first U-boat to be sunk by aircraft (though not the first submarine: this was the French *Fouccault*, sunk on 15 September 1915 in the Adriatic by Austrian aircraft). An RNAS Curtiss H8 Large America flying boat, serial number 8695, crewed by Flt Sub-Lt N.A. Magor, Flt Sub-Lt C. E. S. Lusk, CPO E. A. Boyd and Leading Mechanic R.A. Lucas, sighted a U-boat moving south-east which began to dive on sighting the aircraft. Nevertheless, the aircraft's crew succeeded in dropping two 230lb bombs on the target and were rewarded with the sight of the U-boat rolling over and sinking, followed by the appearance of large air bubble together with considerable quantities of wreckage and oil.

UC21

	Launched	*Commissioned*
	1 Apr 1916	15 Sept 1916
Type	UCII	
CO	*Oberleutnant zur See* von Zerboni di Sposetti (lost)	
Date of loss	September 1917	
Location	English Channel, exact location unknown	
Cause	?	
Casualties	27	
Survivors	None	
Salvaged	No	

Notes *UC21* left Zeebrugge on 13 September for a minelaying operation off the French coast, after which she was to attack any shipping found. She was never heard from again. She may have fallen victim to one of the British fields in the Dover Strait, or one of her own mines may have exploded. Aternatively, the possibility that she was lost through an accident resulting from equipment or drill failure cannot be overlooked.

UC33

	Launched	*Commissioned*
	26 Aug 1916	25 Sept 1916
Type	UCII	
CO	*Oberleutnant zur See* A. Arnold (survived)	
Date of loss	26 September 1917	
Location	St George's Channel, 51°55'N 06°14'W	
Cause	Ramming	
Casualties	27	
Survivors	One	
Salvaged	No	

Notes *UC33* had damaged her hydroplanes in the nets of Waterford while minelaying and was unable to dive. In thick fog in St George's Channel Arnold torpedoed the tanker *San Zeferino* and then tried to make his escape on the surface. However, he was spotted and pursued by *PC61*, one of the convoy's escorts, which engaged the U-boat with gunfire and then turned in to ram. Just before the impact *PC61* stopped her engines so that her bows would drop and have a 'cutting' effect on the U-boat's thin pressure hull. The U-boat sank, leaving oil and wreckage on the surface. A violent underwater explosion brought three men to the surface but *PC61* could only rescue one, who turned out to be Arnold.

UC6

	Launched	*Commissioned*
UC6	20 Jun 1915	24 Jun 1915

Type	UCI
CO	*Oberleutnant zur See* G. Reichenbach (lost)
Date of loss	27 September 1917
Location	North Foreland, 51°30'N 00°34'E
Cause	Mine net
Casualties	16
Survivors	None
Salvaged	No

Notes After sweeping U-boat-laid mines around the Kentish Knock LightVessel, the Royal Navy laid a number of mine nets in the area in case the U-boats should repeat their minelaying operations. At 1430 on the afternoon of 27 September hydrophone operators on the Kentish Knock lightship reported the noises of U-boat motors nearby. At 1630 there were five explosions in the mine nets, followed thirty minutes later by another three explosions.

Surprisingly, the nets were not inspected until January 1918, when pieces of wreckage of German origin and a German type mine sinker were recovered.

UC55

	Launched	*Commissioned*
UC55	2 Aug 1916	15 Nov 1916

Type	UCII
CO	*Oberleutnant zur See* Ruhle von Lilienstern (lost)
Date of loss	29 September 1917
Location	Lerwick, 60°02'N 01°02'W
Cause	Accident
Casualties	10
Survivors	?
Salvaged	No

Notes *UC55* was on a minelaying operation off Lerwick. Just as the minelay was about to commence there was an error in the operation of the compensating tanks used to take in water to make up for the loss of weight of the mines. The tanks were flooded too soon and the submarine lost trim and began to dive deeper. Lilienstern brought the boat under control but surfaced under the guns of the trawler *Moravia* and drifters *Sylvia* and *Tyrade*. The game was up, so Lilienstern threw his confidential books over the side and abandoned the submarine. Under interrogation some of his disgruntled crew blamed sabotage in the dockyard at Heligoland for the submarine's loss.

UC14

	Launched	*Commissioned*
UC14	13 May 1915	5 Jun 1915

Type	UC1
CO	*Oberleutnant zur see der Reserve* Feddersen (lost)
Date of loss	3 October 1917
Location	Zeebrugge, 51°19'N 02°43'E
Cause	Mine
Casualties	17
Survivors	None
Salvaged	No

Notes *UC14* was homeward-bound when she fell victim to a mine cunningly dropped by a British CMB right off the entrance to Zeebrugge harbour. Watchers on the mole at Zeebrugge reported a massive explosion, and some time later Feddersen's body was washed ashore.

UC16

	Launched	*Commissioned*
UC16	1 Feb 1916	26 Jun 1916

Type	UCII
CO	*Oberleutnant zur See* G. Reimarus (lost)
Date of loss	4 (?) October 1917
Location	Zeebrugge (?)
Cause	Mine (?)
Casualties	27
Survivors	None
Salvaged	No

Notes *UC16* was possibly a victim of the same mines which had accounted for *UC14*. She had laid mines off Boulogne on 3 October (the mines were later found and swept) but she did not return to Zeebrugge. On 26 October the body of one of her crew was washed ashore at Noordwijk in the Netherlands.

UB41	*Launched* 6 May 1916	*Commissioned* 25 Aug 1916
Type	UBII	
CO	*Oberleutnant zur See* M. Ploen (lost)	
Date of loss	5 October 1917	
Location	E coast of England, Scarborough, 54°18'N 00°21'W	
Cause	Mine	
Casualties	24	
Survivors	None	
Salvaged	No	

Notes Coast-watchers at Scarborough reported an explosion on 5 October which almost certainly acounted for *UB41*. However, it is not clear whether she was lost in a British field laid early in September or whether, possibly through navigational error, she ran into a German field laid by *UC55* on 9 July.

U106	*Launched* 12 Jun 1917	*Commissioned* 28 Jul 1917
Type	U81	
CO	*Kapitänleutnant* H. Hufnagel (lost)	
Date of loss	7 October 1917	
Location	North Sea	
Cause	Mine	
Casualties	41	
Survivors	None	
Salvaged	No	

Notes Returning from patrol, *U106* was warned of new British minefields at the entrance to German safe passages through Heligoland Bight minefields but she reported that she had not received the signals properly. Although escorts and minesweepers were sent to the old rendezvous, despite the mine risk, she was not met, nor did she respond to any signals. It is almost certain that *U106* was lost in one of these new fields.

UC62	*Launched* 9 Dec 1916	*Commissioned* 8 Jan 1917
Type	UCII	
CO	*Oberleutnant zur See* M. Schmitz (lost)	
Date of loss	14 (?) October 1917	
Location	?	
Cause	?	
Casualties	30	
Survivors	None	
Salvaged	No	

Notes Possibly mined off Portland in a field of deep mines, *UC62* had been ordered to supplement German minefields in the area with an additional field.

UC63	*Launched* 6 Jan 1917	*Commissioned* 30 Jan 1917
Type	UCII	
CO	*Oberleutnant zur See* von Heydebreck	
Date of loss	1 November 1917	
Location	English Channel, Goodwin Sands, 51°23'N 02°00'E	
Cause	Submarine attack	
Casualties	26	
Survivors	1	
Salvaged	No	

Notes British submarines in the Channel made a practice of lurking near known navigational marks to catch U-boats going on or returning from patrol. *E52* had positioned herself off a buoy north of the Dover Barrage and caught *UC63* returning from patrol. There was one survivor.

UC65	*Launched* 8 Jul 1916	*Commissioned* 10 Nov 1916
Type	UCII	
CO	*Kapitänleutnant* Klaus Lafrenz (survived)	
Date of loss	3 November 1917	
Location	English Channel 50°31'N 00°27'E	
Cause	Submarine attack	
Casualties	22	
Survivors	5	
Salvaged	No	

Notes *UC65* was making a fast passage homewards on the surface, Lafrenz trusting to speed and manoeuvrability to get out of any trouble. *UC65* was spotted by the British submarine *C16*, which dived and fired two torpedoes. Lafrenz evaded the first, but the second struck *UC65* amidships.

Under interrogation Lafrenz proved remarkably cooperative and helpful in advising the British on how the Dover defences could be avoided.

UC51	*Launched* 5 Dec 1916	*Commissioned* 6 Jan 1917
Type	UCII	
CO	*Oberleutnant zur See* H. Galster (lost)	
Date of loss	17 November 1917	
Location	English Channel, Start Point, 50 08'N 03 42'W	
Cause	Mine	
Casualties	29	
Survivors	None	
Salvaged	No	

Notes On 17 November the trawler HMS *Lois* was engaged in a routine A/S patrol off Start Point when she was surprised and shaken by an underwater explosion. A U-boat appeared on the surface before sinking, leaving wreckage, including human remains, on the surface. The prize find was a seaboot with the name of one of *UC51*'s crew.

U58	*Launched* 31 May 1916	*Commissioned* 9 Aug 1916
Type	U43	
CO	*Kapitänleutnant* G. Amberger (survived)	
Date of loss	17 November 1917	
Location	Bristol Channel, Milford Haven, 51°32'N 05°21'W	
Cause	Depth charge	
Casualties	2	
Survivors	36	
Salvaged	No	

Notes This was the first sinking of a U-boat by US Navy forces. The US destroyer *Fanning* sighted a periscope and ran over the spot to drop a depth charge. The explosion wrecked *U58*'s hydroplanes and the boat became impossible to control. Amberger surfaced to surrender. The crew went out on to the casing with their hands up to await rescue but two of their number went back into the submarine and set the scuttling charges.

UC47	*Launched* 30 Aug 1916	*Commissioned* 13 Oct 1916
Type	UCII	
CO	*Oberleutnant zur See* von Wigankow (lost)	
Date of loss	18 November 1917	
Location	North Sea, off Flamborough Head, 54°03'N 00°23'E	
Cause	Ramming	
Casualties	28	
Survivors	None	
Salvaged	No	

Notes The patrol boat *P57* sighted what appeared to be a buoy east-south-east of Flamborough Head and closed the object to investigate. As *P57* got nearer the buoy turned into a fully surfaced U-boat. *P57* increased speed and rammed the U-boat just forward of the conning tower. As she passed over the spot a depth charge was dropped before she turned quickly to drop another. While she waited at the scene, a slick of thick oil began to form on the surface. Divers arrived later in the day and recovered publications and papers which identified the boat as *UC47*.

UC57	*Launched* 30 Aug 1916	*Commissioned* 13 Oct 1916
Type	UCII	
CO	*Kapitänleutnant* F. Wissmann (lost)	
Date of loss	Mid-November 1918	
Location	Gulf of Finland, 59°N 23°E	
Cause	?	
Casualties	27	
Survivors	None	
Salvaged	No	

Notes *UC57* had been used to take arms and supplies from Danzig to aid anti-Russian forces in Finland. She arrived in Finnish waters on 17 November and Wissmann told Finnish officers that he had seen Russian forces laying mines in the Gulf of Finland. It is presumed that he fell foul of these mines on his return voyage to Danzig.

U48	*Launched* 3 Oct 1915	*Commissioned* 22 Apr 1916
Type	U43	
CO	*Kapitänleutnant* C. Edeling (lost)	
Date of loss	24 November 1917	
Location	English Channel, Goodwin Sands, 51°11'N 01°31'E	
Cause	Stranding	
Casualties	19	
Survivors	22	

Salvaged	No (although, owing to the movement of the Goodwin Sands, *U48*'s wreck is occasionally thrown to the surface and can be seen at low tide)

Notes *U48* was outward-bound through the Strait of Dover but Edeling had decided to turn back because of exceptionally bright moonlight. Returning to base, *U48* fouled the nets which ran to the north of the Goodwin Sands and then went aground. The following morning she was spotted by the drifters *Paramount*, *Majesty*, *Present Help*, *Feasible*, *Acceptable* and *Claud Hamilton*, which opened fire on her with their 6pdr guns. *U48* returned fire with her 4in gun, but when the Germans saw the destroyer *Gypsy* approaching they set the scuttling charges and surrendered.

UB61	*Launched* 28 Apr 1917	*Commissioned* 23 Jun 1917
Type	UBIII	
CO	*Oberleutnant zur See* T. Schulz (lost)	
Date of loss	29 November 1917	
Location	North Sea, off Vlieland, 53°20'N 04°56'E	
Cause	Mine	
Casualties	25	
Survivors	9	
Salvaged	No	

Notes *UB61* was mined in a field laid at the exit of one of the German 'safe' passages through the Heligoland Bight minefields. The mines had been laid by the British submarine *E51* on 18 November.

UB81	*Launched* 18 Aug 1917	*Commissioned* 23 Jun 1917
Type	UBIII	
CO	*Oberleutnant zur See* Salzwedel (lost)	
Date of loss	2 December 1917	
Location	English Channel, 10m SE of Dunose Head, Isle of Wight, 50°27'N 00°53'W	
Cause	Mine	
Casualties	29	
Survivors	6	
Salvaged	No	

Notes *UB81* had enjoyed a trouble-free passage of the Dover Strait but was forced to dive off Dunose Head. However, while diving her stern struck a mine and she bottomed in 80ft of water. The flooding was isolated and the engineer succeeded in bringing the bow above water. Seven men crawled out through the torpedo tube while the rest waited inside. They fired distress rockets and six hours later the patrol boat *P32* appeared. However the CO of *P32* was unaware of the situation and nudged *UB81*'s bow as he went alongside. Water spilled over and down the open torpedo tube, causing the submarine to sink. Six of the seven survivors were picked up.

UC69	*Launched* 7 Aug 1916	*Commissioned* 23 Dec 1916
Type	UCII	
CO	*Oberleutnant zur See* H. Thielmann	
Date of loss	6 December 1917	
Location	English Channel, Cape Barfleur, 49°47N 01°10'W	
Cause	Rammed in error by *U96*	
Casualties	11	
Survivors	18	
Salvaged	No	

Notes On the surface, at night, *U96* rammed the smaller *UC69*—a collision that was entirely attributable to the poor look-out kept by both boats. To allow *UC69*'s crew time to escape, the CO of *U96* kept his engines going at slow ahead so that his bows were held against the sinking vessel. However, ten minutes after the collision *UC69* sank.

UB18	*Launched* 21 Aug 1915	*Commissioned* 11 Dec 1915
Type	UBII	
CO	*Oberleutnant zur See* G. Niemeyer	
Date of loss	9 December 1917	
Location	English Channel, 49°17'N 05°47'W	
Cause	Ramming	
Casualties	24	
Survivors	None	
Salvaged	No	

Notes *UB18* was rammed and sunk by the trawler *Ben Lawer* escoritng a cross-Channel coal convoy. The trawler rammed her just aft of the conning tower and herself sustained such damage that she was barely able to make port.

UB75	*Launched* 5 May 1917	*Commissioned* 11 Sept 1917

Type UBIII
CO *Oberleutnant zur See* F. Walther (lost)
Date of loss 13 December 1917 (date reported overdue)
Location North Sea, off Flamborough Head, 54°05'N 00°10'E
Cause Mine
Casualties 34
Survivors None
Salvaged No

Notes After making her presence felt off Whitby between 5 and 9 December, *UB75* was not heard from again. She failed to answer all signals and was presumed lost in British minefields off Flamborough Head.

U75	*Launched* 30 Jan 1916	*Commissioned* 26 Mar 1916

Type UE
CO *Kapitänleutnant* Schmolling (survived)
Date of loss 13 December 1917
Location North Sea, Terschelling,
Cause Mine
Casualties 23
Survivors 8
Salvaged No

Notes *U75* had been escorted by two minesweepers through the German fields and out into the North Sea. The minesweepers then picked up the merchant ship *Nordstern* and returned. No sooner had *U75* begun to proceed independently than she struck a mine. Most of the crew got out on to the casing and began signalling to the *Nordstern* which was still in sight. However, in the time it took *Nordstern* to turn around, all but eight of *U75*'s crew had drowned.

UC38	*Launched* 5 Jun 1916	*Commissioned* 19 Oct 1916

Type UCII
CO *Oberleutnant zur See* Hans Wendlandt (survived)
Date of loss 14 December 1917
Location Aegean Sea
Cause Depth charge
Casualties ?
Survivors 25
Salvaged No

Notes *UC38* had just torpedoed the French cruiser *Châteaurenault* and Wendlandt fired a second torpedo to finish her off. The torpedo missed, but the destroyers *Lansquenet* and *Mameluk* ran down the track and dropped depth charges together. The depth charges did considerable damage: both the main and auxiliary ballast pumps were wrecked and water was pouring through the after U-boat's torpedo hatch which had jumped off its seating and become buckled. When the lights failed Wendlandt gave the order to blow everything and *UC38* shot to the surface, where she was abandoned under fire.

UB56	*Launched* 6 Jun 1917	*Commissioned* 19 Jul 1917

Type UBIII
CO *Oberleutnant zur See* H. Valentiner (lost)
Date of loss 19 December 1917
Location Strait of Dover, 50°58'N 01°21'E
Cause Mine
Casualties 37
Survivors None
Salvaged No

Notes The loss of UB56 is directly attributable to the increase in the defences in the Strait of Dover. The Admiralty was aware, through a variety of sources (including the talkative *Kapitänleutnant* Lafrenz of *UC65*), of how U-boats sidestepped the various nets, patrols and minefields which the British placed in their path. On 18 December Vice-Admiral Bacon, Flag Officer Dover, was ordered to increase the defences and illuminate the nets and minefields at night. *UB56* was outward-bound on the night of 19–20 December and Valentiner hoped to pass the defences under cover of darkness. The new flares and searchlights forced him to dive between Le Colbart sandbank and Cap Gris Nez, where the U-boat was mined. Shortly afterwards the destroyer *Gypsy* found two men in the water. One was dead and the other died after an hour on board, though not before he had confirmed the identity of his boat.

	Launched	*Commissioned*
U87	22 May 1916	26 Feb 1917
Type	U87	
CO	*Kapitänleutnant* von Speth-Schulzburg (lost)	
Date of loss	25 December 1917	
Location	Irish Sea	
Cause	Ramming	
Casualties	44	
Survivors	None	
Salvaged	No	

Notes *U87* attacked a convoy in the Irish Sea and was then rammed by the sloop HMS *Buttercup*. She survived this collision though damaged, but was spotted shortly afterwards by *PC56*, which dropped two depth charges and blew her to the surface. The little *PC56* went straight for the U-boat, scoring hits with her 6pdr gun until she rammed her, slicing right through the pressure hull between bow and conning tower. The bow section remained afloat for about ten minutes after the ramming and the crews of *Buttercup* and *PC56* were able to see into the U-boat's interior.

1918

U95

	Launched	Commissioned
U95	20 Jan 1917	19 Apr 1917
Type	U93	
CO	*Kapitänleutnant* A. Prinz (lost)	
Date of loss	7 January 1918	
Location	English Channel, off The Lizard, 49°59'N 05°12'W	
Cause	Ramming	
Casualties	36	
Survivors	None	
Salvaged	No	

Notes *U95* was rammed by the steamer *Braeneil*, which had sighted her quarry in fog less than 100yds away. *Braeneil*'s Master must have had his eye firmly on the reward given the Masters for U-boat sinkings, for after the ramming her went full astern in order to open up the gash torn in *U95*'s hull. German voices were heard in the water but no survivors were rescued.

UB69

	Launched	Commissioned
UB69	7 Aug 1917	12 Oct 1917
Type	UBIII	
CO	*Oberleutnant zur See* A. Klatt (lost)	
Date of loss	9 January 1918	
Location	Mediterranean, off Bizerta, 37°30'N 10°38'E	
Cause	Explosive sweep	
Casualties	31	
Survivors	None	
Salvaged	No	

Notes *UB69* had left Germany on 26 December en route for Pola. On 9 January she attacked a convoy escorted by the sloop HMS *Cyclamen* off Bizerta. When the U-boat's periscope was sighted *Cyclamen* streamed explosive sweeps and was rewarded with a detonation. *UB69*'s bow appeared above the water briefly before sinking amid great gushes of oil. A depth charge was then dropped to finish the submarine off.

UB66

	Launched	Commissioned
UB66	31 May 1917	1 Aug 1917
Type	UBIII	
CO	*Kapitänleutnant* F. Wernicke (lost)	
Date of loss	18 January 1918	
Location	Mediterranean, off Cape Bon, 38°30'N 24°25'E	
Cause	Depth charge	
Casualties	30	
Survivors	None	
Salvaged	No	

Notes *UB66* fired two torpedoes at a ship in a convoy escorted by the sloop HMS *Campanula*. The sloop reacted very quickly, dropping two depth charges over the U-boat's estimated position, and oil and wreckage subsequently came to the surface.

UB22

	Launched	Commissioned
UB22	9 Oct 1915	2 Mar 1916
Type	UBII	
CO	*Oberleutnant zur See* K. Wacker (lost)	
Date of loss	19 January 1918	
Location	North Sea, 54°40'N 06°32'E	
Cause	Mine	
Casualties	22	
Survivors	None	
Salvaged	No	

Notes *UB22* was mined in one of the 'safe' channels through the German minefields in the Heligoland Bight. Her escort, the torpedo boat *S16*, was mined and sank with all hands; *UB22*, following astern of her, suffered the same fate.

U93

	Launched	Commissioned
U93	15 Dec 1916	10 Feb 1917
Type	U93	

CO	*Kapitänleutnant* K. H. Gerlach (lost)
Date of loss	January 1918
Location	West Channel
Cause	?
Casualties	43
Survivors	None
Salvaged	No

Notes *U93* reported her safe arrival in the Western Channel at the end of December 1917 but nothing further was heard from her. It is presumed that she was lost through an accident or mined.

U109

	Launched	Commissioned
U109	25 Sept 1916	7 Jul 1917
Type	U105	
CO	*Kapitänleutnant* O. Ney (lost)	
Date of loss	January 1918	
Location	Strait of Dover	
Cause	?	
Casualties	43	
Survivors	None	
Salvaged	No	

Notes *U109* was outward-bound for the Western Channel via the Strait of Dover. She sailed on 24 January but made no signal confirming that she had successfully passed through the Dover defences. It is therefore presumed that she was mined en route.

U84

	Launched	Commissioned
U84	22 July 1915	6 Jun 1916
Type	U87	
CO	*Kapitänleutnant* W. Röhr (lost)	
Date of loss	26 January 1918	
Location	St George's Channel, 51°53'N 05°44'W	
Cause	Ramming	
Casualties	40	
Survivors	None	
Salvaged	No	

Notes *U84* was sighted by the patrol boat *PC62* which turned towards her and increased speed to ram. Röhr tried to turn away and escape but *PC62* rammed the submarine just aft of the conning tower. The U-boat sank, leaving no survivors but a large oil slick on the surface.

UB35

	Launched	Commissioned
UB35	28 Dec 1915	22 Jun 1916
Type	UBII	
CO	*Oberleutnant zur See* K. Stoter (lost)	
Date of loss	26 January 1918	
Location	English Channel, 51°03'N 01°46'E	
Cause	Depth charge	
Casualties	21	
Survivors	7	
Salvaged	No	

Notes On 25 January *UB35* was engaged in sinking the steamer *Epstatios* (she was seen doing so by *UB58*) and had just put a scuttling party aboard when Stoter was forced to dive by the appearance of *P34*. Six men were left on the *Epstatios* and were taken prisoner. They were the lucky ones. The following day, to the north of Calais, the destroyer HMS *Leven* attacked a submarine whose periscope had been spotted. Oil and wreckage came to the surface together with seven men. However only one could be rescued and he died on board *Leven*—probably from lung damage associated with an escape from depth without any apparatus. The six seamen captured by *P34* confirmed the identity of the boat when shown items of clothing and letters recovered by *Leven* from the water.

UB63

	Launched	Commissioned
UB63	26 May 1917	23 Jul 1917
Type	UBIII	
CO	*Oberleutnant zur See* R. Gebeschus (lost)	
Date of loss	January/February 1918	
Location	North Sea/Irish Sea (?)	
Cause	?	
Casualties	33	
Survivors	None	
Salvaged	No	

Notes *UB63* sailed on 14 January for a patrol in the Western Approaches. She may have been the victim of depth-charge attacks carried out on 28 January 1918 in position 56°10'N 02°00'W by the trawlers *W. S. Bailey* and *Fort George*, but the evidence is not conclusive. At least three other attacks are cited as the cause of the loss of this boat, but again the evidence is inconclusive and sometimes contradictory. In the absence of any firm evidence her loss must remain as due to unknown cause.

UC50	*Launched*	*Commissioned*
	23 Nov 1916	21 Apr 1916
Type	UCIII	
CO	*Kapitänleutnant* R. Seuffer (lost)	
Date of loss	4 February 1918	
Location	Bay of Biscay, 50°49'N 00°59'W	
Cause	Depth charge	
Casualties	29	
Survivors	None	
Salvaged	No	

Notes *UC50* was homeward-bound and had surfaced just to the west of the Dover defences to signal her position and arrival time at Bruges. She was very conspicuous on the surface for she had her wireless masts raised. Her look-outs may have been thinking of the delights of shore leave in Ostend for they failed to notice the approach of the destroyer HMS *Zubian* until she was practically on top of the submarine. Seuffer dived, but too late and too slowly. *Zubian*'s keel scraped along *UC50*'s casing and four depth charges, set shallow, blew the submarine apart.

UB38	*Launched*	*Commissioned*
	1 Apr 1916	19 Jul 1916
Type	UBII	
CO	*Oberleutnant zur See* G. Bachmann (lost)	
Date of loss	8 February 1918	
Location	Strait of Dover, 50°56'N 01°25'E	
Cause	Mine	
Casualties	27	
Survivors	None	
Salvaged	No	

Notes *UB38* was sighted by the drifter *Gowan II* to the north-east of Le Colbart sandbank. The submarine dived at once and twenty minutes later the *Gowan II*, now joined by the duty destroyer and a number of other ships, was shaken badly by a triple underwater explosion. In diving to avoid the drifter Bachmann had most likely dived into a minefield.

U89	*Launched*	*Commissioned*
	6 Oct 1916	21 Jun 1917
Type	U81	
CO	*Kapitänleutnant* W. Bauck (lost)	
Date of loss	13 February 1918	
Location	Atlantic, N of Malin Head, 55°38'N 07°32'W	
Cause	Ramming	
Casualties	43	
Survivors	None	
Salvaged	No	

Notes *U89* was waiting in the area between Malin Head and the Scottish mainland, the funnel of water known as the North Channel through which all Liverpool-bound convoys passed. Bauck sighted a convoy on the night of 10 February but it was going too fast for him to manouevre into an attack position. Two days later *U89* was sighted at a range of 200yds by the cruiser HMS *Roxburgh*, which had escorted the convoy in British coastal waters and was now returning to Liverpool. The cruiser's bow tore through *U89*'s thin plating and in order to increase the damage *Roxburgh* went full astern after the impact.

UXXIII	*Launched*	*Commissioned*
	5 Jan 1917	1 Sept 1917
Type	Havmanden (U20/U23 group)	
CO	*Linienschiffsleutnant* Klemens von Bezard (lost)	
Date of loss	21 February 1918	
Location	Mediterranean, Strait of Otranto, 40°26'N 19°02'E	
Cause	Explosive sweep	
Casualties	12	
Survivors	None	
Salvaged	No	

Notes *UXXIII* was attempting a passage of the Strait of Otranto when she was sighted by the Italian destroyer *Airone*. The destroyer first tried to ram the submarine but when *UXXIII* dived to safety the destroyer steamed her explosive sweep and was rewarded with an underwater explosion followed by the appearance of oil and wreckage on the surface.

UB17	*Launched*	*Commissioned*
	1 Apr 1915	?
Type	UBI	

CO	*Oberleutnant zur See* A. Brandscheid (lost)
Date of loss	March 1918
Location	North Sea
Cause	?
Casualties	21
Survivors	None
Salvaged	No

Notes *UB17* sailed from Zeebrugge on 11 March and was not seen nor heard from again. She might have been depth-charged by *CMB20* in the southern North Sea on 18 March but this would have meant her staying at sea for much longer than her usual five-day patrol. Once again, a verdict of lost through unknown cause must be recorded.

UB54

	Launched	*Commissioned*
UB54	18 Apr 1917	12 Jun 1917
Type	UBIII	
CO	*Oberleutnant zur See* E. Hecht (lost)	
Date of loss	March 1918	
Location	English Channel	
Cause	?	
Casualties	29	
Survivors	None	
Salvaged	No	

Notes *UB54* sailed for patrol on 1 March 1918 and not heard from again. It has been suggested that she was the victim of an attack by HMS *Sturgeon, Thruster* and *Retriever* in 53°15'N 00°45'E, but this attack was made on *UB78* and in any case was far away from *UB54*'s operational area off Portland. Until more definite evidence comes to light, lost by unknown cause is the only answer.

U110

	Launched	*Commissioned*
U110	28 Jul 1917	8 Dec 1917
Type	U81	
CO	*Korvettenkapitän* K. Kroll (lost)	
Date of loss	15 March 1918	
Location	Atlantic, NW of Malin Head, 54°49'N 08°06'W	
Cause	Depth charge	
Casualties	39	
Survivors	4	
Salvaged	No	

Notes *U110* was depth-charged by the destroyers *Michael* and *Moresby*, which had been alerted to the U-boat's presence by an SOS from the steamer *Amazon* which Kroll had just sunk. *U110* surfaced after being badly damaged by the destroyers' depth charges. She tried to escape on the surface but was forced to dive again. Damage to the boat was so severe that the engineer could not maintain a trim. In such a condition Kroll had no option but to surface and abandon the submarine. Only four of her crew survived their brief immersion in the Atlantic

---

U61

	Launched	*Commissioned*
U61	22 Jul 1916	2 Dec 1916
Type	U43	
CO	*Kapitänleutnant* V. Dieckmann (lost)	
Date of loss	26 March 1918	
Location	Irish Sea, 51°48'N 05°32'W	
Cause	Depth charge	
Casualties	36	
Survivors	None	
Salvaged	No	

Notes *U61* was sighted on the surface by the British patrol vessel *PC51* less than 300yds away. *PC51* increased speed and turned to ram but her helm jammed and she made a complete circuit before she found her bows pointing at the U-boat, which was aleady partially submerged. Nevertheless *PC51* ran over the spot and dropped three depth charges. After the explosion of the third there were three underwater detonations and wreckage and human remains came to the surface.

UB33

	Launched	*Commissioned*
UB33	4 Dec 1915	22 Apr 1916
Type	UBII	
CO	*Oberleutnant zur See* F. Gregor (lost)	
Date of loss	11 April 1918	
Location	Strait of Dover, SW of The Varne sandbank, 50°56'N 01°17'E	
Cause	Mine	
Casualties	28	
Survivors	None	
Salvaged	No	

Notes *UB33* was returning to Zeebrugge when she was mined. At 1800 on 11 April the drifter *Ocean Roamer* reported an explosion south-west of The Varne sandbank. She later recovered wreckage and reported that oil was coming to the surface in a thick stream. It took divers some time to find the wreck, largely because *Ocean Roamer* had not given an accurate position, but eventually, on 21 May, they found *UB33*. The divers tried to enter the boat through the conning tower but found Gregor's body blocking the way down—had he been trying to escape when the submarine was mined? His body was recovered and buried ashore, but of much more interest was the recovery of a steel waterproof chest containing *UB33*'s confidential books, signals and ciphers.

	Launched	*Commissioned*
UB82	1 Sept 1917	2 Oct 1917
Type	UBIII	
CO	*Kapitänleutnant* W. Becker	
Date of loss	17 April 1918	
Location	Irish Sea, 55°13'N 05°55'W	
Cause	Depth charge	
Casualties	32	
Survivors	None	
Salvaged	No	

Notes *UB82* was operating in the North Channel and was last heard from on 15 April when she exchanged recognition signals with *U19*. Two days later her periscope was spotted by the drifters *Young Fred* and *Pilot Me*. The drifters dropped four depth charges which blew the U-boat's bow to the surface, where it hung at a 45-degree angle for several minutes before sinking. Two more depth charges were dropped and these brought a mass of wreckage to the surface, including a complete bunk, clothing and personal effects.

	Launched	*Commissioned*
UC79	19 Dec 1916	22 Jan 1917
Type	UCIII	
CO	*Oberleutnant zur See* A. Krameyer (lost)	
Date of loss	19 April 1918	
Location	Strait of Dover, 48°17'N 05°17'W	
Cause	Mine	
Casualties	30	
Survivors	None	
Salvaged	No	

Notes *UC79* was presumed mined in the Dover Barrage on the night of 19/20 April. An explosion was reported, after which oil and air came to the surface for the next 24 hours, but no wreck was ever found.

	Launched	*Commissioned*
UB71	12 Jul 1917	23 Nov 1917
Type	UBIII	
CO	*Kapitänleutnant* K. Schapler (lost)	
Date of loss	21 April 1918	
Location	Mediterranean, Strait of Gibraltar, 35°38'N 05°18W	
Cause	Depth charge	
Casualties	32	
Survivors	None	
Salvaged	No	

Notes *UB71* had left Germany on 4 April and was en route to Pola to reinforce the Mediterranean flotillas. On 21 April she was approaching the Strait of Gibraltar when she ran into a patrol line of MLs which had been established on 17 April. *ML413* first heard the noise of submarine's diesels, then sighted the large bow wave. The submarine passed 30ft ahead of the ML and dived. *ML413* then followed the wake of the U-boat and dropped four depth charges 150ft ahead of the submarine's estimated position. When she stopped to listen on her hydrophones no machinery noises could be heard and at daybreak watchers found oil and wreckage.

	Launched	*Commissioned*
UB55	9 May 1917	1 Jul 1917
Type	UBIII	
CO	*Oberleutnant zur See* Wenninger (survived)	
Date of loss	22 April 1918	
Location	Strait of Dover, 51°01'N 01°20'E	
Cause	Mine	
Casualties	23	
Survivors	6	
Salvaged	No	

Notes *UB55* had left Zeebrugge on 21 April and was hoping to pass through the Strait of Dover on the surface. However, Wenninger was forced to dive just north of The Varne. As *UB55* reached periscope depth she was shaken by a violent explosion aft and began to flood.

Eight men were in the control room and twelve in the fore ends. There were only four Dräger sets as all the others were in the wrecked stern of the U-boat. Pressure in the boat had to equal that outside (at 128ft), so Wenninger ordered the release of HP air from the submarine's storage cylinders and from the torpedoes' air vessels, but there was insufficient air to raise the pressure in order to open the hatches. Wenninger now ordered the compartments to be flooded. The flooding-up period was a dreadful experience. The increasing pressure brought on headaches and earaches while fumes from chlorine gas coming from the battery made breathing difficult. Two men took their own lives, unable to stand the conditions any further. Eventually Wenninger tried the hatch and was literally blown out of the submarine followed by the others. Six got out of the conning tower and twelve from the fore ends. However, a number died on reaching the surface, most likely from burst lungs having escaped from a depth of over 100ft without any apparatus. When rescue arrived nearly two hours later only seven men were still alive and one of those died after being picked up.

U104

	Launched	*Commissioned*
U104	3 Jul 1917	12 Aug 1917
Type	U99	
CO	*Kapitänleutnant* K. Bernis (lost)	
Date of loss	25 April 1918	
Location	St George's Channel, 51°59'N 06°26'W	
Cause	Depth charge	
Casualties	41	
Survivors	1 rating	
Salvaged	No	

Notes *U104* had been damaged in a depth-charge attack on 23 April by the USS *Cushing.* The Americans lacked sufficient evidence to claim a 'kill', but on the morning of the 25th the British sloop HMS *Jessamine* found *U104* on the surface repairing damage to her pressure hull. Bernis dived but *Jessamine* dropped three depth charges over the swirl which caused such damage that he had no choice but to surface. On the way up ten men tried to escape from the fore ends but only one was rescued.

UB85

	Launched	*Commissioned*
UB85	26 Oct 1917	24 Nov 1917
Type	UBIII	
CO	*Kapitänleutnant* Krech (survived)	
Date of loss	30 April 1918	
Location	Irish Sea, 54°47'N 05°23'W	
Cause	Gunfire	
Casualties	None	
Survivors	34	
Salvaged	No	

Notes *UB85* had been sighted by the drifter *Coreopsis* in the North Channel. Had she stayed on the surface and used her speed, she would have escaped. However, Kerch decided to dive. As *UB85* submerged the conning tower was struck by a shell which started a leak. Water poured down into the control room and the battery, generating chlorine gas. Kerch decided to surface and fight it out with the drifter but the flooding in his boat meant that the magazine was inaccessible. Accordingly he fired a white flare to indicate his surrender and then stood by to await rescue. He later told his interrogators that most of his crew were suffering from stomach complaints, which explained their low morale and lack of resistance.

UB31

	Launched	*Commissioned*
UB31	16 Nov 1915	25 Mar 1916
Type	UBII	
CO	*Oberleutnant zur See der Reserve* W. Braun (lost)	
Date of loss	2 May 1918	
Location	Strait of Dover, 51°01'N 01°16'W	
Cause	Mine	
Casualties	26	
Survivors	None	
Salvaged	No	

Notes The circumstances of *UB31*'s sinking may well be interchangeable with those of *UC78* below.

UC78

	Launched	*Commissioned*
UC78	8 Dec 1916	10 Jan 1917
Type	UCIII	
CO	*Kapitänleutnant* H. Kukat (lost)	
Date of loss	2 May 1918	
Location	Strait of Dover	

Cause	Mine
Casualties	29
Survivors	None
Salvaged	No

Notes Two U-boats were lost by mines in the Strait of Dover within hours of one another on 2 May. The first was depth-charged by the drifters *Ocean Roamer* and *Lord Leitrim* between Folkestone and The Varne. The depth-charge attack caused an explosion in the minefield as if the U-boat had been driven into the mines by her assailants. There was another incident on the other side of the Channel, close to Le Colbart, where there was a huge explosion in the minefield followed by the appearance of wreckage and oil on the surface. Both *UC78* and *UB31* were in the area at the time; neither returned from patrol.

UB78

	Launched	*Commissioned*
UB78	2 Jun 1917	20 Oct 1917
Type	UBIII	
CO	*Oberleutnant zur See* A. Stossberg (lost)	
Date of loss	9 May 1918	
Location	English Channel, W of Cherbourg, 49°49'N 01°40'W	
Cause	Ramming	
Casualties	35	
Survivors	None	
Salvaged	No	

Notes *UB78* was on the surface north of Cherbourg when she was spotted and rammed by the transport *Queen Alexandra*. The latter did not stop, but the patrol craft *P35* was ordered to the scene and found oil and battery acid on the surface.

UB70

	Launched	*Commissioned*
UB70	17 Aug 1917	29 Oct 1917
Type	UBIII	
CO	*Kapitänleutnant* J. Remy (lost)	
Date of loss	April/May 1918	
Location	?	
Cause	?	
Casualties	33	
Survivors	None	
Salvaged	No	

Notes *UB70* left Germany on 16 April 1918 en route for Pola. No explanation is available for her loss. It was not until survivors from other boats admitted she was missing that the British became aware of her demise. A drifting mine, accident or drill failure are the most likely causes of *UB70*'s loss.

U32

	Launched	*Commissioned*
U32	28 Jan 1914	3 Sept 1914
Type	U31	
CO	*Kapitänleutnant* K. Albrecht (lost)	
Date of loss	8 May 1918	
Location	Mediterranean, NW of Malta, 36°07'N 13°28'E	
Cause	Depth charge	
Casualties	41	
Survivors	None	
Salvaged	No	

Notes Albrecht attacked a Gibraltar–Alexandria convoy and was first shelled and then depth-charged by the sloop HMS *Wallflower*.

UB16

	Launched	*Commissioned*
UB16	26 Apr 1916	12 May 1916
Type	UBI	
CO	*Oberleutnant zur See* von der Lühe (survived)	
Date of loss	10 May 1918	
Location	North Sea, 52°06'N 02°01'E	
Cause	Submarine attack	
Casualties	15	
Survivors	1	
Salvaged	No	

Notes The British submarine *E34* (Lt R. Pulleyne RN) was returning to Harwich from a minelaying operation when she sighted a submarine bow-on. Pulleyne was in an area where, he had been told, he might encounter other British submarines, so he studied his target through the pericope with some care before firmly identifying it as German. He then fired two torpedoes and recorded two hits (in fact both hit but only one exploded). Surfacing to assess the result of his attack, he was able to pluck von der Lühe from the oily water.

U154

	Launched	*Commissioned*
U154	10 Sept 1917	12 Dec 1917
Type	U151 *U-Kreuzer*	
CO	*Korvettenkapitän* H. Gercke (lost)	
Date of loss	11 May 1918	
Location	Atlantic, W of Cape St Vincent, 36°51'N 11°50'W	
Cause	Submarine attack	

Casualties	77
Survivors	None
Salvaged	No

Notes *U154* was spotted by the British submarine *E35* (Lt-Cdr Guy D'Oyly Hughes RN); the German was slowly zig-zagging on the surface, waiting for a rendezvous with *U62*. Gercke's slow and unpredictable course made setting up the attack extremely difficult. At one stage *E35* was in a perfect position but the range was less than 200yds and at that distance the torpedoes would not have armed. *U154*'s look-outs cannot have been very vigilant for D'Oyly Hughes spent nearly two and a half hours stalking the U-boat, making frequent use of his periscope. Finally *E35* was in the right position and at the right range. A torpedo was fired at 1818, which missed and was not spotted by *U154*'s look-outs. A second torpedo was fired at 1825 which hit *U154* under her after gun. *E35* surfaced and found three men struggling in a widening slick of oil. Just as *E35* was ready to haul them out of the water, a periscope was sighted. This was *U153*, which fired one torpedo which missed. *E35* dived very quickly and left the area, but in the confusion the three survivors of *U154* drowned.

	Launched	*Commissioned*
U103	9 Jun 1917	15 Jul 1917
Type	U81	
CO	*Kapitänleutnant* C. Rucker (survived)	
Date of loss	12 May 1918	
Location	English Channel, 49°16'N 04°51'W	
Cause	Ramming	
Casualties	10	
Survivors	35	
Salvaged	No	

Notes *U103* was one of a group of five boats (with *U46*, *U55*, *U70* and *U94*) concentrated at the western end of the Channel to await a convoy. This was seen as a favourable location since documents captured from an American merchant ship indicated that troop transports were only in convoy as far as the Fastnet; thereafter they proceeded independently. *U103* was on the surface at night waiting for a convoy when her look-outs reported the bow wave of a very large steamer coming straight towards them. The 'steamer' was one of the largest liners in the world, the White Star Line's *Olympic*, carrying American troops to Southampton. It was too late for Rucker to dive or to attack and the *Olympic*, making 24kts, ripped through the submarine. Rucker and 34 of his crew survived: rescued by the USS *Davis*, they were taken to Queenstown.

	Launched	*Commissioned*
UB72	30 Jul 1917	9 Sept 1917
Type	UBIII	
CO	*Oberleutnant zur See* F. Trager (lost)	
Date of loss	12 May 1918	
Location	English Channel, 50°08'N 02°41'E	
Cause	Submarine attack	
Casualties	34	
Survivors	3	
Salvaged	No	

Notes *UB72* was waiting further up-Channel for the same convoy as *U103*. She was spotted by the British submarine *D4*, which had been sent to the area following the interception of German signals about the concentration of U-boats. *D4* was dived and sighted *UB72* on the surface, the U-boat's bridge packed with officers and men all looking zealously to the west—away from *D4*—for the convoy. *D4* fired two torpedoes from a range of 600yds and both hit. When *D4* surfaced she found three survivors swimming in the oily sea.

	Launched	*Commissioned*
UC35	6 May 1916	4 Oct 1916
Type	UCII	
CO	*Oberleutnant zur See* H. P. Korsch (lost)	
Date of loss	17 May 1918	
Location	Mediterranean, SW of Sardinia, 39°48'N 07°42'E	
Cause	Gunfire	
Casualties	20	
Survivors	5 (plus a captured Spanish seaman)	
Salvaged	No	

Notes *UC325* was sunk by gunfire from the French patrol vessel *Ailly*, which Korsch had taken for an escorted steamer. Even though *Ailly*'s first shots had disabled *UC35* by tearing open a ballast tank, the U-boat's gunners kept firing until *UC35* sank beneath them.

UB52	*Launched* 8 Mar 1917	*Commissioned* 9 Aug 1917
Type	UBIII	
CO	*Oberleutnant zur See* Otto Launburg (survived)	
Date of loss	25 May 1918	
Location	Mediterranean, Strait of Otranto, 41°36'N 18°52'E	
Cause	Submarine attack	
Casualties	32	
Survivors	2	
Salvaged	No	

Notes This boat was torpedoed by the British submarine *H4* (Lt Oliver North RN). North had sighted the homeward-bound *UB52* on the surface, chased after her and fired two torpedoes at less than 300yds' range. Both hit and Launburg and his *Obersteuermann*, the two men on the bridge at the time of the attack, were later rescued.

UB74	*Launched* 12 Sept 1917	*Commissioned* 24 Oct 1917
Type	UBIII	
CO	*Oberleutnant zur See* E. Steindorff (lost)	
Date of loss	26 May 1918	
Location	English Channel, 50°32'N 02°32'W	
Cause	Depth charge	
Casualties	35	
Survivors	None	
Salvaged	No	

Notes *UB74* was operating in Lyme Bay when she was spotted by the patrol yacht *Lorna*, which had been warned that a U-boat was in the area. *Lorna* sighted *UB74*'s periscope and dropped two depth charges as she ran over the spot. These had an immediate effect and blew a mass of wreckage, oil and air bubbles to the surface. Four men were seen swimming in the midst of the boil. However, *Lorna*'s CO could not believe that his first 'pattern', dropped by eye, had had such a conclusive effect and so dropped another which killed three of the men. The fourth was dragged on board *Lorna* and later died, though not before confirming the identity of the boat.

UB119	*Launched* 13 Dec 1917	*Commissioned* 9 Feb 1918
Type	UBIII	
CO	*Oberleutnant zur See* W. Kolbe (lost)	
Date of loss	May 1918	
Location	?	
Cause	?	
Casualties	34	
Survivors	None	
Salvaged	No	

Notes *UB119* left Heligoland on 27 April and was known to have sunk a steamer off Belfast on 25 May. Thereafter she disappeared. In the absence of any claim for her loss, it is presumed that she was mined through entering a minefield as a result of navigational error, ran into a drifting mine or was lost as a result of an accident.

UC75	*Launched* 6 Nov 1916	*Commissioned* 6 Dec 1916
Type	UCII	
CO	*Oberleutnant zur See* W. Schmitz (survived)	
Date of loss	31 May 1918	
Location	E coast of England, 53°57'N 00°09'E	
Cause	Ramming	
Casualties	19	
Survivors	14	
Salvaged	No	

Notes *UC75* was attacking an East Coast convoy when she was spotted by the steamer *Blaydonian*, which tried to ram but instead scraped over the casing. Badly damaged in the encounter, *UC75* came to the surface and found herself in the middle of the convoy. The CO of the destroyer HMS *Fairy* could not believe that a U-boat was in his convoy, thought the boat was British and offered the challenge then in force. When no reply was received he rammed the U-boat's stern on the basis that if she was a British boat, all the crew could get out. There was evidently a certain amount of confusion in the submarine for one man in the conning tower indicated that the U-boat was surrendering while others manned the deck gun. *Fairy* then came around for a second deliberate ramming, striking *UC75* between the deck gun and the conning tower. Two of *UC75*'s crew simply jumped from the casing on to *Fairy*'s forecastle, where they stood with their hands raised in surrender. Another twelve were picked up from the water.

However, *Fairy*'s bows were badly damaged in the two rammings—she had been launched in 1897 and had just sunk an opponent one and a half times her size and considerably more stoutly built—and she eventually sank.

U64

	Launched	*Commissioned*
	29 Feb 1916	15 Apr 1916
Type	U43	
CO	*Kapitänleutnant* Robert Moraht (survived)	
Date of loss	17 June 1918	
Location	Mediterranean, SE of Sardinia, 38°07'N 10°27'E	
Cause	Gunfire	
Casualties	38	
Survivors	5	
Salvaged	No	

Notes After attacking a convoy between Sicily and Sardinia *U64* was depth-charged and damaged by the sloop *Lychnis*. *U64* then surfaced and was rammed by *Lychnis*. However, the 'ramming' was more a slight collision and Moraht was able to dive. The submarine proved no easier to control so Moraht surfaced, intending to fight it out. It was an unequal contest. *Lychnis*'s gunners had the advantage of being able to open fire as soon as *U64* surfaced and before her crew could come up on to the casing and man their weapons. In a hail of gunfire *U64* sank almost immediately.

UC64

	Launched	*Commissioned*
	27 Jan 1917	22 Feb 1917
Type	UCII	
CO	*Oberleutnant zur See* F. Schwartz (lost)	
Date of loss	20 June 1918	
Location	Strait of Dover, between Folkestone and The Varne, 50°58'N 01°23'E	
Cause	Mine/depth charge	
Casualties	30	
Survivors	None	
Salvaged	No	

Notes *UC64* was outward-bound for the Bordeaux/Gironde area when she was mined east of The Varne. The explosion was reported by the drifter *Ocean Roamer*, which, together with *Loyal Friend*, began to depth-charge the U-boat which was still moving though leaking oil and air. Oil and air continued to rise for the next seven hours. The identity of the wreck was confirmed on 6 July by divers.

UC11

	Launched	*Commissioned*
	11 Apr 1915	23 Apr 1915
Type	UCI	
CO	*Oberleutnant* K. Utke (survived)	
Date of loss	26 June 1918	
Location	Strait of Dover, 51°55'N 01°1'E	
Cause	Mine	
Casualties	18	
Survivors	1	
Salvaged	No	

Notes *UC11* was mined while proceeding dived north-east of the Sunk Light Vessel. The boat flooded quickly and tanks could not be blown. However, Utke crammed himself into the conning tower and as the water rose in his boat the pressure in the conning tower increased. Eventually he was able to open the hatch and swim to the surface. After swimming for thirty minutes he was rescued by a small boat sent out by the light vessel which had seen the explosion. Utke then unsuccessfully tried to pass himself off as the boat's engineer officer.

An interesting twist to this sinking is that Utke later claimed that *UC11* was mined on a German field. If so, then it was a field laid by *UC11* on an earlier operation.

UXX

	Launched	*Comissioned*
	18 Sept 1916	20 Oct 1917
Type	Havmanden (U20/U23 group)	
CO	*Linienschiffsleutnant* Ludwig Müller (lost)	
Date of loss	4 July 1918	
Location	N Adriatic, 45°29'N 15°2'E	
Cause	Submarine attack	
Casualties	12	
Survivors	None	
Salvaged	Yes (see notes)	

Notes *F12* fired one torpedo while on the surface from a range of 650yds. She subsequently found a large slick of diesel but no wreckage.

UXX's stern was raised on 21 July 1962 and bow on 3 October 1962 by the firm of Sponza and Zuberti of Grado; the crew were buried in the Austrian military cemetery in Wiener Neustadt. The conning tower, one anchor and other relics from the submarine are on display at the Heeresgeschichtliches Museum in Vienna

---

UX

	Launched	*Commissioned*
	16 May 1915	12 June 1915
Type	UB1	
CO	*Linienschiffsleutnant* Johann von Ulmansky (survived)	
Date of loss	9 July 1918	
Location	N Adriatic, between Caorle and mouth of Tagliamento river	
Cause	Mine/grounding	
Casualties	None	
Survivors	13	
Salvaged	Raised by the Austrians 26 July 1918 and towed to Trieste but subsequently declared a constructive total loss and broken up	

Notes *UX* struck a mine but Ulmansky managed to keep his boat afloat long enough to beach her and the crew to get ashore.

UB65

	Launched	*Commissioned*
	26 Jan 1917	18 Aug 1917
Type	UBIII	
CO	*Kapitänleutnant* M. Schelle (lost)	
Date of loss	10 July 1918	
Location	St George's Channel, S of Fastnet Light, 51°07'N 09°42'W	
Cause	Accident	
Casualties	37	
Survivors	None	
Salvaged	No	

Notes *UB65* was lost in an accidental explosion while making an attack on the US Navy submarine *L2* (Lt P. F. Foster USN). The USN's assessment is that *UB65* fired a torpedo fitted with a magnetic exploder which detonated prematurely, catching her within the lethal radius.

UC77

	Launched	*Commissioned*
	2 Dec 1916	29 Dec 1916
Type	UCII	
CO	*Oberleutnant zur See* J. Ries (lost)	
Date of loss	July (?) 1918	
Location	English Channel, exact location unknown	
Cause	?	
Casualties	30	
Survivors	None	
Salvaged	No	

Notes *UC77* sailed on 11 July for the Portland/Owers area and was not heard from again. It may have been this boat (or *UB108*) which was destroyed in an explosion in the Dover Barrage on 14 July 1918, resulting in oil and wreckage being brought to the surface. However, the possibility of loss through accident cannot be ruled out.

UB108

	Launched	*Commissioned*
	21 Jul 1917	1 Mar 1918
Type	UBIII	
CO	*Kapitänleutnant* Walter Amberger (lost)	
Date of loss	July (?) 1918	
Location	?	
Cause	?	
Casualties	36	
Survivors	None	
Salvaged	No	

Notes *UB108* departed on 2 July for the West Channel area and was not heard from again. She may have been the victim of a depth-charge attack by two drifters on 10 July between Folkestone and The Varne which brought wreckage and oil to the surface or she may have been destroyed in an explosion in the Dover Barrage on 14 July 1918.

UB110

	Launched	*Commissioned*
	1 Sept 1917	23 Mar 1918
Type	UBIII	
CO	*Kapitänleutnant* W. Furbringer (survived)	
Date of loss	19 July 1918	
Location	E coast of England, 54°39'N 00°55'E	
Cause	Depth charge	
Casualties	13	
Survivors	21	

Salvaged	Divers were sent down almost immediately; wreck raised on 4 October 1918 and subsequently broken up

Notes Furbringer was making an approach to a convoy when his periscope was spotted by an alert ML. Nearly all the ships in the escort gathered to drop depth charges on the luckless submarine. The hyroplanes jammed, one of the boat's motors short-circuited and the engineer reported leaks in the fuel tanks. Furbringer surfaced, but before he could surrender *UB110* was rammed twice by HMS *Garry*.

	Launched	*Commissioned*
UB124	19 Mar 1918	22 Apr 1918
Type	UBIII	
CO	*Oberleutnant zur See* Wutsdorf (survived)	
Date of loss	20 July 1918	
Location	Irish Sea, 55°43'N 07°51'W	
Cause	Depth charge	
Casualties	2	
Survivors	32	
Salvaged	No	

Notes *UB124* happened to sight the damaged liner *Justicia* (which had been torpedoed by *UB64* the day before) being towed back to Liverpool. Wutsdorf fired two torpedoes at 0910 which hit, but on firing the boat lost trim and broached in full view of the escort. In the next ninety minutes over 50 depth charges were dropped around UB124—a considerable number for 1918 (twenty-five years later Captain Walker's Second Escort Group would expend that number in one attack). By 1750 Wutsdorf thought it safe to surface; conditions in the boat were now very bad. The boat surfaced with a bow-up angle so that battery acid flowed into the bilges, producing chlorine gas. On reaching the surface Wutsdorf found the destroyers *Marne* and *Millbrook* waiting for him. Despite the appalling conditions in the boat he dived and managed to break away despite further depth-charge attacks. Thirty minutes later he surfaced and was leaving the area at best speed when he was sighted again by the destroyers. This time there was no escape. Damage to the battery meant that he could not dive, so Wutsdorf fired the scuttling charges after abandoning *UB124* and waited to be picked up.

	Launched	*Commissioned*
UB107	21 Jul 1917	16 Feb 1918
Type	UBIII	
CO	*Kapitänleutnant* von Prittwitz und Gaffron (lost)	
Date of loss	27 July 1918	
Location	E coast of England, 54°23'N 00°24'E	
Cause	Depth charge	
Casualties	38	
Survivors	None	
Salvaged	No	

Notes Sighted by an ML off Scarborough, *UB107* was hunted relentlessly by an *ad hoc* group of trawlers and MLs reinforced by the destroyer HMS *Vanessa*. In bad weather on the evening of the 27th, *UB107* broached in full view of the trawler *Calvia*. Three trawlers dropped a number of depth charges, after which oil came to the surface together with large air bubbles. The ships remained in the location overnight and the next morning *Vanessa* recovered the headless body of a man in German uniform.

	Launched	*Commissioned*
UB53	9 Mar 1917	21 Aug 1917
Type	UBIII	
CO	*Kapitänleutnant* Sprenger (survived)	
Date of loss	3 August 1918	
Location	Mediterranean, Strait of Otranto, 39°40'N 18°40'E	
Cause	Mine	
Casualties	10	
Survivors	27	
Salvaged	No	

Notes *UB53* was outward-bound from Pola and and Sprenger intended to make his passage through the Otranto Barrage dived. At 1700 he worked out that he was past the defences and that it was safe to surface. Unfortunately the French had recently extended the minefields eastwards, and on coming to the surface *UB53*'s stern was badly damaged by two mines. The boat reached the surface but was sinking. Sprenger threw his charts and confidential books over the side, set the scuttling charges and abandoned the submarine, which sank at 1730. Three and a half hours later the survivors were found and rescued by the destroyer HMS *Martin*.

UC49

	Launched	*Commissioned*
	7 Nov 1916	2 Dec 1916

Type	UCII
CO	*Oberleutnant zur See* H. Kukenthal (lost)
Date of loss	8 August 1918
Location	SW coast of England, off Start Point, 50°20'N 03°30'E
Cause	Depth charge
Casualties	31
Survivors	None
Salvaged	No

Notes *UC49* was ordered to lay mines off Plymouth and Falmouth. On the morning of 8 August she was just beginning her first minelay off Start Point when she fouled one of her own mines. *UC49* was shaken but not badly damaged by the explosion, which, however, was observed by the destroyer HMS *Opossum*, on routine A/S patrol. Kukenthal went to the bottom and lay there with all machinery switched off as the destroyer, joined by a number of MLs, hunted above him. (In these waters in the summer of 1944 Kukenthal's successors in another world war would adopt these very tactics.) At 1520 Kukenthal ordered some machinery to be started to see if the hunters were still there and was rewarded with a depth charge. The same thing happened at 1757. Then *Opossum* indulged in some baiting tactics and noisily withdrew to a spot 2½ miles away in the hope that the U-boat would come up. Just over a quarter of an hour later *UC49* broke surface and was immediately fired on. So intense was the fire that she sank in less than twenty seconds. Depth charges were dropped and oil and bubbles came to the surface.

In a foretaste of proceedings in the next world war the wreck was plastered with depth charges on 9 August in order to break it open and yield definite evidence of a 'kill' (in other words, a body). This was adjudged to have happened when a light bulb bearing the stamp of a Viennese munitions plant came to the surface.

UB30

	Launched	*Commissioned*
	16 Nov 1915	18 Mar 1916

Type	UBII
CO	*Oberleutnant zur See* R. Stier (lost)
Date of loss	13 August 1918
Location	E coast of England, 54°32'N 00°35'E
Cause	Depth charge
Casualties	26
Survivors	None
Salvaged	No

Notes *UB30* had already been lost to the Germans once when she grounded in Dutch waters on 23 February 1917 and was interned. On this occasion diplomatic pressure secured her release. Now she was proceeding dived off Whitby when her periscope was spotted by the trawler *John Gillman*. The trawler went in to ram but the U-boat was diving so that the former scraped noisily over her casing. Two depth charges brought oil and wreckage to the surface, so *John Gillman* dropped a Dan buoy and awaited developments. Two hours later *U30* was sighted surfacing by the trawlers *John Brooker* and *Viola*, which drove her down again with depth charges and gunfire. Ten minutes later *U30* came up again and was fired on and depth-charged by *John Gillman* and *Florio*. The crews of the trawlers could clearly see oil and air pouring out of the holes in the submarine's pressure hull. As the U-boat sank she was followed down by four depth charges. She did not move again. The wreck was located by sweeps that night and later inspected by divers.

UB57

	Launched	*Commissioned*
	21 Jun 1917	31 Jul 1917

Type	UBIII
CO	*Oberleutnant zur See* J. Lohs (lost)
Date of loss	14 August 1918
Location	English Channel, off Zeebrugge, 51°56'N 02°02'E
Cause	Mine
Casualties	34
Survivors	None
Salvaged	No

Notes *UB57* was presumed sunk in a field of ground magnetic mines laid by the 20th Destroyer Flotilla. Lohs' last signal was on 14 August and indicated that he was through the Dover defences and would enter Zeebrugge through a known 'safe' channel. Nothing more was heard, and a week later his body and those of a number of his ship's company were washed ashore near the Schelde. If *UB57* was lost on these mines, then she becomes the first submarine to be sunk by a magnetic mine.

UC70	*Launched* 7 Aug 1916	*Commissioned* 22 Nov 1916
Type	UCII	
CO	*Oberleutnant zur See* K. Dobberstein (lost)	
Date of loss	28 August 1918	
Location	E coast of England	
Cause	Depth charge	
Casualties	31	
Survivors	None	
Salvaged	No	

Notes A patrol aeroplane sighted an oil slick not far from *U30*'s last position. A 250lb bomb was dropped which brought oil and large air bubbles to the surface. The destroyer HMS *Ouse* was sent to investigate and plastered the wreck in a series of depth-charge attacks. Divers sent down on 14 September found *UC70*'s wreck.

It is possible that *UC70* had been damaged earlier in a new British minefield off the Yorkshire coast and was lying on the bottom effecting repairs when the slick was spotted.

UB109	*Launched* 7 Jul 1917	*Commissioned* 31 Dec 1917
Type	UBIII	
CO	*Kapitänleutnant* Ramien (survived)	
Date of loss	29 August 1918	
Location	Strait of Dover, 51°03'N 01°44'E	
Cause	Mine	
Casualties	28	
Survivors	8	
Salvaged	No	

Notes *UB109* was returning from the Bay of Biscay and was passing up the Channel on the English side. She had not received warnings sent to her about new British minefields off Folkestone. At 0305 shore hydrophones at Folkestone registered the noise of *UB109*'s motors. Seventeen minutes later the galvanometer needle indicated that *UB109* was directly over a line of mines and the field was fired. Ramien and seven others managed a bold escape through the conning tower.

UB12	*Launched* 2 Mar 1915	*Commissioned* 29 Mar 1915
Type	UBI	
CO	*Oberleutnant zur See* E. Scholler (lost)	
Date of loss	Between 19 and 31 August 1918	
Location	North Sea, 51°20'N 01°30'E (?)	
Cause	Mine (?)	
Casualties	19	
Survivors	None	
Salvaged	No	

Notes *UB12* sailed on 19 August for a minelay in the Thames estuary. Her loss is unexplained, but equipment or drill failure cannot be ruled out.

U92	*Launched* 12 May 1917	*Commissioned* 22 Oct 1917
Type	U81	
CO	*Kapitänleutnant* G. Ehrlich (lost)	
Date of loss	9 September 1918 (?)	
Location	?	
Cause	?	
Casualties	42	
Survivors	None	
Salvaged	No	

Notes *U92* sailed on 4 September for the Irish Sea and was possibly mined in the Fair Isle Passage. Her last signal was on 9 September when she reported, as instructed, that she was just south of the Passage.

UB83	*Launched* 15 Sept 1917	*Commissioned* 15 Oct 1917
Type	UBIII	
CO	*Oberleutnant zur See* H. Buntebardt (lost)	
Date of loss	10 September 1918	
Location	Orkneys, 58°28'N 01°50W	
Cause	Depth charge	
Casualties	37	
Survivors	None	
Salvaged	No	

Notes *UB83*'s conning tower was sighted from a kite balloon towed by the destroyer HMS *Ophelia*. The destroyer raced to the spot and dropped three depth charges. Oil came up, followed by a massive and violent underwater explosion. The U-boat seemed to be still moving and heading toward the Pentland Firth, so *Ophelia* dropped four more depth charges, after which the target was lying stopped on the bottom.

UB103	*Launched*	*Commissioned*
	7 Jul 1917	18 Dec 1917
Type	UBIII	
CO	*Kapitänleutnant* Paul Hundius (lost)	
Date of loss	16 September 1918	
Location	Strait of Dover	
Cause	Mine	
Casualties	37	
Survivors	None	
Salvaged	No, though divers found and investigated the wreck	

Notes *UB103* was the last U-boat to pass westwards through the Strait of Dover, on 14 September. She may have been damaged in the attempt for on 16 September airship *Z1* sighted an oil slick and followed it for over half an hour. Drifters from the patrol were summoned to the spot and dropped depth charges. The detonations of the depth charges were followed by three large underwater explosions.

The Strait was now effectively closed to U-boats. All passages out into the Atlantic and Western Approaches would have to be made 'north about', a route that would take the U-boats over and through the newly laid Northern Barrage.

UB104	*Launched*	*Commissioned*
	1 Jul 1917	7 Feb 1918
Type	UBIII	
CO	*Oberleutnant zur See* T. Bieber (lost)	
Date of loss	September 1918	
Location	?	
Cause	?	
Casualties	36	
Survivors	None	
Salvaged	No	

Notes *UB104* left Zeebrugge on 6 September and made a successful passage through the Strait of Dover for she exchanged recognition signals with *U57* on the 11th. A week later she was operating in Lyme Bay, but nothing more was heard from her. No *Entente* claim exists to account for her demise and it is possible that she was lost through accident.

UB127	*Launched*	*Commissioned*
	27 Apr 1918	1 Jun 1918
Type	UBIII	
CO	*Oberleutnant zur See* W. Scheffler (lost)	
Date of loss	September 1918	
Location	?	
Cause	?	
Casualties	34	
Survivors	None	
Salvaged	No	

Notes *UB127* was possibly mined south of the Fair Isle Passage. A body wearing German uniform was picked up in this area on 20 September.

U156	*Launched*	*Commissioned*
	14 Apr 1917	28 Aug 1917
Type	U151 *U-Kreuzer*	
CO	*Kapitänleutnant* R. Feldt (lost)	
Date of loss	25 September 1918	
Location	N North Sea	
Cause	Mine	
Casualties	77	
Survivors	None	
Salvaged	No	

Notes *U156* was returning from a very successful patrol in American waters in which her mines had been responsible for the loss of the US cruiser *San Diego* on 19 July. On 24 September Feldt signalled that he would be transiting the Northern Barrage on 25 September and that, as ordered, he would signal when clear. No such signal was received and *U156* was most probably mined.

UB115	*Launched*	*Commissioned*
	4 Nov 1917	26 May 1918
Type	UBIII	
CO	*Oberleutnant zur See* R. Thomsen (lost)	
Date of loss	29 September 1918	
Location	NE coast of England, N of Sunderland, 55°13'N 01°22'W	
Cause	Depth charge	
Casualties	39	
Survivors	None	
Salvaged	No	

Notes The destroyers *Ouse* and *Star* were investigating an oil slick reported by the airship *R39*. The two warships dropped seven depth charges and later three trawlers dropped another ten. The trawlers were fitted with hydrophones and at

1400 they heard a U-boat start her motors. Another twelve depth charges went over the side. An hour later motor noises resulted in more depth charges being dropped. Between 1600 and 1825 the motors were run continuously as if the U-boat were trying to drive herself up to the surface. At 1825 the noise ceased but oil continued to come up all night and for the next two days.

	Launched	*Commissioned*
U102	12 May 1917	18 Jun 1917
Type	U81	
CO	*Kapitänleutnant* K. Beitzen (lost)	
Date of loss	September 1918	
Location	North Sea, exact location unknown	
Cause	?	
Casualties	42	
Survivors	None	
Salvaged	No	

Notes Presumed mined in the Northern Barrage.

	Launched	*Commissioned*
UB113	23 Sept 1917	15 Apr 1918
Type	UBIII	
CO	*Oberleutnant zur See* U. Pilzecker (lost)	
Date of loss	September 1918	
Location	?	
Cause	?	
Casualties	39	
Survivors	None	
Salvaged	No	

Notes *UB113* left Zeebrugge for the West Channel but routed 'north about'. There are some claims that she was mined off Boulogne on 9 October but there is no evidence for this and her loss remains a mystery.

	Launched	*Commissioned*
U34	9 May 1914	5 Oct 1914
Type	U23	
CO	*Kapitänleutnant* J. Klasing (lost)	
Date of loss	October 1918	
Location	Mediterranean	
Cause	?	
Survivors	None	
Salvaged	No	

Notes *U34* sailed on October 18 and was not heard from again. She may have been a victim of a depth charge on the 21st or on 9 November. However the possibility that she was lost through accident cannot be ruled out.

	Launched	*Commissioned*
UB68	4 Jul 1917	5 Aug 1917
Type	UBIII	
CO	*Oberleutnant zur See* Karl Dönitz (survived)	
Date of loss	4 October 1918	
Location	Mediterranean, 150m E of Malta, 35°56'N 16°20'E	
Cause	Gunfire	
Casualties	1	
Survivors	33	
Salvaged	No	

Notes Attacking a convoy, Dönitz sank the 3,883-ton *Oopack* before surfacing to get ahead of the convoy and diving for another attack. On diving, the engineer, *Oberingenieur* Jeschen, had some difficulty in maintaining depth. The boat broached and then went down to 60m before rising again. At 30m the tanks were flooded to stop the boat broaching and this time she went down to 102m (the test depth was 70m) before the engineer could stop her. At this depth hull valves gave way and the boat began to take on water. For a second time all tanks were blown using the last of the HP air, and *UB68* rose with a 45-degree stern-up angle. She surfaced in the middle of the convoy, whose escorts opened a rapid and accurate fire on the U-boat. Dönitz ordered another dive but the LI reported that there was no more HP air left. The *Obersteuermann* reported that the boat had taken two hits on the conning tower and one on the forward casing. Dönitz had no option but to order the crew out and scuttle the boat. *Oberingenieur* Jeschen was ordered by Dönitz to open the vents but he did not come up on to the casing once the boat started to sink. Evidence from the survivors suggests that he accepted that it was his handling of the boat that caused her loss and thus deliberately remained in the control room. Dönitz and the rest of his crew were picked up by HMS *Snapdragon* and taken to Malta.

Oberleutnant zur See Dönitz went on to be *Führer der U-boote* in the Second World War.

UB90	*Launched* 12 Feb 1918	*Commissioned* 21 Mar 1918
Type	UBIII	
CO	*Oberleutnant zur See* G. von Mayer (lost)	
Date of loss	16 October 1918	
Location	Skagerrak, 57°55'N 10°27'E	
Cause	Submarine attack	
Casualties	38	
Survivors	None	
Salvaged	No	

Notes *UB90* had sustained weather damage which prevented her from reaching her operational area in the Bristol Channel. Instead she operated in the North Sea before returning home. Mayer requested an escort to meet him on the 18th, but two days earlier was sighted by HM Submarine *L12*. The British boat was dived and fired four torpedoes at *UB90*'s conning tower. There was a massive explosion and *L12* surfaced in a sea of oil and wreckage and what was identified as half a corpse.

UB123	*Launched* 2 Mar 1918	*Commissioned* 6 Apr 1918
Type	UBIII	
CO	*Oberleutnant zur See* R. Ramm (lost)	
Date of loss	19 October 1918	
Location	Northern Barrage area, exact location unknown	
Cause	Mine	
Casualties	36	
Survivors	None	
Salvaged	No	

Notes *UB123* was homeward-bound and had exchanged signals with *UB125* on the 17th about a safe route through the Northern Barrage. It is most likely that *UB123* was mined while passing through this area.

U78	*Launched* 27 Feb 1915	*Commissioned* 20 Apr 1915
Type	UE	
CO	*Oberleutnant zur See* J. Vollbrecht (lost)	
Date of loss	28 October 1918	
Location	N North Sea, 56°02'N 05°08'	
Cause	Submarine attack	
Casualties	40	
Survivors	None	
Salvaged	No	

Notes HM Submarine *G2* was on patrol in the Skaggerak when her hydrophones picked up the sound of a U-boat giving a recongition signal using an oscillator. She proceeded to attack. Despite an error in the firing drill, one torpedo was fired and the U-boat disintegrated. *G2*'s commanding officer made a brief search for wreckage and survivors but found nothing. Since he believed that another U-boat was in the area he dived and made his exit.

UB116	*Launched* 4 Nov 1917	*Commissioned* 24 May 1918
Type	UBIII	
CO	*Kapitänleutnant* Hans-Joachim Emsmann (lost)	
Date of loss	28 October 1918	
Location	Orkneys, Hoxa Gate to Scapa Flow	
Cause	Mine	
Casualties	36	
Survivors	None	
Salvaged	Wreck inspected by divers but not salved	

Notes This was the last U-boat to be sunk in the First World War. As part of the German Navy's plan for a climactic engagement with the Royal Navy in the winter of 1918, nine U-boats were dispatched on preparatory operations around the British coast on 25 October. *UB116* was to enter the Grand Fleet's base at Scapa Flow and attack the battleships thought to be moored there. Emsman was advised, incorrectly, that the Hoxa Sound was neither mined nor barred by nets and this was he route he chose. However, on the afternoon of 28 October *UB116* was sighted off the Orkneys and the defences were alerted. Hydrophones picked up the noise of her motors and she was tracked through the Hoxa Boom until 2322, when the galvanometer needle in the mine station indicated that she was over a line of mines. The switches were closed and after the explosion there were no more HE noises. The following day divers were sent down and recovered numerous items of interest, including *UB116*'s log.

A Roman Catholic chaplain with the Grand Fleet, Father Tom Bradley, wrote in his diary that after the explosion of the minefield tapping noises could be heard coming from the hull, indicating that there was life on board. Since there was no hope of rescuing the men, the duty destroyer was ordered to drop a depth charge over the wreck to complete the destruction.

Emsmann's operation was courageous but futile: in April 1918 the Grand Fleet had moved south to Rosyth. The massive anchorage which Emsmann died trying to enter was empty. Thirteen days later the war was over.

1939

U39

	Launched	*Completed*
U39	22 Sept 1938	10 Dec 1938

Class: Type IXA
CO: *Kapitänleutnant* Gerhard Glattes (survived)
Date of loss: 14 September 1939
Location: NW of Ireland, 58°32'N 11°49'W
Cause: Depth charge
Casualties: None
Survivors: 43
Salvaged: No

Notes *U39* attacked the aircraft carrier *Ark Royal*, which was engaged in ASW operations, with two torpedoes which exploded prematurely 80m short of the target. The counter-attack by the destroyers *Faulknor*, *Foxhound* and *Firedrake* was swift and accurate. The first attack by *Foxhound* with two charges, set to 250ft and 300ft, damaged the battery and the main motors and extinguished the lights. *Faulknor* then attacked with a full pattern, followed by *Firedrake*, and it was this third attack which did the most damage. The U-boat was making a considerable amount of water, chlorine gas was coming from the battery and the LI could not catch the trim. At 1546 *U39* broke surface and she was abandoned.

U27

	Launched	*Completed*
U27	24 Jun 1936	12 Aug 1936

Class: Type VII
CO: *Kapitänleutnant* Johannes Franz (survived)
Date of loss: 20 September 1939
Location: 60nm W of Hebrides
Cause: Depth charge
Casualties: None
Survivors: 4 officers, 14 senior rates, 20 junior rates
Salvaged: *Fortune*'s engineer officer managed to board *U27* but the boat was beyond salvage.

Notes Reports that a U-boat had been stopping and sinking fishing vessels off the Hebrides prompted a sweep by destroyers of the Home Fleet supported by aircraft of the Fleet Air Arm. On 20 September the destroyers *Fortune* and *Forester* sighted a submarine on the surface and had three torpedoes fired at them which detonated prematurely. *Fortune* then delivered three depth-charge attacks and *Forester* one, which did severe damage to the submarine. One propeller was damaged and the shaft bent, while a considerable amount of water was coming in aft through various pipes and rivets which had started. The main line had fractured, so Franz bought the boat to the surface amid the boil of *Fortune*'s fourth attack. *Fortune* turned to ram and opened fire but stopped on seeing that the crew were gathering on the conning tower and casing. *U27* was ordered to stop and abandon ship, which she did at 0315. From his PoW camp Franz was able to inform BdU, using a basic letter code, that the errant performance of his torpedoes had been his undoing.

U12

	Launched	*Completed*
U12	11 Sept 1935	30 Sept 1935

Class: Type IIB
CO: *Kapitänleutnant* von der Ropp (lost)
Date of loss: 8 October 1939
Location: Strait of Dover, exact location unknown
Cause: Mine
Casualties: 27
Survivors: None
Salvaged: No

Notes *U12* was mined during a transit of the Strait of Dover.

U40	*Launched*	*Completed*
	9 Nov 1938	11 Feb 1939
Class	Type IXA	
CO	*Kapitänleutnant* Wolfgang Barten (lost)	
Date of loss	13 October 1939	
Location	Strait of Dover	
Cause	Mine	
Casualties	38	
Survivors	3	
Salvaged	No	

Notes *U40* was attempting to make a surfaced transit of the Strait of Dover by night some 3½ hours after high water when she struck a mine at 0300 and sank. The monthly Anti Submarine Report for October 1939 commented that Barten had not profited from the experience of his predecessors in the 1914–18 war, who would only transit the Strait at high water so that the mines would be at their maximum dip. Nine men escaped through the after escape hatch from a depth of 115ft using Dräger equipment. One drowned on reaching the surface and five subsequently died from hypothermia before being rescued. The three survivors were eventually rescued after spending nearly ten hours in the water.

U42	*Launched*	*Completed*
	16 Feb 1939	15 Jul 1939
Class	Type IXA	
CO	*Kapitänleutnant* Rolf Dau (survived)	
Date of loss	13 October 1939	
Location	SW of Ireland, 49°12'N 16°00'W	
Cause	Depth charge	
Casualties	25	
Survivors	17	
Salvaged	No	

Notes *U42* attacked the merchant ship *Stonepool*, whose escorts, the destroyers *Imogen* and *Ilex*, had left to proceed to the assistance of a French tanker reported off Cape Clear. The submarine opened fire with her deck gun, which was returned by *Stonepool*, and after about ten minutes of firing the submarine dived. She surfaced some minutes later, apparently to recover her gun's crew who had been left to swim when the boat dived. Dau now tried to work round to a favourable firing position ahead of *Stonepool* to carry out a torpedo attack. In doing so he failed to notice *Imogen* and *Ilex*, which had hastily re-joined their charge on receiving *Stonepool*'s SOS message. At 1855 *Stonepool* sighted *U42*. *Ilex* turned to towards her, firing, and forced her to dive. Both destroyers then started an asdic search and at 1918 *Imogen* was in contact, followed shortly by *Ilex*.

Ilex delivered her first attack at 1927 which caused considerable damage to *U42*. The boat assumed a 45-degree stern-down angle and it proved impossible for the crew to scramble up the deck to their positions. Dau tried to blow the after tanks but the damage to the stern was so severe that the air was merely vented into the sea. In desperation he blew the forward and midships tanks. *U42* began to rise, but it proved impossible to check her ascent at periscope depth and she broke surface at 1930.

Ilex turned in to ram, but she slowed her speed in order to minimise the damage to herself while ensuring that the submarine sank. She was probably doing no more than 6kts when she struck the U-boat's stern. The seventeen survivors included Dau and the IWO. Those in the fore ends and the motor room had shut the watertight doors during the attack and had not been able to reach the conning tower ladder to escape.

U45	*Launched*	*Completed*
	27 Apr 1938	25 Jun 1938
Class	Type VIIB	
CO	*Kapitänleutnant* Alexander Gelhaar (lost)	
Date of loss	14 October 1939	
Location	Atlantic, SW of Ireland, 50°58'N 12°07'W	
Cause	Depth charge	
Casualties	38	
Survivors	None	
Salvaged	No	

Notes *U45* was depth-charged by the British destroyers *Ivanhoe*, *Inglefield* and *Intrepid*.

U16	*Launched*	*Completed*
	28 Apr 1936	16 May 1936
Class	Type IIB	
CO	*Kapitänleutnant* Hannes Weingaertner (lost)	
Date of loss	24 October 1939	
Location	Strait of Dover	

Cause	Depth charge/grounding
Casualties	28
Survivors	None
Salvaged	See notes

Notes *U16* was making a submerged transit of the Dover Strait when she was detected by the St Margaret's Bay Indicator Loop. HM Ships *Puffin* and *Cayton Wyke* were dispatched to investigate and made a series of depth-charge attacks. While trying to avoid her assailants *U16* went aground on the Goodwins and was abandoned.

On 25 October the submarine's hull was located on the Goodwin Sands and the next day a diving boat secured alongside the hull. The hull was found to be extensively damaged forward with a hole in the pressure hull forward of the conning tower. Two officers went down the conning tower but stopped when the water level there reached their necks. Nevertheless a number of items of interest were retrieved. The weather then deteriorated and further diving was impossible until 2 November. By then the submarine had settled further into the sand and divers reported that the hull was full of silt. Bad weather caused the abandonment of further operations.

U16 was the third U-boat to fall victim to the Dover minefields. Her loss had a significant effect on German operations. Henceforth U-boats were forbidden to use the Strait of Dover as a passage through to the Western Approaches and were forced to use the longer route around the north of Scotland. Smaller U-boats, which lacked the endurance for such a long voyage, were therefore confined to the North Sea. However, this disadvantage was overcome by the German conquest of, and use of, French ports on the Atlantic coast some eight months later.

U35

	Launched	*Completed*
	29 Sept 1936	3 Nov 1936
Class	Type VII	
CO	*Kapitänleutnant* Werner Lott	
Date of loss	29 November 1939	
Location	North Sea, 60°53N 02°47E	
Cause	Depth charge	
Casualties	None	
Survivors	4 officers, 14 senior rates, 25 junior rates	
Salvaged	No	

Notes *U35* was sighted at sunrise by the destroyer HMS *Icarus* and was attacked with depth charges. *Icarus* was then joined by *Kashmir* and *Kingston*, which had been detached by Rear-Admiral (D) Home Fleet. *Kingston* was the first to find the submarine, working on the range and bearing of the target as supplied by *Icarus*, and dropped three depth charges with no visible result. She then turned to commence a second run and immediately after the charges had exploded the U-boat was seen to surface in the middle of the depth-charge boil just as *Kashmir* was starting her attack run. *Kingston*'s first attack had damaged the after hydroplanes and jammed them at 'hard arise'. The crew came up on to the casing and made motions as if to man the 88mm gun but a warning shot dissuaded them and they began to abandon ship. *Kashmir* picked up the survivors covered by *Kingston*. *U35* sank by the stern some twenty minutes after surfacing.

An examination of documents found on the survivors, in particular a diary kept by a stoker which listed battery levels throughout the night of 28/29 November, led the British to conclude that *U35* was about to enter Scapa Flow or Sullom Voe since otherwise she would not have spent the night dived.

U36

	Launched	*Completed*
	4 Nov 1936	16 Dec 1936
Class	Type VII	
CO	*Kapitänleutnant* Wilhelm Frolich (lost)	
Date of loss	4 December 1939	
Location	North Sea, 57°00N 02°47E	
Cause	Submarine attack	
Casualties	40	
Survivors	None	
Salvaged	No	

Notes *U36* was outward-bound and 75 miles south-west of the Lister Light when she was sighted by HM Submarine *Salmon*. The British CO, Bickford, originally thought that the U-boat's small conning tower was nothing more than wreckage, but when he noticed that it moved independently he attacked and fired two torpedoes. From *Salmon*'s point of view the attack was not particularly successful as the submarine lost trim on firing and one torpedo broke surface. However, order was restored in time for Bickford to see *U36* vanish in a tremendous explosion, the wreckage from which was blown as high as 300ft in the air.

1940

U55

	Launched	Commissioned
U55	11 Oct 1939	21 Nov 1939
Class	Type VIIB	
CO	*Kapitänleutnant* Werner Heidal (lost)	
Date of loss	30 January 1940	
Location	W of Ushant, 48°47N 07°46W	
Cause	Depth charge/air attack	
Casualties	1	
Survivors	3 officers, 15 senior rates, 23 junior rates	
Salvaged	No	

Notes *U55* had attacked and sunk the tanker *Vaclita* but had been damaged in the counter-attack. She cleared the area and came to the surface, but her damage was such that she could not dive. She was then sighted by Sunderland 'Y' of No 228 Squadron, bombed and strafed. The aircraft then flew off, signalled to the sloop *Fowey* that a U-boat was on the surface and returned to the submarine. When Heidal saw the ships closing in, he took the only course open to him and scuttled the boat. Survivors were picked up by HMS *Fowey*.

U15

	Launched	Commissioned
U15	15 Feb 1946	7 Mar 1936
Class	Type IIB	
CO	*Oberleutnant zur See* Peter Frahm (lost)	
Date of loss	1 February 1940	
Location	Hoofden	
Cause	Collision	
Casualties	25	
Survivors	None	
Salvaged	No	

Notes *U15* was rammed and sunk in error by the torpedo boat *Iltis*. It is not clear whether this loss resulted from navigational error or whether it was a case of mistaken identity.

U41

	Launched	Commissioned
U41	20 Jan 1939	22 Apr 1939
Class	Type IXA	
CO	*Kapitänleutnant* Gustav-Mugler (lost)	
Date of loss	5 February 1940	
Location	S of Ireland, 49°20'N 10°04'W	
Cause	Depth charge	
Casualties	49	
Survivors	None	
Salvaged	No	

Notes *U41* was engaged in operations against convoy OA.84 when she was attacked and depth-charged by the destroyer HMS *Antelope*.

U33

	Launched	Commissioned
U33	11 Jun 1936	25 Jul 1936
Class	Type VII	
CO	*Kapitänleutnant* Hans von Dresky (lost)	
Date of loss	12 February 1940	
Location	Firth of Clyde, 55°25N 05°07W	
Cause	Depth charge	
Casualties	25	
Survivors	17	
Salvaged	No	

Notes *U33* was on a minelaying operation in the Clyde when she was spotted on the surface at night by the minesweeper *Gleaner*. Although the submarine dived quickly, *Gleaner* dropped three patterns of depth charges which did considerable internal damage. Dresky brought his submarine to the surface in the hope that he could get away under cover of darkness, but *Gleaner* was too close and Dresky ordered the boat to be scuttled.

A sequel to the loss of *U33* was that the telegraphist who had been given three of the rotors for the submarine's 'Enigma' coding machine 'forgot' to dispose of them as he went over the side.

As a result the rotors were recovered by the British.

U54	*Launched*	*Commissioned*
	15 Aug 1939	23 Sept 1939
Class	Type VIIB	
CO	*Kapitänleutnant* Kutschmann (lost)	
Date of loss	13 February 1940	
Location	Heligoland Bight , 55°07N 05°05E	
Cause	Mine	
Casualties	41	
Survivors	None	
Salvaged	No	

U53	*Launched*	*Commissioned*
	15 Aug 1939	24 Jun 1939
Class	Type VIIB	
CO	*Korvettenkapitän* Grosse (lost)	
Date of loss	24 February 1940	
Location	W of Orkney, 60°32N 06°14W	
Cause	Depth charge	
Casualties	42	
Survivors	None	
Salvaged	No	

Notes Sunk in a depth-charge attack by the destroyer HMS *Gurkha.*

U63	*Launched*	*Commissioned*
	6 Dec 1939	18 Jan 1940
Class	Type IIC	
CO	*Oberleutnant zur See* Günther Lorentz (survived)	
Date of loss	25 February 1940	
Location	SE of Shetlands, 58°40'N 00°10'W	
Cause	Depth charge/gunfire	
Casualties	1	
Survivors	3 officers, 11 senior rates, 10 junior rates	
Salvaged	No	

Notes *U63* was sighted by the British submarine *Narwhal* which was part of the escort for convoy HN.14. *Narwhal* alerted the escort and the destroyers *Escapade, Escort, Imogen* and *Inglefield* investigated. The U-boat was seen to dive and was then hunted for two hours by the destroyers. Finally the U-boat surfaced and was abandoned by her crew, who were later picked up after 'making a whole lot of noise in the water'.

U31	*Launched*	*Commissioned*
	25 Sept 1936	28 Dec 1936
Class	Type VII	
CO	*Kapitänleutnant* Hans Habecost (lost)	
Date of loss	11 March 1940	
Location	North Sea, Jade river, Schillig Roads, 53°44N 08°04W	
Cause	Air attack	
Casualties	58	
Survivors	None	
Salvaged	Raised 19 March 1940 and recommissioned 30 July 1940	

Notes Blenheim aircraft of No 82 Squadron RAF had been patrolling off the island of Borkum in search of surface craft. Aircraft 'O', flown by Sqn Ldr M.V. Delap RAF, sighted a submarine as it emerged from cloud at 1,000ft. Four bombs were dropped and two hits observed. The submarine sank leaving no wreckage but a large, spreading slick of black oil on the surface.

U44	*Launched*	*Commissioned*
	5 Aug 1939	4 Nov 1939
Class	Type IXA	
CO	*Kapitänleutnant* Ludwig Mathes (lost)	
Date of loss	20 March 1940	
Location	SW of Narvik, 54°14'N 05°26'E	
Cause	Mine	
Casualties	47	
Survivors	None	
Salvaged	No	

Notes *U44* was mined in a field laid by the destroyers HMS *Express*, *Esk*, *Icarus* and *Impulsive* on 3 March 1940. The loss had previously, and incorrectly, been attributed to an attack by the destroyer HMS *Fortune*.

U50	*Launched*	*Commissioned*
	1 Nov 1939	12 Dec 1939
Class	Type VIIB	
CO	*Kapitänleutnant* Max Bauer (lost)	

Date of loss	6 April 1940
Location	NE of Shetlands, 61°59N 00°14W
Cause	Mine
Casualties	44
Survivors	None
Salvaged	No

Notes *U50* was originally thought to have been sunk in a depth-charge attack by the destroyer HMS *Hero* on 10 April, but she is now known to have been mined on 6 April.

U64	*Launched* 20 Sept 1939	*Commissioned* 16 Dec 1939
Class	Type IXB	
CO	*Kapitänleutnant* Wilhelm Schulze (survived)	
Date of loss	13 April 1940	
Location	Norwegian coastal waters, Rombaksfjord, 68°29'N 17°30'E	
Cause	Air attack	
Casualties	8	
Survivors	?	
Salvaged	No	

Notes *U64* was attacked and bombed by the Swordfish from the battleship HMS *Warspite*, the aircraft being flown by P Off F. C. Rice, with Lt-Cdr W. L. Brown as observer and LA M. G. Pacey as TAG, during the Second Battle of Narvik. The Swordfish sighted the U-boat at anchor off Bjerkvik and attacked with bombs, scoring two hits while raking the casing with machine-gun fire. The survivors escaped from the conning tower and made a free ascent to the surface without Dräger equipment.

U49	*Launched* 24 June 1939	*Commissioned* 12 Aug 1939
Class	Type VIIB	
CO	*Kapitänleutnant* Kurt von Goszler (survived)	
Date of loss	15 April 1940	
Location	Vaagsfjord, Norway, 68°53N 16°59E	
Cause	Depth charge	
Casualties	1	
Survivors	4 officers, 16 senior rates, 21 junior rates	
Salvaged	No	

Notes Sunk in a depth-charge attack by the destroyers HMS *Fearless* and HMS *Brazen.*

U1	*Launched* 15 Jun 1935	*Commissioned* 29 Jun 1935
Class	Type IIA	
CO	*Kapitänleutnant* Jurgen Deeke (lost)	
Date of loss	c. 16 April 1940	
Location	North Sea, off Heligoland	
Cause	Mine	
Casualties	24	
Survivors	None	
Salvaged	No	

Notes *U1* had left Germany on 9 April and it has now been established that she was mined off Heligoland. She was previously thought to have been sunk by the British submarine *Porpoise* (Lt-Cdr P. Q. Roberts RN) off Egersund. *Porpoise*'s attack was in fact on *U3*, which escaped unscathed.

U22	*Launched* 28 Jul 1936	*Commissioned* 21 Aug 1936
Class	Type IIB	
CO	*Kapitänleutnant* Karl-Heinz Jenisch (lost)	
Date of loss	25 April 1940	
Location	Skagerrak, Jammer Bay, exact location unknown	
Cause	Mine	
Casualties	27	
Survivors	None	
Salvaged	No	

U13	*Launched* 9 Nov 1935	*Commissioned* 30 Nov 1935
Class	Type IIB	
CO	*Oberleutnant zur See* Max Schulte (survived)	
Date of loss	31 May 1940	
Location	North Sea, N of Newcastle, 55°26'N 02°02'E	
Cause	Depth charge	
Casualties	None	
Survivors	3 officers, 11 senior rates, 12 junior rates	
Salvaged	No	

Notes Sunk in a depth-charge attack by the sloop HMS *Weston*.

U122

	Launched	*Commissioned*
	30 Dec 1939	30 Mar 1940

Class — Type IXB
CO — *Korvettenkapitän* Harald Loof (lost)
Date of loss — 22 June 1940
Location — North Sea
Cause — ?
Casualties — 48
Survivors — None
Salvaged — No

Notes *U122* disappeared while on passage to her patrol area. In the absence of any Allied claim for her loss, her fate can be ascribed either to a drifting mine or to an accident resulting from mechanical or drill failure.

U26

	Launched	*Commissioned*
	14 Mar 1936	11 May 1936

Class — Type IA
CO — *Kapitänleutnant* Heinz Scheringer (survived)
Date of loss — 3 July 1940
Location — SW of Bishop's Rock, 48°03'N 11°30'W
Cause — Depth charge
Casualties — None
Survivors — 4 officers, 17 senior rates, 27 junior rates
Salvaged — No

Notes Sunderland 'H' of No 10 Squadron RAAF sighted the U-boat fifteen minutes after the SS *Zarian* had been torpedoed while in convoy. The aircraft dropped four anti-submarine bombs and a further four when the submarine surfaced in the midst of the explosions. The crew were then seen to abandon ship and the U-boat sank stern first. The survivors were picked up by HMS *Rochester*.

U25

	Launched	*Commissioned*
	14 Feb 1936	11 May 1936

Class — Type IA
CO — *Kapitänleutnant* Heinz Beduhn (lost)
Date of loss — 3 August 1940
Location — North Sea, N of Terschelling, 54°00'N 05°00'E
Cause — Mine
Casualties — 49
Survivors — None
Salvaged — No

Notes Destroyed in the explosion of one of her own mines.

U51

	Launched	*Commissioned*
	11 Jun 1936	6 Aug 1938

Class — Type VIIB
CO — *Kapitänleutnant* D. Knorr (lost)
Date of loss — 20 August 1940
Location — Bay of Biscay, 47°06'N 04°51W
Cause — Submarine attack
Casualties — 43
Survivors — None
Salvaged — No

Notes HM Submarine *Cachalot* (Lt-Cdr J. D. Luce RN) had completed a minelaying operation south of Penmarch on 19 August and was proceeding southwards to Bordeaux when she sighted and attacked *U51*.

U102

	Launched	*Commissioned*
	21 Mar 1940	27 Apr 1940

Class — Type VIIB
CO — *Kapitänleutnant* von Kloth-Heydenfeldt
Date of loss — July 1940
Location — Atlantic
Cause — ?
Casualties — 43
Survivors — None
Salvaged — No

Notes The cause of *U102*'s loss is unknown. She may have been the victim of a depth-charge attack by HMS *Vansittart* in 48°32'N 10°26'W on 1 July 1940. However, other theories to account for her loss, such as a drifting mine or accident resulting from drill or mechanical failure, must be considered.

U57

	Launched	*Commissioned*
	3 Sept 1938	29 Dec 1938

Class — Type IIC
CO — *Oberleutnant zur See* Erich Topp (survived)

Date of loss	3 September 1940
Location	Brunsbüttel Roads
Cause	Collision
Casualties	6
Survivors	19
Salvaged	Yes: recommisioned 3 January 1941 and eventually scuttled at Kiel 3 May 1945

Notes *U57* was rammed by the SS *Rona* while waiting to enter the lock at the Brunsbüttel end of the Kiel Canal. The *Rona* had just left the lock but was caught by a tidal eddy and swung into the submarine, the merchant ship's bow hitting *U57* on the conning tower. *U57* could not develop sufficient astern power on her electric motors to avoid the collision so the order to abandon ship was given (which accounts for the relatively small loss of life). Even so, one man escaped from within the sunken submarine. When Topp inspected the salvaged submarine he found the bodies of two of his crew wedged firmly in the conning tower hatchway.

Korvettenkapitän Erich Topp became the third-ranking U-boat commander with 34 ships grossing 193,684 tons and survived the war. After a brief career as a fisherman and an architect he re-entered the *Bundesmarine* and retired in 1969 with the rank of Rear-Admiral.

U32

	Launched	Commissioned
	25 Feb 1937	5 Apr 1937

Class	Type VII
CO	*Oberleutnant zur See* Hans Jenisch (survived)
Date of loss	30 October 1940
Location	Atlantic, NW of Ireland, 55°37'N 12°20'W
Cause	Depth charge
Casualties	9
Survivors	4 officers, 11 senior rates, 18 junior rates
Salvaged	No

Notes Sunk in a depth charge attack by the destroyers HMS *Harvester* and HMS *Highlander.*

U31

	Launched	Commissioned
	25 Sept 1936	28 Dec 1936

Class	Type VII
CO	*Kapitänleutnant* Wilfrid Prellburg (survived)
Date of loss	2 November 1940
Location	Atlantic, NW of Ireland, 56°26'N 10°18'W
Cause	Depth charge
Casualties	2
Survivors	5 officers, 13 senior rates, 25 junior rates
Salvaged	No

Notes *U31* had recommissioned on 30 July 1940 following her bombing by an RAF Blenheim aircraft on 19 March 1940. Her second existence was to be no more fortunate for she was sunk in a depth-charge attack by the destroyer HMS *Antelope* during operations against convoy OB.237.

U104

	Launched	Commissioned
	25 May 1940	19 Aug 1940

Class	Type IXB
CO	*Kapitänleutnant* Harald Just (lost)
Date of loss	c. 27 November 1940
Location	Atlantic, S of Rockall, exact position unknown
Cause	?
Casualties	49
Survivors	None
Salvaged	No

Notes *U104* was sunk by unknown cause during operations against convoy HX.87. The last transmission received from her was on 27 November, which means that the earlier claim for her sinking by HMS *Rhododendron* during operations in support of convoy OB.224 in position 56°28'N 14°13'W can be discounted.

U560

	Launched	Commissioned
	10 Jan 1941	6 Mar 1941

Class	Type VIIC
CO	*Oberleutnant zur See* Ernst Cordes
Date of loss	November 1940
Location	Baltic, off Memel
Cause	Collision
Casualties	?
Survivors	?
Salvaged	Yes: raised in December 1941 and paid off

Notes *U560* was later commissioned in 1942 for training purposes only and was eventually scuttled at Kiel on 3 May 1945.

1941

U47	29 Oct 1938	17 Dec 1938
Class	Type VIIB	
CO	*Kapitänleutnant* Günther Prien (lost)	
Date of loss	7 March 1941	
Location	North Atlantic, N of Rockall	
Cause	?	
Casualties	45	
Survivors	None	
Salvaged	No	

Notes An attack by the destroyer HMS *Wolverine* on the night of 7/8 March 1941 while escorting convoy OB.293 is usually given as the cause of *U47*'s loss. An examination of the record, however, shows that *Wolverine's* victim was *UA* (the former Turkish submarine *Batiray*), which survived the attack but was badly damaged and forced to break off her patrol.

What is known about *U47*'s loss is that on the morning of 7 March she transmitted a series of shadowing reports on OB.293, the last of which was sent at 0343. She then attacked the convoy together with *U70* and *U99*. Typically Prien selected the biggest ship in the convoy for his attack, the 20,000grt whaling factory ship *Terje Viken*. Although the ship was damaged she did not sink and was eventually scuttled after being attacked by *U99*. Thereafter nothing more was heard from *U47*. BdU enquired of *U47* if she was still in touch with the convoy at 0920/7 and at 2159/7. No reply was received. The request was repeated on 9 March and when no reply was forthcoming the submarine was posted as missing with effect from 7 March.

It is difficult to ascribe *U47*'s loss to a particular cause. Certainly none of the anti-submarine attacks carried out by British forces in the area can account for the submarine's disappearance. A drifting mine is a possibility (a number of drifting mines were sighted in the area), but the most likely possibility is that her loss was the result of an accident. *U47* was an old boat and would almost certainly have been relegated to training duties in the latter half of 1941 had she survived. After a lengthy refit at Lorient, the boat had a diving restriction imposed on her. It is possible that, after the attack on the *Terje Viken*, Prien dived to avoid either a perceived counter-attack or collision with a merchant ship in another column. While diving at speed with a considerable bow-down angle, *U47* possibly went below her safe depth and was crushed. However, this theory, though plausible, is unsubstantiated. In the absence of any firm evidence the cause of the loss of this submarine and her famous commanding officer remains a mystery.

	Launched	*Commissioned*
U70	12 Oct 1940	23 Nov 1940
Class	Type VIIC	
CO	*Kapitänleutnant* Joachim Matz (survived)	
Date of loss	7 March 1941	
Location	Atlantic, N of Rockall, 60°15N 14°00'W	
Cause	Depth charge	
Casualties	20	
Survivors	25	
Salvaged	No	

Notes *U70* was one of possibly four U-boats engaged in attacks on convoy OB.293. Three ships were attacked and sunk early in the morning of 7 March. The Dutch ship *Mijdrecht* had stopped to rescue survivors and was torpedoed herself. While the ship still had some way on, the distinctive feather of a periscope was sighted. The Master, Captain J. Swart, put his helm hard over to ram and passed clean over the submarine. The submarine managed to escape but was damaged. The corvettes *Arbutus* and *Camelia* were quickly on the scene and forced the submarine to the surface with a depth-charge attack, whereupon she was abandoned.

U100	*Launched*	*Commissioned*
	13 Jan 1940	18 Apr 1940
Class	Type VIIB	
CO	*Kapitänleutnant* Joachim Schepke (lost)	
Date of loss	17 March 1941	
Location	Atlantic, NW of Hebrides, 61°04'N 11°30'W	
Cause	Ramming	
Casualties	38	
Survivors	1 officer, 5 ratings	
Salvaged	No	

Notes *U100* was engaged in operations against convoy HX.112. She was attacked by HMS *Walker* at 0137 and again by HMS *Vanoc* at 0157 and 0232. The submarine was not discouraged by this vigilance on the part of the escort for at 0318 she was sighted by *Vanoc* on the surface. *Vanoc* promptly rammed the submarine, striking her at right angles below the conning tower. According to survivors' reports Schepke, who was on the bridge at the time of the ramming, was crushed between *Vanoc*'s bow and his periscopes. He was ranked eleventh in the list of successful U-boat commanders, with 39 ships totalling 159,130 tons.

U99	*Launched*	*Commissioned*
	12 Mar 1940	18 Apr 1940
Class	Type VIIB	
CO	*Kapitänleutnant* Otto Kretschmer (survived)	
Date of loss	17 March 1941	
Location	Atlantic, N of Hebrides, 61°00'N 12°30'W	
Cause	Depth charge	
Casualties	3	
Survivors	40	
Salvaged	No	

Notes *U99* was also engaged in operations against convoy HX.112. According to Kretschmer's post-war account, the submarine was on the surface when a look-out sighted HMS *Walker* rescuing survivors from *U100*. However, the inexperienced OOW gave the order to dive instead of using the U-boat's speed and manoeuvrability to escape on the surface. Once dived, *U99* was detected by the destroyer's asdic and subjected to a depth-charge attack at 0320 which forced her to the surface, where she was abandoned. One of the casualties was *Kapitänleutnant (Ing)* Schroeder , the boat's engineer officer, who volunteered to re-enter the submarine and make sure she was sinking. The boat sank beneath him before he could get back up on to the casing.

Kapitänleutnant Otto Kretschmer was Germany's leading U-boat 'ace' of the Second World War, with 44 ships totalling 266,629 tons. The loss of Kretschmer, Schepke and Prien within a period of just over two weeks represented a serious blow to the U-boat arm of the *Kriegsmarine*.

U551	*Launched*	*Commissioned*
	14 Sept 1940	7 Nov 1940
Class	Type VIIC	
CO	*Kapitänleutnant* Schrott (lost)	
Date of loss	23 March 1941	
Location	Atlantic, Iceland–Faeroes Gap, 62°37'N 16°47'W	
Cause	Depth charge	
Casualties	45	
Survivors	None	
Salvaged	No	

Notes The trawler HMS *Visenda*, operating with the Northern Patrol, made three depth-charge attacks on a submerged submarine and recovered a substantial quantity of wreckage after the third attack.

U76	*Launched*	*Commissioned*
	3 Oct 1940	19 Dec 1940
Class	Type VIIB	
CO	*Oberleutnant zur See* Friedrich von Hippel (survived)	
Date of loss	5 April 1941	
Location	N Atlantic, S of Iceland, 58°35'N 20°20'W	
Cause	Depth charge	
Casualties	1	
Survivors	40	
Salvaged	No	

Notes *U76* was on her first patrol, having left Kiel on 19 March. At 0737 *Wolverine*, part of the escort for convoy SC.26 and searching for a U-boat which had torpedoed the *Athenic* on 4 April, obtained an asdic contact and attacked it with depth charges. She was then joined by *Arbutus* and *Scarborough*, and at 0921 the U-boat surfaced and was quickly abandoned by her crew before sinking stern first. The interrogators subsequently commented on the youth and inexperience of the U-boat's crew and concluded that Hippel 'lacked presence and authority and was somewhat gauche'.

U65	*Launched*	*Commissioned*
	6 Nov 1939	15 Feb 1940
Class	Type IX	
CO	*Kapitänleutnant* Jockel Hoppe (lost)	
Date of loss	28 April 1941	
Location	North Atlantic, 60°04'N 15°45'W	
Cause	Depth charge	
Casualties	50	
Survivors	None	
Salvaged	No	

Notes Depth-charged by the corvette HMS *Gladiolus* during an attack on convoy HX.121.

U110	*Launched*	*Commissioned*
	25 Aug 1940	21 Nov 1940
Class	Type IX	
CO	*Kapitänleutnant* Fritz Julius Lemp (lost)	
Date of loss	9 May 1941	
Location	Atlantic, E of Cape Farewell, 60°22'N 23°12'W	
Cause	Depth charge	
Casualties	15	
Survivors	4 officers, 12 senior rates, 16 junior rates	
Salvaged	*Bulldog* took *U110* in tow but the latter sank on 11 May	

Notes Lemp had begun a submerged attack on convoy OB.318 and fired at three ships from outside the escort screen, sinking the *Esmond* and *Bengore Head*. However, the noise from his motors was picked up by the corvette *Aubretia*, which turned to attack, sighting *U110*'s periscope shortly afterwards. *Aubretia*, joined by *Broadway* and *Bulldog*, delivered three depth-charge attacks, the third of which did the most damage, jamming the hydroplanes and rudder, wrecking the starboard motor and doing much other damage. Although the submarine's main line was damaged, enough air had got into her tanks to bring her to the surface 800yds to port of *Bulldog*.

When Lemp reached the bridge he saw all was hopeless and gave the order to abandon ship. Commander A. J. Baker-Cresswell, in *Bulldog*, was turning to ram the submarine when he realised that it might be possible to board the submarine and retrieve confidential documents. Accordingly the whaler, with an armed crew under the command of Sub-Lt David Balme, was sent away and recovered a boat load of charts, documents, code-books and other ephemera. The prize was an 'Enigma' machine complete with rotors which a telegraphist thought was a typewriter but 'pressed the keys and, finding the results peculiar, sent it up the hatch'.

Lemp had commanded *U30* and was responsible for the sinking of the *Athenia* on 3 September 1939. A good deal of rumour surrounds the circumstances attending Lemp's death, various sources having him being shot by the British while attempting to reboard *U110* (when he saw that she was not sinking), or claiming that he took his own life. The truth is more prosaic: Lemp was thrown to the deck and concussed in the third depth-charge attack. He was then bundled up the conning tower ladder and, literally, thrown over the side. Left on his own in the bitterly cold water, he drowned.

One of the survivors was a journalist from a *Propaganda Kompanie*, Helmut Ecke, on board to write publicity material on the U-boat war.

U147	*Launched*	*Commissioned*
	16 Nov 1940	11 Dec 1940
Class	Type IID	
CO	*Oberleutnant zur See* Wetjen (lost)	
Date of loss	2 June 1941	
Location	Atlantic, W of Skerryvore, 56°38'N 10°24'W	
Cause	Depth charge	
Casualties	26	
Survivors	None	
Salvaged	No	

Notes Depth-charged by HM Ships *Wanderer* and *Periwinkle* escorting convoy OB.329.

U138	*Launched*	*Commissioned*
	18 May 1940	27 Jun 1940
Class	Type II	
CO	*Kapitänleutnant* Franz Gramitsky (survived)	
Date of loss	18 June 1941	
Location	Atlantic, W of Cape Trafalgar, 36°04'N 07°29'W	

Cause	Depth charge/gunfire
Casualties	None
Survivors	4 officers, 11 senior rates, 12 junior rates
Salvaged	No

Notes *U138* was unfortunate enough to fall in with the entire 6th Destroyer Flotilla (HM Ships *Faulknor, Fearless, Forester, Foresight* and *Foxhound*), which was returning from Operation 'Tracer'. She was depth-charged, blown to the surface and finished off with gunfire.

	Launched	*Commissioned*
U556	7 Dec 1940	6 Feb 1941
Class	Type VIIC	
CO	*Kapitänleutnant* Herbert Wohlfarth (survived)	
Date of loss	27 June 1941	
Location	Atlantic, E of Cape Farewell, Greenland, 60°24'N 29°00'W	
Cause	Depth charge/gunfire	
Casualties	1 officer, 4 ratings	
Survivors	5 officers, 14 senior rates, 21 junior rates	
Salvaged	No	

Notes *U556* was engaged in operations against convoy HX.133. She ran in on the surface to make her attack but was spotted by HMS *Nasturtium*; the latter dropped six depth charges, which did some damage. Wohlfarth decided to surface, torpedo his assailant and escape on the surface. However, when he reached the surface he found *U555* ringed by three corvettes which prevented his escape. The U-boat was fired on by *Nasturtium*, *Celandine* and *Gladiolus* and abandoned, her engineer officer remaining on board to make sure that she sank.

Wohlfarth, known as 'Parsifal' on account of his fastidiousness on a pre-war cruise, was one of the characters of the U-boat service.

	Launched	*Commissioned*
U651	21 Dec 1940	12 Feb 1941
Class	Type VIIC	
CO	*Kapitänleutnant* Peter Lohmeyer (survived)	
Date of loss	29 June 1941	
Location	Atlantic, S of Iceland , 59°52'N 18°36'W	
Cause	Depth charge	
Casualties	None	
Survivors	44	
Salvaged	No	

Notes The second U-boat to fall victim to the escort of HX.133, *U651* was depth-charged by the destroyers *Malcolm* and *Scimitar* and forced to the surface, where she was abandoned.

	Launched	*Commissioned*
U144	24 Aug 1940	2 Oct 1940
Class	Type IID	
CO	*Kapitänleutnant* Gerd von Mittelstaedt (lost)	
Date of loss	28 July 1941	
Location	Gulf of Finland, near Dago, 59N°23E approx.	
Cause	Submarine attack	
Casualties	28	
Survivors	None	
Salvaged	No	

Notes *U144* was one of five Type IID boats dispatched to the Eastern Baltic to attack Soviet submarines working from ports on the Baltic coast. After sinking the Soviet boat *M78*, she was torpedoed by the Soviet submarine *Shch-307* (Lt-Cdr A.V. Petrov).

	Launched	*Commissioned*
U401	16 Dec 1940	10 Apr 1941
Class	Type VIIC	
CO	*Kapitänleutnant* Zimmermann (lost)	
Date of loss	3 August 1941	
Location	Atlantic, SW of Ireland, 50°27'N 19°50'W	
Cause	Depth charge	
Casualties	44	
Survivors	None	
Salvaged	No	

Notes *U401* was sunk in a depth-charge attack by the destroyers *Wanderer* and *St Albans* and corvette *Hydrangea* during operations in support of convoy SL.81.

	Launched	*Commissioned*
U452	29 Mar 1941	29 May 1941
Class	Type VIIC	
CO	*Kapitänleutnant* Jurgen March (lost)	

Date of loss	25 August 1941
Location	Atlantic, W of Faeroe Islands, 61°30'N 15° 30'W
Cause	Air attack
Casualties	42
Survivors	None
Salvaged	No

Notes *U452* was on her first patrol, having left Trondheim on 20 August. Catalina 'J' of No 209 Squadron RAF, flown by Fg Off E.A. Jewiss RAF, had taken off from Iceland at 1630 on the 24th. Some ten hours later, the aircraft having exchanged signals with the trawler *Vascama*, *U452* was sighted on the surface. Four depth charges were dropped as the U-boat dived. The U-boat surfaced in the middle of the depth-charge boil and then sank stern first.

U570

	Launched	*Commissioned*
U570	20 Mar 1941	15 May 1941
Class	Type VIIC	
CO	*Kapitänleutnant* Hans Joachim Rahmlow (survived)	
Date of loss	27 August 1941	
Location	Atlantic, 62°15'N 18°35'W	
Cause	Air attack	
Casualties	None	
Survivors	44	
Salvaged	Taken in tow on 28 Aug 1941 and brought to Britain	

Notes *U570* had sailed on her first patrol and had the misfortune to surface at 1050 directly beneath Hudson 'S' of No 269 Squadron RAF flown by Sqn Ldr J. H. Thompson. The result was a depth-charge attack which left Rahmlow so shocked that he surrendered to the aircraft by fixing a white-backed chart to the periscope. The Hudson circled the U-boat, relieved by a Catalina of No 209 Squadron, until the trawler *Northern Chief* arrived at 2250. The next day the destroyer *Burwell* and trawler *Windermere* unsuccessfully attempted to take the submarine in tow and it was not until the arrival of the trawler *Kingston Agate*, which was specially fitted for towing, that a line could be passed. By 1800 on 28 August the crew had all been taken off by the destroyer *Niagara* and the U-boat was making steady progress under tow to Thorlakshafn in Iceland, where she arrived on 29 August. She was taken to Britain and on 21 September 1941 was recommissioned as HMS *Graph*.

When they reached the prisoner-of-war camp at Grizedale Hall, Rahmlow and his officers faced an 'Honour Court' (so-called to circumvent regulations forbiddding PoWs to court martial each other) chaired by *Korvettenkapitän* Otto Kretschmer of *U99*. The LI and 2WO were acquitted, but Rahmlow and the 1WO were found 'guilty'. Rahmlow was to spend the rest of the war in a state of virtual isolation. However the 1WO, *Leutnant zur See* Bernhard Berndt, was offered a bizarre chance to clear his name. Through newspapers, gossip and over-talkative guards, the Germans learned that *U570* was at Barrow, so Berndt was provided with forged papers and told that if he escaped, succeeded in making his way to Barrow and was able to sink the submarine his name would be cleared. Although he managed to escape from the camp, he was picked up by a Home Guard patrol. He was evidently fearful of his reception back at the camp having failed in his mission, so he tried to escape. He was challenged by the Home Guard and, when he failed to stop, he was shot.

In British service *Graph* was used largely for experimental purposes, though she did conduct operational patrols. She ran aground at Islay on 20 March 1944 en route to the breakers.

U501

	Launched	*Commissioned*
U501	25 Jan 1941	30 Apr 1941
Class	Type IX	
CO	*Kapitänleutnant* Hugo Forster (survived)	
Date of loss	10 September 1941	
Location	Atlantic, S of Greenland, 62°50'N 37°50'W	
Cause	Depth charge	
Casualties	12 (see notes)	
Survivors	37	
Salvaged	No	

Notes *U501* was engaged in operations against convoy SC.42 which consisted of 64 ships with an escort of one destroyer and three corvettes, all RCN. Submarine attacks, in which a quarter of the convoy was sunk, began on 9 September and went on until the 18th, by which time substantial reinforcements had been received. Just after midnight on 10 September the corvette *Chambly* obtained a firm contact, which was classified as 'Sub' only 700yds away. Although the target was well within the 1,200yd minimum range for depth-charge attacks, it was decided to attack at once and the pattern was fired at 0038, only two minutes after the contact was reported. As *Chambly* turned for a second run, *U501* surfaced almost alongside the corvette *Moose Jaw* which was following. *Moose Jaw* drew alongside the U-boat so that Forster was able to step from his bridge to the forecastle without so much as getting his feet wet.

Fearing an armed and more determined boarding party from *U501*, *Moose Jaw* withdrew and, as *U501* passed across her bows, rammed her while at the same time raking her with gunfire to prevent the deck armament being manned. The U-boat's crew began to gather on the casing wearing lifejackets, so *Chambly* went alongside and sent over a boarding party under the command of Lt Edward Simmons. After failing to persuade any of *U501*'s crew to re-enter the submarine, despite being threatened at gunpoint, Simmons and his party went down into the control room. There they found that the interior of the boat had been completely wrecked, either in the depth-charge attack or deliberately. There was the sound of incoming water so Simmons and his party hurriedly returned to the casing. However Stoker W. I. Brown was unable to reach the casing and drowned as *U501* took her final plunge.

U207

	Launched	*Commissioned*
U207	24 Apr 1941	7 Jun 1941
Class	Type VIIC	
CO	*Kapitänleutnant* Fritz Meyer (lost)	
Date of loss	11 September 1941	
Location	Atlantic, Denmark Strait, 63°59'N 34°48'W.	
Cause	Depth charge	
Casualties	41	
Survivors	None	
Salvaged	No	

Notes Another victim of SC.42's escort, *U207* was sunk in a depth-charge attack by the British destroyers *Leamington* and *Veteran*.

U111

	Launched	*Commissioned*
U111	6 Sept 1940	19 Dec 1940
Class	Type IXB	
CO	*Kapitänleutnant* Wilhelm Kleinschmidt (lost)	
Date of loss	4 October 1941	
Location	Atlantic, WSW of Tenerife, 27°15'N 20°27'W	
Cause	Depth charge	
Casualties	9	
Survivors	44	
Salvaged	No	

Notes At 0840 the trawler *Lady Shirley* (Lt-Cdr A. H. Callaway RANVR) sighted what was thought to be the funnel of a ship but what on later observation turned out to be a U-boat's conning tower. At 1004 the trawler was in asdic contact and a pattern of depth charges was dropped. The U-boat then surfaced and the trawler's helm was put hard over to port to bring the 4in gun to bear. The submarine was engaged as soon as possible and there was fire from machine guns on the bridge wings. Although this fire stopped the U-boat's crew from manning their 88mm deck gun, light machine guns fired from the submarine's bridge killed the trawler's gunlayer, whose place was immediately taken by Sub-Lt F. E. French RNR. The *Lady Shirley's* fire was so effective that Kleinschmidt, three of his officers and five ratings were killed. As the *Lady Shirley* was preparing to run alongside the U-boat and drop a shallow pattern of depth charges, the U-boat showed signs of surrender. *Kapitänleutnant* Heinecke, a prospective commanding officer on board for 'experience', gave orders to abandon and scuttle *U111*, which sank by the stern at 1023. During the voyage back to Gibraltar nine uninjured members of the *Lady Shirley*'s crew were responsible for 44 uninjured Germans who were, frankly, resentful at having been sunk by such a minor vessel of war.

Flag Officer Commanding North Atlantic, Vice-Admiral Sir G. Frederick Edward-Collins KCVO KCB, commented that 'this splendid achievement resulted from an alert look-out supported by all-round efficiency.' Sadly, the *Lady Shirley* was torpedoed by *U374* on 11 December 1941 in the Strait of Gibraltar. There were no survivors.

U204

	Launched	*Commissioned*
U204	23 Jan 1941	8 Mar 1941
Class	Type VIIC	
CO	*Kapitänleutnant* Walter Kell (lost)	

Date of loss	19 October 1941
Location	Strait of Gibraltar, 35°46'N, 06°02'W
Cause	Depth charge
Casualties	46
Survivors	None
Salvaged	No

Notes Towards mid-October 1941 strong evidence suggested a concentration of U-boats off the Strait of Gibraltar. Following the torpedoing of the corvette *Fleur de Lys* on 14 October, the 37th Escort Group was ordered to hunt for U-boats in this area. At 2050 on the 19th the sloop *Rochester* and corvette *Mallow* attacked a firm contact off Cape Spartel. A quantity of oil was observed, and twenty-four hours later the corvette *Bluebell* picked up the air vessel, fuel bottle and water bottle of a German torpedo within a few miles of the attack position.

U580

	Launched	*Commissioned*
	28 May 1941	24 Jul 1941
Class	Type VIIC	
CO	*Oberleutnant zur See* Kuhlmann	
Date of loss	11 November 1941	
Location	Baltic Sea, off Memel	
Cause	Collision	
Casualties	12	
Survivors	32	
Salvaged	No	

Notes Lost following a collision with the target vessel *Angelburg* during a night exercise.

U583

	Launched	*Commissioned*
	26 Jun 1941	14 Aug 1941
Class	Type VIIC	
CO	*Kapitänleutnant* Ratsch (lost)	
Date of loss	15 November 1941	
Location	Baltic, 55°20'N 17°30'E	
Cause	Collision	
Casualties	45	
Survivors	None	
Salvaged	No	

Notes Sunk in a collision with *U153*.

U433

	Launched	*Commissioned*
	15 Mar 1941	24 May 1941
Class	Type VIIC	
CO	*Oberleutnant zur See* Ey (survived)	
Date of loss	16 November 1941	
Location	Mediterranean, S of Malaga, 36°13'N, 04°42'W	
Cause	Depth charge	
Casualties	6	
Survivors	38	
Salvaged	No	

Notes The corvette *Marigold* was proceeding independently to catch up with a convoy ahead of her when she made a radar contact with an object at 4,000yds. While she was turning towards the target it was identified as a U-boat, which dived before *Marigold* could ram. The first depth-charge attack was made by asdic with five charges set to 50ft. Contact was then lost but regained fifteen minutes later. The second attack consisted of ten charges set to 150 and 300ft. The U-boat surfaced astern of *Marigold* amid the depth-charge boil and was engaged by gunfire. The U-boat was abandoned and sank very quickly.

Marigold's commanding officer subsequently received a personal signal from the First Sea Lord, Admiral Sir Dudley Pound, congratulating him and his ship's company.

U95

	Launched	*Commissioned*
	18 Jul 1940	31 Aug 1940
Class	Type VIIC	
CO	*Kapitänleutnant* Gerd Schreiber (survived)	
Date of loss	28 November 1941	
Location	Mediterranean, E of Gibraltar, 36°24'N 03°20'W	
Cause	Submarine attack	
Casualties	33	
Survivors	4 officers, 3 senior rates, 5 junior rates	
Salvaged	No	

Notes *U95* was sunk in a torpedo attack by the Dutch submarine *O.21* (Lt-Cdr J. F. van Dulm RNethN), which was returning to Gibraltar from an uneventful patrol off Naples. At 0030 on 28 November, in clear weather and bright moonlight, *U95* sighted the Dutch submarine first but was reluctant to attack since Schreiber knew that other German boats were in the area. Instead he challenged her using the signal code then in force. Van Dulm was operating with no such inhibitions. Directly the German challenge was made Dulm fired one torpedo at 2,000yds, which missed; a second was fired at the U-boat, which saw it coming but, while turning to starboard to comb the track, ran right into it.

U206	*Launched*	*Commissioned*
	4 Apr 1941	17 May 1941
Class	Type VIIC	
CO	*Kapitänleutnant* Herbert Opitz (lost)	
Date of loss	30 November 1941	
Location	Bay of Biscay, W of St Nazaire, 46°55'N 07°16'W	
Cause	Air attack	
Casualties	46	
Survivors	None	
Salvaged	No	

Notes During a routine A/S patrol Whitley 'B' of No 502 Squadron, flown by Fg Off R. W. G. Holdsworth, made S/E contact with the submarine at a range of five miles. The U-boat dived and was fully submerged before the aircraft was within attacking range. Nevertheless, Holdsworth dropped three depth charges ahead of and across the U-boat's probable track and then turned to port and released three more 100yds ahead of the swirl marking the point where the U-boat had dived. After the attack the water turned a dirty brown colour. Nothing further was seen, although the aircraft remained overhead for a further 32 minutes. *U206* failed to answer further signals from BdU so was adjudged to have been sunk in this attack.

U208	*Launched*	*Commissioned*
	21 May 1941	5 Jul 1941
Class	Type VIID	
CO	*Kapitänleutnant* Alfred Schlieper (lost)	
Date of loss	7 December 1941	
Location	W of Gibraltar, 35°51'N 07°45'W	
Cause	Depth charge	
Casualties	45	
Survivors	None	
Salvaged	No	

Notes Depth-charged and sunk by HM Ships *Harvester* and *Hesperus*.

U127	*Launched*	*Commissioned*
	4 Feb 1941	24 Apr 1941
Class	Type IX	
CO	*Kapitänleutnant* Bruno Hansmann (lost)	
Date of loss	15 December 1941	
Location	Atlantic, SW of Cape St Vincent	
Cause	Depth charge	
Casualties	51	
Survivors	None	
Salvaged	No	

Notes *U127* had the misfortune to run into Force H's destroyer screen which was carrying out a routine A/S patrol in response to intelligence reports that a large concentration of U-boats was developing off Gibraltar. She was detected on *Nestor*'s asdic, depth-charged and sunk.

U557	*Launched*	*Commissioned*
	22 Dec 1940	13 Feb 1941
Class	Type VIIC	
CO	*Kapitänleutnant* Ottokar Paulssen (lost)	
Date of loss	16 December 1941	
Location	Mediterranean, SW of Crete, 35°33'N 23°14'E	
Cause	Collision	
Casualties	43	
Survivors	None	
Salvaged	No	

Notes *U557* was sunk following a collision with the Italian torpedo boat *Orione*. The submarine was returning to port when she was rammed by *Orione*, which was heading for North Africa with a cargo of cased petrol. An investigation by the *Supermarina* attributed the sinking to an 'accident', but it is not clear whether the collision was an accident resulting from navigational error or whether the attack was deliberate.

U131	*Launched*	*Commissioned*
	1 Apr 1941	1 July 1941
Class	Type IX	
CO	*Korvettenkapitän* Arend Baumann (survived)	
Date of loss	17 December 1941	
Location	Atlantic, off Cape St Vincent, 34°12'N 13°35'W	
Cause	Gunfire	
Casualties	None	

Survivors	55
Salvaged	No

Notes *U131* was the first of four U-boats of *Gruppe Seeraber* to be sunk in operations against convoy HG.76 (Gibraltar–UK). At 0918 *U131* was sighted by a Martlet aircraft flying from the escort carrier *Audacity* 22 miles on the port beam of the convoy. The sloop HMS *Stork* (Cdr F. J. Walker RN), destroyers *Blankney*, *Exmoor* and *Stanley* and corvette *Penstemon* set off in pursuit. The U-boat altered course towards the convoy but was detected on *Penstemon*'s asdic and depth-charged. Contact was lost but quickly regained when the U-boat was sighted making off on the surface. A Martlet of 802 NAS flown by Sub-Lt George Fletcher RNVR attacked *U131* but was shot down. The escorts then opened a sustained fire on the U-boat and scored a number of hits which holed the pressure hull. Baumann had no option but to scuttle his submarine.

U434

	Launched	*Commissioned*
U434	1 Apr 1941	21 Jun 1941
Class	Type VIIC	
CO	*Kapitänleutnant* Heyda (survived)	
Date of loss	18 December 1941	
Location	Atlantic, off Cape St Vincent, 36°15'N 15°48'W	
Cause	Depth charge	
Casualties	2	
Survivors	44	
Salvaged	No	

Notes At 0906 *U434* was sighted by *Stanley* on the convoy's port quarter. *Stanley* and *Blakeney* attacked with depth charges. Forty-three were dropped within a very short period as an example of Walker's dictum to 'Hit them quickly and as often as possible before they have time to think'. At 0948 the U-boat surfaced. Both destroyers opened fire and *Blankney* attempted to ram. A whaler was lowered in the hope of boarding the submarine but the latter sank very quickly.

U574

	Launched	*Commissioned*
U574	18 Apr 1941	12 Jun 1941
Class	Type VIIC	
CO	*Oberleutnant zur See* Dietrich Gengelbach (lost)	
Date of loss	19 December 1941	
Location	Atlantic, off Lisbon, 38°12'N 17°23'W	
Cause	Ramming	
Casualties	27	
Survivors	4 officers, 16 senior and junior rates	
Salvaged	No	

Notes At 0415 HMS *Stanley* was torpedoed in her position astern of the convoy. *Stork* counter-attacked twice with depth charges. The depth-charge attack did tremendous damage: the pressure hull was dished in where a frame had fractured; there was an electrical fire in the control room; and bottles of compressed air had broken which increased the pressure in the boat, making conditions very difficult and painful. The LI wanted to surface whereas Gengelbach wanted to remain submerged, and there was a heated argument between the two before Gengelbach ordered the crew to put on their Dräger breathing apparatus and prepared to surface. *U574* surfaced 200yds in front of *Stork*, which tried to ram but found that the U-boat was turning inside the sloop's turning circle. The range was so close that *Stork*'s 4in guns were at maximum depression and would not fire: the guns' crews were reduced to shaking their fists at the U-boat, which seemed to be almost alongside the sloop. Gengelbach gave the order to scuttle the submarine (although he refused to leave his command) and *U574* continued to turn on her own before *Stork* struck her a glancing blow on her starboard quarter. The U-boat rolled over, hung on *Stork*'s bow and then hung on her asdic dome before passing under the sloop to be finished off by a pattern of depth charges. Five survivors from *U574* were subsequently killed when HMS *Deptford* collided with HMS *Stork*.

U451

	Launched	*Commissioned*
U451	5 Mar 1941	3 May 1941
Class	Type VIIC	
CO	*Kapitänleutnant* Eberhard Hoffmann (lost)	
Date of loss	21 December 1941	
Location	Strait of Gibraltar, off Tangier, 35°55'N 06°08'W.	
Cause	Air attack	
Casualties	44	
Survivors	1	
Salvaged	No	

Notes Swordfish 'A' of 812 NAS flying from RAF North Front, Gibraltar, took *U451* completely by surprise off Cape Spartel. Three depth charges were dropped, one of which is thought to have exploded beneath the U-boat. The sole survivor, the boat's 1WO, was later rescued by the corvette *Myosotis*.

U567

	Launched	*Commissioned*
	6 Mar 1941	24 Apr 1941

Class Type VIIC
CO *Kapitänleutnant* Engelbert Endrass (lost)
Date of loss 21 December 1941
Location Atlantic, W of Cape Finisterre, 44°02'N 20°10'W
Cause Depth charge
Casualties 47
Survivors None
Salvaged No

Notes At 2241 the sloop HMS *Deptford*, stationed on the convoy's port beam, detected a hydrophone effect. The contact was illuminated with starshell and a U-boat was sighted closing the convoy. *Deptford* carried out a series of depth-charge attacks. After the third attack a large double underwater explosion was observed. At 0105 on the 22nd, her primary object of putting the U-boat down having been achieved, she rejoined the convoy. No wreckage was found but the subsequent German admission that *U567* was missing makes her the most likely victim *of Deptford's* attack.

Endrass had been Prien's 1WO in *U47* and had fired the torpedoes which sank *Royal Oak* in Scapa Flow. However, by December 1941 he was worn out and exhausted and was probably unfit for sea service.

U79

	Launched	*Commissioned*
	25 Jan 1941	13 Mar 1941

Class Type VIIC
CO *Kapitänleutnant* Wolfgang Kaufmann (survived)
Date of loss 23 December 1941
Location Mediterranean, off Bardia, 32°15'N 25°19'E
Cause Depth charge
Casualties None
Survivors 44
Salvaged No

Notes The destroyers *Hasty* and *Hotspur*, part of the escort for convoy AT.5, attacked a contact and carried out a sustained hunt which lasted over 3½ hours. Eventually *U79* surfaced and was abandoned.

U75

	Launched	*Commissioned*
	18 Oct 1940	19 Dec 1940

Class Type VIIB
CO *Kapitänleutnant* Helmuth Ringelmann (lost)
Date of loss 28 December 1941
Location Mediterranean, off Mersa Matruh, 31°50'N 26°40'E
Cause Depth charge
Casualties 14
Survivors 2 officers, 10 senior rates, 18 junior rates
Salvaged No

Notes Depth-charged by HMS *Kipling* after a hunt lasting 2½ hours.

1942

U374

	Launched	Commissioned
U374	10 May 1941	21 Jun 1941

Class Type VIIC
CO *Oberleutnant zur See* Unno von Fischel (lost)
Date of loss 12 January 1942
Location Mediterranean, off Cape Spartivento, 37°50'N 16°00'E
Cause Submarine attack
Casualties 43
Survivors 1
Salvaged No

Notes *U374* was torpedoed by HM Submarine *Unbeaten* (Lt-Cdr E.A.Woodward RN) in a snap attack, less than two minutes elapsing from the time the U-boat was sighted in poor visibility to when the full salvo of four Mk VIII torpedoes was fired. Two torpedoes were seen to hit the submarine. Although he was only four miles from the coast, Woodward surfaced to rescue the sole survivor.

U577

	Launched	Commissioned
U577	15 May 1941	3 Jul 1941

Class Type VIIC
CO *Kapitänleutnant* Schauenburg (lost)
Date of loss 15 January 1942
Location Mediterranean, NW of Mersa Matruh, 32°40 25°48'E
Cause Air attack
Casualties 43
Survivors None
Salvaged No

Notes Sunk by Swordfish 'G' of 815 NAS, Fleet Air Arm.

U93

	Launched	Commissioned
U93	8 Jun 1940	30 Jul 1940

Class Type VIIC
CO *Oberleutnant zur See* Horst Elfe (lost)
Date of loss 15 January 1942
Location Atlantic, W of Cape St Vincent, 36°40'N 15°42'W
Cause Ramming/depth charge/ gunfire
Casualties 6
Survivors 5 officers, 35 ratings
Salvaged No

Notes The destroyers HMS *Hesperus* and *Laforey* were sweeping six to eight miles on the port quarter of convoy SL.97G when at about 0045 *Hesperus* obtained a simultaneous radar contact at 2,400yds and asdic contact at 2,000yds. When the range came down to 1,000yds *Hesperus*'s 'A' gun opened fire with starshell and the U-boat was seen heading away at 17kts. *Hesperus* overtook the submarine and rammed her on the port side. As *Hesperus* passed the submarine she delivered a pattern of depth charges (set to shallow) and fired a number of rounds from 'X' gun.

U581

	Launched	Commissioned
U581	12 Jun 1941	31 Jul 1941

Class Type VIIC
CO *Kapitänleutnant* Werner Pfeifer (survived)
Date of loss 2 February 1942
Location Atlantic, off Pico Island in the Azores, 38°24'N 28°30'W
Cause Ramming/depth charge
Casualties 4
Survivors 39
Salvaged No

Notes *U581* was off the Azores with the intention of attacking the troopship *Llangibby Castle* which had been damaged by *U402* and had put into Horta for repairs. While the damaged troopship was en route for Gibraltar one of her escorts, the destroyer HMS *Westcott*, sighted the conning tower of a U-boat steering towards Pico Island. She attempted to ram but missed. As *Westcott* passed the U-boat she fired a pattern of depth charges before turning to make another attempt at ramming. This time she struck the U-boat just aft of the conning tower and the submarine rolled over and sank.

The survivors were picked up by *Westcott* (one intrepid officer swimming ashore to Pico Island and subsequently being repatriated to Germany). *Kapitänleutnant* Pfeifer made a stout protest to *Westcott*'s commanding officer concerning the circumstances in which his boat had been sunk. Pfeifer claimed that *U581* had been sunk inside Portuguese waters and demanded that he and his crew be put ashore and interned. *Westcott*'s CO checked that at the time of sinking *U581* lay 3.1 miles from the coast and was thus in international waters. According to the Staff History, he 'ignored the protest and his (Pfeifer's) pretentious request for internment in a neutral country'.

U82	*Launched* 15 Mar 1941	*Commissioned* 14 May 1941
Class	Type VIIC	
CO	*Oberleutnant zur See* Siegfried Rollmann (lost)	
Date of loss	6 February 1942	
Location	North Atlantic, 44°10'N 23°52'W	
Cause	Depth charge	
Casualties	45	
Survivors	None	
Salvaged	No	

Notes While returning from operations off the east coast of the USA, *U82* encountered convoy OS.18 and was sunk in a depth-charge attack by HM Ships *Rochester* and *Tamarisk*.

U656	*Launched* 8 Jul 1941	*Commissioned* 17 Sept 1941
Class	Type VIIC	
CO	*Kapitänleutnant* Kroning (lost)	
Date of loss	1 March 1942	
Location	Atlantic, S of Cape Race, 46°15'N 53°15'W	
Cause	Air attack	
Casualties	45	
Survivors	None	
Salvaged	No	

Notes Sunk by a Catalina of USN patrol squadron VP-82.

U133	*Launched* 28 Apr 1941	*Commissioned* 5 Jul 1941
Class	Type VIIC	
CO	*Kapitänleutnant* Eberhard Mohr (lost)	
Date of loss	14 March 1942	
Location	Mediterranean, off Salamis, 37°59'N 29°35'E	
Cause	Mine	
Casualties	45	
Survivors	None	
Salvaged	No	

Notes *U133* strayed into a German minefield through navigational error and was sunk.

U503	*Launched* 5 Apr 1941	*Commissioned* 10 Jul 1941
Class	Type IXC	
CO	*Kapitänleutnant* Gericke (lost)	
Date of loss	15 March 1942	
Location	Atlantic, SW of Newfoundland, 45°50'N 48°50'W	
Cause	Air attack	
Casualties	51	
Survivors	None	
Salvaged	No	

Notes Sunk by a Hudson aircraft of USN patrol squadron VP-82 flying in support of convoy ON.72.

U655	*Launched* 5 Jun 1941	*Commissioned* 11 Aug 1941
Class	Type VIIC	
CO	*Kapitänleutnant* Otto Dumrese (lost)	
Date of loss	24 March 1942	
Location	Arctic, SE of Bear Island, 73°00'N 21°00'E	
Cause	Ramming	
Casualties	45	
Survivors	None	
Salvaged	No	

Notes *U655* was engaged in operations against convoy QP.9 when she was sighted by the minesweeper HMS *Sharpshooter*. The minesweeper rammed *U655* at 13kts, rolling the submarine right over.

U587	*Launched*	*Commissioned*
	23 Jul 1941	11 Sept 1941
Class	Type VIIC	
CO	*Kapitänleutnant* Borcherdt (lost)	
Date of loss	27 March 1942	
Location	Atlantic, W of Ushant, 47°10'N 21°39'W	
Cause	Depth charge	
Casualties	42	
Survivors	None	
Salvaged	No	

Notes Sunk during operations in support of WS.17, a fast troop convoy on its way to the Middle East. The convoy was repeatedly shadowed by U-boats and on the forenoon of 26 March a determined hunt by the destroyers *Javelin* and *Inconstant* put down one of the shadowers though without result. At 0713 on the 27th a U-boat surfaced seven miles astern of the convoy and was attacked by the destroyers *Leamington Spa, Grove, Aldenham* and *Volunteer*. At 1040 *Leamington Spa* reported that the hunt was being abandoned since all depth charges had been expended. The assessors considered the attack had been a 'Category C' success, i.e. that the U-boat had 'probably' been damaged. However, post-war analysis revealed that *U567* was the victim of this attack.

U585	*Launched*	*Commissioned*
	9 Jul 1941	28 Aug 1941
Class	Type VIIC	
CO	*Kapitänleutnant* Lohse (lost)	
Date of loss	30 March 1942	
Location	Arctic, N of Murmansk, 70°10'N 34°00'W	
Cause	Mine	
Casualties	44	
Survivors	None	
Salvaged	No	

Notes Mined on the German Bantos field into which the boat had strayed, probably as a result of navigational error. Some German sources claim that the U-boat was in the right place but it was the mine that had drifted—a typically Germanic explanation of such an event. The end result, however, was the same.

U585's loss was previously attributed to an attack by HMS *Fury* on 29 March. *Fury*'s contact on that occasion had been *U378*, which had escaped unscathed.

U702	*Launched*	*Commissioned*
	24 May 1941	3 Sept 1941
Class	Type VIIC	
CO	*Kapitänleutnant* Wolf von Rabeneau (lost)	
Date of loss	April 1942	
Location	North Sea	
Cause	?	
Casualties	44	
Survivors	None	
Salvaged	No	

Notes The possibility that this U-boat was lost as a result of an accident arising from mechanical or drill failure cannot be ruled out.

U85	*Launched*	*Commissioned*
	10 Apr 1941	7 Jun 1941
Class	Type VIIB	
CO	*Kapitänleutnant* Eberhard Grueger (lost)	
Date of loss	14 April 1942	
Location	Atlantic, off Cape Hatteras, 35°55'N 75°13'W	
Cause	Depth charge	
Casualties	45	
Survivors	None	
Salvaged	No	

Notes A few minutes after midnight on 14 April the USS *Roper* was proceeding south off Cape Hatteras when she obtained a radar contact at 2,700yds. *Roper* closed to 2,100yds, when a wake and a small silhouette were sighted heading away from the destroyer at speed. *Roper* increased speed to follow, and when the range came down to 700yds a torpedo was seen to pass close down the destroyer's port side. Soon afterwards the target, now identified as a submarine, turned to starboard across *Roper*'s bows but was caught in the searchlight and fired on by the forward 3in and machine guns. At least one hit was seen on the conning tower before the U-boat dived. Roper then attacked with depth charges, but in view of reports that a number of U-boats were in the vicinity her commanding officer decided to clear the area until dawn. When he returned at 0715 the scene was littered with wreckage and bodies, and from papers recovered it was possible to learn the identity of the boat.

U252	*Launched*	*Commissioned*
	14 Aug 1941	4 Oct 1941

Class Type VIIC
CO *Kapitänleutnant* Kai Lerchen (lost)
Date of loss 14 April 1942
Location Atlantic, NW of Cape Finisterre, 47°00'N 18°14'W
Cause Depth charge
Casualties 44
Survivors None
Salvaged No

Notes *U252* was shadowing convoy OG.82 when she was detected by the corvette HMS *Vetch*. The initial contact was made by radar but the submarine was revealed on the surface when starshell was fired. *U252* fired two torpedoes which passed down the corvette's port side, narrowly missing her by 30ft. *U252* headed away on the surface, chased by *Vetch* which was joined by the Senior Officer's ship, HMS *Stork*. The chase ended at 2239 when the U-boat dived. Both ships then remained in contact and attacked with depth charges up to 2311. The sound of ballast tanks being blown was heard and it was considered that the U-boat might have been attempting to surface. However, these noises were classified as 'Non-Sub'. Both ships then hunted unsuccessfully to the north-west in case the U-boat had broken away, but when they returned to the position of the original attack they found wreckage, including a sheepskin coat, gloves, trousers made in Stuttgart and human remains.

U573	*Launched*	*Commissioned*
	17 Apr 1941	5 Jun 1941

Class Type VIIC
CO *Kapitänleutnant* Heinrich Heinsohn (survived)
Date of loss 1 May 1942
Location Mediterranean, E of Cartagena, 37°00'N 01°00'E
Cause Air attack
Casualties 1
Survivors 43
Salvaged Purchased by Spanish government 10 August 1943 and redesignated *G7*; redesignated *S01* 15 June 1960 and sold for breaking up 2 May 1970.

Notes *U573* was attacked by Hudson 'M' of No 233 Squadron RAF with three depth charges. One appeared to be a direct hit on the starboard side aft of the conning tower and another exploded about 12yds from the hull further aft. The boat 'heaved out of the water' and then dived, leaving a large oil slick behind her on the surface. The aircrew then watched as the bow appeared perpendicularly and then slid back, and soon afterwards the submarine surfaced at a steep angle with white smoke issuing from the conning tower. Ten men appeared on the bridge with their arms raised as if in surrender. Since they made no effort to man the U-boat's AA armament, no further attacks were made by the Hudson. However, half an hour later the Hudson had to leave the scene owing to lack of fuel and the U-boat was able to reach sanctuary in the Spanish port of Cartagena on 2 May, where she was interned.

The Admiralty was extremely annoyed that a U-boat had been allowed to 'get away' after using the surrender as a *ruse de guerre*. On 24 June 1942 instructions were issued to aircrew that they were in no position to accept the surrender of a U-boat until surface forces were available physically to take possession of the boat. Until that time 'offensive action with all available weapons is to continue'.

U74	*Launched*	*Commissioned*
	31 Aug 1940	31 Oct 1940

Class Type VIIB
CO *Leutnant zur See* Karl Friedrich (lost)
Date of loss 2 May 1942
Location Mediterranean, S of Cartagena, 37°16'N 01°00'W
Cause Air attack/depth charge
Casualties 46
Survivors None
Salvaged No

Notes *U74* was sighted on the surface by Catalina 'C' of No 202 Squadron, flown by Flt Lt R.Y. Powell, and attacked with seven Mk 8 depth charges from a height of 50ft. No wreckage or bubbles were seen, but the Catalina remained on station until 1745, when the destroyers *Wishart* and *Wrestler* arrived. The ships were soon in contact with the submarine, and they destroyed her in a number of depth-charge attacks.

U352	*Launched*	*Commissioned*
	7 May 1941	28 Aug 1941
Class	Type VIIC	
CO	*Kapitänleutnant* Helmut Rathke (survived)	
Date of loss	9 May 1942	
Location	Atlantic, 34°12'N 76°35'W	
Cause	Depth charge	
Casualties	13	
Survivors	3 officers, 14 senior rates, 16 junior rates	
Salvaged	No	

Notes The US Coast Guard cutter *Icarus* obtained a sonar contact at the very short range of 1,200yds at 2025 while on patrol off the coast of North Carolina. Four minutes later a torpedo passed down her port side and exploded 200yds off her port quarter. Course was reversed and a five-charge pattern was dropped, followed quickly by three more charges. A further depth charge was dropped just before the submarine surfaced at 2109 and was abandoned.

U568	*Launched*	*Commissioned*
	6 Mar 1941	1 May 1941
Class	Type VIIC	
CO	*Kapitanleitnant* Joachim Preuss (survived)	
Date of loss	28 May 1942	
Location	Mediterranean, off Tobruk, 32°42'N 24°53'E	
Cause	Depth charge/gunfire	
Casualties	None	
Survivors	47	
Salvaged	No	

Notes At 1115 on 27 May the destroyer *Eridge* detached the destroyers *Hero* and *Hurworth* from the escort of convoy AT.47 to search for a U-boat which had been reported by an aircraft in position 32°24'N 24°55'E. Contact was made two hours later and the U-boat was subjected to series of depth-charge attacks throughout the day. HMS *Eridge* joined the hunt at 1750 and by 2000 only one pattern of depth charges remained among the three ships. However, contact was held throughout the night in the knowledge that the U-boat must eventually surface for air. At 2355 the U-boat surfaced, but she dived almost immediately on being engaged by gunfire. Contact was maintained until 0330/28, when she surfaced again. This time Preuss had had enough. He had done all that could be expected of him: he could not evade his assailants and his battery was virtually exhausted. Accordingly he ordered the submarine abandoned and scuttled.

U652	*Launched*	*Commissioned*
	7 Feb 1941	3 Apr 1941
Class	Type VIIC	
CO	*Kapitänleutnant* Georg Werner Fraatz (survived)	
Date of loss	2 June 1942	
Location	Mediterranean, off Sollum, 31°55'N 25°13'E	
Cause	Scuttling	
Casualties	None	
Survivors	45	
Salvaged	No	

Notes *U652* had been damaged in an attack by Swordfish 'L' of 815 NAS and was disabled. The boat was unable to dive and so Fraatz transmitted a signal requesting assistance. *U81* (*Kapitänleutnant* Friedrich Guggenberger) picked up the signal—fortunately being on the surface at the time—and headed for *U652* at maximum speed. Guggenberger found *U652* down by the stern and in a sinking condition. After taking off the crew Guggenberger allowed Fraatz the privilege of sinking his command by firing one torpedo from *U81*'s stern tube: *U652* was hit amidships and disintegrated immediately.

U81 returned *U652*'s crew to Salamis, where they arrived on 3 June. Fraatz later commanded *U529* and was killed in her on 30 January 1943.

U157	*Launched*	*Commissioned*
	5 Jun 1941	15 Sept 1941
Class	Type IXC	
CO	*Korvettenkapitän* Wolf Henne (lost)	
Date of loss	13 June 1942	
Location	Caribbean, N of Havana, 24°13'N 82°03'W	
Cause	Depth charge	

Casualties 52
Survivors None
Salvaged No
Notes Sunk in a depth-charge attack by the US Coast Guard cutter *Thetis*.

	Launched	*Commissioned*
U158	21 Jun 1941	25 Sept 1941

Class Type IXC
CO *Korvettenkapitän* Erwin Rostin (lost)
Date of loss 30 June 1942
Location Caribbean, W of Bermuda, 32°50'N 67°28'W
Cause Air attack
Casualties 54
Survivors None
Salvaged No
Notes *U158* had enjoyed a successful patrol in the Gulf of Mexico, sinking over 62,000 tons of shipping. On her return she was located by HF/DF and sunk by a Mariner aircraft of USN squadron VP-74.

	Launched	*Commissioned*
U215	9 Oct 1941	22 Nov 1941

Class Type VIID
CO *Kapitänleutnant* Fritz Hoeckner (lost)
Date of loss 3 July 1942
Location Atlantic, E of Nova Scotia, 41°48'N 66°35'W
Cause Depth charge
Casualties 48
Survivors None
Salvaged No
Notes Hoeckner attacked convoy BA.2 off Nova Scotia and sank the *Alexander Macomb*. Retribution was swift for he was spotted by the escort, the French trawler *Le Tigre*, and sunk.

	Launched	*Commissioned*
U502	18 Feb 1941	31 May 1941

Class Type IXC/40
CO *Kapitänleutnant* Jurgen von Rosenstiel (lost)
Date of loss 6 July 1942
Location Bay of Biscay, W of La Rochelle, 46°10'N 06°40'W
Cause Air attack
Casualties 52
Survivors None
Salvaged No
Notes Wellington 'H' of No 172 Squadron picked up an S/E contact at a range of seven miles at 0445. The contact was held until the range had come down to one mile, when the aircraft's Leigh Light was switched on, illuminating a U-boat on the surface. As the U-boat dived four depth charges were released across the bows from starboard to port at a height of 50ft. The rear gunner opened fire as the Wellington passed over and saw a swirling mass of water as the depth-charge boil subsided. The aircraft then dropped flares and observed the water to be a different colour from the surrounding sea. The Wellington stayed in the area until 0513 but made no further contact.

This was the first successful attack by a Wellington aircraft and the first by an aircraft fitted with the Leigh Light. The pilot, P Off W. B. Howell, was an American volunteer who later transferred to the US Navy and reached the rank of Captain. He was awarded the DFC for this attack.

	Launched	*Commissioned*
U701	14 Apr 1941	16 Jul 1941

Class Type VIIC
CO *Kapitänleutnant* Horst Degen
Date of loss 7 July 1942
Location Atlantic, W of Cape Hatteras, 34°50'N 74°55'W
Cause Air attack
Casualties 39
Survivors 17 (see notes)
Salvaged No
Notes *U701* was lying in wait for shipping off Cape Hatteras, spending the days dived to conserve fuel and surfacing at night. However, by the early afternoon of 7 July the atmosphere in the boat was so foul that Degen decided to surface and ventilate. His record for crash-diving was 28 seconds, but on this occasion the look-outs may have been suffering from the effects of breathing too much carbon dioxide for they failed to notice a Liberator of the 396th Bomb Squadron USAAF dive out of the sun. Although Degen gave the order to dive, *U701* was hit aft by two bombs which tore open the pressure hull. Tanks were blown and sufficient buoyancy was maintained

for seventeen men (including Degen) to scramble out of the conning tower. They remained afloat, supported by Dräger apparatus, until 9 July when a US Navy airship sighted them and dropped a raft. At 1605/9 a US Coast Guard seaplane picked up the seven survivors, ten having died one by one while drifting for over 60 miles under a blazing sun in the Gulf Stream.

	Launched	*Commissioned*
U136	5 Jul 1941	30 Aug 1941

Class	Type VIIC
CO	*Kapitänleutnant* Heinz Zimmermann (lost)
Date of loss	11 July 1942
Location	Atlantic, NW of Madeira, 33°30'N 22°52'W
Cause	Depth charge
Casualties	45
Survivors	None
Salvaged	No

Notes Sunk during operations against convoy OS.33 in a determined depth-charge attack by the sloop *Pelican*, frigate *Spey* and French destroyer *Léopard*.

	Launched	*Commissioned*
U153	5 Apr 1941	19 Jul 1941

Class	Type IXC
CO	*Korvettenkapitän* Wilfrid Reichmann (lost)
Date of loss	13 July 1942
Location	Caribbean, off Colón
Cause	Depth charge
Casualties	52
Survivors	None
Salvaged	No

Notes Reichmann attacked a netlayer off the eastern entrance to the Panama Canal but was forced to submerge by the patrol craft *PC458*. An intensive air and sea search followed before *U153* was sunk by the US destroyer *Lansdowne*.

	Launched	*Commissioned*
U576	30 Apr 1941	26 Jun 1941

Class	Type VIIC
CO	*Kapitänleutnant* Hans-Dieter Heinicke (lost)
Date of loss	15 July 1942
Location	Atlantic, off Cape Hatteras, 34°50'N 75°22'W.
Cause	Gunfire/ramming
Casualties	45
Survivors	None
Salvaged	No

Notes *U576* attacked a convoy off the US East Coast and sank the *Bluefields* and damaged the *Chilore* (which sank later while under tow). However, the submarine was spotted and attacked by an aircraft of VS-9 based at Cherry Point. She was then fired on by the Armed Guard Detachment aboard the SS *Unicoi* of the same convoy, which finally ended *U576*'s career by ramming her.

	Launched	*Commissioned*
U751	16 Nov 1940	31 Jan 1941

Class	Type VIIC
CO	*Korvettenkapitän* Gerhard Bigalk (lost)
Date of loss	17 July 1942
Location	Atlantic, NW of Cape Ortegal, 45°14'N 12° 22'W
Cause	Air attack
Casualties	44
Survivors	None
Salvaged	No

Notes *U751* was sighted on the surface by Whitley 'H' of No 502 Squadron and attacked with depth charges. The submarine made no attempt to dive but seemed to reduce speed and began to circle to port. The Whitley then climbed to 700ft and dropped two 100lb anti-submarine bombs before the U-boat was seen to submerge stern first. An hour later Lancaster 'F' of No 61 Squadron (a Bomber Command squadron 'on loan' to Coastal Command) saw the U-boat resurface about a mile away. The Lancaster's captain, Flt Lt P. R. Casement, was not aware of the Whitley's attack and attacked again with depth charges and anti-submarine bombs. The Lancaster's gunners also raked the U-boat's casing with machine-gun fire to prevent the crew from manning the AA armament. The U-boat was seen to sink stern first while the crew abandoned ship.

	Launched	*Commissioned*
U90	25 Oct 1941	20 Dec 1941

Class	Type VIIC

CO	*Kapitänleutnant* Hans Olldoerp (lost)
Date of loss	24 July 1942
Location	Atlantic, E of Cape Race, 48°12'N 40°56'W
Cause	Depth charge
Casualties	44
Survivors	None
Salvaged	No

Notes Sunk during operations against convoy ON.113. *U90* had been put down after being detected on the surface by the Canadian destroyer *St Croix* at a range of 6,000yds. *St Croix*, joined by HMS *Burnham*, made two depth-charge attacks. After the second attack a good deal of wreckage, oil, human remains and Dräger apparatus with remnants of flesh attached came to the surface.

U213

	Launched	Commissioned
	24 Jul 1941	30 Aug 1941
Class	Type VIID	
CO	*Oberleutnant zur See* Hans von Varendorf (lost)	
Date of loss	31 July 1942	
Location	Atlantic, S of Azores, 36°45'N 22°50'W	
Cause	Depth charge	
Casualties	50	
Survivors	None	
Salvaged	No	

Notes Sunk by HM Ships *Erne*, *Sandwich* and *Rochester* during operations in support of convoy OS.35. The U-boat was attacked ahead of the convoy and after a number of depth-charge attacks a good deal of wreckage, including human remains, was sighted. Subsequent assessment concluded that the boat was *U213*.

U588

	Launched	Commissioned
	23 Jul 1941	11 Sept 1941
Class	Type VIIC	
CO	*Kapitänleutnant* V. Vogel (lost)	
Date of loss	31 July 1942	
Location	Atlantic, NE of St John's, Newfoundland, 49°59'N 36°36'W	
Cause	Depth charge	
Casualties	46	
Survivors	None	
Salvaged	No	

Notes Convoy ON.115 was shadowed by a pack of six or more U-boats which were in contact from the 29th onwards. The escorts, the Canadian C3 group, did not have HF/DF or effective radar, but evasive manoeuvring and the vigorous prosecution of U-boat contacts which presented themselves kept the U-boats at bay. On the night of the 30th the Canadian destroyer *Skeena* sighted a U-boat and, supported by *Wetaskiwin*, went after it. *Skeena* delivered a series of unsuccessful attacks and then lost contact before *Wetaskiwin* arrived. Just before 0900 on the 31st contact was regained, but it was lost again after two attacks by *Skeena* and one by *Wetaskiwin*. At 1000 contact was regained and *Skeena* delivered the final attack, a five-charge pattern set to explode at depths between 350 and 550ft and fired at longer intervals to compensate for the longer descent time. Underwater explosions—distinct from the charges—were heard shortly afterwards. A considerable amount of wreckage, including human remains, was blown to the surface, confirming the boat's destruction. Subsequent assessment concluded that the boat was *U588*.

U754

	Launched	Commissioned
	5 Jul 1941	28 Aug 1941
Class	Type VIIC	
CO	*Kapitänleutnant* Johannes Ostermann (lost)	
Date of loss	31 July 1942	
Location	Atlantic, S of Nova Scotia, 43°02'N 64°52'W	
Cause	Air attack	
Casualties	44	
Survivors	None	
Salvaged	No	

Notes Sunk by a Hudson of No 113 Squadron RCAF which was flying in support of convoy ON.113.

U166

	Launched	Commissioned
	1 Nov 1941	23 Mar 1942
Class	Type IXC	
CO	*Oberleutnant zur See* Hans Kuhlmann (lost)	
Date of loss	1 August 1942	
Location	Gulf of Mexico, Mississippi estuary, 28°37'N 09°45'W	

Cause Air attack
Casualties 52
Survivors None
Salvaged No
Notes Sunk in an attack by a US Coast Guard aircraft.

	Launched	*Commissioned*
U335	15 Oct 1941	17 Dec 1941

Class Type VIIC
CO *Kapitänleutnant* Hans-Hermann Pelkner (lost)
Date of loss 3 August 1942
Location N of Shetlands, 62°48'N 00°12'W
Cause Submarine attack
Casualties 41
Survivors One
Salvaged No
Notes HM Submarine *Saracen* (Lt M. G. R. Lumby RN) was on her working-up patrol north of the Shetlands when orders were received from Flag Officer Submarines on 1 August 1942 to shift patrol in response to intelligence reports that a number of U-boats were outward-bound to the Atlantic. At 2159 on 3 August, just before sunset and while the boat was dived, a U-boat surfaced less than a mile away. In a snap attack Lumby fired all six bow tubes and the U-boat disintegrated in a huge explosion.

Saracen surfaced amid a considerable amount of wreckage and a spreading oil slick. Three men were in the water, one of whom was dead while the other deliberately avoided rescue and sank. The third was picked up and proved to be *U335*'s signalman. He said that one torpedo had struck amidships and exploded but that a second had struck the engine room and had penetrated the pressure hull without exploding. BdU was unaware of *U335*'s loss and continued to 'operate' her until 11 August, when she was declared lost.

	Launched	*Commissioned*
U372	8 Mar 1941	19 Apr 1941

Class Type VIIC
CO *Kapitänleutnant* Hans-Joachim Neumann (survived)
Date of loss 4 August 1942
Location Mediterranean, SW of Haifa, 32°28'N 34°37'E
Cause Depth charge
Casualties None
Survivors 4 officers, 16 senior rates, 26 junior rates, 1 Lebanese civilian
Salvaged No
Notes At 2123/3 an ASV-equipped Wellington of No 231 Squadron obtained a submarine contact south-west of Haifa and marked the spot with a flare. The destroyers *Sikh* and *Zulu*, which were cooperating with the aircraft, hunted throughout the night and the next morning. Soon after noon on 4 August the destroyers *Croome* and *Tetcott* joined the hunt since the two 'Tribals' had expended virtually their entire outfit of depth charges. Their perseverance was rewarded when *Sikh* sighted a U-boat on the surface leaking oil. Neumann had tried to break contact with his pursuers and, with the air in the boat by now extremely foul, had surfaced to see if he could escape in this way. Faced by four destroyers, Neumann took the only option open to him and scuttled the boat.

The identity and purpose of the Lebanese civilian recovered with the survivors of *U372* has not been established from those records open to public scrutiny. He was, however, without doubt an agent of some sort.

	Launched	*Commissioned*
U612	9 Jan 1942	5 Mar 1942

Class Type VIIC
CO ?
Date of loss 6 August 1942
Location Baltic
Cause Collision
Casualties 1
Survivors 44
Salvaged Yes (See notes)
Notes Sunk following a collision with *U444*. The submarine was raised in August 1942 and paid off. She recommissioned as a training boat on 31 May 1943. She was finally scuttled at Warnemünde 2 May 1945 as part of Operation *'Regenbogen'*.

	Launched	*Commissioned*
U210	23 Dec 1941	21 Feb 1942

Class Type VIIC
CO *Kapitänleutnant* Rudolf Lemcke (lost)

Date of loss	6 August 1942
Location	North Atlantic, 40°15'N 39° 37'W
Cause	Ramming
Casualties	6
Survivors	2 officers, 10 senior rates, 25 junior rates
Salvaged	No

Notes The first of two U-boats sunk during operations against convoy SC.94, which lost eleven out of 36 ships to U-boats. At 1125/6 the Canadian destroyer *Assiniboine* sighted a U-boat and a hunt was carried out in company with HMS *Dianthus*, both escorts and the U-boat dodging in and out of the fog banks. At 1851 a U-boat was sighted on the surface and *Assiniboine* gave chase while opening fire. The U-boat returned fire but was rammed squarely by *Assiniboine* and left wallowing on the surface, her conning tower wrecked after a direct hit from a 4.7in shell which had killed the commanding officer and all those on the bridge. *Assiniboine* turned and rammed the U-boat a second time, after which the submarine sank at 1914.

The return fire from the U-boat had been heavy and accurate. A number of hits from 40mm shells ignited a ready-use petrol store outside *Assiniboine*'s wheelhouse. The coxswain, CPO Max Bernays, remained at his post and proceeded to execute the 141 helm orders given during the chase, despite the fire raging outside the compartment and the wheelhouse being repeatedly hit by further fire from *U210*.

U379

	Launched	Commissioned
	16 Oct 1941	29 Nov 1941
Class	Type VIIC	
CO	*Kapitänleutnant* Paul Hugo Kettner (lost)	
Date of loss	9 August 1942	
Location	North Atlantic, 57°11'N 30°57'W	
Cause	Ramming	
Casualties	36	
Survivors	3 senior rates, 2 junior rates	
Salvaged	No	

Notes The second U-boat to fall victim to SC.94's escort. At dusk on the 8th two U-boats had been sighted on the surface by the corvette HMS *Dianthus*, which opened fire, forcing the U-boats to dive, after which *Dianthus* carried out a fruitless asdic search. Just after 2330 a sharp-eyed signalman with night glasses sighted a U-boat on the surface, which promptly dived when *Dianthus* turned towards the submarine. A quick and accurate depth-charge attack blew the submarine to the surface. *Dianthus* opened fire on the U-boat with every gun that would bear and rammed her no fewer than four times before she sank at 0006/9. Some of the U-boat's crew were left swimming in the water but *Dianthus*, badly damaged and taking water forward, could only stop to rescue five of them although a Carley float with rations was thrown over for the remainder.

Although SC.04's escort had disposed of two U-boats, the success had cost the them two of their number. *Assiniboine* had turned for home and a dockyard while *Dianthus* took up position as one of the convoy. Ramming was an effective and satisfying means of sinking a U-boat, but it could result in a Pyrrhic victory.

U578

	Launched	Commissioned
	15 May 1941	10 Jul 1941
Class	Type VIIC	
CO	*Korvettenkapitän* Ernst-August Rehwinkel (lost)	
Date of loss	10 August 1942	
Location	Western Approaches, W of Land's End, 49°59'N 07°44'W	
Cause	Air attack	
Casualties	49	
Survivors	None	
Salvaged	No	

Notes Wellington 'H' of No 311 (Czech) Squadron RAF, flown by Fg Off Josef Nyvlt, sighted the U-boat on the surface and attacked, dropping only three depth charges in the first run since Nyvlt judged that his speed was too high. As Nyvlt came round for a second pass he was fired on by the U-boat, which then began to dive. The three depth charges exploded around the conning tower and stern. Nyvlt then circled the area and observed a large oil slick forming over the position where the U-boat had dived.

U464

	Launched	Commissioned
	20 Dec 1941	30 Apr 1942
Class	Type XIV	
CO	*Kapitänleutnant* Otto Harms (survived)	

Date of loss	20 August 1942
Location	Atlantic, SE of Iceland, 61°58'N 17°05'W
Cause	Air attack
Casualties	2
Survivors	52
Salvaged	No

Notes This was the first of the ten Type XIV tanker U-boats to be sunk. These were large (and unarmed, other than AA guns for self defence), 1688/2300t submarines designed to supply other U-boats with food, fuel and torpedoes in mid-Atlantic. For their successful operation they depended on efficient (and safe) wireless communication with BdU, and this requirement would, eventually, prove their undoing.

U464 was outward-bound on her first operation when she strayed within the area covered by air patrols supporting convoy SN.73. In rough weather she was completely surprised by Catalina 'R' of USN squadron VP-73. The aircraft dropped five 325lb depth bombs and saw three of them explode close alongside the U-boat. Although damaged, *U464* could still make about 8kts, but Harms was advised by the LI that diving was out of the question until repairs could be effected. Harms realised that the air attack merely heralded the arrival of surface forces and that the large, unarmed U-tanker would stand little chance. Accordingly he scuttled the boat and the crew headed for a nearby Icelandic trawler with the intention of boarding her and returning to Germany. Fortunately the destroyers *Castleton* and *Newark* intervened and took off the survivors.

U94

	Launched	*Commissioned*
	12 Jun 1940	10 Aug 1940
Class	Type VIIC	
CO	*Kapitänleutnant* Otto Ites (survived)	
Date of loss	28 August 1942	
Location	Caribbean, off Haiti, 17°40'N 74°30'W	
Cause	Ramming	
Casualties	19	
Survivors	2 officers, 9 senior rates, 15 junior rates	
Salvaged	No	

Notes *U94* was detected on the surface and attacked by a PBY from US Navy squadron VP-92. Although the submarine dived on being sighted, she was blown to the surface by four 650lb depth charges. Fortunately the Canadian corvette *Oakville* was nearby (attached to the USN's Eastern Sea Frontier Force) and was called up by the aircraft. She found *U94* on the surface and rammed her.

It was particularly appropriate that *U94* should have been sunk by a Canadian vessel: in May 1942 the submarine had sunk a number of ships in ONS.92, escorted by a largely Canadian group.

U756

	Launched	*Commissioned*
	18 Oct 1941	30 Dec 1941
Class	Type VIIC	
CO	*Kapitänleutnant* Klaus Harney (lost)	
Date of loss	1 September 1942	
Location	North Atlantic, 57°41'N 31°30'W	
Cause	Depth charge	
Casualties	43	
Survivors	None	
Salvaged	No	

Notes Sunk in a depth-charge attack by HMCS *Morden*, escorting convoy SC.97.

U222

	Launched	*Commissioned*
	28 Mar 1942	23 May 1942
Class	Type VIIC	
CO	*Kapitänleutnant* Rolf von Jessen (lost)	
Date of loss	2 September 1942	
Location	Baltic, off Danzig	
Cause	Collision	
Casualties	42	
Survivors	4	
Salvaged	No	

Notes Sunk in a collision with *U626*.

U162

	Launched	*Commissioned*
	1 Mar 1941	9 Sept 1941
Class	Type IXC	
CO	*Fregattenkapitän* Jurgen Wattenburg (survived)	
Date of loss	3 September 1942	
Location	Caribbean, near Trinidad, 12°19'N 59°33'W	
Cause	Ramming	

Casualties	2
Survivors	3 officers, 16 senior rates, 30 junior rates
Salvaged	No

Notes The destroyers *Pathfinder*, *Quentin* and *Vimy* were en route for Port of Spain in Trinidad after escorting the battleship HMS *Queen Elizabeth* to Norfolk, Virginia, for repairs when they encountered *U162* during routine asdic sweeping. All three ships attacked with depth charges and a torpedo fired by the submarine was neatly avoided by *Quentin*. No visible results were apparent until five hours after the attack, when *Vimy* obtained a radar contact, sighted the submarine soon afterwards on the surface, opened fire and headed in to ram. A consequence of the ramming was that *Vimy*'s port shaft was damaged and the ship required docking.

Fregattenkapitän Wattenberg had been a gunnery officer in the pocket battleship *Admiral Graf Spee* and had escaped from internment in Argentina to return to Germany.

U705

	Launched	*Commissioned*
	23 Oct 1941	30 Dec 1941
Class	Type VIIC	
CO	*Kapitänleutnant* Karl-Horst Horn (lost)	
Date of loss	3 September 1942	
Location	Atlantic, W of Ushant, 46°42'N 11°07'W	
Cause	Air attack	
Casualties	45	
Survivors	None	
Salvaged	No	

Notes Whitley 'P' of No 77 Squadron RAF, flown by Flt Sgt A. A. MacInnes, made visual contact with *U705* from an altitude of 2,500ft at five miles. MacInnes attacked with depth charges dropped from a height of 50ft and appeared to take the U-boat completely by surprise. One depth charge hit the U-boat's saddle tank on the port side before exploding, while another exploded 20ft off the port side. MacInnes prepared for a second attack but his quarry had sunk before he could get the Whitley lined up. The intense glare from the sun made observation of any oil or wreckage very difficult, but subsequent analysis confirmed that *U705* had been the victim of this attack.

U705 is often credited to Whitley 'V' of No 77 Squadron, flown by P Off T. Lea. This attack was made on *U660*, which was undamaged.

U88

	Launched	*Commissioned*
	16 Aug 1941	15 Oct 1941
Class	Type VIIC	
CO	*Kapitänleutnant* Heino Bohmann (lost)	
Date of loss	12 September 1942	
Location	Arctic, NW of Bear Island, 75°04'N 04°49'E	
Cause	Depth charge	
Casualties	46	
Survivors	None	
Salvaged	No	

Notes *U88* was sunk by the destroyer HMS *Faulknor* during operations against convoy PQ.18 and was the first of a number U-boats to be sunk in this epic convoy battle. *Faulknor* was crossing ahead of the convoy when her asdic located a firm contact. *Faulknor* attacked six minutes later and was in the act of turning to deliver a second pattern when the asdic operator reported distinctive breaking-up noises. Later a considerable silver-grey oil slick was seen on the surface.

U589

	Launched	*Commissioned*
	6 Aug 1941	25 Sept 1941
Class	Type VIIC	
CO	*Kapitänleutnant* Hans Joachim Horrer (lost)	
Date of loss	14 September 1942	
Location	Arctic, NW of North Cape, 70°40'N 20°32'E	
Cause	Air attack/depth charge	
Casualties	44	
Survivors	None	
Salvaged	No	

Notes *U589* had been shadowing convoy PQ.18 when she was detected by a Swordfish aircraft of 825 NAS flying from the escort carrier HMS *Avenger*. The Swordfish attacked but was driven off by a Bv 138 reconnaissance aircraft (thus providing a very rare example of *Luftwaffe/Kriegsmarine* co-operation). The destroyer HMS *Onslow* was dispatched to the scene and sighted the U-boat on the surface at 1020. *Onslow* made her first attack at 1055 and continued for three hours, after which a quantity of oil fuel, together with green vegetables and pieces of the U-boat's casing, was seen on the surface.

U261

	Launched	*Commissioned*
	16 Feb 1942	28 Mar 1942
Class	Type VIIC	
CO	*Kapitänleutnant* Hans Lange (lost)	
Date of loss	15 September 1942	
Location	Atlantic, NW of Cape Wrath, 59°49'N 09°28'W	
Cause	Air attack	
Casualties	43	
Survivors	None	
Salvaged	No	

Notes At 1500hrs Whitley 'B' of No 58 Squadron, flown by Sgt B. F. Snell, sighted a U-boat on the surface at a distance of seven miles. Attacking through low cloud, Snell dropped three depth charges, one of which hit the conning tower while the other two straddled the submarine. When the depth-charge boils subsided the bows of the U-boat were seen protruding from the water. Snell attacked again, dropping his remaining depth charges around the boat, which then sank stern first. Debris, wooden wreckage and an oil drum were then observed on the surface.

U457

	Launched	*Commissioned*
	4 Oct 1941	5 Nov 1941
Class	Type VIIC	
CO	*Korvettenkapitän* Karl Brandenburg (lost)	
Date of loss	16 September 1942	
Location	Arctic, NE of North Cape, 75°05'N 43°15'E	
Cause	Depth charge	
Casualties	45	
Survivors	None	
Salvaged	No	

Notes Just after 0300 *U457* penetrated the screen of convoy PQ.18 but was spotted by the destroyer HMS *Impulsive*. The destroyer gained asdic contact and delivered an immediate attack with depth charges set to 50ft. *Impulsive* then kept the submarine in contact despite having to manouevre in and out of the lines of merchantmen. When *Impulsive* finally emerged at the rear of the convoy the sea was found to be thick with oil fuel and wreckage, which included a black leather gauntlet.

U446

	Launched	*Commissioned*
	11 Apr 1942	20 Jun 1942
Class	Type VIIC	
CO	?	
Date of loss	21 September 1942	
Location	Baltic, off Danzig, exact position unknown	
Cause	Mine	
Casualties	23	
Survivors	?	
Salvaged	Raised 8 November 1942 and paid off; subsequent fate unknown	

Notes Sunk off Danzig after striking an Allied air-laid mine.

U253

	Launched	*Commissioned*
	30 Aug 1941	21 Oct 1941
Class	Type VIIC	
CO	*Kapitänleutnant* Adolf Friedrich (lost)	
Date of loss	25 September 1942	
Location	Atlantic, NW of Iceland, 67°00'N 23°00'W	
Cause	Mine	
Casualties	45	
Survivors	None	
Salvaged	No	

Notes Mined in a British field off Iceland. An attack by Catalina 'U' of No 210 Squadron on 23 September, which is often cited as the cause of the loss of this submarine, was in fact made on *U255*, which escaped undamaged.

U165

	Launched	*Commissioned*
	15 Aug 1941	3 Feb 1942
Class	Type IXC	
CO	*Kapitänleutnant* Eberhard Hoffmann (lost)	
Date of loss	c. 27 September 1942	
Location	Bay of Biscay	
Cause	Unknown	
Casualties	50	
Survivors	None	
Salvaged	No	

Notes Being mined is one explanation for *U165*'s loss, but the possibility that she was lost by accident arising from mechanical or drill failure cannot be discounted.

	Launched	*Commissioned*
U512	9 Oct 1941	20 Dec 1941

Class	Type IXC
CO	*Kapitänleutnant* Wolfgang Schultze (lost)
Date of loss	2 October 1942
Location	Caribbean, N of Cayenne, 06°50'N 52°25'W
Cause	Air attack
Casualties	51
Survivors	1
Salvaged	No

Notes A B-18A from the 99th Bombardment Squadron USAAF sighted *U512* from fifteen miles and attacked from dead ahead, dropping four bombs from a height of 50ft. Two bombs were seen to hit the submarine before she could crash dive and oil and air were observed coming to the surface for half an hour after the attack.

One man was seen to reach the surface, having made an escape from the submarine using his Dräger apparatus. The aircraft saw him in the water and dropped a life raft. The man spent ten days on this raft before being rescued on 12 October by the USS *Ellis*. During this period he sustained himself by killing and eating some of the seabirds which attacked him.

	Launched	*Commissioned*
U582	12 Jun 1941	7 Aug 1941

Class	Type VIIC
CO	*Kapitänleutnant* W. Schulte (lost)
Date of loss	5 October 1942
Location	Atlantic, S of Iceland, 58°25'N 21°42'W
Cause	Air attack
Casualties	46
Survivors	None
Salvaged	No

Notes Sunk by Catalina 'I' of VP-73, US Navy.

	Launched	*Commissioned*
U619	9 May 1942	23 Apr 1942

Class	Type VIIC
CO	*Oberleutnant zur See* Kurt Makowski (lost)
Date of loss	5 October 1942
Location	North Atlantic, 58°41'N 22°58'W
Cause	Air attack
Casualties	44
Survivors	None
Salvaged	No

Notes *U619* was sunk in an attack by Hudson 'N' of No 269 Squadron flown by Fg Off J. Markham. Flying ahead of convoy ONS.136, Markham sighted a U-boat at five miles from an altitude of 4,000ft. The Hudson dived to 20ft and attacked with four Mk XI depth charges and strafing fire. The U-boat was diving as Markham was attacking, but as he circled the area first oil and then wreckage came to the surface. Hudson 'W' of the same squadron overflew the area some 30 minutes later and confirmed that oil and wreckage were still rising.

The loss of this boat was previously attributed to an attack by HMS *Viscount*, whose contact was actually *U661*.

	Launched	*Commissioned*
U179	18 Nov 1941	7 Mar 1942

Class	Type IXD2
CO	*Fregattenkapitän* Ernst Sobe (lost)
Date of loss	8 October 1942
Location	S Atlantic, W of Cape Town, 33°28'S 17°05'W
Cause	Depth charge/gunfire
Casualties	61
Survivors	None
Salvaged	No

Notes Sunk by HMS *Active*.

	Launched	*Commissioned*
U171	22 Jul 1941	25 Oct 1941

Class	Type IXC
CO	*Kapitänleutnant* Günther Pfeffer (survived)
Date of loss	9 October 1942
Location	Bay of Biscay, near Lorient, 47°30'N 03°30'W
Cause	Mine
Casualties	22
Survivors	?
Salvaged	No

Notes Mined outside Lorient harbour.

U597	*Launched* 11 Oct 1941	*Commissioned* 20 Nov 1941
Class	Type VIIC	
CO	*Kapitänleutnant* Eberhard Bobst (lost)	
Date of loss	12 October 1942	
Location	Atlantic, SW of Iceland, 56°50'N 28°05'W	
Cause	Air attack	
Casualties	49	
Survivors	None	
Salvaged	No	

Notes Liberator 'H' of No 120 Squadron RAF, flown by Sqn Ldr T. M. Bulloch DFC RAF, was flying in support of convoy ONS.136. At 1218 the aircraft homed in on a radar contact and at 1223 a U-boat was sighted on the surface. Bulloch attacked with depth charges as the U-boat dived. Subsequently oil and wreckage were observed on the surface.

U661	*Launched* 11 Dec 1941	*Commissioned* 12 Feb 1942
Class	Type VIIC	
CO	*Oberleutnant zur See* Erich von Lilienfeld (lost)	
Date of loss	15 October 1942	
Location	North Atlantic, 53°42'N 35°56'W	
Cause	Ramming/gunfire/depth charge	
Casualties	44	
Survivors	None	
Salvaged	No	

Notes Convoy SC.104 was first sighted by a U-boat on 11 October and shadowed by several more thereafter. In night attacks on 13 and 14 October eight merchant ships were sunk but in turn the escorts sank two U-boats, the first of which was *U661*.

HMS *Viscount* obtained a radar contact on her port bow, range 6,200yds, at 0131. The contact appeared to be steering a parallel course at a speed of 9kts. By 0142 the range had come down to 2,000yds, so *Viscount* increased speed to 26kts and set course to ram. Two minutes later the U-boat was sighted in a fully buoyant condition, fine on the port bow. The U-boat altered course to starboard but *Viscount* was unable to turn quickly enough so crossed the submarine's track while under starboard helm. For some reason which will never be known, the U-boat then turned back to port—straight across *Viscount*'s bows. The U-boat was struck just aft of the conning tower and hung on *Viscount*'s bows for about 15 seconds before dragging off to port. As the shattered hull passed down the destroyer's port side, it was engaged with close-range weapons and given the *coup de grâce* with the firing of a Mk X depth charge set to 140ft. The U-boat sank stern first at 0147.

U353	*Launched* 11 Nov 1941	*Commissioned* 31 Mar 1942
Class	Type VIIC	
CO	*Oberleutnant zur See* Wolfgang Romer (survived)	
Date of loss	16 October 1942	
Location	North Atlantic, 53°54'N 29°30'W	
Cause	Depth charge	
Casualties	6	
Survivors	3 officers, 14 senior rates, 16 junior rates	
Salvaged	No	

Notes The second of two U-boats sunk in the battle for SC.104. The destroyer HMS *Fame* followed up a radar contact and pounced on *U353*. Again the U-boat was rammed and then engaged with gunfire and depth charges. It appears that the submarine was taken by surprise, for the commanding officer was in his bunk when the boat was attacked, believing that he was shadowing the convoy from a safe distance. *Fame* managed to put a boarding party aboard the sinking *U353*, but they had barely got down into the control room when they had to abandon the submarine and no documents were recovered.

U116	*Launched* 3 May 1941	*Commissioned* 26 Jul 1941
Class	Type XB	
CO	*Oberleutnant zur See* Wilhelm Grimme (lost)	
Date of loss	19 October 1942	
Location	North Atlantic	
Cause	?	
Casualties	55	

Survivors None
Salvaged No
Notes *U116* left for patrol on 22 September 1942. When she failed to answer all signals she was declared missing. No Allied claim exists for her loss, and it is presumed that she was the victim of an accident, a mine or the detonation of her own mines.

U216

	Launched	*Commissioned*
	23 Oct 1941	15 Dec 1941

Class Type VIIC
CO *Kapitänleutnant* Karl Schultze (lost)
Date of loss 20 October 1942
Location Atlantic, W of Ushant, 48°21'N 19°25'W
Cause Air attack
Casualties 45
Survivors None
Salvaged No
Notes Liberator 'H' of No 224 Squadron RAF, flown by Fg Off D. M. Sleep, sighted the U-boat and attacked with depth charges. Six were dropped from a height of 30ft. The pattern was accurately dropped for the rear gunner saw wreckage from the submarine fly into the air as the depth charges exploded. He then saw the submarine sink. However, the low altitude from which the charges had been dropped meant that the aircraft sustained damage to her elevators: she was down by the tail and all loose gear had to be ditched. The flight home to the Isles of Scilly was accomplished with all the crew in the forward part of the aircraft in order to keep the tail up.

U412

	Launched	*Commissioned*
	15 Dec 1941	29 Apr 1942

Class Type VIIC
CO *Kapitänleutnant* Walter Jahrmarker (lost)
Date of loss 22 October 1942
Location Atlantic, N of Shetlands, 63°55'N 00°24'W
Cause Air attack
Casualties 47
Survivors None
Salvaged No
Notes During a routine A/S patrol north of the Shetlands Wellington 'B' of No 179 Squadron, flown by Flt Sgt A. D. Martin, obtained a radar contact at 2255/21 but immediately lost it. A further contact was made at 0106/22 at a range of five miles and the aircraft began to close the target. At a range of 1.5 miles the Leigh Light was switched on and a U-boat was illuminated on the surface. Four depth charges were dropped from 150ft which exploded in pairs on either side of the submarine. Oil and air bubbles were seen but no further wreckage.

U412, adjudged the victim of this attack, had left Kiel just five days earlier on her first patrol.

U599

	Launched	*Commissioned*
	15 Oct 1941	4 Dec 1941

Class Type VIIC
CO *Kapitänleutnant* Breithaupt (lost)
Date of loss 24 October 1942
Location Atlantic, NW of Cape Finisterre, 46°07'N 17°40'W
Cause Air attack
Casualties 44
Survivors None
Salvaged No
Notes Liberator 'G' of No 224 Squadron RAF, flown by P Off B. P. Liddington, had been tasked to fly cover for convoy KX.2 but had failed to meet it. At 1650 a fully surfaced U-boat was sighted and attacked with depth charges. Although the U-boat dived during the attack, a large oil slick was observed forming on the surface shortly afterwards.

U627

	Launched	*Commissioned*
	29 Apr 1942	?

Class Type VIIC
CO *Kapitänleutnant* Robert Kindelbacher (lost)
Date of loss 27 October 1942
Location Atlantic, SW of Iceland, 59° 14'N 22°49'W
Cause Air attack
Casualties 44
Survivors None
Salvaged No
Notes Fortress 'F' of No 206 Squadron, flown by P Off R. L. Cowey, was providing cover to convoy SC.105 when a U-boat was sighted at 1125. An attack was made with seven depth charges, which fell about 25yds ahead of the swirl

as the boat dived. The straddle appeared to go across the estimated track of the submarine. After the explosions had cleared a patch of light, iridescent oil was visible on the surface.

U520	*Launched*	*Commissioned*
	2 Mar 1942	19 May 1942
Class	Type IXC	
CO	*Kapitänleutnant* Schwarzkopf (lost)	
Date of loss	30 October 1942	
Location	Atlantic, E of Newfoundland, 47° 47'N 49°50'W	
Cause	Air attack	
Casualties	53	
Survivors	None	
Salvaged	No	

Notes Sunk by a Digby bomber of No 10 Squadron RCAF during operations in support of convoy SC.107.

U559	*Launched*	*Commissioned*
	8 Jan 1941	27 Feb 1941
Class	Type VIIC	
CO	*Kapitänleutnant* Hans Heidtmann	
Date of loss	30 October 1942	
Location	Mediterranean, NE of Port Said, 32°30'N 33°00'E	
Cause	Depth charge	
Casualties	7	
Survivors	?	
Salvaged	No	

Notes At 0500 on the 30th a Sunderland of No 201 (Naval Cooperation) Group reported a U-boat in position 31°47'N 33°24'E. The destroyer *Hero*, on passage south from Haifa, proceeded to the position and began to search. Meanwhile Captain (D)12 in *Pakenham*, with *Petard*, *Dulverton* and *Hurworth*, sailed from Port Said to relieve *Hero*, which continued her passage. Contact was made with the submarine by *Pakenham* and the first attack was made at 1257. The four destroyers continued to attack throughout the day, assisted by Wellesley 'N' of No 47 Squadron RAF. Over 300 depth charges were expended, some of which had soap stuffed into the hydrostatic fuse in order that the charge should sink beyond the maximum 500ft setting before exploding. At 2240 the persistence of the hunters was rewarded when the submarine surfaced and was immediately engaged with 4in, 12pdr and 20mm fire.

The U-boat was boarded by Lt Anthony Fasson, AB Colin Grazier and the fifteen-year-old canteen assistant, Tommy Brown, who had swum over to the submarine. Since the submarine's crew had abandoned the vessel, the boarding party made its way into the control room and began to seize documents and such equipment as could be detached, to be passed to *Pakenham*'s whaler which was now alongside under the command of Sub-Lt G. G. Connell. The U-boat was now sinking fast, and although Brown came up on to the casing, Fasson and Grazier remained inside the control room, refusing to heed the advice to leave, and continued to pass up documents until the submarine sank beneath them.

Fasson's and Grazier's self-sacrifice was to pay enormous dividends. The haul of documents included copies of the Short Signal Book and the Short Weather Cipher which the codebreakers at Bletchley Park were able to use to break the new four rotor setting on the German Shark 'Enigma' cipher used by BdU to communicate with boats in the Atlantic and which had been unbroken since its inception. On the evening of 13 December Bletchley Park broke Shark and a stream of intelligence flowed to the Submarine Tracking Room—intelligence that would be of priceless value in the critical convoy battles of 1943.

The authorities decreed that Fasson and Grazier could not be awarded the VC since they had not been in action with the enemy. However, both were posthumously awarded the George Cross.

U658	*Launched*	*Commissioned*
	11 Sept 1941	9 Nov 1941
Class	Type VIIC	
CO	*Kapitänleutnant* Senkel (lost)	
Date of loss	30 October 1942	
Location	N Atlantic, NE of St John's, Newfoundland, 50°32'N 46°32'W	
Cause	Air attack	
Casualties	48	
Survivors	None	
Salvaged	No	

Notes Sunk by Hudson 'Y' of No 45 Squadron RCAF. At the time *U658* was part of a patrol line scouting for an eastbound convoy.

U132	*Launched* 10 Apr 1941	*Commissioned* 29 May 1941
Class	Type VIIC	
CO	*Kapitänleutnant* Ernst Vogelsang (lost)	
Date of loss	5 November 1942	
Location	North Atlantic, 55° 38'N 39°52'W	
Cause	Explosion	
Casualties	47	
Survivors	None	
Salvaged	No	

Notes It had been accepted for some time that *U132* was the victim of an attack by a Liberator of No 120 Squadron on 6 November during operations in support of convoy SC.107. However, it is now accepted that she was destroyed in the explosion of her last victim, the ammunition ship *Hatimura*, which blew up with considerable violence after being hit. *U132* was probably within the lethal radius of this explosion.

U408	*Launched* 16 Jul 1941	*Commissioned* 19 Nov 1941
Class	Type VIIC	
CO	*Kapitänleutnant* Reinhard von Hymmen (lost)	
Date of loss	5 November 1942	
Location	N Atlantic, N of Iceland, 67°40'N 18°32'W	
Cause	Air attack	
Casualties	45	
Survivors	None	
Salvaged	No	

Notes Catalina 'H' of USN squadron VP-84, flown by Lieutenant Millard, attacked and sank *U408* during a routine patrol south of Iceland.

U272	*Launched* 15 Aug 1942	*Commissioned* 7 Oct 1942
Class	Type VIIC	
CO	*Kapitänleutnant* Horst Hepp (lost)	
Date of loss	12 November 1942	
Location	Baltic, off Hela, 54°45'N 18°50'E	
Cause	Collision	
Casualties	28	
Survivors	?	
Salvaged	No	

Notes Sunk following a collision with an unidentified vessel during a training exercise. No further details are available concerning this loss.

U660	*Launched* 17 Nov 1941	*Commissioned* 12 Feb 1942
Class	Type VIIC	
CO	*Kapitänleutnant* G. Bauer (sur vived)	
Date of loss	12 November 1942	
Location	Mediterranean, N of Oran, 36°07'N 01°00'W	
Cause	Depth charge	
Casualties	None	
Survivors	45	
Salvaged	No	

Notes *U660* was preparing to attack convoy TE.3 when she was detected by the corvette HMS *Lotus* and attacked with depth charges at 0931while warning the convoy to alter course. After three attacks *Lotus* re-joined the convoy, her place being taken by *Starwort*, which continued the hunt. At 1059 the U-boat surfaced and surrendered before sinking stern first at 1105.

U411	*Launched* 15 Nov 1941	*Commissioned* 18 Mar 1942
Class	Type VIIC	
CO	*Kapitänleutnant* Johann Spindlegger (lost)	
Date of loss	13 November 1942	
Location	Atlantic, SW of Gibraltar, 36°00'N 09°35'W	
Cause	Air attack	
Casualties	46	
Survivors	None	
Salvaged	No	

Notes Hudson 'D' of No 500 Squadron RAF, flown by Sqn Ldr J. B. Ensor, attacked a surfaced U-boat with four depth charges which fell ahead of the boat as she was diving. No results were observed. *U411* was originally thought to have been lost, cause unknown, on or around 28 November. However, subsequent analysis shows that she was sunk in this attack.

U605	*Launched* 27 Nov 1941	*Commissioned* 15 Jan 1942
Class	Type VIIC	

CO	*Kapitänleutnant* H.V. Schutze (lost)
Date of loss	14 November 1942
Location	Mediterranean, N of Algiers, 36°20'N 01°01'W
Cause	Air attack
Casualties	46
Survivors	None
Salvaged	No

Notes Sunk in an attack by Hudson 'B' of No 233 Squadron. The loss of this boat was incorrectly attributed to a depth-charge attack off Algiers by HM Ships *Lotus* and *Poppy*, whose real victim was *U77*, which survived the encounter with minor damage.

U595	*Launched*	*Commissioned*
	17 Sept 1941	6 Nov 1941
Class	Type VIIC	
CO	*Kapitänleutnant* Jurgen Quaet-Faslam (survived)	
Date of loss	14 November 1942	
Location	Mediterranean, W of Oran	
Cause	Air attack/beaching	
Casualties	?	
Survivors	?	
Salvaged	No	

Notes *U595* was sighted by Hudsons 'C' and 'D' of No 608 Squadron and attacked with depth charges. The charges straddled the U-boat, which dived but resurfaced after a short interval: *U595* had been so badly damaged that she could not dive, so Quaet-Faslam decided to beach her. She was repeatedly attacked with depth charges and machine-gun fire by the two Hudsons. These attacks left the submarine in a very parlous state: she was flooding aft, so much so that her bows were out of the water. Some half-hearted support appeared at this stage in the form of a Ju 88, but the aircraft made off after being fired on by Hudson 'C'. At this point Hudsons 'F', 'J', 'K', 'X' and 'W' of No 500 Squadron joined the action. Despite the overwhelming odds and being unable to dive, U595 kept up a brisk return fire, hitting 'F', 'K' and 'X'. Eventually Quaet-Faslam beached *U595* near Ténès on the Algerian coast. The crew were captured by the French. The U-boat's loss was officially credited to Hudsons 'C' and 'D' of No 608 Squadron since Quaet-Faslam admitted that it was the attacks by these aircraft which had done the most damage.

U259	*Launched*	*Commissioned*
	30 Dec 1941	18 Feb 1942
Class	Type VIIC	
CO	*Kapitänleutnant* Klaus Kopke (lost)	
Date of loss	15 November 1942	
Location	Mediterranean, off Algiers, 37°20'N 03° 05'E	
Cause	Air attack	
Casualties	48	
Survivors	None	
Salvaged	No	

Notes Hudson 'S' of No 500 Squadron RAF, flown by Fg Off M.A. Ensor DFC RAF, attacked a surfaced U-boat north of Algiers. The rear gunner reported that the boat had 'blown up'. However, the aircraft was badly damaged in the explosion of the depth charges. Ensor kept the Hudson airborne for as long as possible but eventually he and his crew of three baled out and were rescued by HM Ships *Erne* and *Leath*.

U98	*Launched*	*Commissioned*
	31 Aug 1940	18 Apr 1940
Class	Type VIIC	
CO	*Oberleutnant zur See* Kurt Eichmann (lost)	
Date of loss	15 November 1942	
Location	Atlantic, W of Gibraltar, 36°09'N 07°42'W	
Cause	Depth charge	
Casualties	46	
Survivors	None	
Salvaged	No	

Notes Sunk by HMS *Wrestler*.

U173	*Launched*	*Commissioned*
	11 Aug 1941	15 Nov 1941
Class	Type IXC	
CO	*Oberleutnant zur See* Hans Schweichel (lost)	
Date of loss	16 November 1942	
Location	Mediterranean, off Casablanca	
Cause	Depth charge	
Casualties	57	
Survivors	None	
Salvaged	No	

Notes Sunk in a depth-charge attack by the US destroyers *Woolsey*, *Swanson* and *Quick*.

U331	*Launched*	*Commissioned*
	20 Dec 1940	31 Mar 1941
Class	Type VIIC	
CO	*Kapitänleutnant* Hans Dietrich *Freiherr* von Tiesenhausen (survived)	
Date of loss	17 November 1942	
Location	Mediterranean,, off Cape Caxine, 37°00'N 02°10'E	
Cause	Air attack	
Casualties	32	
Survivors	4 officers, 4 senior rates, 9 junior rates	
Salvaged	No	

Notes *U331* was sighted on the surface and attacked by Hudson 'Z' of No 500 Squadron RAF which dropped four depth charges from a height of 20ft, inflicting severe damage. 'Z' was then joined by Hudsons 'L' and 'C', which attacked with four and three depth charges respectively. 'Z' then attacked with anti-submarine bombs and machine-gun fire until *U331* indicated that she was surrendering. The destroyer *Wilton* had been ordered to the scene under aircraft control, but before she could reach the area an Albacore from the carrier HMS *Formidable* attacked with a torpedo and sank the submarine. Fourteen survivors were left swimming in the water, two being taken as a sample by a Walrus from Algiers, leaving the remainder to be picked up later. Among them was von Tiesenhausen, who had sunk the battleship *Barham* on 25 November 1941.

Admiral Sir Andrew Cunningham commented that credit for the sinking should go to the Hudsons since the Albacore had merely 'finished off a cripple already heavily damaged'.

U184	*Launched*	*Commissioned*
	21 Feb 1942	29 May 1942
Class	Type IXC/40	
CO	*Kapitänleutnant* Günther Dangschat (lost)	
Date of loss	20 November 1942	
Location	Mid-Atlantic, 24°25'N 45°25'W	
Cause	Depth charge	
Casualties	50	
Survivors	None	
Salvaged	No	

Notes *U184* was shadowing convoy ONS.144 when she was attacked and sunk early on the morning of the 20th by the Norwegian-manned corvette HMS *Potentilla*. The homing signals broadcast by *U184* for other U-boats had instead brought down the corvette with her tough and experienced crew.

U517	*Launched*	*Commissioned*
	30 Dec 1941	2 Mar 1942
Class	Type IXC	
CO	*Korvettenkapitän* Paul Hartwig (survived)	
Date of loss	21 November 1942	
Location	Atlantic, WNW of Cape Finisterre, 46°10'N 17°08'W	
Cause	Air attack	
Casualties	1	
Survivors	51	
Salvaged	No	

Notes At 1100 an Albacore aircraft from HMS *Victorious*, on passage from Gibraltar to Greenock, sighted *U517* diving and attacked immediately with depth charges. *U517* was blown to the surface, where the Albacore observed that the depth charges had blown the bridge and a large portion of the conning tower away. Meanwhile the destroyer *Opportune* had been detached from the screen in response to the Albacore's sighting report, but by the time she reached the spot *U517* had been scuttled.

The interrogators noted that Hartwig was 'an extremely competent submarine officer and a hard drinker, apparently admired by his crew in both capacities'.

U254	*Launched*	*Commissioned*
	20 Sept 1941	8 Nov 1941
Class	Type VIIC	
CO	*Kapitänleutnant* Odo Loewe (survived)	
Date of loss	8 December 1942	
Location	Atlantic, SE of Greenland, 58°20'N 33°25'W	
Cause	Collision	
Casualties	41	
Survivors	4	
Salvaged	No	

Notes *U254* was rammed by *U221* while both boats were manoeuvring on the surface during operations against convoy HX.217. *U221* sustained superficial damage but *U254* sank quickly. Although a number of the crew were able to abandon the submarine, the rough weather meant that only four could be rescued.

The attack by Liberator 'B' of No 120 Squadron, which is often given as the cause of *U254*'s loss, was made against *U611*.

U611

	Launched	*Commissioned*
U611	8 Jan 1942	26 Feb 1942

Class: Type VIIC
CO: *Kapitänleutnant* Nikolaus von Jakobs (lost)
Date of loss: 8 December 1942
Location: Atlantic, SE of Cape Discord, Greenland, 57°25'N 35°19'W
Cause: Air attack
Casualties: 45
Survivors: None
Salvaged: No

Notes Sunk by Liberator 'B' of No 120 Squadron RAF during operations in support of convoy HX.217. Six depth charges were dropped and after the attack the aircrew observed wreckage and human remains on the surface.

U611's loss is usually attributed to an attack by PBY-5A Catalina 'H' of VP-84, US Navy, on 10 December. However, the victim of this attack was *U609*, which received but slight damage.

U626

	Launched	*Commissioned*
U626	15 Apr 1942	11 Jun 1942

Class: Type VIIC
CO: *Leutnant zur See* Bade (lost)
Date of loss: 15 December 1942
Location: N Atlantic, SW of Iceland, 56°46'N 27° 12'W
Cause: Depth charge
Casualties: 47
Survivors: None
Salvaged: No

Notes Sunk by the US Coast Guard cutter *Samuel D. Ingham*.

U357

	Launched	*Commissioned*
U357	31 Mar 1942	18 Jun 1942

Class: Type VIIC
CO: *Kapitänleutnant* Adolf Kellner (lost)
Date of loss: 26 December 1942
Location: Atlantic, SW of Rockall, 57°10'N 15°40'W
Cause: Depth charge/ramming
Casualties: 37
Survivors: 2 petty officers, 5 junior rates
Salvaged: No

Notes *U357* was shadowing convoy HX.219 when she was detected and attacked by HMS *Hesperus*, joined by HMS *Vanessa*. It took 5½ hours of persistent depth-charging to blow *U357* to the surface, where she was rammed by *Vanessa* and again by *Hesperus* before sinking.

The interrogators were surprised to find that, of the U-boat's officers, only Kellner had any submarine experience, while, of the ratings, only three had previously undertaken a war patrol.

U356

	Launched	*Commissioned*
U356	11 Sept 1941	20 Dec 1941

Class: Type VIIC
CO: *Kapitänleutnant* Günther Ruppelt (lost)
Date of loss: 27 December 1942
Location: Atlantic, NW of Cape Finisterre, 45° 30'N 25°40'W
Cause: Depth charge
Casualties: 45
Survivors: None
Salvaged: No

Notes *U356* had made two passes through convoy ONS.154, sinking three ships, *Empire Union*, *Melrose Abbey* and *King Edward*, and damaging a fourth, *Soekaboemi*. She was caught on the surface and engaged by the Canadian destroyer *St Laurent* at 0330Z with 20mm and 4.7in shellfire; at least one of the latter rounds is thought to have struck home. As she dived *St Laurent* laid a shallow depth-charge pattern over the swirl, followed by a ten-charge pattern on a good, firm asdic contact. *St Laurent*'s asdic operator reported hearing eleven detonations, the last being 'delayed and intense'. As the destroyer closed for a third attack, the target appeared stopped and a large oil slick was spreading on the surface. Only after the war was it learned that *U356* was the victim of this attack. This was the sole U-boat sinking to compensate for thirteen merchant ships of ONS.154 sunk by U-boat attack.

1943

U164

	Launched	*Commissioned*
U164	1 May 1941	28 Nov 1941
Class	Type IXC/40	
CO	*Korvettenkapitän* Otto Fechner (lost)	
Date of loss	6 January 1943	
Location	Atlantic, NW of Pernambuco, 01°58'S 39°22'W	
Cause	Air attack	
Casualties	54	
Survivors	2	
Salvaged	No	

Notes A PBY-5A of VP-83 was returning to its base at Natal in Brazil from covering a convoy when it surprised *U164* on the surface. The aircraft attacked from a height of 50ft and dropped four depth charges manually. The submarine appeared to rise up amidst the depth-charge explosions and break in two. Several bodies and a good deal of wreckage were seen. The aircraft dropped a life raft to three men swimming and two of them, a Petty Officer and a junior rating, subsequently landed on the north coast of Brazil, where they were made prisoners-of-war.

U224

	Launched	*Commissioned*
U224	7 May 1942	20 Jun 1942
Class	Type VIIC	
CO	*Oberleutnant zur See* Hans Kosbadt (lost)	
Date of loss	13 January 1943	
Location	Mediterranean, W of Algiers, 36°28'N 00°49'E	
Cause	Depth charge/ramming	
Casualties	44	
Survivors	1	
Salvaged	No	

Notes The corvette HMCS *Ville de Quebec* was escorting convoy TE.13 when she detected *U224* and delivered an extremely accurate depth-charge attack which blew the submarine to the surface. The IWO, *Leutnant zur See* Danckworth, was sent up to the bridge to survey the damage. On opening the upper hatch his first sight was that of *Ville de Quebec* bearing down to ram. Danckworth was the only survivor, being thrown clear when the U-boat was rammed. He was rescued some 30 minutes later by HMCS *Port Arthur.*

U507

	Launched	*Commissioned*
U507	15 Jul 1941	8 Oct 1941
Class	Type IXC	
CO	*Korvettenkapitän* Schacht (lost)	
Date of loss	13 January 1943	
Location	NW of Natal, 01°38'S 39°52'W	
Cause	Air attack	
Casualties	54	
Survivors	None	
Salvaged	No	

Notes Sunk by a Catalina aircraft of USN patrol squadron VP-83.

U337

	Launched	*Commissioned*
U337	25 Mar 1942	6 May 1942
Class	Type VIIC	
CO	*Oberleutnant zur See* Kurt Ruhwiedel (lost)	
Date of loss	16 January 1943	
Location	N Atlantic, SW of Iceland, 57°40'N 27°10'W	
Cause	Air attack	
Casualties	47	
Survivors	None	
Salvaged	No	

Notes Fortress 'G' of No 208 Squadron, flown by P Off L. G. Clark, was patrolling in support of convoy ON.160 when a surfaced submarine was sighted at 1440 between five and six miles on the port bow. Clark attacked from 80ft and dropped seven Mk VIII depth charges; four of them straddled the submarine but the others failed to release. As the aircraft passed over the U-boat the rear gunner fired some 300 rounds of .5in ammunition. The U-boat was observed to sink by the stern until the bows were nearly at the vertical. Air bubbles and foam continued to reach the surface for six minutes after the boat sank.

	Launched	*Commissioned*
U301	25 Mar 1942	9 May 1942
Class	Type VIIC	
CO	*Kapitänleutnant* Willi Korner (lost)	
Date of loss	21 January 1943	
Location	Mediterranean, W of Bonifacio, 41° 27'N 07°04'E	
Cause	Submarine attack	
Casualties	45	
Survivors	1 officer	
Salvaged	No	

Notes HM Submarine *Sahib* (Lt J. H. Bromage RN) was returning to Algiers after a successful patrol in the Gulf of Genoa when she surprised and sank *U301* which had surfaced to take sun sights.

The sole survivor was a midshipman who was picked up with a broken jaw. He spent the rest of the patrol in *Sahib*'s coxswain's bunk being fed soup through a gauge jar. Nevertheless he offered much useful information, including the fact that no zig-zag or listening watch had been kept since Korner had been adamant that no British submarines could possibly be in the area!

	Launched	*Commissioned*
U553	7 Nov 1940	23 Dec 1940
Class	Type VIIC	
CO	*Korvettenkapitän* Karl Thurmann (lost)	
Date of loss	January 1943	
Location	North Atlantic	
Cause	?	
Casualties	47	
Survivors	None	
Salvaged	No	

Notes Lost during operations in the North Atlantic, between 20 and 28 January. The possibility that the submarine was lost as a result of an accident arising from mechanical or drill failure cannot be ruled out.

	Launched	*Commissioned*
U265	23 Apr 1942	6 Jun 1942
Class	Type VIIC	
CO	*Oberleutnant zur See* Leonhard Aufhammer (lost)	
Date of loss	3 February 1943	
Location	N Atlantic, SW of Iceland, 56°35'N 22°48'W	
Cause	Air attack	
Casualties	45	
Survivors	None	
Salvaged	No	

Notes Flying in support of convoy HX.224, Fortress 'N' of No 220 Squadron, flown by P Off K. Ramsden, sighted the U-boat on the surface through a gap in the clouds at a range of four miles at 1106. Gaining position so that the sun was behind him, Ramsden dropped seven Mk IX depth charges from 50ft. The aircraft then turned to port to make a second run but the submarine had disappeared and all that remained was a spreading slick of oil.

	Launched	*Commissioned*
U187	16 Mar 1942	23 Jul 1942
Class	Type IXC/40	
CO	*Kapitänleutnant* Ralph Münnich (lost)	
Date of loss	4 February 1943	
Location	N Atlantic, 50°12'N 36°35'W	
Cause	Depth charge	
Casualties	9	
Survivors	3 officers, 13 senior rates, 29 junior rates	
Salvaged	No	

Notes *U187* made a sighting report of convoy SC.118 at noon. The transmission was brief—no more than fifteen to twenty seconds—but was enough to seal the submarine's fate. The Senior Officer's ship, *Vanessa*, was fitted with HF/DF, as was the rescue ship *Toward* and the US Coast Guard cutter *Bibb*. The destroyers *Vimy* and *Beverley* were sent off down the bearing at full speed. *Beverley* sighted the submarine fifteen miles ahead of the convoy and tried to open fire at a range of 1,500yds, but heavy seas meant that the submarine kept disappearing in the troughs and fire control was extremely difficult. In the event no rounds were fired before the boat dived at 4,000yds. *Vimy* gained an asdic contact at 1235 and made four attacks with depth charges and Hedgehog, after which *U187* surfaced. Both destroyers opened fire, *Vimy*'s gunfire striking home. *U187* listed to port and sank by the stern, her crew out of the conning tower. The survivors were picked up by both ships and *U187* went down at 1343, one hour and forty-three minutes after her fateful signal.

This attack could be said to illustrate the classic use of HF/DF and also the important role played by rescue ships which were all HF/DF fitted. The Merchant Navy radio officers in the rescue ships were experts at their craft, as shown on this occasion.

	Launched	*Commissioned*
U609	23 Dec 1941	12 Feb 1942

Class	Type VIIC
CO	*Kapitänleutnant* Klaus Rudloff (lost)
Date of loss	7 February 1943
Location	N Atlantic, W of Bloody Foreland, 55°17'N 26°38'W
Cause	Depth charge
Casualties	46
Survivors	None
Salvaged	No

Notes The second U-boat to be sunk in the battle for convoy SC.118. *U609* was attacked by the French corvette *Lobelia*. However, the evidence was inconclusive and it was not until after the war that *U609* was adjudged the victim of this attack.

	Launched	*Commissioned*
U624	31 Mar 1941	28 May 1942

Class	Type VIIC
CO	*Kapitänleutnant* Ulrich Graf von Soden-Frauenhofen (lost)
Date of loss	7 February 1943
Location	N Atlantic, W of Rockall, 55°42'N 26°17'W
Cause	Air attack
Casualties	45
Survivors	None
Salvaged	No

Notes Fortress 'J' of No 220 Squadron, flown by P Off G. Robertson, was flying in support of convoy SC.118 when the U-boat was sighted some nine miles away. Robertson used the heavy cloud cover to manoeuvre into a favourable attacking position and finally broke through the cloud only three-quarters of a mile away from the U-boat to attack with seven depth charges from 50ft. The bomb-aimer and rear gunner saw the U-boat pass beneath them and saw depth charges 4 and 5 straddle the hull. After the depth charge boil had subsided an oil slick was observed on the surface together with wooden wreckage.

	Launched	*Commissioned*
U519	12 Feb 1942	7 May 1942

Class	Type IXC
CO	*Kapitänleutnant* Günther Eppen (lost)
Date of loss	10 February 1943
Location	Atlantic, SW of Ireland, 47°05'N 18°34'W
Cause	Air attack
Casualties	50
Survivors	None
Salvaged	No

Notes Liberator 'T' *Tidewater Tillie* of the 2nd Squadron, 480th Group USAAF, attached to RAF Coastal Command and flown by 1/Lt William L, Sandford, picked up a radar contact at 0910 at a range of between three and four miles and homed in to sight a U-boat on the surface. However the U-boat had dived by the time the Liberator made its attacking run, although the top and rear turret fired into the swirl. At 0928 the aircraft had resumed patrol when the port waist gunner sighted a U-boat at a range of four miles. Sandford attacked as the U-boat was diving and dropped six depth charges, all of which overshot. The U-boat came to the surface and was attacked for a second time with three depth charges. On the third run the aircraft's navigator observed that the submarine had a list to starboard, and seconds later it disappeared amid the boil of a further three depth charges.

The attack was originally assessed as a 'possibly damaged', but subsequent enquiry revealed that *U519* had been sunk.

U442	*Launched* 12 Jan 1942	*Commissioned* 22 Mar 1943
Class	Type VIIC	
CO	*Korevettenkapitän* Joachim Hesse (lost)	
Date of loss	12 February 1943	
Location	Atlantic, W of Cape St Vincent, 37°32'N 11°56'W	
Cause	Air attack	
Casualties	48	
Survivors	None	
Salvaged	No	

Notes Hudson 'F' of No 48 Squadron RAF, flown by Fg Off G. R. Mayhew, sighted a fully surfaced U-boat at 1402 and dived to attack from dead astern from 40ft. One depth charge exploded directly alongside the conning tower on the port side while the other two exploded ahead of the submarine. The U-boat sank amid the depth-charge boil and Mayhew subsequently circled the spot photographing oil and debris.

U620	*Launched* 9 Mar 1942	*Commissioned* 30 Apr 1942
Class	Type VIIC	
CO	*Oberleutnant zur See* Heinz Stein (lost)	
Date of loss	13 February 1943	
Location	Atlantic, NW of Lisbon, 39°27'N 39°24'W	
Cause	Air attack	
Casualties	46	
Survivors	None	
Salvaged	No	

Notes Catalina 'J' of No 202 Squadron was flying in support of convoy KMS.6 when a U-boat was sighted on the surface at 2240 but submerged before an attack could be mounted. Nearly an hour later another U-boat was sighted and attacked with five depth charges, all of which overshot. At 0105 third U-boat was sighted on the surface and attacked while diving with the remaining two depth charges. No results of this attack were visible because all was in darkness behind the aircraft.

Subsequent analysis showed that the victim of the first attack was *U381*, which was damaged but survived. *U620* was the victim of the second attack.

U225	*Launched* 28 May 1942	*Commissioned* 11 Jul 1942
Class	Type VIIC	
CO	*Oberleutnant zur See* Wolfgang Leimkuhler (lost)	
Date of loss	15 February 1942	
Location	North Atlantic, 55°45'N 31°09'W	
Cause	Air attack	
Casualties	46	
Survivors	None	
Salvaged	No	

Notes Sunk by Liberator 'S' of No 120 Squadron RAF, flown by Fg Off R. F. T. Turner, during operations in support of convoy SC.119. The U-boat was sighted on the surface and attacked with six depth charges dropped from 70ft. The U-boat was diving but the depth charges were dropped while the conning tower was still visible. Oil and wreckage were subsequently observed on the surface.

This loss of *U225* is often incorrectly attributed to an attack on 21 February 1943 by the US Coast Guard cutter *Spencer*. However *Spencer's* quarry was *U604*, which escaped the encounter unscathed.

U529	*Launched* 15 Jul 1942	*Commissioned* 30 Sept 1942
Class	Type IXC/40	
CO	*Kapitänleutnant* Georg Fraatz (lost)	
Date of loss	c. 15 February 1943	
Location	N Atlantic, E of Newfoundland	
Cause	?	
Casualties	48	
Survivors	None	
Salvaged	No	

Notes *U529* may have been sunk in an air attack in approximately 55°45'N 31°09'W but the evidence is not conclusive. In the absence of any reason to account for her loss, the boat's fate can be ascribed either to a drifting mine or to an accident resulting from mechanical or drill failure.

U69	*Launched* 19 Sept 1940	*Commissioned* 2 Nov 1940
Class	Type VIIC	
CO	*Kapitänleutnant* Ulrich Graf (lost)	

Date of loss 17 February 1943
Location N Atlantic, 50°50'N 40°50'W
Cause Ramming
Casualties 46
Survivors None
Salvaged No

Notes Sunk by the destroyer HMS *Viscount* during operations against convoy ONS.165. *U69* and *U201* (see below) struggled through mountainous seas and storm force winds in order to reach the convoy. When they reached the convoy, they reported the contact and this proved their undoing. The destroyer *Viscount* raced down the HF/DF bearing and rammed and sank *U69*.

	Launched	*Commissioned*
U201	7 Dec 1940	25 Jan 1941

Class Type VIIC
CO *Oberleutnant zur See* Günther Rosenberg (lost)
Date of loss 17 February 1943
Location Atlantic, NE of Newfoundland, 50°36'N 40°50'W
Cause Depth charge
Casualties 49
Survivors None
Salvaged No

Notes *U201* was the second U-boat to contact ONS.165. Once again HF/DF proved her undoing and she was sunk by the destroyer HMS *Fame*.

U201 had previously been commanded by *Kapitänleutnant* Adalbert Schnee, one of the most successful U-boat commanders. After winning his laurels before the pendulum swung decisively against the U-boats, Schnee went on to serve on BdU's staff before being appointed to command *U2511*, a Type XXI U-boat, in which he survived the war.

	Launched	*Commissioned*
U205	20 Mar 1941	3 May 1941

Class Type VIIC
CO *Oberleutnant zur See* Friedrich Burgel (survived)
Date of loss 17 February 1943
Location Mediterranean, NW of Derna, 32°56'N 22°01'E
Cause Depth charge/gunfire
Casualties 8
Survivors 3 officers, 17 senior rates, 22 junior rates
Salvaged No

Notes Sunk by the British destroyer HMS *Paladin*, assisted by Bisley aircraft of the South African Air Force. *Paladin* managed to get a boarding party embarked but the U-boat sank as a tow was being attached.

	Launched	*Commissioned*
U268	9 Jun 1942	29 Jul 1942

Class Type VIIC
CO *Oberleutnant zur See* Ernst Heydemann (lost)
Date of loss 19 February 1943
Location Atlantic, Bay of Biscay, 47°03'N 05°56'W
Cause Air attack
Casualties 45
Survivors None
Salvaged No

Notes Sunk by Wellington 'B' of No 172 Squadron flown by P Off G. D. Lundon. The aircraft picked up the U-boat on radar at a range of four miles. When the range had come down to one mile the U-boat was sighted on the surface at 0150 (visibility was good even though there was a 10/10 cloud base at 2,000ft). The Leigh Light was switched on when the aircraft was a quarter of a mile away and it was clear that the U-boat had been taken by surprise. Three men were seen on the bridge and another three clustered around the deck gun, all cowering in the glare of the searchlight. Four depth charges were dropped around the submarine: one exploded off the port quarter, another by the conning tower and a third off the port bow. The U-boat appeared to stop (judging by its position relative to the flame float which was dropped at the same time as the depth charges) and then sink, leaving bubbles and oil on the surface. The aircraft circled the area until 0225 but nothing further was seen.

	Launched	*Commissioned*
U562	24 Jan 1941	20 Mar 1941

Class Type VIIC
CO *Kapitänleutnant* Horst Hamm (lost)
Date of loss 19 February 1943

Location	Mediterranean, NE of Benghazi, 32°57'N 20°54'E
Cause	Depth charge
Casualties	49
Survivors	None
Salvaged	No

Notes Wellington 'S' of No 38 Squadron RAF, flown by Fg Off I. B. Butler AFC, was covering a British convoy off the Libyan coast when the rear gunner, Sgt J. I. Brown, spotted *U562* directly below the aircraft, at periscope depth and in an ideal position for an attack on the convoy. Butler's attempt at an attack was not successful, so he called up the destroyers *Isis* and *Hursley* from the escort, which destroyed the U-boat in a series of depth-charge attacks.

U623

	Launched	*Commissioned*
	31 Mar 1942	21 May 1942
Class	Type VIIC	
CO	*Oberleutnant zur See* Hermann Schroeder (lost)	
Date of loss	21 February 1943	
Location	North Atlantic, 55°42'N 26°17'W	
Cause	Air attack	
Casualties	46	
Survivors	None	
Salvaged	No	

Notes Liberator 'T' of No 120 Squadron RAF, flown by Sqn Ldr D. J. Isted DFC, was patrolling under the control of the SO of the escort to convoy ON.166 when the U-boat was sighted nine miles from the aircraft and fifteen miles from the convoy. Isted used the cloud cover to approach the submarine, breaking cover when three or four miles away, only to sight a second U-boat on the surface. Undeterred, Isted pressed on with his attack on the U-boat first sighted, diving to 50ft and releasing six depth charges The entire stick exploded alongside the conning tower but the submarine made no attempt to dive (the other U-boat had by now dived to safety). As Isted circled, the U-boat was seen to remain almost awash on the surface with only the top of the conning tower and the gun platform above the water. When the U-boat finally submerged Isted marked the spot for two of the escorting warships which had been detached by the SNO to investigate. They found nothing but two large slicks of oil despite an extensive asdic search.

U606

	Launched	*Commissioned*
	27 Nov 1941	22 Jan 1942
Class	Type VIIC	
CO	*Oberleutnant zur See* Hans Dohler (lost)	
Date of loss	22 February 1943	
Location	North Atlantic, 47°44'N 33°43'W	
Cause	Depth charge	
Casualties	36	
Survivors	12	
Salvaged	No	

Notes *U606* was participating in an attack against convoy ON.166. After dark she penetrated the screen from astern and sank the *Chatanooga City* and damaged the *Empire Redshank* and the *Expositor* (both of which were sunk later). After pressing home Dohler began a turn to port to take him out of the convoy when he was spotted by the Polish destroyer *Burza* and attacked.

Dohler dived but the boat went out of control and sank to below 200m before the LI caught a trim. Meanwhile *Burza* was plastering the area with depth charges, one of which exploded directly above the bridge. During an inspection of the pressure hull the LI discovered a crack near to the after diving tank and recommended that *U606* be brought to the surface. Dohler concurred but as the boat was rising the 1WO, *Leutnant zur See* Werner Boulanger, panicked and had to be forcibly restrained from trying to make an escape via the galley hatch.

On reaching the surface the LI decided that things were not quite as bad as he had thought. However, Dohler could not open the conning tower hatch, which had been damaged as a result of *Burza*'s depth-charging, and thus *U606* was running blind on the surface. It was while she was in this condition that she was spotted by the US Coast Guard vessel *Campbell*. The latter dropped two depth charges which exploded close alongside and then opened fire with 3in, 20mm and small arms. Meanwhile Dohler had reached the casing via the torpedo loading hatch and had managed to open the conning tower hatch from the outside. A number of the crew then joined him on deck wearing their Dräger escape gear. However, their flashlights drew more fire from *Campbell* and it was at this stage that Dohler was killed. The fire only ceased when one of the crew flashed what was described as a distress signal. All the other officers had stayed in the boat, leaving the *Obersteuermann* as the senior officer on the casing. He gave the order to abandon ship and the men jumped into the water and were not seen again. Those who remained in the boat fared slightly better. The LI claimed to have opened the main vents before going up on to the bridge with eleven others. There they fortified themselves by consuming the wardroom wine stores while awaiting rescue. Five were picked up by *Campbell* and seven by *Burza*.

The interrogators were amazed at the low state of morale on board *U606*, the LI and 1WO being particularly unpopular for their harsh discipline and poor professional performance. Just before abandoning *U606* one of the petty officers is alleged to have struck Boulanger, saying, 'I've been waiting to do this for a long time.'

	Launched	*Commissioned*
U443	31 Jan 1942	18 Apr 1942

Class — Type VIIC
CO — *Oberleutnant zur See* Konstantin von Puttkamer (lost)
Date of loss — 23 February 1943
Location — Mediterranean, NW of Algiers, 36°55'N 02°25'E
Cause — Depth charge
Casualties — 48
Survivors — None
Salvaged — No

Notes *U443* was initially detected by shore radar at Algiers at 2125 on 20 February and the 'Hunt' class destroyers *Bicester*, *Lamerton* and *Wheatland* were sent to investigate. There followed a three-day hunt which, in words of the Staff History, 'demonstrated the value of persistent effort' before *U443* was depth-charged to destruction.

	Launched	*Commissioned*
U522	1 Apr 1942	11 Jun 1942

Class — Type IXC
CO — *Kapitänleutnant* H. Schneider (lost)
Date of loss — 23 February 1943
Location — Atlantic, SW of Madeira, 31°27'N 26°22'W
Cause — Depth charge
Casualties — 51
Survivors — None
Salvaged — No

Notes Attacked and depth-charged by the ex-US Coast Guard cutter *Totland* escorting convoy UC.1.

	Launched	*Commissioned*
U649	30 Sept 1942	19 Nov 1942

Class — Type VIIC
CO — *Oberleutnant zur See* Tiesler
Date of loss — 24 February 1943
Location — Baltic, exact position unknown
Cause — Collision
Casualties — 35
Survivors — ?
Salvaged — No

Notes Sank following a collision with *U232*.

	Launched	*Commissioned*
U83	9 Dec 1940	8 Feb 1941

Class — Type VIIB
CO — *Kapitänleutnant* Gerhard Worisshoffer (lost)
Date of loss — 4 March 1943
Location — Mediterranean, E of Cartagena, 37°10'N 00°05'E
Cause — Air attack
Casualties — 50
Survivors — None
Salvaged — No

Notes Hudson 'V' of No 500 Squadron RAF, flown by Sgt G. Jacimov, was on an anti-submarine patrol when at 1002 the wake of a U-boat was sighted in bad visibility. The U-boat made no attempt to dive but began evasive manoeuvring. The Hudson made two attacks, dropping three 100lb A/S bombs on the first run and three 150lb depth charges on the second. After the second attack white smoke was seen coming from the conning tower and the U-boat settled in the water as a number of her crew gathered in the after end of the conning tower. The U-boat then sank, leaving men in the water, swimming in the middle of a growing oil slick. Jacimov ordered two dinghies to be dropped, but both sank on hitting the water.

	Launched	*Commissioned*
U87	21 June 1941	19 Aug 1941

Class — Type VIIB

CO	*Kapitänleutnant* Joachim Berger (lost)
Date of loss	4 March 1943
Location	North Atlantic, W of Leixoes, 41°36'N 13°31'W
Cause	Depth charge
Casualties	49
Survivors	None
Salvaged	No

Notes Depth-charged by the corvettes HMCS *Shediac* and *St Croix* which were escorting convoy KMS.10.

	Launched	Commissioned
U156	21 May 1941	4 Sept 1941
Class	Type IXC	
CO	*Korvettenkapitän* Werner Hartenstein (lost)	
Date of loss	8 March 1943	
Location	Caribbean, E of Barbados, 12°38'N 54°39'W	
Cause	Air attack	
Casualties	53	
Survivors	None	
Salvaged	No	

Notes Sunk by a USN aircraft from VP-53.

	Launched	Commissioned
U633	10 Jun 1942	30 Jul 1942
Class	Type VIIC	
CO	*Oberleutnant zur See* Bernhard Müller (lost)	
Date of loss	10 March 1943	
Location	Atlantic, SW of Iceland, 58°51'N 19°55'W	
Cause	Ramming	
Casualties	42	
Survivors	None	
Salvaged	No	

Notes *U633* was rammed by the SS *Scorton* in convoy SC.121. The attack by Fortress 'J' of No 220 Squadron on 7 March, previously thought to have accounted for this submarine, was in fact made on *U641*, which escaped unscathed.

	Launched	Commissioned
U444	1 Jan 1942	9 May 1942
Class	Type VIIC	
CO	*Oberleutnant zur See* Albert Langfeld	
Date of loss	11 March 1943	
Location	Atlantic, 51°14'N 29°18'W	
Cause	Depth charge/ramming	
Casualties	41	
Survivors	5	
Salvaged	No	

Notes *U444* was engaged in operations against convoy HX.228 when she was detected at night on radar by the destroyer HMS *Harvester* (Cdr A. A. Tait RN). *Harvester* ran down the bearing and forced *U444* to submerge. Tait then delivered an accurate depth-charge attack which blew *U444* to the surface, where she was rammed. *Harvester* went over the U-boat, which bumped and scraped her way along the destroyer's keel until she became wedged under her propellers. Thus locked together, the two ships remained for some time until the U-boat broke free. However, *Harvester* had suffered so much damage that she was reduced to a slow crawl. At this point the French corvette *Aconit* (Lt A. Lavasseur) arrived, and, finding that *U444* was still on the surface, rammed her and sent her to the bottom.

	Launched	Commissioned
U432	3 Feb 1941	26 Apr 1941
Class	Type VIIC	
CO	*Kapitänleutnant* Hermann Eckhardt (lost)	
Date of loss	11 Mar 1943	
Location	North Atlantic, 51°35'N 04°42'W	
Cause	Depth charge/gunfire	
Casualties	20	
Survivors	24	
Salvaged	No	

Notes The sinking of *U444* had not gone unnoticed. *U432* observed *Harvester* making slow progress back to join the convoy and torpedoed her with considerable loss of life shortly after midday. *Aconit* saw the distant pall of smoke which marked this event and turned back, despite her buckled bows. Gaining contact within the hour, *Aconit* blew *U432* to the surface with depth-charge attacks before ramming her. The survivors said they had been celebrating their sinking of the *Harvester* when *Aconit* arrived: 'I hope they appreciated their dessert of my ten grenades,' wrote Lavasseur.

U130	*Launched* 14 Mar 1941	*Commissioned* 11 Jun 1941
Class	Type IXC	
CO	*Oberleutnant zur See* Siegfried Keller (lost)	
Date of loss	12 March 1943	
Location	Atlantic, W of Azores	
Cause	Depth charge	
Casualties	53	
Survivors	None	
Salvaged	No	

Notes Sunk by the USS *Champlin*.

U163	*Launched* 1 May 1941	*Commissioned* 21 Oct 1941
Class	Type IXC	
CO	*Korvettenkapitän* Kurt Engelmann (lost)	
Date of loss	12/13 March 1943	
Location	Bay of Biscay	
Cause	Depth charge	
Casualties	57	
Survivors	None	
Salvaged	No	

Notes Returning from patrol, *U163* ran into the escort for convoy MKS.9 and was depth-charged and sunk by the US destroyer *Prescott*.

U5	*Launched* 14 Aug 1935	*Commissioned* 31 Aug 1935
Class	Type IIA	
CO	*Leutnant zur See* Hermann Rahn (lost)	
Date of loss	19 March 1943	
Location	Baltic, W of Pillau, 54°25'N 19°50'E	
Cause	Accident	
Casualties	21	
Survivors	4	
Salvaged	No	

Notes Sunk while diving during exercises.

U384	*Launched* 28 May 1942	*Commissioned* 18 Jul 1942
Class	Type VIIC	
CO	*Oberleutnant zur See* Heinz Achim von Rosenberg-Grusczynski (lost)	
Date of loss	20 March 1943	
Location	Atlantic, W of Malin Head, 54°18'N 26°15'W	
Cause	Air attack	
Casualties	47	
Survivors	None	
Salvaged	No	

Notes Fortress 'B' of No 206 Squadron, flown by P Off L. G. Clark, was escorting convoy HX.229 and sighted a surfaced U-boat at 0924. After an attack with depth charges a large oil slick formed on the surface which was still visible when sighted hours later by some of the convoy's escorts.

An attack by an aircraft of No 201 Squadron on a U-boat on 20 March, previously assessed as being on *U384*, was in fact made on *U631*, which escaped undamaged.

U524	*Launched* 30 Apr 1942	*Commissioned* 8 Jul 1942
Class	Type IXC	
CO	*Kapitänleutnant* Walter *Freiherr* von Steinaecker	
Date of loss	22 March 1943	
Location	Atlantic, S of Madeira, 30°15'N 18°13'W	
Cause	Air attack	
Casualties	52	
Survivors	None	
Salvaged	No	

Notes The B-24 Liberator *Tidewater Tillie* of the 1st Squadron, 480th Group USAAF, flown by Lt William L. Sandford, sighted a broad wake five miles on the starboard beam. Sandford elected to make a beam attack, which allowed him to approach from out of the sun. *Tidewater Tillie* roared over the U-boat at 200ft, dropping four US Mk 37 650lb depth charges in a perfect straddle. The stern of the U-boat was completely enveloped in the explosions before the bows were seen to rise and the boat sank by the stern, leaving a number of survivors clinging to wreckage amidst a spreading oil slick.

U665	*Launched* 9 Jun 1942	*Commissioned* 22 Jul 1942
Class	Type VIIC	
CO	*Oberleutnant zur See der Reserve* Hans-Jurgen Haupt (lost)	

Date of loss	22 March 1943
Location	Atlantic, W of St Nazaire, 48°04'N 10°26'W
Cause	Air attack
Casualties	46
Survivors	None
Salvaged	No

Notes Whitley 'V' of No 10 OTU, flown by Sgt J. A. Marsden, was flying in bad weather when the rear gunner reported the wake of a periscope just beneath the port wing at 1152. However, nothing else was seen, and when the periscope was lowered the Whitley continued with its patrol. That afternoon, at 1503, a surfaced U-boat was sighted. Marsden was flying only 100ft above the waves, so he went straight in and attacked from the starboard beam, dropping six depth charges. As the boat dived the rear gunner saw the depth charges explode, straddling the track of the submarine. The weather was so bad that the results of this attack could not be assessed, and it was only in the post-war analysis that *U665* was deemed to have been the victim.

The attack by Wellington 'G' of No 172 Squadron, previously thought to have accounted for *U665*, was made on *U488*, which escaped unscathed.

U469

	Launched	*Commissioned*
	8 Aug 1942	7 Oct 1942
Class	Type VIIC	
CO	*Oberleutnant zur See* Clausen (lost)	
Date of loss	25 March 1943	
Location	Atlantic, W of Faeroe Islands, 62°12'N 16°40'W	
Cause	Air attack	
Casualties	46	
Survivors	None	
Salvaged	No	

Notes Fortress 'L' of No 206 Squadron RAF was flying in support of convoy RU.67 when she sighted *U469*. The U-boat was making a surface passage to join *Gruppe Seawolf* to operate against convoy SC.123, whose position had been located by *xB-Dienst*, when she was attacked and sunk.

U169

	Launched	*Commissioned*
	6 Jun 1942	16 Nov 1942
Class	Type IXC	
CO	*Kapitänleutnant* Hermann Bauer (lost)	
Date of loss	27 March 1943	
Location	Atlantic, S of Iceland, 60°54'N 15°25'W	
Cause	Air attack	
Casualties	54	
Survivors	None	
Salvaged	No	

Notes *U169* had been ordered to join *Gruppe Seawolf* to operate against convoy SC.123, whose position had been located by *xB-Dienst*. In coming up to join the patrol line, *U169* came within the area covered by the convoy's air patrols and was attacked and sunk by Fortress 'L' of No 206 Squadron RAF, flown by Fg Off A. Samuel. As the aircraft dived it was fired on by the U-boat, but Samuel placed his depth charges carefully along the submarine's port side. The explosions rolled the U-boat over on to its beam ends before it disappeared. As the bows reappeared, canted up at a steep angle, Samuel made a second depth-charge attack. The boat then sank vertically by the stern. Three men were seen on the conning tower as she sank but were not sighted in the water.

U77

	Launched	*Commissioned*
	23 Nov 1940	18 Jan 1941
Class	Type VIIC	
CO	*Kapitänleutnant* Otto Hartmann (lost)	
Date of loss	29 March 1943	
Location	Mediterranean, E of Cape Palos, 37°42'N 00°10'E	
Cause	Air attack	
Casualties	38	
Survivors	9	
Salvaged	No	

Notes On 28 March Hudsons 'L' of No 48 Squadron and 'L' of No 233 Squadron had both attacked a submarine but had been unable to pursue these attacks to a conclusion because they were operating at the limits of their endurance. On the following day Hudson 'V' of No 48 Squadron was on A/S patrol between Cape San Antonio and Ibiza and sighted the U-boat heading north-east. The aircraft attacked from dead astern, and although the U-boat dived her periscope was still visible when four depth charges were dropped. The first exploded just aft of the persicope and the other three fell in a salvo ahead of the swirl.

No oil or wreckage was visible after this attack, even when the Hudson returned half an hour later. However, on 30 March nine survivors from *U77* were landed by a Spanish fishing boat at Altoa.

U416	*Launched* 9 May 1942	*Commissioned* 4 Nov 1942
Class	Type VIIC	
CO	?	
Date of loss	30 March 1943	
Location	Baltic, off Bornholm	
Cause	Mine	
Casualties	?	
Survivors	?	
Salvaged	Raised 8 April 1943	

Notes Lost in a minefield laid by the Soviet submarine *L-3* (Frunzevez). Following her salvage the boat was used for training. She was finally sunk on 12 December 1944 north-west of Pillau in position 54°58'N 19°33'E following a collision with the minesweeper *M203*.

U124	*Launched* 9 Mar 1940	*Commissioned* 11 Jun 1940
Class	Type IXB	
CO	*Korvettenkapitän* Johann Mohr (lost)	
Date of loss	3 April 1943	
Location	Atlantic, W of Oporto, 41°02'N 15°39'W	
Cause	Depth charge	
Casualties	53	
Survivors	None	
Salvaged	No	

Notes Sunk by the corvette HMS *Stonecrop* and sloop HMS *Black Swan* during operations in support of convoy OS.45.

U635	*Launched* 24 Jun 1942	*Commissioned* 13 Aug 1942
Class	Type VIIC	
CO	*Oberleutnant zur See* Eckelmann (lost)	
Date of loss	5 April 1943	
Location	Atlantic, SW of Iceland, 58°20'N 31°52'W	
Cause	Air attack	
Casualties	47	
Survivors	None	
Salvaged	No	

Notes Liberator 'N' of No 120 Squadron RAF, flown by Fg Off G. Hatherly, was en route to meet convoy HX.231, and when 10 miles north of the convoy the crew sighted a U-boat surfacing in front of them. An attack was carried out from an altitude of 50ft as the Liberator flew directly towards the target. The depth charges were released just as the U-boat disappeared beneath the aircraft's nose and fell in a straddle. The submarine vanished in the explosions and was not seen again.

The sinking of *U635* had incorrectly been ascribed to a depth-charge attack by HMS *Tay* on 6 April, but the victim of this attack was in fact *U306*.

U167	*Launched* 5 Mar 1942	*Commissioned* 4 Jul 1942
Class	Type IXC/40	
CO	*Korvettenkapitän* Kurt Sturm	
Date of loss	6 April 1943	
Location	Atantic, Canary Islands, 27°47'N 15°00'W	
Cause	Scuttled	
Casualties	?	
Survivors	?	
Salvaged	Raised 1951	

Notes *U167* was attacked twice, by Hudsons 'W' and 'L' of No 233 Squadron, flown by Flt Sgt K. R. Dalton and Flt Lt W. E. Willets respectively, which were escorting convoy RS.3. *U167* sustained severe damage in these two attacks and Sturm was badly wounded. Accordingly the boat was scuttled east of Grand Canary island and the crew made their way ashore for internment.

Following her salvage *U167* was used commercially in Spain as a film set and subsequently broken up.

U632	*Launched* 27 May 1942	*Commissioned* 23 Jul 1942
Class	Type VIIC	
CO	*Kapitänleutnant* Hans Karpf (lost)	
Date of loss	6 April 1943	
Location	Atlantic, SW of Iceland, 58°02'N 28°42'W	
Cause	Air attack	

Casualties	48
Survivors	None
Salvaged	No

Notes Liberator 'R' of No 86 Squadron, flown by Flt Lt C. W. Burcher, sighted a surfaced U-boat while on patrol 18 miles from convoy HX.231. Burcher carried out two attacks, dropping five depth charges as the submarine dived. An oil slick subsequently formed on the surface over the spot where the U-boat had sunk.

U644	*Launched*	*Commissioned*
	20 Aug 1942	15 Oct 1942
Class	Type VIIC	
CO	*Oberleutnant zur See* Eberhard Dahlhaus (lost)	
Date of loss	7 April 1943	
Location	Arctic, SE of Jan Mayen Island, 69°30'N 05°40'W	
Cause	Submarine attack	
Casualties	45	
Survivors	None	
Salvaged	No	

Notes At the end of March the British became aware of a German U-boat patrol line established east of Jan Mayen Island awaiting the passage of the next JW-series convoy to Russia. HM Submarine *Tuna* (Lt D. S. R. Martin RN) was dispatched from Lerwick on 3 April to investigate. At 2105 on 7 April a U-boat was sighted at a range of 5,000yds. Martin closed to 1,200yds before firing five torpedoes. A hit was observed before Martin surfaced to survey the scene and rescue any survivors. One man was seen, without a lifejacket, struggling in a slick of diesel but he drowned before the submarine could close and rescue him.

On the 14th another U-boat, *U302* (*Kapitänleutnant* Herbert Sickel), was sighted and attacked with eight torpedoes. However the U-boat was able to comb the tracks and report the attack, with the result that the patrol line was moved fifty miles to the north-east.

U376	*Launched*	*Commissioned*
	10 Jul 1941	21 Aug 1941
Class	Type VIIC	
CO	*Kapitänleutnant* Friedrich Marks (lost)	
Date of loss	10 April 1943	
Location	Atlantic, Bay of Biscay, 49°48'N 09°00'W	
Cause	Air attack	
Casualties	47	
Survivors	None	
Salvaged	No	

Notes Wellington 'C' of No 172 Squadron, flown by P Off G. H. Whitley, picked up a radar contact at 2240 on the port side of the aircraft at a range of six miles. The aircraft homed in on the contact and at a range of a quarter of a mile exposed the Leigh Light, which revealed *U376* on the surface. The attack with depth charges was made from the U-boat's starboard quarter, and although the charges were seen to straddle the submarine, only three exploded. Nevertheless, on circling the area the aircraft saw nothing and no radar contact was made.

U526	*Launched*	*Commissioned*
	3 Jun 1942	12 Aug 1942
Class	Type IXC/40	
CO	*Kapitänleutnant* Moglich	
Date of loss	14 April 1943	
Location	Bay of Biscay, 47°30'N 03°45'W	
Cause	Mine	
Casualties	42	
Survivors	?	
Salvaged	No	

Notes Mined off Lorient.

U175	*Launched*	*Completed*
	2 Sept 41	1941
Class	Type IXC	
CO	*Kapitänleutnant* Heinrich Bruns (survived)	
Date of loss	17 April 1943	
Location	Atlantic, W of Land's End	
Cause	Depth charge/gunfire	
Casualties	13	
Survivors	5 officers, 12 senior rates, 24 junior rates	
Salvaged	No	

Notes U175 was sunk after being forced to the surface by two depth-charge attacks, a total of 22 charges being expended by the US Coast Guard cutter *John C. Spencer*, which was sweeping ahead of convoy HX.233. The submarine broached 48 minutes after the attack began. On the surface the U-boat and the cutters *Spencer* and *Duane* engaged in a close-in gun duel. Bruns was killed by a direct hit on the conning tower. When merchant ships in the convoy joined in the firing, *Spencer* suffered a 5in (127mm) hit from a merchant ship. In all, eight Coast Guardsmen on board *Spencer* were wounded in the firefight with *U175*, one fatally (Radioman 3rd Class J.T. Petralla). Coast Guardsmen were able to board the stricken U-boat, but she sank before any documents or equipment could be salvaged.

	Launched	*Commissioned*
U191	3 Jul 1942	20 Oct 1942
Class	Type IXC/40	
CO	*Kapitänleutnant* Herbert Fiehn (lost)	
Date of loss	23 April 1943	
Location	Atlantic, SE of Cape Farewell, 56°45'N 34°25'W	
Cause	Hedgehog	
Casualties	55	
Survivors	None	
Salvaged	No	

Notes Sunk in a Hedgehog attack by HMS *Hesperus* during the passage of convoy ONS.4.

	Launched	*Commissioned*
U710	11 May 1942	2 Sept 1942
Class	Type VIIC	
CO	*Oberleutnant zur See* Dietrich von Carlowitz (lost)	
Date of loss	24 April 1943	
Location	Atlantic, SE of Iceland, 61°25'N 19°48'W	
Cause	Air attack	
Casualties	49	
Survivors	None	
Salvaged	No	

Notes Fortress 'D' of No 206 Squadron, flown by Fg Off Robert Cowey, was flying a parallel track sweep for convoy ONS.5 when a submarine was sighted well trimmed down on the surface. The aircraft attacked with depth charges, despite being engaged by the 20mm gun on the submarine's conning tower. Six depth charges straddled the boat at right angles and the explosions 'seemed to lift the boat out of the water'. The aircraft made a second attack, after which 25 casualties were seen swimming amid the wreckage.

	Launched	*Commissioned*
U203	4 Jan 1941	18 Feb 1941
Class	Type VIIC	
CO	*Kapitänleutnant* Hermann Kottmann (survived)	
Date of loss	25 April 1943	
Location	Atlantic, SE of Greenland, 55°05'N 42°25'W	
Cause	Depth charge	
Casualties	10	
Survivors	6 officers, 7 senior rates, 26 junior rates	
Salvaged	No	

Notes This was the first occasion on which aircraft from an escort carrier, a Swordfish of 811 NAS aboard HMS *Biter*, played in part in the destruction of a U-boat. The carrier was escorting convoy ONS.4. The Swordfish sighted the U-boat and called up the destroyer *Pathfinder*, one of the convoy's escorts, which blew the U-boat to the surface in a series of depth-charge attacks.

	Launched	*Commissioned*
U174	21 Aug 1941	26 Nov 1941
Class	Type IXC	
CO	*Oberleutnant zur See* Wolfgang Grandefeld (lost)	
Date of loss	27 April 1943	
Location	Atlantic, S of Newfoundland, 43°35'N 56°18'W	
Cause	Air attack	
Casualties	53	
Survivors	None	
Salvaged	No	

Notes Sunk by a Ventura flown by Lt Thomas Kinaszczuk USNR from USN squadron VB-125.

	Launched	*Commissioned*
U602	30 Oct 1941	29 Dec 1941
Class	Type VIIC	
CO	*Kapitänleutnant* Philipp Schuler (lost)	
Date of loss	April 1943	
Location	Mediterranean	
Cause	?	
Casualties	48	
Survivors	None	
Salvaged	No	

Notes The original finding of the Assessment Committee was that *U602* was lost to unknown cause, possibly accident. This was revised when the report of an attack by Hudson 'N' of No 500 Squadron on 23 April was received, and her sinking was credited to this aircraft. However, a more detailed examination of the circumstances of the Hudson's attack reveals that the victim was *U453*, which so damaged the aircraft with flak on the run-in that the attack was not carried through. Therefore the original finding of the Assessment Committee stands.

U332	*Launched*	*Commissioned*
	20 Mar 1941	7 Jun 1941

Class Type VIIC
CO *Oberleutnant zur See* Eberhard Huttemann (lost)
Date of loss 29 April 1943
Location Atlantic, NW of Cape Ortegal, 45°08'N 09°33'W
Cause Air attack
Casualties 45
Survivors None
Salvaged No

Notes Sunk by Liberator 'D' of No 224 Squadron in Operation 'Derange', an anti-U-boat sweep by RAF Coastal Command in the Bay of Biscay.

U227	*Launched*	*Commissioned*
	9 Jul 1942	22 Aug 1942

Class Type VIIC
CO *Kapitänleutnant* Jurgen Kuntze (lost)
Date of loss 30 April 1943
Location Atlantic, N of Faeroe Islands, 64°05'N 06°40'W
Cause Air attack
Casualties 49
Survivors None
Salvaged No

Notes A Hampden of No 455 Squadron RAAF, flown by Flt Sgt J. S. Freeth, sighted *U227* in rough weather on the surface at 0955. The submarine began to dive, engaging the aircraft with flak as it did so. Freeth dropped six depth charges from a height of 50ft, three of which exploded on the starboard side of the U-boat and the other three astern. The stern came out of the water as the Hampden made a second attack, dropping two more depth charges which exploded either side of the bow. The U-boat's bow rose out of the water almost to the vertical before sliding back, leaving some thirty men in the water wearing Dräger apparatus together with one liferaft.

U465	*Launched*	*Commissioned*
	30 Apr 1942	20 May 1942

Class Type VIIC
CO *Kapitänleutnant* H. Wolf (lost)
Date of loss 2 May 1943
Location Atlantic, NW of Cape Ortegal, 44°48'N 08°58'W
Cause Air attack
Casualties 48
Survivors None
Salvaged No

Notes Sunk by Sunderland 'M' of No 461 Squadron RAAF, flown by Flt Lt E. C. Smith RAAF. Smith dropped eight depth charges, after which the U-boat was seen sinking stern first with the crew leaping over the side.

U209	*Launched*	*Commissioned*
	28 Aug 1941	11 Oct 1941

Class Type VIIC
CO *Kapitänleutnant* Heinrich Brodda (lost)
Date of loss May 1943
Location N Atlantic, approx. 52°N 38°W
Cause ?
Casualties 46
Survivors None
Salvaged No

Notes The cause of *U209*'s loss in unknown but was probably damage inflicted in an attack by Canso 'W' of No 5 Squadron RCAF on 4 May 1943.

U439	*Launched*	*Commissioned*
	10 Aug 1941	20 Dec 1941

Class Type VIIC
CO *Oberleutnant zur See* Helmut von Tippelskirch (lost)
Date of loss 4 May 1943
Location Atlantic, NW of Cape Finisterre, 43°32'N 13°30'W

Cause	Collision
Casualties	40
Survivors	9
Salvaged	No

Notes Sunk in a collision with *U659* (see next entry for details).

U659

	Launched	*Commissioned*
	14 Oct 1941	9 Dec 1941
Class	Type VIIC	
CO	*Kapitänleutnant* Hans Stock (lost)	
Date of loss	4 May 1943	
Location	Atlantic, NW of Cape Finisterre, 43°32'N 13°30'W	
Cause	Collision	
Casualties	44	
Survivors	3	
Salvaged	No	

Notes Both *U439* and *U659* were engaged in the pursuit of two southbound convoys, one a flight of landing craft and the other composed of fifteen MTBs, all bound for the Mediterranean. At 0120 on 4 May *U439* was shadowing the MTB convoy from a position about four miles ahead of it. Meanwhile *U659* had tried to find the landing craft convoy but failed. In fact *U659* had gone so far across the convoy's track that she was now ahead of the MTB convoy. Stock had no idea where either convoy was and, believing that both had passed ahead of him, altered course to the south and increased speed. In *U439* a less than perfect look-out was being maintained since the 1WO, 'who by nature was lazy and easy going', was watching the pyrotechnic display as another U-boat got in amongst the MTBs and not his allotted sector on the port side. As a result he failed to see *U659* coming up from astern and overtaking on the port side. At this moment von Tippelskirch came on to the bridge and ordered an alteration of course to port.

The two boats did not just merely collide. *U439*, travelling at 7kts, struck *U659*, travelling at about 15kts, on her starboard side abreast the control room. Water flooded in through the gash and moments later a large wave washed over *U659*, sending her to the bottom. Meanwhile *U439* had gone astern but in doing so had been pooped in the heavy seas and her diesel exhausts were flooded. At the same time she began sinking by the bow because of the damage sustained in the collision. She began to founder, and sank after a heavy sea swept over her. At the time she foundered the conning tower hatch was shut, so she may have drifted just below the surface for some time. The trawler HMS *Coverley* reported striking a submerged object in the area two hours later and this may have been the *coup de grâce* for the hull of *U439*. At about 0300 *MTB. 670*, leading the starboard column of the MTB convoy, ran into diesel fumes and smoke and saw twelve ring lifejackets in the water. These were the combined survivors of *U439* and *U659*.

U630

	Launched	*Commissioned*
	12 May 1942	9 Jul 1942
Class	Type VIIC	
CO	*Oberleutnant zur See* Werner Winkler (lost)	
Date of loss	4 May 1943	
Location	N Atlantic, NE of Cape Race, 56°38'N 42°32'W	
Cause	Air attack	
Casualties	47	
Survivors	None	
Salvaged	No	

Notes Sunk in an attack by a Canso of No 5 Squadron RCAF.

U192

	Launched	*Commissioned*
	31 Jul 1942	16 Nov 1942
Class	Type IXC/40	
CO	*Kapitänleutnant* Werner Happe (lost)	
Date of loss	5 May 1943	
Location	N Atlantic, S of Greenland, 54°56'N 43°44'W	
Cause	Depth charge	
Casualties	55	
Survivors	None	
Salvaged	No	

Notes The first of five U-boats (*U192*, *U638*, *U125*, *U531* and *U438*) sunk in the battle for convoy ONS.5 By early May BdU had achieved a concentration of 41 U-boats in the North Atlantic. The convoy was escorted by the very experienced B7 escort group commanded by Cdr Peter Gretton, but bad weather on 2, 3 and 4 May scattered the convoy and forced Gretton to take his destroyer HMS *Duncan* and three others back to Newfoundland since they could not fuel from the oiler in such heavy seas. The corvette HMS *Pink* was escorting a group of five merchant ships which had straggled when she came across *U192* and depth-charged her to destruction.

U638	*Launched* 8 Jul 1942	*Commissioned* 3 Sept 1942
Class	Type VIIC	
CO	*Kapitänleutnant* Staudinger (lost)	
Date of loss	5 May 1943	
Location	N Atlantic, N of Cape Race, 53°06'N 45°02'W	
Cause	Depth charge	
Casualties	44	
Survivors	None	
Salvaged	No	

Notes Caught on the surface while attempting to penetrate the screen of ONS.5 by the corvette HMS *Loosestrife*, which sank her with depth charges as she dived.

U125	*Launched* 10 Dec 1940	*Commissioned* 3 Mar 1941
Class	Type IXC	
CO	*Kapitänleutnant* Ulrich Folkers (lost)	
Date of loss	6 May 1943	
Location	N Atlantic, E of Newfoundland, 52°13'N 44°50'W	
Cause	Gunfire/ramming	
Casualties	54	
Survivors	None	
Salvaged	No	

Notes In the fog that descended on the evening of 6 May the destroyer *Oribi* came across *U125* and rammed her. Although the destroyer thought that the ramming had been successful as *U125* staggered off into a rain squall, the U-boat was just seaworthy, though possibly unable to dive. Some time later *U125* was caught by the corvette HMS *Snowflake*. The latter had expended her entire outfit of depth charges on *U531*, but her 4in gun was still in good order and she sank *U125* by gunfire.

U531	*Launched* 12 Aug 1942	*Commissioned* 28 Oct 1942
Class	Type IXC/40	
CO	*Kapitänleutnant* Neckel (lost)	
Date of loss	6 May 1943	
Location	N Atlantic, NE of Newfoundland, 52°31'N 44°50'W	
Cause	Depth charge	
Casualties	54	
Survivors	None	
Salvaged	No	

Notes *U531* had endured a severe depth-charging from the corvette HMS *Snowflake* and had been forced to the surface but was able to make off in the poor visibility. The destroyer HMS *Vidette* was sweeping back to her position in the screen after investigating a radar contact when she obtained an asdic contact at a range of 900yds. The target, moving right with a slight opening doppler, was assessed as a submarine and was engaged with the Hedgehog. All the bombs hit the water, and after an interval following the last splash two distinct underwater explosions were heard and flashes observed. Shortly afterwards *Vidette*'s asdic operator reported the noise of tanks being blown together with various banging noises, and the bridge was warned that the U-boat appeared to be coming up along the starboard side. In the event all that came to the surface was a large disturbance and upheaval, which was most likely the air from within the submarine. An asdic sweep was carried out but no contact was made.

U438	*Launched* 30 Jul 1941	*Commissioned* 22 Nov 1941
Class	Type VIIC	
CO	*Kapitänleutnant* Heinrich Heinsohn (lost)	
Date of loss	6 May 1943	
Location	N Atlantic, 52°00'N 45°10'W	
Cause	Depth charge	
Casualties	48	
Survivors	None	
Salvaged	No	

Notes The sloop HMS *Pelican*, leading EG1, had been ordered up to support ONS.5's hard-pressed escort. On the morning of 6 May *Pelican* detected *U438* by radar and dispatched her with depth charges.

At the same time as *U438* was making her final dive BdU called off the attack on ONS.5. It was a signal victory: five U-boats accounted for by the convoy escort together with *U630* meant that six boats had been sunk and many badly damaged. Writing later, the official British historian said of the battle for ONS.5: 'The seven-day battle fought against thirty U-boats is marked only by latitude and longitude and has no name by which it will be remembered; but it was, in its own way, as decisive as Quiberon Bay or the Nile.'

U109	*Launched*	*Commissioned*
	14 Sept 1940	5 Dec 1940

Class — Type IXB
CO — *Oberleutnant zur See* Joachim Schramm (lost)
Date of loss — 7 May 1943
Location — Atlantic, S of Ireland, 47°22'N 22°40'W
Cause — Air attack
Casualties — 52
Survivors — None
Salvaged — No

Notes Liberator 'P' of No 86 Squadron RAF, flown by P Off J. C. Green, was flying in support of convoy HX.236 and sighted a U-boat at 1835. Four depth charges were expertly placed, two on either side of the conning tower. When the boil had subsided, the U-boat had vanished and all that could be seen was wooden wreckage amid a large and growing patch of oil.

U447	*Launched*	*Commissioned*
	30 Apr 1942	11 Jul 1942

Class — Type VIIC
CO — *Oberleutnant zur See* Bothe (lost)
Date of loss — 7 May 1943
Location — Atlantic, SW of Cape St Vincent, 35°30'N 11°55'W
Cause — Air attack
Casualties — 48
Survivors — None
Salvaged — No

Notes Hudson 'X' of No 233 Squadron, flown by Sgt J. V. Holland, sighted a surfaced U-boat and attacked with four depth charges. The U-boat appeared to be blown clear of the water by the explosions and was then attacked by Hudson 'I' of No 233 Squadron, flown by Sgt J. W. McQueen. Both aircraft then carried out a series of machine-gun passes over the submarine, which was seen to be sinking by the stern.

U663	*Launched*	*Commissioned*
	26 Mar 1942	14 May 1942

Class — Type VIIC
CO — *Kapitänleutnant* H. Schmid (lost)
Date of loss — 8 May 1943
Location — Atlantic, Bay of Biscay, 47°06'N 10°58'W
Cause — Air attack/accident
Casualties — 49
Survivors — None
Salvaged — No

Notes Attacked by Sunderland 'W' of No 10 Squadron RAAF, then sunk in a submarine accident.

U528	*Launched*	*Commissioned*
	1 Jul 1942	16 Sept 1942

Class — Type IXC/40
CO — *Oberleutnant zur See* G. von Rabenau
Date of loss — 11 May 1943
Location — North Atlantic, SW of Ireland, 46°55'N 14°44'W
Cause — Depth charge
Casualties — 11
Survivors — ?
Salvaged — No

Notes Returning from patrol, having been damaged by a USN Catalina, *U528* came within the air patrols covering convoy OS.47. She was first sighted and attacked by Halifax 'D' of No 58 Squadron RAF, flown by P Off J. B. Stark. Stark attacked the U-boat from the port bow and saw it lift out of the water and roll over as his depth charges exploded. He then noticed a secondary explosion before the boat sank by the stern, leaving an oil slick forming on the water. Stark flew back to the convoy to report the attack and subsequently saw the sloop HMS *Fleetwood* and corvette *Mignonette* detach from the screen and head for the area. The two ships blew the damaged *U528* to the surface, where she was abandoned.

U186	*Launched*	*Commissioned*
	11 Mar 1942	10 July 1942

Class — Type IXC/40

CO	*Kapitänleutnant* Siegfried Hessemann (lost)
Date of loss	12 May 1943
Location	Atlantic, N of the Azores, 41°54'N 31°49'W
Cause	Depth charge
Casualties	53
Survivors	None
Salvaged	No

Notes Depth-charged by the destroyer HMS *Hesperus* during operations against convoy SC.129. Caught on the surface, *U186* managed to let BdU know that she was under attack. Following the attack a large quantity of debris with German markings was recovered.

U89

	Launched	Commissioned
	20 Sept 1941	19 Nov 1941
Class	Type VIIC	
CO	*Kapitänleutnant* Dietrich Lohmann	
Date of loss	12 May 1943	
Location	Atlantic, N of the Azores, 46°30'N 25°40'W	
Cause	Depth charge	
Casualties	48	
Survivors	None	
Salvaged	No	

Notes Sunk during operations against convoy HX.237. *U89* was spotted by Swordfish 'B' of 811 NAS from the escort carrier *Biter*, which summoned up the destroyer *Broadway* and frigate *Lagan* from the escort. *Broadway* and *Lagan* delivered a number of depth-charge attacks before *Lagan* finished off the boat with Hedgehog.

U456

	Launched	Commissioned
	21 Jun 1941	18 Sept 1941
Class	Type VIIC	
CO	*Kapitänleutnant* Max Martin Teichert (lost)	
Date of loss	13 May 1943	
Location	Atlantic, NW of Cape Ortegal, 46°40'N 26°20'W	
Cause	Air attack	
Casualties	49	
Survivors	None	
Salvaged	No	

Notes Liberator 'B' of No 86 Squadron, flown by Flt Lt J. Wright, attacked a surfaced U-boat in poor visibility near to convoy HX.237. The U-boat dived on seeing the aircraft, but Wright dropped a Fido which functioned perfectly, hitting the U-boat, which then surfaced. Wright then informed the convoy's SOE, who detached a destroyer from the screen. However, by the time she reached the spot the boat had gone, either having sunk as a result of the attack or having been scuttled by the crew.

This attack was originally assessed as having been unsuccessful, and *U456* was credited to a combined attack by Sunderland 'G' of No 423 Squadron RAF, HMS *Lagan* and HMCS *Drumheller*. However, recent reassessment shows that *U753* was the victim of this attack. It is therefore *U456* which was the first casualty of a Fido air-dropped acoustic homing torpdo.

U753

	Launched	Commissioned
	26 Apr 1941	18 Jun 1941
Class	Type VIIC	
CO	*Korvettenkapitän* Alfred Mannhart von Manstein	
Date of loss	13 May 1943	
Location	Atlantic, Bay of Biscay, 48°37'N 22°39'W	
Cause	Air attack/depth charge	
Casualties	47	
Survivors	None	
Salvaged	No	

Notes Sunderland 'G' of No 423 Squadron RAF, piloted by Flt Lt J. Musgrave, was flying in support of HX.237 and at 0830 sighted a fully surfaced U-boat 10 miles from the convoy. Musgrave made effective use of the cloud and only broke cover when he was a mile from the target. Even so, the U-boat opened fire and showed no intention of diving. Accordingly, Musgrave broke off his attack and circled the U-boat while calling up the convoy's SOE to request that an escort be detached. HMS *Lagan* and HMCS *Drumheller* were sent, but when they had just got to within gun range of the U-boat she dived. This was the Sunderland's chance: Musgrave attacked and dropped two depth charges from 50ft, both of which were seen to explode. *Lagan* and *Drumheller* continued the attack until oil and wreckage appeared on the surface.

The sinking of three U-boats (with only the sinking of three stragglers in return) by the escort of HX.237 represented a blow to BdU since excellent intelligence on the convoy had been available. BdU attributed the Allied success entirely to radar and made no mention of the lengthy signals U-boats were required to make which were so often the cause of their downfall.

U657

	Launched	*Commissioned*
	12 Aug 1941	8 Oct 1941

Class: Type VIIC
CO: *Kapitänleutnant* Gollnitz (lost)
Date of loss: 14 May 1943
Location: Atlantic, SW of Iceland, 60°10'N 31°52'W
Cause: Air attack
Casualties: 47
Survivors: None
Salvaged: No

Notes Sunk by a Catalina of USN patrol squadron VP-82 using a Mk 24 mine.

U176

	Launched	*Commissioned*
	12 Sept 1941	15 Dec 1941

Class: Type IXC
CO: *Korvettenkapitän* Reiner Dierksen (lost)
Date of loss: 15 May 1943
Location: Caribbean, NW of Havana, 23°21'N 80°18'W
Cause: Air attack/depth charge
Casualties: 53
Survivors: None
Salvaged: No

Notes Sunk by a USN aircraft from VS-62 and the Cuban patrol craft *SC13*.

U266

	Launched	*Commissioned*
	11 May 1942	24 Jun 1942

Class: Type VIIC
CO: *Kapitänleutnant* Ralf von Jessen (lost)
Date of loss: 15 May 1943
Location: Atlantic, N of the Azores, 47°28'N 10°20'W
Cause: Air attack
Casualties: 47
Survivors: None
Salvaged: No

Notes *U266* was spotted by Halifax 'M' of No 58 Squadron and carefully stalked from out of the sun until the pilot, Wg Cdr W. E. Oulton RAF, was able to attack. Oulton attacked from the port quarter, the depth charges seeming to explode right underneath the submarine. The bows then rose to the vertical, where they hung for several minutes before sinking vertically, leaving a scum of light blue oil on the surface.

U266 was originally thought to have been the victim of Liberator 'B' of No 86 Squadron RAF. The boat attacked on this occasion was, however, *U403*, which was not damaged.

U463

	Launched	*Commissioned*
	20 Dec 1941	2 Apr 1942

Class: Type XIV
CO: *Korvettenkapitän* Leo Wolfbauer (lost)
Date of loss: 15 May 1943
Location: Western Approaches, SW of Isles of Scilly, 48°28'N 10°20'W
Cause: Air attack
Casualties: 56
Survivors: None
Salvaged: None

Notes *U463* was spotted on the surface at 1820 by Halifax 'R' of No 58 Squadron, flown by Fg Off A. Birch. The U-boat dived on seeing the aircraft, but the attack was carried through, the depth charges falling ahead of, within and astern of the swirl. After the explosions had subsided a pool of blue oil formed on the surface, with items of unidentified wreckage floating in it.

U463 was originally adjudged to have been sunk by Halifax 'M' of No 58 Squadron on 15 May; her victim was *U266* (q.v.). The attack by aircraft 'R' was originally thought to have been made on the Italian submarine *Tazzoli*.

Wolfbauer was unusual in that he had originally been commissioned into the Austro-Hungarian Navy (*KuK Kriegsmarine*) and had graduated from the Naval Academy at Fiume in 1913. However, following the *Anschluss* in 1938 he, like a number of former KuK officers, elected to serve in the new *Kriegsmarine*.

U182

	Launched	*Commissioned*
	3 Mar 1942	30 June 1942

Class: Type IX D2
CO: *Kapitänleutnant* Nicolai Clausen (lost)

Date of loss	16 May 1943
Location	Atlantic, N of Tristan da Cunha, 33°55'S 20°35'W
Cause	Depth charge
Casualties	61
Survivors	None
Salvaged	No

Notes *U182* was returning from profitable operations off the Cape of Good Hope when she encountered the convoy UGS.8. Two depth-charge attacks by the destroyers USS *Mackenzie* and *Lamb* brought wreckage to the surface.

U128

	Launched	*Commissioned*
	10 Feb 1941	12 May 1941
Class	Type IXC	
CO	*Kapitänleutnant* Hermann Steinert (survived)	
Date of loss	17 May 1943	
Location	Atlantic, S of Pernambuco, 10°00'N 35°35'W	
Cause	Gunfire	
Casualties	7	
Survivors	4 officers, 7 petty officers, 36 junior rates	
Salvaged	No	

Notes *U128* had been operating in the South Atlantic, but her frequent and lengthy use of wireless enabled her position to be fixed by HF/DF. Air searches were mounted from 9 April, but it was not until the 16th that she was sighted. The destroyers *Moffett* and *Jouett* were detached from a nearby convoy while American and Brazilian aircraft conducted further searches. *U128* was sighted by two Mariner aircraft, which delivered such effective and damaging attacks that when Steinert saw the two destroyers closing he abandoned the submarine, which was sunk by gunfire.

U640

	Launched	*Commissioned*
	23 Jul 1942	17 Sept 1942
Class	Type VIIC	
CO	*Oberleutnant zur See* Karl-Heinz Nagel (lost)	
Date of loss	17 May 1943	
Location	Atlantic, S of Cape Farewell, 58°54'N 42°	
Cause	Depth charge	
Casualties	49	
Survivors	None	
Salvaged	No	

Notes *U640* was enaged in operations against convoy ONS.7. At 0037 on 17 May *U640* penetrated the screen and sank the 5,196-ton *Aymeric.* The frigate HMS *Swale* counter-attacked: her final attack was timed at 0138 and the result assessed as 'probably sunk', the evidence being inconclusive. It was not until after the war that *U640* was adjudged the victim of this attack.

U646

	Launched	*Commissioned*
	3 Sept 1942	29 Oct 1942
Class	Type VIIC	
CO	*Oberleutnant zur See* Wulf	
Date of loss	17 May 1942	
Location	Atlantic, W of Faeroe Islands, 62°10'N 14°30'W	
Cause	Air attack	
Casualties	46	
Survivors	None	
Salvaged	No	

Notes *U646* was setting out on her first patrol when she was spotted by Hudson 'J' of No 269 Squadron, flown by Sgt F.W. James. Visibility was perfect, with no clouds to hide in, so James approached at low level, pulling up to 50ft to drop four depth charges which fell in a perfect straddle. The boat was seen to sink, leaving wreckage and debris on the surface together with an oil slick which was visible five miles away.

U273

	Launched	*Commissioned*
	2 Sept 1942	21 Oct 1942
Class	Type VIIC	
CO	*Oberleutnant zur See* Hermann Rossmann (lost)	
Date of loss	19 May 1943	
Location	N Atlantic, SW of Iceland, 59°25'N 24°33'W	
Cause	Air attack	
Casualties	46	
Survivors	None	
Salvaged	No	

Notes The first of four U-boats sunk by the escorts of convoy SC.130. Hudson 'M' of No 269 Squadron, flown by Fg Off J. N. Bell, sighted a U-boat which promptly dived before the aircraft could attack. Bell then carried out baiting tactics and sighted the U-boat again at 1625. This time the attack went in and Bell dropped four depth charges in a perfect straddle on either side of the conning tower. The boat was seen to turn to starboard as an oil slick grew and spread around her. A number of men in the conning tower fired on the Hudson, but the fire stopped when Bell made a strafing pass. The U-boat began to sink as Bell made another strafing pass, after which wreckage was seen amid the oil.

U381

	Launched	*Commissioned*
	14 Jan 1942	24 Feb 1942

Class Type VIIC
CO *Kapitänleutnant Graf* von Puckler und Limpurg (lost)
Date of loss 19 May 1943
Location N Atlantic, 54°41'N 34°45'W
Cause Depth charge
Casualties 47
Survivors None
Salvaged No

Notes The corvette HMS *Snowflake*, one of SC.130's escorts, detected a U-boat on her asdic coming in to attack from the starboard side of the convoy. *Snowflake* dropped one pattern but was then relieved by the destroyer *Duncan* (Cdr P. Gretton RN), whose first pattern went down as the ships of the convoy were passing around her. *U381* went deep and Gretton decided to attack with Hedgehog. The first salvo produced no result but the second produced one hit and a large oil slick.

German sources say that the victim of this attack was *U636*, which escaped (despite one hit from a Hedgehog?), and that *U381*'s fate is unknown.

U258

	Launched	*Completed*
	13 Dec 1941	4 Feb 1942

Class Type VIIC
CO *Kapitänleutnant* Wilhelm von Massenhausen (lost)
Date of loss 20 May 1943
Location North Atlantic, 55°18'N 27°49'W
Cause Air attack
Casualties 49
Survivors None
Salvaged No

Notes Liberator 'P' of No 120 Squadron RAF, flown by Sqn Ldr J. R. E. Proctor RAF, had already attacked two U-boats around SC.130. The third sighting came at 1924 when Proctor attacked a U-boat on the surface with cannon fire and a single 600lb depth charge. After the attack Proctor observed the U-boat down by the stern and wallowing in heavy seas. He requested that the SOE detach an escort to finish off the U-boat but this was refused. Eventually he saw the U-boat sink stern first.

U954

	Launched	*Commissioned*
	28 Oct 1942	23 Dec 1942

Class Type VIIC
CO *Oberleutnant zur See* Loewe (lost)
Date of loss 19 May 1943
Location N Atlantic
Cause Air attack
Casualties 47
Survivors None
Salvaged No

Notes *U954*'s loss is often attributed to an attack by Liberator 'T' of No 120 Squadron. However, the aircraft's target was in fact *U753*, which escaped undamaged. The credit for sinking *U954* goes to the frigates *Jed* and *Sennen*.

The sinking of *U954* brought the tally of U-boats lost against convoy SC.130 to five. Among the casualties in *U954* was *Leutnant zur See* Peter Dönitz, son of *Grossadmiral* Karl Dönitz.

U303

	Launched	*Commissioned*
	16 May 1942	17 Jul 1942

Class Type VIIC
CO *Kapitänleutnant* Karl-Franz Heine (lost)
Date of loss 21 May 1943
Location Mediterranean, S of Toulon, 42°50'N 06°00'E
Cause Submarine attack
Casualties 19
Survivors ?
Salvaged No

Notes HM Submarine *Sickle* (Lt J. R. Drummond RN) was on patrol off the south of France. On the 19th Drummond found what was evidently the U-boat exercise area off Toulon, for two U-boats were sighted independently on the 19th and another on the 20th. The last was unsuccessfully attacked with a full salvo of six Mk VIII** torpedoes. At 1510 on the 21st another U-boat was sighted heading south. Two Mk VIII** torpedoes were fired at a range of 2,600yds on a 100-degree track angle, one of which struck the U-boat just aft of the conning tower. Drummond was able to watch her sink through his periscope before returning to Algiers, where he arrived on the 25th.

U569	*Launched* 20 Mar 1941	*Commissioned* 8 May 1941
Class	Type VIIC	
CO	*Oberleutnant zur See der Reserve* Hans Johannsen	
Date of loss	22 May 1943	
Location	Mid-Atlantic, SE of Cape Farewell, 50°40'N 35°21'W	
Cause	Air attack/scuttling	
Casualties	19	
Survivors	24	
Salvaged	No	

Notes U569 was a member of the *Donau-Mosel* group which was operating against convoy ON.184. This convoy had the additional protection of the escort carrier USS *Bogue*, with the air group VC-9 embarked, and four destroyers. *Bogue*'s aircraft had had a busy day throughout 22 May with many U-boat sightings and a number of attacks, all unsuccessful. At 1623 HF/DF placed *U569* only twenty miles from the convoy, where she was found by an TBM Avenger—flown by Lt (jg) William F. Chamberlain—cruising unconcernedly on the surface as if her crew had not a care in the world. Chamberlain attacked and dropped four depth charges and the U-boat dived. Lt H. S. Roberts relieved Chamberlain, and when *U569* surfaced at 1740 she was attacked again. In a crash dive, compounded by damage from the depth charges, *U569* plunged to 350ft before the LI could catch a trim. She returned to the surface, where she was seen to break surface with a 30-degree bow-up angle.

The crew, some of whom were waving white cloths, now spilled out on to the casing, despite strafing fire coming from Roberts' and Chamberlain's aircraft. The Canadian destroyer *St Laurent* had been detached from the convoy's escort and arrived on the scene to discover *U569* barely afloat. The LI had done his work very well and the boat sank before the destroyer could send over a boarding party.

This was the first U-boat to be sunk by USN hunter-killer teams operating from escort carriers.

U752	*Launched* 29 Mar 1941	*Commissioned* 24 May 1941
Class	Type VIIC	
CO	*Kapitänleutnant* Karl-Ernst Schroeter (lost)	
Date of loss	23 May 1943	
Location	Atlantic, W of River Shannon, 51°48'N 29°32'W	
Cause	Air attack	
Casualties	29	
Survivors	13	
Salvaged	No	

Notes *U752* was shadowing convoy HX.239 but dived on closing the convoy since Schroeter thought he had been sighted. An SBT was discharged but no attack developed. However, *U752* was the first boat in contact with HX.239 so Schroeter was keen to surface and transmit a contact report. His haste to make such a report evidently caused him to be less than prudent. It was suspected that aircraft were about and the search periscope (fitted with a sky search facility) was not manned before the boat surfaced.

Swordfish 'G' of 819 NAS, flying from the escort carrier *Archer*, had already sighted *U752*'s periscope and was turning to attack when the U-boat came to surface in front of her. No sooner had the look-outs reached their places on the bridge than they sighted the Swordfish and Schroeter gave the order to dive. By then the Swordfish had attacked and dropped a bomb which penetrated No 4 tank and blew a hole in the pressure hull. A stream of water entered the wardroom and poured down into the battery. Schroeter then ordered the boat to the surface, where he intended to fight it out. Martlet 'B' of 892 NAS (also from *Archer*) joined the engagement, sweeping the bridge and casing with cannon fire. Schroeter was killed, as was a midshipman on the bridge, while the 2WO, who was standing between them, was unscathed. On hearing of Schroeter's death the LI, who was supervising the flow of ammunition at the foot of the conning tower ladder, gave the order to abandon ship but remained in the boat to ensure that the main vents were open. The 1WO remained on the bridge until the submarine sank beneath him, leaving the 2WO as the senior survivor.

U752 was the first U-boat to be sunk by rockets, which had only been issued for front-line service to 819 NAS three weeks before this sinking.

	Launched	*Commissioned*
U414	25 Mar 1942	1 Jul 1942
Class	Type VIIC	
CO	*Oberleutnant zur See* Walter Huth (lost)	
Date of loss	21 May 1943	
Location	Mediterranean, 36°01'N 00°34'E	
Cause	Depth charge	
Casualties	47	
Survivors	None	
Salvaged	No	

Notes Sunk in a depth-charge attack by the American destroyer USS *Nields* during an attack on a convoy.

	Launched	*Commissioned*
U467	16 May 1942	15 Jul 1942
Class	Type VIIC	
CO	*Kapitänleutnant* Kummer (lost)	
Date of loss	25 May 1943	
Location	Atlantic, W of Faeroe Islands, 62°25'N 14°52'W	
Cause	Air attack	
Casualties	46	
Survivors	None	
Salvaged	No	

Notes Heading out in to the Atlantic on patrol, *U467* was attacked by Catalina 'F', flown by Lt R. C. Millard, of patrol squadron VP-84 USN. Millard dropped three depth charges on his first run, but as he banked to begin the second the U-boat dived. Rather than expend more depth charges, Millard dropped a Fido and was rewarded with an underwater explosion and the appearance of oil and wreckage on the surface.

	Launched	*Commissioned*
U436	21 Jun 1941	27 Sept 1941
Class	Type VIIC	
CO	*Kapitänleutnant* Siebicke (lost)	
Date of loss	26 May 1943	
Location	Atlantic, W of Cape Ortegal, 43°49'N 15°56'W	
Cause	Depth charge	
Casualties	47	
Survivors	None	
Salvaged	No	

Notes Returning to port from patrol, *U467* blundered into the escort for convoy KX.10 and was sunk in a depth-charge attack by the Indian corvette *Hyderabad* and the frigate HMS *Test*.

	Launched	*Commissioned*
U304	13 Jun 1942	5 Aug 1942
Class	Type VIIC	
CO	*Oberleutnant zur See* Heinz Koch (lost)	
Date of loss	28 May 1943	
Location	N Atlantic, 54°50'N 37°20'W	
Cause	Air attack	
Casualties	46	
Survivors	None	
Salvaged	No	

Notes Sunk in an attack by Liberator 'E' of No 120 Squadron RAF.

	Launched	*Commissioned*
U755	23 Aug 1941	3 Nov 1941
Class	Type VIIC	
CO	*Kapitänleutnant* Walter Going	
Date of loss	28 May 1943	
Location	Mediterranean, NE of Valencia, 39°58'N 01°41'E	
Cause	Air attack	
Casualties	40	
Survivors	?	
Salvaged	No	

Notes Attacked and sunk by Hudson 'M' of No 608 Squadron RAF. This was the second U-boat to be sunk using rockets, and the first by the RAF.

	Launched	*Commissioned*
U440	1 Sept 1941	24 Jan 1942
Class	Type VIIC	
CO	*Oberleutnant zur See* Werner Schwaff (lost)	
Date of loss	31 May 1943	
Location	Atlantic, NW of Cape Ortegal, 45°38'N 13°04'W	

Cause	Air attack
Casualties	46
Survivors	None
Salvaged	No

Notes While heading out into the Atlantic, *U440* was attacked and sunk in an attack by Sunderland 'R' of No 201 Squadron RAF flown by Flt Lt D. M. Gall. Gall attacked immediately on sighting the U-boat as he did not want the German to see him and dive while he was flying around looking for the best angle from which to make his run. As Gall came in it appeared as if the U-boat was trying to send a signal by light, and for one brief moment he thought he was attacking a British submarine. However, the rear gunner cleared up any doubts by confirming that the flashing was in fact gunfire. The Sunderland returned the fire—effectively, as a number of dead were seen on the conning tower as the aircraft flew over. The four depth charges fell way off track, but fortuitously the U-boat altered course and steered right into the middle of the pattern. The submarine's bow was observed to lift out of the water with the explosions, rise up to the vertical and then sink.

	Launched	*Commissioned*
U563	5 Feb 1941	27 Mar 1941
Class	Type VIIC	
CO	*Oberleutnant zur See* Borchardt (lost)	
Date of loss	31 May 1943	
Location	Atlantic, SW of Isles of Scilly, 46°35'N 10°40'W	
Cause	Air attack	
Casualties	49	
Survivors	None	
Salvaged	No	

Notes *U563* was sighted and attacked at 1545 by Halifax 'R' of No 58 Squadron, flown by Wg Cdr W. E. Oulton. After a second attack the boat appeared to be settling and was observed leaking oil. As Oulton had run out of depth charges he circled the U-boat until Halifax 'J' of the same unit arrived. However, this aircraft's charges all fell short. At 1650 Sunderland 'E' of No 10 Squadron RAAF, flown by Flt Lt M. Mainprize RAAF, appeared and attacked the U-boat with eight depth charges. By now it had become clear that the U-boat was sinking: the crew began to gather on the casing wearing their lifejackets. At this juncture Sunderland 'X' of No 228 Squadron (Fg Off W. M. French) joined the fray and made two further attacks. In the second of these bodies were blown into the air and by the time the explosions had subsided the U-boat had disappeared, leaving a large number of men in the water.

	Launched	*Commissioned*
U202	10 Feb 1941	22 Mar 1941
Class	Type VIIC	
CO	*Kapitänleutnant* Günther Poser (survived)	
Date of loss	2 June 1943	
Location	North Atlantic, 56°12'N 39°52'W	
Cause	Depth charge/gunfire	
Casualties	18	
Survivors	30	
Salvaged	No	

Notes *U202* surfaced on the morning of 1 June to transmit her daily report to BdU. The transmission was picked up on HF/DF by HMS *Starling* (Capt F. J. Walker DSO RN), the senior ship of the Second Support Group which was en route from Iceland to screen convoy HX.241. The ships ran down the bearing and detected *U202* by asdic just after 1000. *Starling* began to deliver a series of depth-charge attacks but *U202* proved a wily opponent, altering course and changing depth while releasing a number of SBTs. The hunt went on until just after midnight, when *U202*, her battery exhausted and the air in the submarine foul, came to the surface. *Starling* turned to ram but Walker checked her speed when he saw the U-boat's crew preparing to abandon ship. Instead he passed down *U202*'s starboard side, raking the conning tower and casing with 20mm fire and administering the *coup de grâce* with a pattern of depth charges, set shallow, fired from the portside throwers. It seemed as if *U202* was blown clear of the water by the explosions before she was seen to sink.

Walker subsequently commented, 'I am most grateful to *Kapitänleutnant* Poser for an excellent bit of Group training' and later that morning signalled 'Splice the mainbrace.'

	Launched	*Commissioned*
U418	11 Jul 1942	21 Oct 1942
Class	Type VIIC	

CO	*Oberleutnant zur See* G. Lange (lost)
Date of loss	1 June 1943
Location	Bay of Biscay, 56°31'N 08°55'W
Cause	Air attack
Casualties	48
Survivors	None
Salvaged	No

Notes Beaufighter 'B' of No 236 Squadron, flown by Fg Off M. C. Bateman (with Lt-Cdr F. J. Brookes RN, a specialist ASW officer, on board as observer), was on routine patrol when the wake of a surfaced submarine was sighted. Bateman attacked immediately, firing four 25lb rockets. After the attack all that could be seen was a large patch of greenish water. Bateman's estimate was that his attack had been successful, but the absence of evidence meant that the victim was graded as 'seriously damaged'. However, in September 1943 Bateman heard that the sinking had been confirmed, and with this confirmation came the award to him of a DFC.

U105

	Launched	Commissioned
	15 Jun 1940	10 Sept 1940
Class	Type IXB	
CO	*Kapitänleutnant* Jurgen Nissen (lost)	
Date of loss	2 June 1943	
Location	Mid-Atlantic, off Dakar, 14°15'N 17°35'W	
Cause	Air attack	
Casualties	54	
Survivors	None	
Salvaged	No	

Notes Sunk by a French aircraft of No 141 Squadron operating from Dakar and escorting convoy SL.130.

U521

	Launched	Commissioned
	17 Mar 1942	3 Jun 1942
Class	Type IXC	
CO	*Kapitänleutnant* Bargsten (survived)	
Date of loss	2 June 1943	
Location	N Atlantic, SE of Baltimore, 37°43'N 73°16'W	
Cause	Depth charge	
Casualties	51	
Survivors	None	
Salvaged	No	

Notes *U521* was sunk by the submarine-chaser *PC565* ecsorting a New York–Guantanamo (Cuba) convoy. *PC565* obtained a firm echo and attacked with a five-charge pattern. The noise of the sonar followed the explosion of the depth charges, which took *U521* by surprise: evidence reluctantly given by her CO showed that he had not been aware of *PC565*'s presence nor of the the convoy pounding up only a mile astern of her. The depth charges did great damage and Bargsten ordered the boat to the surface, where, confronted by *PC565* with all guns blazing and turning to ram, he gave the order to abandon ship. However, before any more of her crew could get to the conning tower *U521* sank, hastened by another depth-charge pattern from the American vessel, leaving Bargsten as the sole survivor.

U308

	Launched	Commissioned
	31 Oct 1942	23 Dec 1942
Class	Type VIIC	
CO	*Oberleutnant zur See* Karl Muhkenfordt (lost)	
Date of loss	4 June 1943	
Location	N Atlantic, NE of Faeroe Islands, 64°28'N 03°09'W	
Cause	Submarine attack	
Casualties	44	
Survivors	None	
Salvaged	No	

Notes HM Submarine *Truculent* (Lt-Cdr R. L. Alexander RN) was on patrol north of the Faeroes when she was warned that a number of outward-bound U-boats would be passing through her area. *U308*, which had left Kiel on 29 May, was sighted and, after MkVIII** torpedoes were fired, was seen to sink. BdU was unaware of her loss until nearly two weeks later, when it was thought she was the victim of an air attack.

U594

	Launched	Commissioned
	3 Sept 1941	30 Oct 1941
Class	Type VIIC	
CO	*Kapitänleutnant* Friedrich Mumm (lost)	
Date of loss	4 June 1943	
Location	Atlantic, S of Cape St Vincent, 39°55'N 09°25'W	
Cause	Air attack	

Casualties	50
Survivors	None
Salvaged	No

Notes *U594* was attacked and sunk by Hudson 'F' of No 48 Squadron RAF, flown by Fg Off H. C. Bailey DFM. Bailey attacked out of the sun with rockets; the first four went 'over' but at least one of the second four struck home. The U-boat was diving during the attack but later resurfaced, lost way and then sank slowly on a even keel. No wreckage was seen on the surface but an oil slick began to form.

U217

	Launched	*Commissioned*
	15 Nov 1941	31 Jan 1942
Class	Type VIID	
CO	*Kapitänleutnant* Kurt Reichenbeich-Klinke (lost)	
Date of loss	5 June 1943	
Location	North Atlantic, 30°18'N 42°50'W	
Cause	Air attack	
Casualties	50	
Survivors	None	
Salvaged	No	

Notes *U217* was part of the *Trutz* group shadowing the convoy UGS.9 when she was attacked by an F4F/Avenger pair of VC-9 flying from the escort carrier *Bogue* at 0650. The F4F eliminated the flak gunners on its first pass, so that when Lt (jg) McAuslan brought his Avenger in to attack he was virtually unopposed. Four depth charges were dropped from 100ft, and when the boil subsided *U217* was seen sinking in a very steep dive.

U417

	Launched	*Commissioned*
	6 Jun 1942	26 Sept 1942
Class	Type VIIC	
CO	*Oberleutnant zur See* Schreiner (lost)	
Date of loss	11 June 1943	
Location	Atlantic, NW of Faeroe Islands, 63°20'N 10°30'W	
Cause	Air attack	
Casualties	46	
Survivors	None	
Salvaged	No	

Notes *U417* was heading out into the Atlantic when she was sighted and attacked by Fortress 'R' of No 206 Squadron RAF. The U-boat opened a heavy and accurate fire on the aircraft as it ran in and scored several hits. Nevertheless, the Fortress dropped all four depth charges and obtained a perfect straddle. The U-boat was completely enveloped by the explosions and sank with her bows rising to the vertical. However, the aircraft was so badly damaged that the crew had time just to overfly the position and send out an SOS before ditching in the sea. A US Navy PBY5A sighted the men some eight hours later but was itself damaged on landing and sank in twenty minutes. During the night of 11–12 June a gale separated the two parties of airmen and it was not until the 14th that a specially lightened Catalina with a volunteer crew found the Fortress crew and took them to Sullom Voe after 3 days, 2 hours and 24 minutes in a rubber dinghy in the Atlantic. The US Catalina survivors were not sighted until the 16th and it was another twenty-four hours before the USS *Symbol* could rescue them, by which time only one was alive. The Atlantic is fearfully impartial.

U118

	Launched	*Commissioned*
	23 Sept 1941	6 Dec 1941
Class	Type XB	
CO	*Korvettenkapitän* Werner Czygan (lost)	
Date of loss	12 June 1943	
Location	Atlantic, W of Canary Islands, 30°49'N 38°21'W	
Cause	Air attack	
Casualties	43	
Survivors	16	
Salvaged	No	

Notes *U758* was damaged in an attack by *Bogue*'s aircraft on 8 June but managed to beat off the aircraft using her newly installed quadruple 20mm guns. BdU now ordered *U118* and *U460* to go to her assistance. These messages, and the subsequent traffic from *U118* and *U460* to the effect that they could not find *U758*, were all read by Tenth Fleet planners and the boats' positions fixed by HF/DF. The USS *Bogue* was notified of the area of U-boat activity and her aircraft began to search accordingly. They missed the rendezvous, which took place on the 9th, but at 1145 on the 12th they found *U118* cruising placidly on the surface only 20 miles astern of the carrier.

U118 dived as the F4F/Avenger pair came in, but later surfaced to fight it out, the CO evidently thinking that he could emulate *U758*.The German gunners, confident of being able to deal with two aircraft, were very surprised to find another eight circling and preparing to attack. After a series of concerted attacks in which fourteen 325lb depth charges, 4,410 rounds of .50in ammunition and 800 rounds of .30in ammunition had been expended, *U118* finally exploded after an attack by Lt (jg) Chamberlain. The submarine was blown in half, oil and debris being flung 500ft into the air. Sixteen survivors, all senior and junior rates, some of whom were wounded from *U758* who had been transferred to *U118*, were subsequently rescued by the DE *Osmond Ingram*.

U118's demise was seen, heard and reported by *U172*, which was waiting only a few miles away to fuel from her.

U334

	Launched	*Commissioned*
U334	15 Aug 1941	9 Oct 1941
Class	Type VIIC	
CO	*Oberleutnant zur See* Heinz Erich (lost)	
Date of loss	14 June 1943	
Location	Atlantic, W of Butt of Lewis, 58°16'N 38°20'W	
Cause	Depth charge	
Casualties	47	
Survivors	None	
Salvaged	No	

Notes *U334* was located by the frigates *Pelican* and *Jed*, which were part of the 1st Support Group supporting convoy ONS.10, and was depth-charged to destruction.

U564

	Launched	*Commissioned*
U564	7 Feb 1941	3 Apr 1941
Class	Type VIIC	
CO	*Oberleutnant zur See* Fiedler (lost)	
Date of loss	14 June 1943	
Location	Bay of Biscay, 44°17'N 10°25'W	
Cause	Air attack	
Casualties	28	
Survivors	?	
Salvaged	No	

Notes On 13 June *U564* was one of a group of five U-boats (gathered together for mutual protection) attacked by Sunderland 'U' of No 228 Squadron, flown by Fg Off L. B. Lee, in position 44°30N 15°00'W. The Sunderland was shot down and all the crew were killed. However, *U564* had sustained such damage that Fiedler was obliged to break off his patrol and return to Bordeaux. BdU ordered *U185* to escort the damaged boat and provide her with additional cover. It was while both boats were proceeding east at 1439 on 14 November that they were spotted by Whitley 'G' of No 10 OTU flown by Sgt A. J. Benson. Benson shadowed the two boats for over two hours, broadcasting homing signals, before he was authorised to deliver an attack. He attacked with depth charges, one of them exploding directly under the U-boat, causing her bow to lift out of the water before she sank by the stern. Survivors could be seen swimming in the middle of a large oil slick.

However aircraft 'G' had been hit in the attack and Benson became more preoccupied with keeping the Whitley airborne. The hydraulics were damaged and at 1920 the starboard engine stopped. The crew survived the ditching and then spent three days in their dinghy before being rescued by a French fishing boat. Benson tried to persuade the French skipper to head for England but he refused, afraid of what the Germans would do to his family. Eventually Benson and his crew were put ashore at Morgat, south of Brest, and went into captivity.

The survivors of *U564* were picked up by *U185* and were later transferred to the destroyers *Z24* and *Z25* which had put out from Le Verdon to meet them.

U97

	Launched	*Commissioned*
U97	15 Aug 1940	14 Sept 1940
Class	Type VIIC	
CO	*Kapitänleutnant* Hans-Georg Trox (lost)	
Date of loss	16 June 1943	
Location	Mediterranean, W of Haifa, 33°00'N 34°00'E	
Cause	Air attack	
Casualties	27	
Survivors	2 officers, 8 senior rates, 11 junior rates	
Salvaged	No	

Notes U97 was sunk by Hudson 'T' of No 459 Squadron RAAF, flown by Flt Sgt D. T. Barnard RAAF. Barnard was supposed to be engaged in a joint air–sea search for a U-boat but proceeded independently when he failed to meet the ships. At 1437 a U-boat was sighted four miles away. Barnard attacked out of the sun with four 250lb charges. As he overflew the submarine Barnard saw what he took to be a number of ratings sun-bathing on the casing, who jumped overboard as the Hudson roared overhead. One of the four depth charges exploded ahead of the U-boat, two were near misses but the fourth exploded on impact. The U-boat was seen circling to port as her crew poured out of the conning tower. Five minutes later her bows rose up to the vertical and she sank, leaving the survivors in the water.

The Hudson had sustained considerable damage when the fourth depth charge had exploded. The blast had hurled the aircraft 400ft up into the air and torn over 100 holes in the fuselage.

	Launched	*Commissioned*
U388	12 Nov 1942	31 Dec 1942
Class	Type VIIC	
CO	*Oberleutnant zur See* Peter Suss (lost)	
Date of loss	20 June 1943	
Location	Atlantic, SE of Cape Farewell, 57°36'N 31°20'W	
Cause	Air attack	
Casualties	47	
Survivors	None	
Salvaged	No	

Notes *U388* was sunk by Catalina 'I' of VP-84 USN based in Iceland, flown by Lt E. W. Wood USNR. The Catalina was sweeping ahead of convoy ON.189 when a surfaced U-boat was sighted fourteen miles away. Wood attacked first with three depth charges, but as he was turning for a second run he saw the boat diving and instead dropped a Fido on the swirl. Although there was no sign of the usual explosion associated with the Fido hitting the target, bubbles and oil began to appear on the surface. These were followed by the appearance of the submarine's stern. As Wood overflew the spot he saw that the U-boat's hull had been blown open and that the interior of the boat was visible. As the stern sank large amounts of wreckage were left on the surface.

	Launched	*Commissioned*
U119	6 Jan 1942	2 Apr 1942
Class	Type XB	
CO	*Kapitänleutnant* Horst-J. von Kamecke (lost)	
Date of loss	24 June 1943	
Location	Atlantic, NW of Cape Ortegal, 44°59'N 12°24'W	
Cause	Ramming/gunfire	
Casualties	575	
Survivors	None	
Salvaged	No	

Notes HMS *Starling* (Cdr F. J. Walker RN) and the Second Support Group were working in the Bay of Biscay, unencumbered by convoy escort duties, in cooperation with RAF Coastal Command to catch U-boats transiting through the Bay to and from the Atlantic. At 0800 on the 24th *Starling* obtained an asdic contact which was quickly classified as a submarine and the ship went into the attack—with the First Lieutenant, who had been in his bath, dashing to the quarterdeck clad in nothing more than his towel and a duffle coat. A pattern of ten charges set to 150ft and 350ft was dropped at 0822. As *Starling* turned for a second run, the U-boat surfaced astern of her and was engaged with gunfire by every ship in the group.

Starling headed towards the U-boat with Walker intending to ram. The swell lifted the sloop so that she descended on to *U119*'s casing just aft of the conning tower and rode over her. As she passed under the quarterdeck a full pattern was dropped right on top of the U-boat even though *Starling* was moving too slowly to get clear. The U-boat was finished off by a final attack by *Woodpecker* moving across *Starling*'s stern. A considerable amount of wreckage was left on the surface, including human remains.

	Launched	*Commissioned*
U194	22 Sept 1942	8 Jan 1943
Class	Type IXC/40	
CO	*Korvettenkapitän* Hermann Hesse (lost)	
Date of loss	24 June 1943	
Location	Atlantic, S of Iceland, 58°15'N 25°25'W	
Cause	Air attack	
Casualties	54	
Survivors	None	
Salvaged	No	

Notes *U194* was heading out into the Atlantic when she came within the area covered by the air patrols for convoy ONS.11. Catalina 'G' of USN SquadronVP-84, flown by Lt (jg) J.W. Beach USNR, sighted the U-boat on the surface. However, the first attack was a failure as the depth charges hung up. In a second attack two depth charges were released manually: one fell short and the other exploded just aft of the stern. During neither attack did the U-boat make any attempt to dive but instead engaged the Catalina with gunfire. However, after the second attack she submerged and it is considered that she later sank as a result of damage sustained.

U194 was originally thought to have been sunk by Liberator 'H' of 120 Squadron RAF. This aircraft's attack was made on *U200* (q.v.) and was equally successful.

U200	*Launched*	*Commissioned*
	20 Aug 1942	22 Dec 1942
Class	Type IXD2	
CO	*Korvettenkapitän* Heinrich Schonder (lost)	
Date of loss	24 June 1943	
Location	Atlantic, SW of Iceland, 58°15'N 25°25'W	
Cause	Air attack	
Casualties	62	
Survivors	None	
Salvaged	No	

Notes En route for the Far East, *U200* was sunk by Liberator 'H' of No 120 Squadron, flown by Flt Lt A.W. Fraser. As Fraser dived to attack, *U200* replied with some very accurate flak which damaged the Liberator's port wing and fuselage, damaged the hydraulic system and started a leak from a wing tank. Only two of the four depth charges released, but they landed abreast the U-boat in a perfect straddle. In a second attack run Fraser tried to drop a 600lb depth charge but this too hung up. However, the damage had been done: the U-boat had disappeared, leaving oil, wreckage and about fifteen men on the surface.

U449	*Launched*	*Commissioned*
	13 Jun 1942	22 Aug 1942
Class	Type VIIC	
CO	*Oberleutnant zur See* Otto (lost)	
Date of loss	24 June 1943	
Location	Atlantic, NW of Cape Ortegal, 45°00'N 11°59'W	
Cause	Depth charge	
Casualties	49	
Survivors	None	
Salvaged	No	

Notes Shortly after *U119* had been dispatched, *Wren* and *Wild Goose* were in contact with another U-boat. Walker transferred from the damaged *Starling* to *Wild Goose* to direct operations. This U-boat was a wily opponent, diving deep and firing large numbers of SBTs. Walker was concerned that the U-boat was using her hydrophones to detect when the escort had steadied on her attacking course and then manoeuvre accordingly: before the first charges had exploded the U-boat had a good chance of being elsewhere. Walker now directed *Kite* and *Woodpecker* in a series of creeping attacks, which finally brought a mass of wreckage to the surface.

U126	*Launched*	*Commissioned*
	31 Dec 1940	22 Mar 1941
Class	Type IXC	
CO	*Oberleutnant zur See* Siegfried Kietz (lost)	
Date of loss	3 July 1943	
Location	Atlantic, NW of Cape Ortegal, 46°02'N 11°23'W	
Cause	Air attack	
Casualties	55	
Survivors	None	
Salvaged	No	

Notes Sunk by Wellington 'R' of No 172 Squadron RAF flown by Flt Sgt A. Coumbis. The U-boat was detected by radar, and when three-quarters of a mile away Coumbis illuminated the target with his Leigh Light. Eight depth charges were dropped, which fell on either side of the submarine. The rear gunner saw the charges explode but when Coumbis flew over the site just one minute later nothing could be found either visually or by a radar search. Nevertheless, *U126* was the victim of this attack: the sinking had been witnessed and reported to BdU by *U154* which was nearby.

U628	*Launched*	*Commissioned*
	29 Apr 1942	25 Jun 1942
Class	Type VIIC	
CO	*Kapitänleutnant* Heinrich Hasenschar (lost)	

Date of loss	3 July 1943
Location	Atlantic, NW of Cape Ortegal, 44°11'N 08°45'W
Cause	Air attack
Casualties	49
Survivors	None
Salvaged	No

Notes Sunk by Liberator 'J' of No 224 Squadron RAF flown by Sqn Ldr P. J. Cundy DFC. At 1402 a radar contact was reported and one minute later the wake of a U-boat was sighted, followed by the boat herself. Cundy made two attacks, the first with depth charges and A/S bombs and the second with depth charges alone. After the second attack the U-boat disappeared, leaving a number of bodies floating in a large brown oil slick.

U535

	Launched	*Commissioned*
	8 Oct 1942	23 Dec 1942
Class	Type IXC/40	
CO	*Kapitänleutnant* Ellmennreich (lost)	
Date of loss	5 July 1943	
Location	Atlantic, NE of Cape Finisterre, 43°38'N 09°13'W	
Cause	Air attack	
Casualties	55	
Survivors	None	
Salvaged	No	

Notes *U535*, *U536* and *U170* were returning from patrol. In accordance with BdU's new doctrine, formulated as a result of *U758*'s success against VC-9, all three boats were proceeding on the surface in the hope that their combined flak armament would be effective. However, the wireless messages required to organise the group transit had put the 2nd Escort Group to work looking for the three boats. On this occasion Walker was unsuccessful, but the three U-boats were found by Liberator 'G' of No 53 Squadron, which dispatched *U535* despite being badly damaged in the encounter.

U951

	Launched	*Commissioned*
	14 Oct 1942	3 Dec 1942
Class	Type VIIC	
CO	*Oberleutnant zur See* Pressel (lost)	
Date of loss	7 July 1943	
Location	North Atlantic, 37°40'N 15°30'W	
Cause	Air attack	
Casualties	46	
Survivors	None	
Salvaged	No	

Notes Liberator 'K' of the 1st Squadron, 480th Group USAAF, flown by Lt Walter S. McDonnell, sighted a fully surfaced U-boat at the same time as the SC317 operator reported a target. The U-boat made no attempt to dive but instead manoeuvred so as to keep her stern (and therefore her flak armament) towards her assailant. McDonnell roared in barely 50ft above the waves to deliver seven Mk 37 350lb Torpex depth charges. The charges straddled the U-boat, which appeared to break up aft of the conning tower.

McDonnell did not make a second run for his aircraft had been hit hard by flak. The navigator, co-pilot, bombardier and assistant radio operator were wounded and the radio compass and most of the cockpit instrumentation were destroyed. The navigator's wounds were serious and he could not assist the pilot in shaping course for land. For the next 3½ hours McDonnell used his magnetic compass and eventually made landfall not far from the airfield at Port Lyaeutey in French North Africa.

U232

	Launched	*Commissioned*
	15 Oct 1942	28 Nov 1942
Class	Type VIIC	
CO	*Kapitänleutnant* Ernst Ziehm (lost)	
Date of loss	8 July 1943	
Location	Atlantic, SW of Cape Finisterre, 40°37'N 13°41'W	
Cause	Air attack	
Casualties	46	
Survivors	None	
Salvaged	No	

Notes Liberator 'Q' of the 2nd Squadron, 480th Anti Submarine Group USAAF, was patrolling over the Bay if Biscay when the aircraft's radar picked up a possible contact, 18 miles ahead and to starboard. The pilot, 1/Lt James H. Darden, took full advantage of cloud cover to position the aircraft so that he approached the U-boat out of the sun. Visual contact was made at eight miles and the aircraft crossed the submarine at 50ft, dropping four Mk 37 depth charges. When the explosions subsided the U-boat was seen to be settling by the stern in the water and circling as if out of control. Darden came in for a second run and this time the U-boat's flak gunners put up an accurate fire which did much damage to the aircraft, making it impossible for the depth charges to be released. The crew succeeded in opening the bomb bay doors by hand as Darden came round for a third run, but even though two depth charges were released it was clear that *U232* was sinking by the stern.

U514	*Launched*	*Commissioned*
	18 Nov 1941	24 Jan 1942
Class	Type IXC	
CO	*Kapitänleutnant* Hans-Jurgen Auffermann (lost)	
Date of loss	8 July 1943	
Location	Atlantic, NE of Cape Finisterre, 43°37'N 08°59'W	
Cause	Air attack	
Casualties	54	
Survivors	None	
Salvaged	No	

Notes On her way out to the Far East *U514* was attacked and sunk by Liberator 'R' of No 224 Squadron RAF flown by Sqn Ldr T. M. Bulloch DSO DFC. Bulloch's Liberator was specially modified to carry rockets and was attached to No 224 Squadron for operational trials. While he was on patrol in conditions of exceptional visibility, a U-boat was spotted lurking amidst a group of Spanish fishing vessels. Bulloch attacked with eight rockets and at least six were seen to hit. The submarine, which had been putting up some heavy flak in response, sank, then her stern reappeared, only to sink back again. Bulloch then decided to drop a Fido to assure the U-boat's destruction. A few minutes after the weapon had been dropped an object was observed travelling on or just below the surface. It was not clear whether this was the Fido or the U-boat, but Bulloch decided to attack it with two depth charges. When these exploded there was a third, larger explosion accompanied by a bright flash. It was later considered that Bulloch had attacked his own Fido which was running rogue and he was commended for doing so. Fido was then a top secret weapon and the chance of one being picked up in these waters by a Spanish fishing vessel would mean that its details would be known in Berlin within days.

U435	*Launched*	*Commissioned*
	31 May 1941	30 Aug 1941
Class	Type VIIC	
CO	*Kapitänleutnant* Siegfried Strelow (lost)	
Date of loss	9 July 1943	
Location	North Atlantic, 39°48'N 14°22'W	
Cause	Air attack	
Casualties	48	
Survivors	None	
Salvaged	No	

Notes Sunk by Wellington 'R' of No 179 Squadron RAF, flown by P Off E. J. Fisher. Up until 1800 on 9 July Fisher had been having a frustrating patrol, with numerous contacts reported but never materialising into anything firm enough to attack. Then at 1811 a fully surfaced U-boat was sighted. As Fisher made his attack the U-boat made no attempt to dive nor to return the machine-gun fire coming from the Wellington's front turret. Did *U435*'s crew think that the twin-engine Wellington was a German aircraft? Four depth charges were dropped which straddled the submarine. The U-boat appeared to lose way and stop, and then sink by the bows before being shaken by two violent explosions which blew debris high into the air. The U-boat then rolled over on to her beam ends and sank, leaving foaming water and wreckage on the surface.

U590	*Launched*	*Commissioned*
	6 Aug 1941	2 Oct 1941
Class	Type VIIC	
CO	*Oberleutnant zur See der Reserve* Werner Kruer (lost)	
Date of loss	9 July 1943	
Location	Off mouth of River Amazon, 03°22'N 48°38'W	
Cause	Air attack	
Casualties	45	
Survivors	None	
Salvaged	No	

Notes Sunk by a Catalina of VP-94 USN, flown by Lt (jg) S. E. Auslander USNR.

U409

	Launched	*Commissioned*
U409	23 Sept 1941	21 Jan 1942

Class Type VIIC
CO *Kapitänleutnant* Hans-Ferdinand Massmann
Date of loss 12 July 1943
Location Mediterranean, NE of Algiers, 37°12'N 04°00'E
Cause Depth charge
Casualties 11
Survivors 35
Salvaged No

Notes Sunk by the British destroyer HMS *Inconstant* off Dellys on the Algerian coast. The destroyer was escorting convoy MKF.19A when she obtained an asdic contact. She had already made a number of contacts which had been assessed as fish, so a single depth charge was dropped. When the contact failed to disperse, it was hurriedly upgraded to 'Submarine' and the first pattern of depth charges went over the side at 0722. After six attacks the U-boat's bow came up vertically and then disppeared. The whole submarine then surfaced on an even keel. She was fired on and the conning tower was wrecked. The crew abandoned ship as the submarine sank. This action was subsequently described in the Monthly Anti Submarine Report for July 1943 as 'An excellent example of a single ship hunt.'

U506

	Launched	*Commissioned*
U506	20 Jun 1941	15 Sept 1941

Class Type IXC
CO *Kapitänleutnant* Erich Wuerdermann (lost)
Date of loss 12 July 1943
Location N Atlantic, W of Vigo, 42°30'N 16°30'W
Cause Air attack
Casualties 54
Survivors 6
Salvaged No

Notes Bound for the Far East, *U506* was sunk in a surprise attack by B-24 Liberator 'C' of the 480th Group USAAF, flown by 2/Lt Ernest Salm on his first flight as aircraft commander. The Liberator gained contact using the SC317 10cm radar set which the U-boat could not detect, and Salm made skilful use of cloud cover while descending from 5,600ft to 200ft to emerge one mile off the U-boat's starboard bow. Seven Mk XI depth charges were dropped which straddled the submarine. As Salm turned for a second run, the U-boat was seen to break in two and sink, leaving some fifteen men in the water.

Salm dropped a liferaft for the survivors and a smoke float to mark their position. Of the fifteen or so who escaped *U506*'s sinking, only six survived to be rescued by a British destroyer on 15 July.

U561

	Launched	*Commissioned*
U561	23 Jan 1941	13 Mar 1941

Class Type VIIC
CO *Oberleutnant zur See* F. Henning
Date of loss 12 July 1943
Location Mediterranean, Straits of Messina, 38°16'N 15°39'E
Cause Torpedo
Casualties 42
Survivors ?
Salvaged No

Notes Torpedoed by *MTB.81* in the Straits of Messina—the only occasion on which a U-boat was known to be sunk by British coastal forces.

U487

	Launched	*Commissioned*
U487	17 Oct 1942	21 Dec 1942

Class Type XIV
CO *Oberleutnant zur See* Konstantin Metz (lost)
Date of loss 13 July 1943
Location Mid-Atlantic, S of the Azores, 27°15'N 34°18'W
Cause Air attack
Casualties 31
Survivors 33
Salvaged No

Notes *U487* was caught on the surface with most of her crew sunning themselves on the casing (Metz evidently believing that his location was far enough away from Allied aircraft) by a TBM Avenger and F4F pair from VC-13 embarked aboard the escort carrier USS *Core*, which was covering convoy GUS.9. The F4F, flown by Lt (jg) Earl F. Steiger, went in first to strafe the boat, followed by Lt Robert P. Williams in his TBM Avenger who dropped four 250lb depth charges.

Two depth charges exploded on either bow while the other two exploded off the port side. Metz had now come to his senses, for *U487*'s flak crews were now closed up and putting up intense AA fire. Steiger made another strafing pass but was shot down and killed. Lt-Cdr Charles F. Brewer made a strafing pass in his F4F (using 1,200 rounds of ammunition) while another pair of Avengers delivered more depth charges. Two exploded under the U-boat while the other two exploded by the starboard bow and port quarter. When the boil subsided only 30ft of the boat's stern could be seen raised at an acute angle, with several men swimming in the water. The survivors were rescued by the DE USS *Barker*.

U607	*Launched*	*Commissioned*
	11 Dec 1941	29 Jan 1942
Class	Type VIIC	
CO	*Oberleutnant zur See* Jeschonnek	
Date of loss	13 July 1943	
Location	Atlantic, NW of Cape Ortegal, 45°02'N 09°14'W	
Cause	Air attack	
Casualties	45	
Survivors	7	
Salvaged	No	

Notes Sunk by Sunderland 'N' of No 228 Squadron RAF, flown by Fg Off R. D. Hanbury. *U607* was one of three U-boats (the other two being *U613* and *U445*) sighted by Hanbury. The aircraft was fired on while circling the U-boats, broadcasting homing signals. For some reason *U607* broke away from the other two, whereupon she was immediately attacked by Hanbury. In a devastating attack seven depth charges were dropped which blew off *U607*'s bows and conning tower. Hanbury counted about 25 survivors in the water and dropped a dinghy. However, only seven of the men survived to be rescued by HMS *Wren* the next day.

U160	*Launched*	*Commissioned*
	12 Jul 1941	16 Oct 1941
Class	Type IXC	
CO	*Oberleutnant zur See* Gerd von Pommer-Esche (lost)	
Date of loss	14 July 1943	
Location	Atlantic, S of the Azores, 33°54'N 27°13'W	
Cause	Air attack	
Casualties	57	
Survivors	None	
Salvaged	No	

Notes *U160* was on her maiden voyage out to the Far East, where she was operate with the *Monsun* group. However, HF/DF fixes plotted at Tenth Fleet placed *U160* as operating close to the escort carrier *Santee* with VC-13 embarked. The carrier was signalled accordingly, and on the morning of the 14th an F4F/TBM team spotted the submarine on the surface. Lt 'Brink' Bass strafed the submarine in his F4F as she began to crash dive. Lt (jg) John H. Ballentine followed in his TBM and dropped a Mk 24 Fido 200yds ahead and 100yds to the right of where the submarine had dived. As he circled back, Ballentine saw a pronounced shock wave form in the water followed by a ring of foam.

U135	*Launched*	*Commissioned*
	12 June 1941	16 Aug 1941
Class	Type VIIC	
CO	*Oberleutnant zur See* Otto Luther (survived)	
Date of loss	15 July 1943	
Location	N Atlantic, 28°20'N 13°17'W	
Cause	Depth charge/ramming	
Casualties	5	
Survivors	4 officers, 6 senior rates, 31 junior rates	
Salvaged	No	

Notes *U135* ignored BdU's standing orders that attacks on convoys should not be attempted and attacked OS.51. He damaged the 4,762-ton freighter *Twickenham* but was spotted by the escort. The sloop *Rochester* and corvettes *Balsam* and *Mignonette* launched a series of depth-charge attacks which blew the submarine to the surface, where she was rammed by *Rochester*.

The subsequent interrogation of *U135*'s crew revealed that the boat was still seaworthy after the depth-charging and that Luther had been the first man to abandon her. He had not sunk anything for over a year and was desperate to do so before the end of his patrol—hence his disregard of BdU's orders.

U159	*Launched*	*Commissioned*
	1 Jul 1941	4 Oct 1941
Class	Type IXC	

CO	*Oberleutnant zur See* Hermann Beckmann (lost)
Date of loss	15 July 1943
Location	Caribbean, S of Haiti, 15°58'N 73°44'W
Cause	Air attack
Casualties	53
Survivors	None
Salvaged	No

Notes One of ten U-boats dispatched to the Caribbean by BdU in July in the hope that they would meet less opposition there than in mid-Atlantic, *U159* was surprised by a Mariner ofVP-32 flown by Lt R. C. Mayo USNR which flew so low during her attacking run that Mayo could see the lights of the control room through the conning tower hatch. As Mayo banked to begin his second run, he saw *U159* disappear. When he returned for a second run there was no sign of the target.

U509

	Launched	*Commissioned*
	19 Aug 1941	4 Nov 1941
Class	Type IXC	
CO	*Kapitänleutnant* W. Witte (lost)	
Date of loss	15 July 1943	
Location	Atlantic, NW of Madeira, 34°02'N 26°01'W	
Cause	Air attack	
Casualties	54	
Survivors	None	
Salvaged	No	

Notes Following the loss of *U160* (q.v.), BdU received a report via a Spanish merchant ship of a 'large aircraft carrier' operating in the area where *U160* had last been heard from. Accordingly BdU ordered all boats to move west of the Azores. This signal was received by Tenth Fleet and duly re-transmitted to the CVE groups at sea, which acted accordingly. At 0818 on the morning of 15 July Lt (jg) Claude N. Barton, flying a TBM Avenger ofVC-29 embarked in USS *Santee*, sighted a U-boat on the surface. His F4F partner, Ensign Jack D. Anderson, began strafing runs while Barton lowered flaps and undercarriage in order to bring the speed of the Avenger down for a successful Fido launch. As Anderson finished his fourth strafing run, the submarine dived and Barton dropped the Fido ahead and to the right of the swirl. A few seconds later a shock wave was seen in the water followed by a large oil slick.

U67

	Launched	*Commissioned*
	30 Oct 1940	22 Jan 1941
Class	Type IXB	
CO	*Kapitänleutnant* G. Müller-Stockheim (lost)	
Date of loss	16 July 1943	
Location	Atlantic, Sargasso Sea, 30°05'N 44°17'W	
Cause	Air attack	
Casualties	48	
Survivors	1 officer, 1 senior rate, 1 junior rate	
Salvaged	No	

Notes Another helpful 'fix' from the Tenth Fleet helped put VC-13 from the USS *Core* on to *U67*. She was sighted on the surface by Lt J. Williams, who used cloud cover to approach the submarine undetected. When he broke cover the U-boat's crew did not have time to react before four Mk 47 depth charges fell around them. One exploded beneath the boat while the other three exploded along the port side. The U-boat's bow came out of the water and iridescent blue oil was seen spreading round her hull. In less than five seconds the boat had vanished. Three survivors were subsequently rescued by the USS *McCormick*. They had all been on the bridge when Williams attacked and had been blown overboard by the explosions.

U513

	Launched	*Commissioned*
	9 Oct 1941	10 Jan 1942
Class	Type IXC	
CO	*Kapitänleutnant* Friedrich Guggenberger (survived)	
Date of loss	19 July 1943	
Location	S Atlantic, SE of San Francisco do Sul, 27°17'S 47°32'W	
Cause	Air attack	
Casualties	46	
Survivors	7	
Salvaged	No	

Notes Guggenberger had been having a successful time off the Brazilian coast, where opposition was fairly weak. Unfortunately he chose to inform BdU of this state of affairs in a lengthy signal which served to home in a Mariner ofVP-74, flown by Lt (jg) R. S. Whitcomb. *U513* put up a lot of flak but the aircraft delivered two hits which were sufficient to sink the submarine. Twenty of her crew survived the attack but only seven stayed afloat long enough to be rescued by *Barnegat* five hours later.

Guggenberger had torpedoed and sunk the British aircraft carrier HMS *Ark Royal* while in command of *U81* on 13 December 1941.

U558	*Launched*	*Commissioned*
	23 Dec 1940	20 Feb 1940
Class	Type VIIC	
CO	*Kapitänleutnant* Günther Krech (survived)	
Date of loss	20 July 1943	
Location	Atlantic, NW of Cape Ortegal, 45°10'N 09°42'W	
Cause	Air attack	
Casualties	41	
Survivors	5	
Salvaged	No	

Notes *U558* was first spotted transiting the Bay of Biscay on her return from patrol on 15 July by a Wellington of No 179 Squadron RAF, but heavy and accurate flak drove off the aircraft. Two days later she was attacked by a Liberator of No 224 Squadron RAF but again survived the encounter. On 20 July her luck finally ran out when she was spotted by Liberator 'F' of the 19th Squadron, 479th Submarine Group USAAF, flown by 1/Lt Charles F. Gallmeier.

Gallmeier had been having a frustrating time. The first radar contact on the 20th turned out to be two U-boats being menaced by an RAF Liberator and a Sunderland. When Gallmeier tried to join, the U-boats were lost in a rain squall and dived into safety. A second radar contact was not found, but 45 minutes later the SCR-717A radar picked up a third contact. Visual contact was made at five miles and Gallmeier went straight into the attack, dropping seven depth charges which all fell along the port side. As Gallmeier circled for a second run his No 2 engine, damaged by flak, cut out. As an RAF Halifax ('E' of No 58 Squadron) was approaching, Gallmeier jettisoned his remaining depth charges and headed for home on three engines.

On board *U558* the situation was critical. Gallmeier's attack had badly damaged the battery and the boat was filling with chlorine gas as sea water poured into the hull. Another eight depth charges delivered by Halifax 'E' ensured that there would be no recovery and the order to abandon ship was given. Although a number of the crew managed to leave the submarine only five men (including Krech) survived five days in a single open raft to be rescued by HMCS *Athabaskan*. The 'kill' was shared between No 58 Squadron and the 479th Anti Submarine Group.

U662	*Launched*	*Commissioned*
	22 Jan 1942	9 Apr 1942
Class	Type VIIC	
CO	*Kapitänleutnant* H. E. Müller (survived)	
Date of loss	21 July 1943	
Location	Atlantic, 03°56'N 48°46'N	
Cause	Air attack	
Casualties	44	
Survivors	3	
Salvaged	No	

Notes *U662* was operating just north of the Amazon estuary and had been unsuccessfully attacked by a USAAF B-24 based in Surinam after Müller had attempted to attack convoy TF.2. On 20 July a USAAF B-18 unsuccessfully attacked *U662* about 200 miles south-west of Cayenne. Müller was not giving up and continued his pursuit of TF.2, only to be attacked by USN Catalinas of VP-94 based at Amapa in Brazil. One, flown by Lt 'Stan' Auslander, had an hour long engagement with *U662*, but it fell to a second Catalina, flown by Lt (jg) R. H. Howland USNR, to sink the boat on the 21st. Müller and three of his men survived for a week in an open raft before being picked up by *PC494*.

U613	*Launched*	*Commissioned*
	29 Jan 1942	12 Mar 1942
Class	Type VIIC	
CO	*Kapitänleutnant* Helmut Koppe (lost)	
Date of loss	23 July 1943	
Location	Atlantic, S of the Azores, 35°32'N 28°36'W	
Cause	Depth charge	
Casualties	49	
Survivors	None	
Salvaged	No	

Notes The destroyer USS *George E. Badger* was part of *Bogue*'s group covering convoy UGS.12. Although there had been a number of HF/DF 'fixes' plotted during the convoy's passage, none of these had resulted in any firm contacts. On the morning of 23 July *Badger* obtained a sonar contact at a range of 1,000yds in almost perfect weather and sea conditions. At 0923 the first pattern went over the side, followed by another two. *Badger*'s CO, Lt Thomas H. Byrd USNR, made skilful use of his rudder and engines to stay within the U-boat's much smaller turning circle and delivered a third attack only seven minutes later. Breaking-up noises were heard on sonar and were followed by the appearance of a large amount of wreckage and human remains on the surface, including a copy of a German translation of Poe's *Murders in the Rue Morgue.*

U527

	Launched	*Commissioned*
	3 Jun 1942	2 Sept 1942
Class	Type IXC/40	
CO	*Kapitänleutnant* Herbert Uhlig	
Date of loss	23 July 1943	
Location	Atlantic, S of the Azores, 35°25'N 27°56'W	
Cause	Air attack	
Casualties	42	
Survivors	13	
Salvaged	No	

Notes Two hours after the sinking of *U613*, *U527* was caught in the act of fuelling *U648* by an Avenger flown by Lt (jg) Stearns of VC-9 from the USS *Bogue*. The attack took the Germans by surprise. *U648*, a Type VIIC, dived quickly but the larger Type IX was less manouevrable. Uhlig headed for a fog bank, hoping that his flak would keep the Avenger away. However, Stearns was too close for flak to be effective and he dropped four depth charges from dead astern. From the air it looked as though *U527*'s pressure hull had been torn open aft of the conning tower. The boat turned slowly to starboard as the bow rose high into the air almost to the vertical before sinking, leaving thirteen survivors to be rescued by the DE *Clemson.*

U598

	Launched	*Commissioned*
	2 Oct 1941	27 Nov 1941
Class	Type VIIC	
CO	*Kapitänleutnant* Gottfried Holtorf (lost)	
Date of loss	23 July 1943	
Location	S Atlantic, NE of Cape San Roque, 04°05'S 33°23'W	
Cause	Air attack	
Casualties	43	
Survivors	2	
Salvaged	No	

Notes *U598* was sighted by a Liberator of VB-107 flown by the squadron's executive officer, Lt-Cdr Renfro Turner USN, while on a training flight on 22 July. There followed a series of attacks on the U-boat throughout 22 July and into the morning of the 23rd. *U598* sustained considerable damage in these attacks and was unable to dive. On the morning of the 23rd a Liberator flown by Lt (jg) George E. Waugh USNR of VB-107 USN attacked but flew so low that the aircraft was caught in the blast of its own depth charges and crashed, killing the crew of twelve. A second Liberator, flown by Lt William R. Ford, was more prudent and finally finished off the U-boat. Two of her crew were later rescued by the tug *Seneca.*

U459

	Launched	*Commissioned*
	13 Sept 1941	15 Nov 1941
Class	Type XIV	
CO	*Korvettenkapitän* von Wilamowitz-Mollendorf	
Date of loss	24 July 1943	
Location	Atlantic, NW of Cape Ortegal, 45°53'N 10°38'W	
Cause	Air attack	
Casualties	19	
Survivors	?	
Salvaged	No	

Notes Wellington 'Q' of No 172 Squadron (Fg Off W. H. Jennings) was flying an anti-submarine patrol in the Bay of Biscay in a 'Musketry' area (an area specially cleared for A/S operations) when she made radar contact with a surfaced U-boat at a range of six miles. The Wellington broke through the cloud at five miles and attacked through dense flak. The flak was so accurate that the Wellington crashed on to the casing, though not before one depth charge had exploded underneath the U-boat while another lodged in the after casing. This was rolled over the side by a hastily assembled casing party, where it promptly exploded. The sole survivor from the aircraft, Sgt A. A. Turner, saw smoke pouring from the U-boat, which began to settle in the water. Then a Wellington of No 549 Squadron attacked with depth charges and *U459*'s crew abandoned the submarine, which sank shortly afterwards.

The survivors were later resuced by the destroyer ORP *Orkan*, which also picked up Sgt Turner who was floating in splendid isolation a short distance away.

U622	*Launched* 29 Mar 1942	*Commissioned* 14 May 1942
Class	Type VIIC	
CO	*Kapitänleutnant* Horst-Thilo Queck (?)	
Date of loss	24 July 1943	
Location	Norway, Trondheim	
Cause	Air attack	
Casualties	?	
Survivors	?	
Salvaged	No	

Notes Sunk in a daylight bombing raid by the US Eighth Air Force on Trondheim.

U759	*Launched* 30 May 1942	*Commissioned* 15 Aug 1942
Class	Type VIIC	
CO	*Kapitänleutnant* Rudolf Friedrich (lost)	
Date of loss	26 July 1943	
Location	Caribbean, SE of Jamaica, 18°06'N 75°00'W	
Cause	Air attack	
Casualties	47	
Survivors	None	
Salvaged	No	

Notes Attacked and sunk by a Mariner of VP-32 flown by Lt R. W. Rawson USN. Rawson was sweeping ahead of a convoy when he sighted the boat before dawn. After illuminating it with flares, he dropped depth charges and saw the submarine disappear in the midst of the boil.

U359	*Launched* 11 Jun 1942	*Commissioned* 5 Oct 1942
Class	Type VIIC	
CO	*Oberleutnant zur See* Heinz Forster (lost)	
Date of loss	28 July 1943	
Location	Caribbean, S of San Domingo, 15°57'N 68°30'W	
Cause	Air attack	
Casualties	47	
Survivors	None	
Salvaged	No	

Notes Sunk by an aircraft of patrol squadron VP-32 USN.

U404	*Launched* 6 Apr 1942	*Commissioned* 6 Aug 1941
Class	Type VIIC	
CO	*Oberleutnant zur See* Adolf Schoenberg (lost)	
Date of loss	28 July 1943	
Location	N Atlantic, 45°53'N 09°25'W	
Cause	Air attack	
Casualties	50	
Survivors	None	
Salvaged	No	

Notes Outward-bound from St Nazaire, *U404* was sighted by Liberator 'Y' of the 4th Squadron, 479th Anti Submarine Group USAAF, flown by Maj Stephen D. McElroy. A radar contact was quickly confirmed by a visual sighting. However, as the aircraft ran in to attack, the depth charges failed to release and *U404* was able to escape unscathed. Nearly three hours after the first attack Schoenberg brought *U404* to the surface. The same Liberator made another attack through fierce flak (which damaged the aircraft) and released eight depth charges manually. Black oil was seen on the surface after the explosions but McElroy could not remain in the area as his No 3 engine was losing oil pressure. However *U404*'s location was known and Liberator 'N' from the same unit, flown by 1/Lt Arthur J. Hammer, was on the scene and attacked just as *U404* was surfacing half an hour after the previous attack. Schoenberg began to manouevre *U404* in a series of tight S-turns to complicate the Liberator's attack. Hammer pressed on and made two attacks, dropping a total of twelve depth charges despite sustaining severe flak damage. At this juncture an RAF Liberator, 'W' of No 224 Squadron, flown by Fg Off R. Sweeney, appeared, to deliver another seven depth charges. *U404* dived, then surfaced again and sank, leaving ten men in the water.

It had taken three Liberators and twenty-seven depth charges to send *U404* to the bottom. All three aircraft lost one engine during the attacks.

U614

	Launched	Commissioned
U614	29 Jan 1942	19 Mar 1942

Class Type VIIC
CO *Kapitänleutnant* Wolfgang Strater (lost)
Date of loss 29 July 1943
Location Atlantic, NW of Cape Ortegal, 12°38'N 64°15'W
Cause Air attack
Casualties 49
Survivors None
Salvaged No

Notes Sunk in an attack by Wellington 'G' of No 172 Squadron RAF, flown by Wg Cdr R. Musson. Flying in cloudy weather, the aircraft obtained a radar contact which was assessed as being a U-boat. Musson made effective use of the cloud so that when he finally broke cover he was less than a mile away from the target. Six depth charges were dropped: the rear gunner saw four of them explode on the starboard side and two off the port side. When the explosions had subsided the U-boat had gone and all that remained was an oil slick and some survivors in the water.

U43

	Launched	Commissioned
U43	23 May 1939	26 Aug 1939

Class Type IX
CO *Kapitänleutnant* Hans-Joachim Schwantke (lost)
Date of loss 30 July 1943
Location Atlantic, SW of the Azores, 34°57'N 35°11'W
Cause Air attack
Casualties 55
Survivors None
Salvaged No

Notes *U43* was caught refuelling *U403* by an F4F/Avenger pair from the USS *Santee*'s VC-29 which was covering convoy GUS.10. As Lt (jg) van Vranken went into suppress the flak in his F4F, *U403* dived to safety, but as *U43* was diving Lt (jg) Richmond's Avenger dropped a Fido. The torpedo began to circle and moments later there was a massive underwater explosion, causing a mushroom boiling effect on the surface. *U43* had been carrying mines which were to be laid off Lagos, and their detonation was the cause of the unusually large explosion.

U375

	Launched	Commissioned
U375	7 Jun 1941	19 Jul 1941

Class Type VIIC
CO *Kapitänleutnant* Jürgen Koenenkamp (lost)
Date of loss 30 July 1943
Location Mediterranean, NW of Malta, 36°40'N 12°28'E
Cause Depth charge
Casualties 45
Survivors None
Salvaged No

Notes Sunk by *PC624* while attempting to transit the Sicilian Channel in order to operate in the Aegean. Ironically, this was an area where a number of British submarines had also been sunk.

U461

	Launched	Commissioned
U461	8 Nov 1941	30 Jan 1942

Class Type XIV
CO *Kapitänleutnant* Stiebler (survived)
Date of loss 30 July 1943
Location Atlantic, NW of Cape Ortegal, 45°33'N 10°48'W
Cause Air attack
Casualties 53
Survivors None
Salvaged No

Notes See the circumstances attending the loss of *U504* below.

U462

	Launched	Commissioned
U462	29 Nov 1941	5 Mar 1942

Class Type XIV
CO *Oberleutnant zur See* Bruno Vowe(survived)
Date of loss 30 July 1943
Location Atlantic, NW of Cape Ortegal, 45°33'N 10° 38'W
Cause Air attack
Casualties 1
Survivors 53
Salvaged No

Notes See the circumstances attending the loss of *U504* below.

U504

	Launched	*Commissioned*
U504	24 Apr 1941	30 Jul 1941
Class	Type IXC/40	
CO	*Kapitänleutnant* Luis (lost)	
Date of loss	30 July 1943	
Location	Atlantic, NW of Cape Ortegal, 45°33'N 10°56'W	
Cause	Depth charge	
Casualties	53	
Survivors	None	
Salvaged	No	

Notes On 30 July the Second Support Group (Senior Officer Cdr F. J. Walker RN) were hunting in the Bay of Biscay supported by a Sunderland and a Catalina. At 0714 *Wild Goose* picked up an HF/DF bearing on a U-boat sending a long signal and the Group, now joined by an American Liberator and two Halifaxes, closed the position at speed. At 1005 three conning towers were visible and Walker hoisted the signal 'General chase'. The U-boats were in line abreast with *U461* flanked by *U462* and *U504*. Their combined firepower had already beaten off the first air attacks but the standing *Luftwaffe* patrol of nine Ju 88s had insufficient fuel to reach them.

The aircraft returned for a second attack and a Halifax of No 502 Squadron damaged *U462* so that she could not dive. Then US Liberator 'O' of the 53rd Squadron went in low—so low that it drew the concentrated fire of all three boats, was badly shot up and had to head for safety of Portugal following the attack. Taking advantage of the diversion caused by the Liberator's attack, Sunderland 'U' of No 461 Squadron came in from astern and sank *U461*, which went down very quickly. By this time the ships of 2SG were within range and they opened up on *U462*, firing a total of 112 rounds. *Kite* registered a hit at the remarkable range of 13,050yds and was rewarded by a message from a Halifax viewing proceedings that the U-boat was sinking. Vowe saw the sloops coming up and, with his boat damaged by gunfire, decided to scuttle.

U504 had dived when the shells from 2SG started to fall around her. *Kite* was quickly in contact but Walker took his time, allowing *U504* to move away from the large number of survivors from *U461* and *U462*, who were in their dinghies on the surface. The first two attacks were unsuccessful and it was clear that *U504* had gone deep. A series of creeping attacks was launched, with the *coup de grâce* being given by *Woodpecker* and *Wild Goose*. The echo on *Kite*'s asdic faded and the usual grim evidence of a 'kill' came to the surface.

U591

	Launched	*Commissioned*
U591	20 Aug 1941	9 Oct 1941
Class	Type VIIC	
CO	*Oberleutnant zur See* Ziesmer (survived)	
Date of loss	30 July 1943	
Location	S Atlantic, SE of Recife, 08°36'S 34°34'W	
Cause	Air attack	
Casualties	19	
Survivors	28	
Salvaged	No	

Notes *U591* was taken completely by surprise in an attack by PV-1 Ventura of VB-127 flown by Lt (jg) Walter C. Young USNR sweeping 25 miles ahead of a convoy. Young dropped six depth charges and saw the boat disappear in the midst of the boil. The survivors were subsequently rescued by *Saucy*.

U199

	Launched	*Commissioned*
U199	12 July 1942	28 Nov 1942
Class	Type IXD2	
CO	*Kapitänleutnant* Werner Kraus (survived)	
Date of loss	31 July 1943	
Location	S Atlantic, E of Rio de Janeiro, 23°54'S 42°54'W	
Cause	Air attack	
Casualties	49	
Survivors	4 officers, 1 senior rate, 7 junior rates	
Salvaged	No	

Notes *U199* had enjoyed a profitable time off the west coast of South America and had even shot down an attacking Mariner on 27 June. Now she headed north for a Milch Cow but on 31 July was attacked near St Paul's Rocks by a Mariner flown by Lt (jg) William F. Smith. Smith attacked with six depth charges and damaged the submarine so that she could not dive. After expending all his depth charges, Smith kept the U-boat under fire until a Hudson and a Catalina of the Brazilian Air Force arrived to finish her off. The survivors were later rescued by the *Barnegat*.

U383

	Launched	*Commissioned*
U383	22 Apr 1942	6 Jun 1942

Class Type VIIC
CO *Oberleutnant zur See* Horst Kremser (lost)
Date of loss 1 August 1943
Location Atlantic, NW of Cape Ortegal, 47°24'N 12°10'W
Cause Air attack
Casualties 52
Survivors None
Salvaged No

Notes Sunk in an attack by Sunderland 'V' of No 228 Squadron RAF, flown by Flt Lt S.White. White sighted the U-boat in poor weather at 2002. As the Sunderland attacked it was met with heavy and accurate flak from the U-boat which did so much damage that White was forced to break off. On a second run seven depth charges were dropped, and once the explosions had subsided the U-boat was seen listing with men jumping into the sea from the conning tower. However, the damage sustained by the aircraft meant that White could not linger, so he headed for home.

U383 did not sink immediately. Kremser's LI achieved wonders keeping the boat afloat while a signal was sent to BdU reporting the situation. BdU ordered *U218*, *U706* and *U54* to render assistance, but the weather deteriorated during the night of 1–2 August and *U383* foundered.

U454

	Launched	*Commissioned*
U454	30 Apr 1941	24 Jul 1941

Class Type VIIC
CO *Kapitänleutnant* Burkhard Hacklander (survived)
Date of loss 1 August 1943
Location Atlantic, NW of Cape Ortegal, 45°36'N 10°23'W
Cause Air attack
Casualties 32
Survivors 13
Salvaged No

Notes Sunk by Sunderland 'B' of No 10 Squadron RAAF in an accurate attack in which the aircraft was shot down just as the ships of Walker's 2SG hove in sight. The two pilots were killed but the aircrew of six were picked by *Wren*; thirteen survivors from *U454* were rescued by *Kite*. Once on board *Kite* Hacklander initially refused to give anything other than his name, rank and number but totally lost his composure when the commanding officers of *U461* and *U462* were paraded before him.

U106

	Launched	*Commissioned*
U106	17 Jun 1940	8 Oct 1940

Class Type IXB
CO *Oberleutnant zur See* Wolf-Dietrich Damerow (lost)
Date of loss 2 August 1943
Location Atlantic, NW of Cape Ortegal, 46°35'N 11°55'W
Cause Air attack
Casualties 22
Survivors ?
Salvaged No

Notes *U106* was sunk in an attack by Sunderlands 'N' of No 228 Squadron (Fg Off R. D. Hanbury) and 'M' of No 461 Squadron RAAF (Flt Lt I. A. Clark RAAF). The boat had been damaged by a Mosquito of 407 Squadron RCAF and had requested assistance, and BdU ordered the boats and aircraft which were still looking for *U383* to look for *U106* instead. Damerow was being very cautious. He reached the spot where he was to rendezvous with three torpedo boats (in reality small destroyers) and remained at periscope depth while listening for their engines on his hydrophones. Their engine noises were heard, but when they drew away to the north Damerow surfaced in order to catch up with them. This was his undoing, for he was spotted by the two flying boats. Both aircraft carried out a series of attacks despite fierce flak put up by *U106*, but in the end the LI reported that both motors had been destroyed together with the port diesel and that chlorine gas was coming from the battery. Damerow gave the order to abandon ship. Five ratings continued to man the flak guns while the rest of the crew got clear before they too went over the side, Damerow being the last to leave. Shortly afterwards there was a heavy explosion inside the submarine and she sank stern first. The survivors were later rescued by the three torpedo boats sent out to escort them back to harbour.

U706

	Launched	*Commissioned*
U706	24 Nov 1941	16 Mar 1942

Class Type VIIC

CO	?
Date of loss	2 August 1943
Location	Atlantic, NW of Cape Ortegal, 46°15'N 10°25'W
Cause	Air attack
Casualties	42
Survivors	15?
Salvaged	No

Notes *U706* had just survived an attack by Hampden 'A' of No 415 Squadron RCAF. Now, attacking from out of the sun, Liberator 'T' of the 4th Squadron, 479th Anti Submarine Group USAAF, flown by Capt Joseph L. Hamilton, came in at 50ft despite fierce flak. All twelve depth charges were dropped manually—following the embarrassing failure of the intervalometer during McElroy's attack on *U404*, use of the automatic release gear was prohibited—and fell in a perfect straddle. The U-boat was seen to sink stern first, leaving fifteen men in the water. Hamilton dropped a liferaft and the survivors were subsequently rescued by HMS *Waveney*.

This was the last U-boat sunk by the A/S squadrons of the USAAF. Under a 'horse trade' conducted at high level, ASW would become the responsibility of the USN and all USAAF ASW squadrons in Great Britain and North Africa were to be replaced by USN squadrons. Their departure was a matter for regret. The USAAF fliers had proved to be true brothers-in-arms to RAF Coastal Command, and relations with the USN fliers would not be so smooth.

	Launched	*Commissioned*
U572	5 Apr 1941	29 May 1941
Class	Type VIIC	
CO	*Oberleutnant zur See* Heinz Kummetat (lost)	
Date of loss	3 August 1943	
Location	Caribbean, NE of Georgetown, 11°33'N 54°05'W	
Cause	Air attack	
Casualties	47	
Survivors	None	
Salvaged	No	

Notes Presumed sunk by a Mariner of patrol squadron VP-205 flown by Lt (jg) Clifford C. Cox USN. At 0025 on 3 August Cox radioed his command in Trinidad that he was attacking a U-boat. He was never heard from again and neither was *U572*. A careful search revealed neither survivors nor wreckage, so the story of that particular night encounter will never be told.

	Launched	*Commissioned*
U647	16 Sept 1942	5 Nov 1942
Class	Type VIIC	
CO	*Kapitänleutnant* Willi Hertin	
Date of loss	?	
Location	?	
Cause	?	
Casualties	48	
Survivors	None	
Salvaged	No	

Notes Lost at some time between 28 July and 10 August 1943, possibly as a result of striking a mine in the Faeroes–Iceland mine barrage. However, the possibility that *U647* was lost by accident as a result of drill or equipment failure cannot be ruled out.

	Launched	*Commissioned*
U489	24 Dec 1942	8 Mar 1943
Class	Type XIV	
CO	*Oberleutnant zur See* Adalbert Schmandt	
Date of loss	4 August 1943	
Location	Atlantic, SE of Iceland, 61°11'N 14°38'W	
Cause	Air attack	
Casualties	1	
Survivors	53	
Salvaged	No	

Notes Sunk by a Sunderland of No 424 Squadron RCAF. The Sunderland sighted the U-boat four miles away and turned to attack. At 1,200yds the front gunner opened fire to suppress any flak, but the U-boat's gunners were on their mettle and the aircraft was soon hit and on fire. This did not deter the pilot, who dropped depth charges which destroyed *U469*. The Sunderland had to ditch, and it sank about four minutes later. The destroyer *Castleton* rescued six of the eleven crew of the Sunderland and 53 survivors from *U469*.

	Launched	*Commissioned*
U34	17 Jul 1936	12 Sept 1936
Class	Type VII	
CO	*Oberleutnant zur See* Horst Frenski	

Date of loss	5 August 1943
Location	Baltic, off Memel, 55°42'N 21°09'E
Cause	Collision
Casualties	4
Survivors	?
Salvaged	Raised 24 August but paid off 8 September 1943; subsequent fate unknown

Notes Sunk in a collision with the depot ship *Lech*, the exact circumstances of which are unknown.

	Launched	*Commissioned*
U117	26 Jul 1941	25 Oct 1941
Class	Type XB	
CO	*Korvettenkapitän* Hans-Walter Neumann (lost)	
Date of loss	7 August 1943	
Location	N Atlantic, 39°42'N 38°21'W	
Cause	Air attack	
Casualties	62	
Survivors	None	
Salvaged	No	

Notes *U66* had been badly damaged and had her CO wounded in an attack by an Avenger/Wildcat team from the USS *Card* on 3 August 1943. Accordingly, BdU directed her to rendezvous with *U117* for assistance and a new commanding officer. The amount of wireless traffic necessary for arranging this meeting was considerable. It was read with much interest by *Card*, and although the exact location of the meeting was not known the general area was narrowed down considerably.

On the morning of 7 August Lt (jg) Ashbury H. Sallenger sighted a 'large white object' which turned out to be *U117* and *U66* on the surface. There was no cloud cover, but the Germans were so intent on the replenishment operation that they failed to see or hear the TBF until he was 400yds away. Sallenger dropped two depth charges which fell alongside *U117*, and the boat began to smoke and make large, erratic turns. Meanwhile *U66* was diving, but a Fido attack on her by Sallenger came to nothing when the torpedo failed to acquire the target.

U117 was now attacked by another pair of Avengers and Wildcats, with depth charges from the Avengers landing alongside to port and starboard while the Wildcats kept strafing the casing. The U-boat appeared to be diving, but she wallowed on the surface before disappearing stern first. The Avengers attacked with Fidos. One dropped by Lt Charles R. Stapler was launched on the starboard side of the swirl while that dropped by Lt (jg) Junior C. Forney went in on the port side. Five minutes after launch an area of light blue water filled with bubbles appeared—the sign of a successful strike.

	Launched	*Commissioned*
U615	29 Jan 1942	26 Mar 1942
Class	Type VIIC	
CO	*Kapitänleutnant* Ralf Kapitzky	
Date of loss	7 August 1943	
Location	Caribbean, W of Grenada, 12°38N 64°15'W	
Cause	Air attack	
Casualties	4	
Survivors	43	
Salvaged	No	

Notes *U615* sank a small tanker off Curaçao on 27 July and the CO reported his success to BdU in a lengthy signal which also served to call down a massive American air search for his boat.

The first to find *U615* was a B-18 of the 10th Squadron USAAF on 29 July, and this aircraft made an unsuccessful attack. On 1 August *U615* was bombed by a B-24 and depth-charged by *PC1196*. On the night of 5 August she was again attacked unsuccessfully, this time by a US Navy Mariner of VP-205; another Mariner of the same squadron made a further attack on 6 August, only to be shot down. A third Mariner from VP-205 found *U615* on the afternoon of 6 August and attacked, inflicting some damage. At 1635 a Ventura attacked and straddled *U615*, which dived, only to surface again shortly.

There were now two Mariners and a Ventura overhead. All three aircraft made a concerted attack, during which the pilot of one of the Venturas was killed. The action continued all night with another two Mariners joining the fray together with an Army B-18. *U615* was still afloat on the morning of 7 August and was sighted by yet another Mariner, which dropped flares but made no attack since the pilot (showing a restraint rare in Allied aircrew) was uncertain whether the submarine was friendly. The end for *U615* came with the approach of the destroyer *Walker*. Kapitzky realised that his crew could not take on a destroyer so he ordered the survivors into the liferafts before scuttling the submarine. Kapitzky remained on board during *U615*'s final dive.

U664

	Launched	*Commissioned*
U664	28 Apr 1942	17 Jun 1942

Class Type VIIC
CO *Kapitänleutnant* Adolf Graef
Date of loss 9 August 1943
Location Atlantic, NW of the Azores, 40°12'N 37°29'W
Cause Air attack
Casualties 7
Survivors ?
Salvaged No

Notes *U664* had already survived one attack by aircraft from VC-1 embarked in the USS *Card* on 8 August in which an Avenger and an F4F were shot down. That evening Graef attacked *Card* (which he identified as a tanker) but missed. At 1216 on the following day *U664* was on the surface charging batteries when she was spotted by Lt (jg) C. G. Hogan USNR. *Card*'s aircrew had devised new tactics to deal with U-boats which consisted of fighting it out on the surface, and the team dispatched to deal with *U664* now comprised an F4F and two Avengers, one aircraft armed with two impact-fused 500lb bombs and the other with two depth charges and a Fido. Lt Hodson, flying the F4F, was the first to attack with a strafing run, followed by Lt (jg) Gerald C. Hogan with two 500lb bombs. Ten seconds later Lt (jg) Forney roared in and dropped two depth charges. *U664*, which had been diving, was blown back to the surface again.

Inside the U-boat there was pandemonium. The LI requested permission to abandon ship but this question was treated as an order by some fourteen of the crew, who rushed up on to the casing, to be killed in Hodson's second strafing pass. Graef now decided to dive, but at a depth of 50ft it was clear that the hull was leaking so badly that he had no alternative but to surrender. Then, met by further strafing and bombing attacks, Graef gave the order to abandon ship. *U664*'s bow rose higher and higher out of the water and at 1420 she sank stern first. The survivors were rescued by the DE *Borie*, which had to break off operations when attacked by another U-boat.

U468

	Launched	*Commissioned*
U468	16 May 1942	12 Aug 1942

Class Type VIIC
CO *Oberleutnant zur See* Klemens Schamong
Date of loss 11 August 1943
Location Atlantic, SW of Dakar, 12°20'N 20°07'W
Cause Air attack
Casualties 42
Survivors 7
Salvaged No

Notes *U468* was sighted by Liberator 'D' of No 200 Squadron RAF flown by Fg Off Lloyd Trigg DFC RNZAF. The U-boat put up a barrage of flak which set the aircraft on fire before it began its attack. Trigg, however, held on, and dropped six depth charges with perfect accuracy: the U-boat sank before the aircraft crashed with the loss of all its crew. Searching for the missing Liberator, the corvette *Clarkia* found seven of *U468*'s crew in a dinghy which had broken loose from the aircraft. In their subsequent interrogation the survivors, three of whom were officers, confirmed the circumstances of their sinking and the loss of the aircraft. They also 'expressed their admiration for the coolness and courage of the doomed bomber crew in making an accurate attack with their aircraft heavily on fire before crashing in the sea at 250mph.'

This evidence resulted in the posthumous award of the Victoria Cross to Fg Off L. A. Trigg. His was the first VC awarded to aircrew engaged in anti-submarine operations and is doubly unique in that testimony from his victims was instrumental in securing the award.

U525

	Launched	*Commissioned*
U525	20 May 1942	30 Jul 1942

Class Type IXC/40
CO *Kapitänleutnant* Hans Joachim Drewitz (lost)
Date of loss 11 August 1943
Location Atlantic, NW of the Azores, 41°29'N 38°55'W
Cause Air attack
Casualties 54
Survivors None
Salvaged No

Notes *U525* was spotted on the surface by an Avenger/Wildcat team from the USS *Card*. The

Wildcat, flown by Ensign Jack H. Stewart, made a strafing pass, and this was followed by an attack with two 500lb depth charges by the Avenger, flown by Lt (jg) Charles G. Hewitt. The two depth charges exploded close to the boat's port side, midway between the conning tower and the stern, and she began to dive, leaking oil. The water was so clear that Stewart could see the submarine under the surface. He watched in fascination as Hewitt dropped a Fido just ahead of the submarine's swirl and saw the torpedo swing towards the U-boat and strike just aft of the conning tower. A brownish column of water erupted into the air, followed by a large air bubble and quantities of oil.

Discussing this attack, Capt Arnold J. Isbell USN of *Card* commented that the main purpose of the depth charges was to force the U-boat to depth where a successful Fido attack could be mounted. He concluded: 'It is believed that the Mk 24 mine is far more effective than commonly given credit. It is acknowledged that our eggs are in one basket. However, when the mine functions as it is supposed to, the show is over and there is no further argument by either the enemy or ourselves.'

	Launched	*Commissioned*
U604	16 Nov 1941	8 Jan 1942
Class	Type VIIC	
CO	*Kapitänleutnant* Horst Holtring (survived, but see entry for *U185* below)	
Date of loss	11 August 1943	
Location	S Atlantic, 05°00'S 20°00'W	
Cause	Air attack/scuttling	
Casualties	None (but see notes)	
Survivors	9	
Salvaged	No	

Notes On 30 July *U604* was badly damaged by a Ventura of VB-129 USN. Further damage was inflicted on 3 August by a Liberator of VB-107 USN and the following day *U604* was attacked by the USS *Moffett*. By now the boat was in no state to complete the patrol or return to base, and a rendezvous was arranged with *U185* and *U172*. After the crew (23 to *U172* and the remainder, including Holtring, to *U185*) and essential supplies had been transferred the boat was scuttled. Fourteen of her crew were subsequently killed when *U185* was sunk.

	Launched	*Commissioned*
U403	26 Dec 1940	25 Jun 1941
Class	Type VIIC	
CO	*Kapitänleutnant* Heine (lost)	
Date of loss	17 August 1943	
Location	Atlantic, SW of Dakar, 14°11'N 17°40'W	
Cause	Air attack	
Casualties	49	
Survivors	None	
Salvaged	No	

Notes Hudson 'O' of No 200 Squadron RAF, flown by Fg Off P. R. Horbat, was escorting convoy SL.135 when a U-boat was sighted at 0929 and attacked with four depth charges. Horbat flew off to warn the SOE and when he returned to the scene of the attack the spot was marked by a large oil slick on the water. The honours for this sinking were shared with Wellington 'HZ' of No 697 (Free French) Squadron RAF, which had also been involved.

	Launched	*Commissioned*
U197	21 May 1942	10 Oct 1942
Class	Type IXD2	
CO	*Kapitänleutnant* Robert Bartels (lost)	
Date of loss	20 August 1943	
Location	Indian Ocean, S of Madagascar, 28°40'S 42°36'E	
Cause	Air attack	
Casualties	67	
Survivors	None	
Salvaged	No	

Notes *U197* was sunk by Catalinas 'C' of No 259 Squadron, flown by Flt Lt L. O. Bennett, and 'N' of No 265 Squadron, flown by Fg Off C. E. Robin RCAF. While on a routine A/S patrol aircraft 'C' sighted a U-boat and attacked with six depth charges. After the attack the aircrew observed that the U-boat was slowing down and had a list to port, although her flak gunners still had plenty of fight left in them. The Catalina had expended all her depth charges so shadowed the U-boat until 1605 when 'N' appeared and attacked, dropping three depth charges. Two landed alongside the submarine as she was diving but the third landed on the casing and exploded when *U197* passed a depth of 25ft.

U670	*Launched* 15 Dec 1942	*Commissioned* 26 Jan 1943
Class	Type VIIC	
CO	*Oberleutnant zur See* Hyronimus	
Date of loss	20 August 1943	
Location	Baltic, position unknown	
Cause	Collision	
Casualties	21	
Survivors	?	
Salvaged	No	

Notes Lost in a collision with the SS *Bolkoburg*, the exact circumstances of which are unknown.

U458	*Launched* 4 Oct 1941	*Commissioned* 12 Dec 1941
Class	Type VIIC	
CO	*Kapitänleutnant* Kurt Diggins (survived)	
Date of loss	22 August 1943	
Location	Mediterranean, SE of Pantellaria, 36°25'N 12°39'E	
Cause	Depth charge	
Casualties	8	
Survivors	43	
Salvaged	No	

Notes While escorting convoy MKF.22 the destroyer HMS *Easton* attacked a contact. She made two depth-charge attacks and was reinforced by the Greek destroyer *Pindos* which made one. The U-boat then surfaced and was fired on. *Easton* then rammed the U-boat at 20kts and sustained such damage that she had to be towed by *Pindos* to Malta for repairs.

U185	*Launched* 2 Mar 1942	*Commissioned* 13 Jun 1942
Class	Type IXC/40	
CO	*Kapitänleutnant* August Maus	
Date of loss	24 August 1943	
Location	Atlantic, 27°00'N 37°06'W	
Cause	Air attack	
Casualties	29 (plus 14 from *U604*)	
Survivors	36 (of which 9 were from *U604*)	
Salvaged	No	

Notes *U185* was waiting for a rendezvous with the Type XIV *U847* when she was spotted shortly after 0700 on the surface by an Avenger, flown by Lt Robert P. Williams, and a Wildcat, flown by Lt (jg) Martin G. O'Neill, from the USS *Core*. The weather was perfect, with good visibility and cloud cover, so both aircraft were able to approach the submarine undetected and attack from astern. After O'Neill strafed the submarine (wounding all personnel on the bridge), Williams attacked with two Mk 47 depth charges, one of which hit the 105mm gun while the other exploded under the boat aft of the conning tower. As the boil subsided, *U185* was seen settling by the stern and listing to port.

Inside the submarine the depth charge had ruptured the pressure hull. Sea water was pouring into the battery, generating chlorine gas. *U604*'s CO took his own life in Wagnerian circumstances in the fore ends after shooting a critically wounded member of his own crew. Meanwhile another Wildcat/Avenger team arrived and began attacking the stricken submarine. Eventually *U185* sank stern first, leaving 36 survivors in the water who were eventually rescued by the USS *Barker*.

U84	*Launched* 26 Feb 1941	*Commissioned* 29 Apr 1941
Class	Type VIIB	
CO	*Oberleutnant zur See* Horst Uphoff (lost)	
Date of loss	24 August 1943	
Location	North Atlantic, 27°09'N 37°03'W	
Cause	Air attack	
Casualties	46	
Survivors	None	
Salvaged	No	

Notes At approximately noon Lt (jg) William A. Felter, flying a VC-13 TBF from the USS *Core*, sighted a U-boat emerging from a rain squall not ten miles from the spot where *U185* had been sunk. Felter bored in to attack with a Fido as the U-boat began to dive. The torpedo performed perfectly, marking the end of *U84*.

U134	*Launched* 17 May 1941	*Commissioned* 26 Jul 1941
Class	Type VIIC	
CO	*Kapitänleutnant* Hans-Georg Brosin (lost)	
Date of loss	24 August 1943	
Location	Atlantic, SW of Cape Finisterre, 42°07'N 09°30'W	
Cause	Air attack	

Casualties	48
Survivors	None
Salvaged	No

Notes Sunk in an attack by Wellington 'J' of No 179 Squadron RAF. On 18 July 1943 this boat had achieved the unique distinction of shooting down the US Navy 'blimp' *K74*.

U523

	Launched	*Commissioned*
	15 Apr 1942	25 Jun 1942

Class	Type IXC
CO	*Kapitänleutnant* Werner Pietsch (survived)
Date of loss	25 August 1943
Location	N Atlantic, W of Vigo, 42°03'N 18°02'W
Cause	Depth charge
Casualties	16
Survivors	4 officers, 3 senior rates, 30 junior rates
Salvaged	No

Notes *U523* literally blundered into convoy OG.92/KMS.24. She received no warning about the presence of this convoy from either BdU or her own search receiver. The destroyer HMS *Wanderer* obtained a radar contact and turned towards it. The U-boat dived and *Wanderer* ran over the spot and dropped a pattern of depth charges. *U532* released a number of SBTs and went deep. *Wanderer*'s next attack was with Hedgehog and did slight damage aft, but her second depth-charge attack did massive damage to the engines and motors. The boat plunged to 270m before the LI could stop her. She surfaced and all discipline in the crew collapsed. The officers and senior rates gathered in the conning tower and control room and a large number were killed when a 4in shell burst on the conning tower.

U847

	Launched	*Commissioned*
	5 Sept 1942	23 Jan 1943

Class	Type IXD2
CO	*Kapitänleutnant* Herbert Kuppisch (lost)
Date of loss	27 August 1943
Location	Atlantic, Sargasso Sea, 28°19'N 37°58'W
Cause	Air attack
Casualties	62
Survivors	None
Salvaged	No

Notes *U847* had originally been ordered to Penang but the loss of *U117* and *U489* had forced BdU to change his plans and use *U847* as a supply boat operating in the mid-Atlantic. On 27 August aircrew from the USS *Card* had delivered an unsuccessful Fido attack on *U508*, which had escaped. Lt Ralph Long in his Avenger, escorted by two F4Fs, had been ordered up to assist in the hunt for *U508* when another submarine was sighted heading south-east at 12kts. Long ordered the fighters to strafe the U-boat and force her to dive so that he could use Fido. The tactic worked, and as *U847* went down Long dropped the torpedo which could be seen turning towards the submarine before disappearing from sight. About fifteen seconds later there was a underwater explosion followed by a 'mound-shaped mass of water' rising up several feet above the surface. Considerable quantities of oil started to come up before there was another underwater explosion. *U508*, several miles away, heard the detonations.

U639

	Launched	*Commissioned*
	22 Jul 1942	10 Sept 1942

Class	Type VIIC
CO	*Oberleutnant zur See* Walter Wichmann (lost)
Date of loss	25 August 1943
Location	Arctic, Kara Sea, 76°40'N 60°40'E
Cause	Submarine attack
Casualties	47
Survivors	None
Salvaged	No

Notes The Soviet submarine *S-101* (Capt Lt Y. Trofimov) was on patrol in the Kara Sea when her (British trained) asdic operators detected a surfaced U-boat's diesels. Climatic conditions in the Arctic meant that Soviet doctrine was to use asdic for the initial approach and only use the periscope in the final moments of the attack. This was precisely the course followed by Trofimov, who, when 1,000yds from the submarine, fired three torpedoes. Trofimov heard one explosion and then surfaced to recover evidence identifying the boat as *U639*.

U634

	Launched	Commissioned
	10 June 1942	6 Aug 1942

Class Type VIIC
CO *Oberleutnant zur See* Eberhard Dahlhaus (lost)
Date of loss 30 August 1943
Location Atlantic, W of Cape Finisterre, 40°13'N 19°24'W
Cause Depth charge
Casualties 47
Survivors None
Salvaged No
Notes Sunk in a depth-charge attack by HM Ships *Stork* and *Stonecrop*.

U669

	Launched	Commissioned
	6 Dec 1942	16 Dec 1942

Class Type VIIC
CO *Oberleutnant zur See* Kurt Kohl (lost)
Date of loss 7 September 1943
Location N Atlantic, 45°36'N 10°13'W
Cause Air attack
Casualties 52
Survivors None
Salvaged No
Notes This boat was sunk by Wellington 'W' of No 407 Squadron RCAF, flown by P Off E. M. O'Donnell RCAF. Investigating a radar contact, the crew switched on the aircraft's Leigh Light when three-quarters of a mile away and revealed a U-boat. O'Donnell was not happy with his approach so he flew astern of the target to turn, hotly pursued by flak. This time he came in from astern and illuminated the boat with the Leigh Light when one mile away. Five depth charges were dropped around the conning tower. No oil or wreckage were seen but subsequent assessment showed that *U669* was the victim of this overwhelming attack.

U760

	Launched	Commissioned
	21 Jun 1942	15 Oct 1942

Class Type VIIC
CO *Oberleutnant zur See* Otto Erich Bluhm (survived)
Date of loss 8 September 1943
Location Vigo
Cause Interned
Casualties None
Survivors ?
Salvaged No
Notes This boat was damaged in an attack by VB-103, US Navy, on 12 August 1943 and put into Vigo on 8 September, where she was interned by the Spanish authorities: the tide of war having turned in the Allies' favour, the Spanish were not going to be seen to be cooperating too closely with the Germans. On 23 July 1945 *U760* arrived at Loch Ryan and was subsequently sunk on 13 December in Operation 'Deadlight'.

U983

	Launched	Commissioned
	12 May 1943	16 Jun 1943

Class Type VIIC
CO *Leutnant zur See* Reimers
Date of loss 8 September 1943
Location Baltic, N of Leba, 54°56'N 17°14'E
Cause Collision
Casualties 5
Survivors ?
Salvaged No
Notes Sunk following a collision with *U988*, the exact circumstances of which are unknown.

U617

	Launched	Commissioned
	19 Feb 1942	9 Apr 1942

Class Type VIIC
CO *Kapitänleutnant* Albrecht Brandi (survived)
Date of loss 12 September 1943
Location N African coast, near Melilla, 35°13'N 03°29'W
Cause Beaching/scuttling
Casualties None
Survivors 49
Salvaged No
Notes *U617* was attacked by Wellingtons 'P' and 'J' of No 179 Squadron, having been detected by radar and then illuminated with Leigh Light. Aircraft 'P' (Sqn Ldr D. Hodgkinson RCAF) was the first to spot the U-boat at 0050 and he dropped six depth charges, after which the target was seen leaking oil and steering an erratic course. At 0315 aircraft 'J' (P Off W. H. Brunini) arrived and delivered another six depth charges despite fierce flak which killed the aircraft's rear gunner. After this *U617* was seen down by the stern, smoke and flames coming from the conning tower.

At daybreak *U617* could be seen lying on her port side on the shore with her conning tower awash. The crew had abandoned the boat since dinghies were seen on the shore and later men could be seen drying their clothes. Hudson aircraft of Nos 48 and 233 Squadrons attacked the wreck with rockets together with Swordfish of 833 and 886 NAS. The wreck was finally destroyed by gunfire from HM Ships *Hyacinth* and *Harlem* and HMAS *Woollongong*. The Spanish government made noises about a violation of Spanish waters but the British government justified its actions by the doctrine of continuous pursuit.

Brandi was one of the more experienced and decorated U-boat commanders to fall into Allied hands. As well as *U617*, he had commanded *U380* and *U967* and had been awarded the Knight's Cross with Oak Leaves, Swords and Diamonds.

U341	*Launched*	*Commissioned*
	10 Oct 1942	28 Nov 1942

Class — Type VIIC
CO — *Oberleutnant zur See* Dietrich Epp (lost)
Date of loss — 19 September 1943
Location — Atlantic, S of Iceland, 58°40'N 25°30'W
Cause — Air attack
Casualties — 50
Survivors — None
Salvaged — No

Notes Liberator 'A' of No 10 Squadron RCAF, flown by Flt Lt R. F. Fisher RCAF, was sweeping round convoy ONS.18 when a fully surfaced U-boat was sighted. The first attack was aborted since Fisher flew over the boat at too great a height, but on his second attack he dropped six depth charges which exploded alongside the submarine. After the detonation of the depth charges there was a second explosion at the U-boat's bow which blew much debris into the air. The U-boat then slowed, stopped and sank as the Liberator carried out a third attack with four depth charges.

U338	*Launched*	*Commissioned*
	2 Apr 1942	25 Jun 1942

Class — Type VIIC
CO — *Kapitänleutnant* Manfred Kinzel (lost)
Date of loss — 20 September 1943
Location — Atlantic, SW of Iceland, 57°40'N 29°48'W
Cause — Air attack
Casualties — 51
Survivors — None
Salvaged — No

Notes Liberator 'F' of No 120 Squadron RAF attacked *U338* (without result), and this attack is often given as the cause of this submarine's loss. However, *U338* made three signals after the attack, the last of which was at 1707/20. The submarine was then engaged by the corvette HMCS *Drumheller*, which had been detached from the convoy's escort in response the Liberator's report. *Drumheller* engaged the U-boat with gunfire until the submarine dived, whereupon the Canadian vessel gained asdic contact. The corvette was shaken by a underwater explosion of some violence, the cause of which is unknown. It might have been *U338* (damaged by *Drumheller*'s gunfire) collapsing, having gone beyond her crush depth, or it might been have been a Gnat fired by *U338* exploding near or under *Drumheller*. Either way, *U338* failed to answer signals from 21 September.

U346	*Launched*	*Commissioned*
	13 Apr 1943	7 Jun 1943

Class — Type VIIC
CO — *Oberleutnant zur See* Arno Leisten (lost)
Date of loss — 20 September 1943
Location — Baltic, off Hela, 54°25'N 19°50'E
Cause — Accident
Casualties — 37
Survivors — None
Salvaged — No

Notes Lost in a diving accident, the exact circumstances of which are unknown.

U229	*Launched*	*Commissioned*
	20 Aug 1942	3 Oct 1942

Class — Type VIIC
CO — *Oberleutnant zur See* Robert Schetelig (lost)
Date of loss — 22 September 1943
Location — North Atlantic, 54°36'N 36°25'W

Cause	Depth charge
Casualties	50
Survivors	None
Salvaged	No

Notes Sunk in operations against convoy ON.202, a series of battles which marked the return of the U-boats to the North Atlantic. HMS *Keppel* followed a DF bearing of *U229* transmitting a homing signal, ran down the bearing and rammed and sank the boat.

U161

	Launched	*Commissioned*
	1 Mar 1941	8 Jul 1941

Class	Type IXC
CO	*Kapitänleutnant* Albrecht Achilles (lost)
Date of loss	27 September 1943
Location	South Atlantic, NE of Bahia, 12°30'S 35°35'W
Cause	Air attack
Casualties	53
Survivors	None
Salvaged	No

Notes Sunk by a Mariner of VP-74 flown by Lt (jg) Harry G. Patterson USNR.

U221

	Launched	*Commissioned*
	14 Mar 1942	9 May 1942

Class	Type VIIC
CO	*Kapitänleutnant* Hans Trojer (lost)
Date of loss	27 September 1943
Location	Atlantic, NW of Cape Finisterre, 47°00'N 18°00'W
Cause	Air attack
Casualties	50
Survivors	None
Salvaged	No

Notes Sunk by Halifax 'B' of No 58 Squadron RAF flown by Fg Off E. L. Hartley. Hartley dropped eight depth charges in a perfect straddle which fell from port bow to starboard quarter. The rear gunner saw the U-boat's bows rise up to the vertical amidst the explosions before dropping back and sinking.

U336

	Launched	*Commissioned*
	1 Dec 1941	14 Feb 1942

Class	Type VIIC
CO	*Kapitänleutnant* Hans Hunger (lost)
Date of loss	4 October 1943
Location	N Atlantic, SW of Iceland, 62°43'N 27°17'W
Cause	Air attack
Casualties	50
Survivors	None
Salvaged	No

Notes Hudson 'F' of 269 Squadron, flown by Flt Sgt G. C. Allsop, sighted a fully surfaced U-boat while flying in support of convoy ONS.19. Allsop attacked with eight rockets fired in pairs, flying through a heavy flak barrage which ceased abruptly the moment the first salvo of rockets struck home. The first pair of rockets hit the U-boat forward of the conning tower and silenced the flak. The second pair hit on the waterline just aft of the conning tower while one of the salvo also hit forward of the conning tower With five holes in her pressure hull, there was no possibility that the U-boat could survive such an attack. The boat stopped and smoke began to pour from the conning tower. The stern rose up in the air and the submarine sank at a very steep angle, although even as the she sank some determined seamen continued to fire at the aircraft. Some fifteen men were seen in the water, but when Allsop overflew the area the survivors and the wreckage had vanished, leaving a large, spreading oil slick on the water.

The loss of *U336* was previously attributed to Ventura 'B' of VP-128 USN, flown by Cdr C. L. Westhofen. His victim was in fact *U279*.

U279

	Launched	*Commissioned*
	16 Dec 1942	3 Feb 1943

Class	Type VIIC
CO	*Kapitänleutnant* Otto Finke (lost)
Date of loss	4 October 1943
Location	North Atlantic, 60°51'N 29°26'W
Cause	Air attack
Casualties	48
Survivors	None
Salvaged	No

Notes Ventura 'B' of VP-128 USN, flown by Cdr C. L. Westhofen, sighted and attacked *U305*, which dived and survived the encounter. The aircraft retired and commenced baiting tactics. A little later another U-boat was sighted on the surface, twelve miles from the first attack position. As the Ventura dived the U-boat swung round to present her stern (and flak armament) to the aircraft. Westhofen attacked through the flak and dropped three Mk 44 depth charges which exploded along the starboard side under the stern, conning tower and bows. As the Ventura turned for a second run, the U-boat could be seen settling in the water with smoke pouring from the conning tower. The crew could then be seen abandoning the submarine as a large oil slick began to form and spread. The U-boat then sank, leaving a number of men in four or five dinghies with others swimming in the sea. Westhofen was unable to summon any rescue for the survivors since his W/T had been damaged in the attack.

The loss of *U279* was previously attributed to Liberator 'X' of No 120 Squadron, whose victim was actually *U389*.

U460

	Launched	*Commissioned*
U460	3 Sept 1941	30 Jan 1942
Class	Type XIV	
CO	*Kapitänleutnant* Heinrich Schnoor (lost)	
Date of loss	4 October 1943	
Location	Atlantic, N of the Azores, 43°13'N 28°58'W	
Cause	Air attack	
Casualties	62	
Survivors	None	
Salvaged	No	

Notes On 4 October Lt (jg) R. L. Stearns USNR of VC-9, now embarked in the USS *Card*, was on the last leg of his dawn A/S patrol when he sighted four U-boats ahead of him. The tanker *U460* had fuelled *U264* and was getting ready to fuel *U422* while *U455* was waiting her turn. While *Card* launched more aircraft Stearns attacked at once and planted a 500lb bomb between *U264* and *U460* while their commanding officers were arguing about who should dive first, thus ignoring BdU's orders that the tanker boats should dive first and be protected by the others. As more aircraft arrived *U455* dived and escaped while the other three put up a solid curtain of flak. All three boats were damaged by strafing before *U422* decided to dive, leaving one U-boat on the surface for each Avenger. Stearns saw *U264* diving and, thinking that she was the tanker, went after her with his Fido. However, he lost sight of her diving position and, unwilling to waste his Fido, switched his attack to *U460*. About 25 seconds later there was a well-defined shock wave, followed by the appearance of a considerable amount of fuel and wreckage on the surface.

U422

	Launched	*Commissioned*
U422	10 Oct 1942	10 Feb 1943
Class	Type VIIC	
CO	*Oberleutnant zur See* Poeschel (lost)	
Date of loss	4 October 1943	
Location	Atlantic, N of the Azores, 43°18'N 28°58'W	
Cause	Air attack	
Casualties	49	
Survivors	None	
Salvaged	No	

Notes Three hours after the sinking of *U460*, *U422* surfaced three miles from the position of the original attack. Three thousand feet above her were an F4F and an Avenger from VC-9. Ensign Joseph D. Horn dived down to 50ft in a strafing run as *U422* began to dive. Lt (jg) Stewart B. Holt was right behind him in the Avenger and dropped the Fido, which he saw explode midway between the conning tower and the stern. A plume of water was thrown up into the air, followed by an quantity of wreckage including a raft.

U389

	Launched	*Commissioned*
U389	11 Dec 1942	6 Feb 1943
Class	Type VIIC	
CO	*Kapitänleutnant* Siegfried 'Udo' Heilmann (lost)	
Date of loss	5 Oct 1943	
Location	N Atlantic, SW of Iceland, 60°51'N 29°26'W	
Cause	Air attack	
Casualties	50	
Survivors	None	
Salvaged	No	

Notes Liberator 'X' of No 120 Squadron, flown by Flt Lt W. J. McEwen, was tasked to support convoy ONS.19. Another Liberator from the same unit, escorting the same convoy, sent a U-boat sighting report but when McEwen arrived on the scene he found nothing. After resuming the patrol a Hudson on passage to Britain reported sighting a U-boat and gave the position.

After starting a square search a U-boat was spotted perfectly positioned between the aircraft and the setting sun and McEwen attacked with depth charges. The U-boat disappeared after the attack, leaving a number of men in the water. McEwen dropped emergency food packs, first aid containers and three K-type one-man dinghies.

U419

	Launched	*Commissioned*
	22 Aug 1942	18 Nov 1942

Class	Type VIIC
CO	*Oberleutnant zur See* Dietrich Giersberg (survived)
Date of loss	8 October 1943
Location	North Atlantic, 56°31'N 27°05'W
Cause	Air attack
Casualties	48
Survivors	1
Salvaged	No

Notes *U419* was shadowing convoy SC.143 when she was sighted and attacked by Liberator 'R' of No 86 Squadron, flown by Flt Lt J. Wright DFC, which was carrying out a Cobra 12 patrol around the convoy. Badly damaged in this attack, *U419* came back to the surface, where she was again attacked by 'R' at 0954. Two depth charges exploded alongside the hull and there was a violent detonation. When the smoke cleared, *U419*'s bows could be seen protruding vertically out of the water. Some fifteen men were seen swimming amid the debris and an oil slick, but by the time an escort had been detached from the convoy to rescue them only Giersberg was alive.

U643

	Launched	*Commissioned*
	20 Aug 1942	8 Oct 1942

Class	Type VIIC
CO	*Kapitänleutnant* Hans Spiedel (survived)
Date of loss	8 October 1943
Location	Atlantic, S of Iceland, 56°14'N 26°55'W
Cause	Air attack
Casualties	30
Survivors	21
Salvaged	No

Notes *U643* was another boat in contact with SC.143 and had been sighted on the surface and attacked with machine-gun fire by Liberator 'R' of No 86 Squadron. However, the aircraft was obliged to return to base, so it homed in 'Z', flown by Flt Lt C. W. Burcher DFC, which found the U-boat at 1137. The U-boat began to dive but was attacked with four depth charges which produced some scum and oil on the surface but no more. An hour later Burcher returned to the spot and found Liberator 'T' of No 120 Squadron, flown by Fg Off D. C. Webster DFC, attacking a surfaced U-boat. Both aircraft made depth-charge attacks, followed by repeated machine-gun strafing attacks. The tactical situation was now quite crowded, with 'G' of No 120 and 'L' of No 86 Squadron attacking *U762*.

After these attacks the U-boat's crew could be seen congregating on the bridge wearing lifejackets and breaking out liferafts from their stowage on the casing, while the U-boat was seen to be down by the bows. The aircraft dropped smoke floats to mark the spot while homing in HMS *Orwell* from the escort to rescue the survivors. At 1445 there was a violent explosion, indicating that Spiedel had fired the scuttling charges, and the U-boat sank. The survivors were subsequently picked up by *Orwell*.

U610

	Launched	*Commissioned*
	24 Dec 1941	19 Feb 1942

Class	Type VIIC
CO	*Kapitänleutnant Baron* Walter von Freyberg-Eisenberg-Allmendingen (lost)
Date of loss	8 October 1943
Location	Atlantic, SW of Rockall, 55°45'N 24°33'W
Cause	Air attack
Casualties	51
Survivors	None
Salvaged	No

Notes Sunderland 'J' of No 423 Squadron RCAF met convoy SC.143 at 1734. The aircraft patrolled astern of the convoy and after coming out of some low cloud sighted the wake of a fully surfaced U-boat. The U-boat was strafed with machine-gun fire as the Sunderland flew over before banking round and dropping four depth charges. One hung up, but, of the other three, two exploded alongside the conning tower, lifting the boat out of the water. When the explosions had subsided, nothing could be seen except for wreckage and approximately fifteen men in the water.

U402

	Launched	Commissioned
U402	28 Dec 1940	21 May 1941
Class	Type VIC	
CO	*Korvettenkapitän Baron* Siegfried von Forstner	
Date of loss	13 October 1943	
Location	North Atlantic, 48°56'N 29°41'W	
Cause	Air attack	
Casualties	50	
Survivors	None	
Salvaged	No	

Notes The USS *Card* had been ordered to break up a fuelling rendezvous for boats of the *Rossbach* group 200m north of Flores and there had been a number of failed attacks. Aircraft from *Card* had unsuccessfully attacked *U488* and *U731* on the 12th and *U378* on the 13th. While combing the area in the hope that *U378* might reappear, Lt-Cdr Howard M. Avery USN sighted another U-boat, *U402*, which he thought was diving. He went in to attack with his Fido but realised that the boat was on the surface with her casing being washed over by heavy seas. He was now too low to drop the 500lb weapon so he merely strafed the U-boat and then shadowed it, waiting for reinforcements. *U402*'s gunners were so engrossed with Avery that they failed to notice Ensign Barton C. Sheelah, who dived in from astern to drop a 500lb bomb. Although the bomb fell wide of the mark, von Forstner decided to dive. This was Avery's chance, and he came in to drop the torpedo, which began its run and turned left. Seconds later there was an underwater explosion, followed by the appearance of oil and wreckage on the surface.

U470

	Launched	Commissioned
U470	8 Aug 1942	7 Jan 1943
Class	Type VIIC	
CO	*Oberleutnant zur See der Reserve* Günther Grave (lost)	
Date of loss	16 October 1943	
Location	Atlantic, SW of Iceland, 58°20'N 29°20'W	
Cause	Air attack	
Casualties	46	
Survivors	2	
Salvaged	No	

Notes *U470*, shadowing convoy ON.206, had been attacked by Sunderland 'S' of No 422 Squadron RCAF but had managed to shoot the aircraft down. She was then attacked by Liberators 'E' (Flt Lt H. Kerrigan) and 'Z' (Flt Lt B. Peck) of No 120 Squadron, which were sweeping ahead of the convoy and were directed by the SNO to *U470*'s position. Both aircraft delivered one attack and were then joined by Liberator 'C' of No 59 Squadron, flown by P Off W. G. Loney, which had been directed to the scene by the SNO. Loney delivered one attack after Peck and then Peck attacked for a second time. In this attack *U470* was blown clear of the water before sinking vertically, leaving 15–20 men in the water.

The destroyer *Duncan* was ordered to rescue survivors but her commanding officer, Cdr Peter Gretton RN (who had led the defence of ONS.5 and SC.130), elected not to stop since a number of U-boats had been reported in the area and he did not want to risk his ship. Instead he steamed by the survivors with grappling nets rigged, but only two men, *Marinegefreiter* Gerhard Tacken and *Marinegefreiter* Heinz Knappe, were able to grab hold and be pulled to safety.

Subsequent interrogation of the prisoners revealed that *U470*'s hull had been coated with a rubber compound code-named *'Alberich'* to reduce the effects of asdic transmissions. Another interesting aspect of this attack is that it was the first occasion on which sonobuoys had been deployed by the RAF. It had not been possible to use them during the attack as *U470* was on the surface, but one was dropped as the submarine sank and the breaking-up noises were clearly audible to the crew in Liberator 'Z'.

Oberleutnant zur See Günther Grave had been radio officer of the German tanker *Altmark* during her epic voyage back from the South Atlantic in 1939–40.

U533

	Launched	Commissioned
U533	11 Sept 1942	25 Nov 1942
Class	Type IXC/40	
CO	*Kapitänleutnant* Helmut Hennig (lost)	
Date of loss	16 October 1943	
Location	Indian Ocean, Gulf of Oman, 25°28'N 56°50'E	
Cause	Air attack	
Casualties	52	
Survivors	2	
Salvaged	No	

Notes *U533* was heading into the Gulf of Oman to operate against tanker traffic when she was attacked by a Bisley aircraft of No 244 Squadron RAF. The U-boat was taken completely by surprise, and although Henning dived, the four 250lb depth charges stove in the pressure hull.

Two men, an officer and a junior rating, escaped from the submarine without breathing apparatus. They simply unclipped a hatch and waited for the rapidly rising pressure in the boat as she sank to blow them clear and up to the surface. On reaching the surface the officer was unconscious but his companion kept him afloat for about an hour before exhaustion made him let go. The rating spent a further 28 hours in the water before reaching land at Khor Fakkan, where he was rescued by HMIS *Hiravati*.

U844

	Launched	*Commissioned*
U844	30 Dec 1942	7 Apr 1943
Class	Type IXC/40	
CO	*Oberleutnant zur See* Günther Moller (lost)	
Date of loss	16 October 1943	
Location	Atlantic, SW of Iceland, 58°30'N 27°16'W	
Cause	Air attack	
Casualties	53	
Survivors	None	
Salvaged	No	

Notes *U844* had been attacked by the destroyers *Duncan* (Lt-Cdr P. Gretton RN) and *Vanquisher*, part of the escort for convoy ONS.206, on the night of 15/16 October and was held down until dawn when Gretton had to return to the convoy. Thereafter the hunt was carried on by aircraft.

Liberator 'L' of No 86 Squadron, flown by Flt Lt E. A. Bland, found the U-boat on the surface and attacked. However, the aircraft was so badly damaged by flak that the depth charges would not release. Bland could do little more than circle the submarine and broadcast homing signals for other aircraft. Liberator 'S' of No 59 Squadron, flown by P Off W. J. Thomas, arrived and attacked through heavy flak to drop four depth charges around the U-boat. After the explosions had subsided another detonation was observed with a dark red flash. The U-boat started to dive and Thomas dropped another four depth charges ahead of the swirl.

Meanwhile aircraft 'L' was so badly damaged that Bland decided to ditch near the convoy and await rescue. However, the aircraft broke up on ditching, two of the crew were killed and Bland and his navigator were injured. The five survivors were eventually rescued by HMS *Pink*.

U964

	Launched	*Commissioned*
U964	30 Dec 1942	18 Feb 1943
Class	Type VIIC	
CO	*Oberleutnant zur See* Emmo Hummerjohann	
Date of loss	16 October 1943	
Location	Atlantic, 58°34'N 05°46'W	
Cause	Air attack	
Casualties	47	
Survivors	3	
Salvaged	No	

Notes Liberator 'Y' of No 86 Squadron, flown by Fg Off G. D. Gamble DFC BEM, was operating in support of convoy ON.206 when she sighted and attacked a U-boat at 1735. The first attack was unsuccessful, and because of the intense flak put up by the U-boat Gamble held off while calling the convoy's SNO to detach an escort vessel. The SNO declined, so at 1910 a second attack was mounted and one of the three depth charges fell alongside the hull. Within minutes the U-boat was down by the bows and she slowly sank, leaving 35 men in the water. Although Gamble informed the SNO of the survivors' position it was not possible to rescue them because night had fallen and it was not until some time after this that the three remaining survivors were rescued by *U231*.

U540

	Launched	*Commissioned*
U540	18 Dec 1942	10 Mar 1943
Class	Type IXC/40	
CO	*Kapitänleutnant* Lorenz Kasch (lost)	
Date of loss	17 October 1943	
Location	Atlantic, E of Cape Farewell, 58°38'N 31°56'W	
Cause	Air attack	
Casualties	55	
Survivors	None	
Salvaged	No	

Notes *U540* had already been attacked on the previous day by Liberator 'S' of No 59 Squadron, which had just disposed of *U844*. On the 17th *U540* was found on the surface by Liberators 'D' of No 58 Squadron (Flt Lt Eric Knowles DFM) and 'H' of No 120 Squadron (WO B.W. Turnbull RNZAF). Knowles was first to attack but his depth charges overshot. At the same time Turnbull, who was already committed to the run-in, roared overhead at 150ft (to avoid a collision) in an attempt to distract the U-boat's flak gunners. Knowles' second attack was a straddle, but Turnbull's attack ended the engagement. As his aircraft flew over the U-boat the rear gunner reported that he could see bows and stern pointing up to the vertical: the explosion of the eight depth charges had broken the submarine in two. *U540* managed to transmit one last signal to BdU informing him that she was under attack, and so when she failed to answer further signals there could be no doubt as to her fate.

U631	*Launched*	*Commissioned*
	27 May 1942	16 Jul 1932
Class	Type VIIC	
CO	*Oberleutnant zur See* Kruger (lost)	
Date of loss	17 October 1943	
Location	N Atlantic, SE of Cape Farewell, 58°13'N 32°29'W	
Cause	Depth charge	
Casualties	53	
Survivors	None	
Salvaged	No	

Notes HMS *Sunflower*, one of the escorts for ON.206, detected *U631* on her asdic and made two attacks in foul weather with heavy seas washing over her quarterdeck. The weather made any assessment very difficult but a large oil slick was subsequently observed on the surface. Post-war analysis confirmed that *U631* was the victim.

U841	*Launched*	*Commissioned*
	21 Oct 1942	6 Feb 1943
Class	Type IXC/40	
CO	*Kapitänleutnant* Werner Bender (lost)	
Date of loss	17 October 1943	
Location	N Atlantic, E of Cape Farewell, 59°57'N 31°06'W	
Cause	Depth charge	
Casualties	26	
Survivors	1 officer, 5 senior rates, 21 junior rates	
Salvaged	No	

Notes *U841* was surprised by an aircraft while closing convoy ON.206, and, although she was able to dive, her battery was damaged and sea water was leaking into the boat through a damaged torpedo tube and a fuel connection. She was then spotted by the DE HMS *Byard* trailing ON.206 at a range of nine miles. *Byard*'s attack compounded the damage and Bender brought the boat to the surface and scuttled her. As his crew swarmed out on to the casing, Bender was seen firing at *Byard* with a small arm. However, a more realistic member of his ship's company waved a white flag and 27 of the crew were rescued.

This was the first sinking of a U-boat by a US-built DE in British service. *Byard*'s commanding officer sent a message to her builders, the Bethlehem-Hingham Shipyard: 'Have credited your account with one fat U-boat.'

U378	*Launched*	*Commissioned*
	13 Sept 1941	30 Oct 1941
Class	Type VIIC	
CO	*Kapitänleutnant* Erich Mader (lost)	
Date of loss	20 October 1943	
Location	North of the Azores, N Atlantic, 47°40'N 28°27'W.	
Cause	Air attack	
Casualties	52	
Survivors	None	
Salvaged	No	

Notes Sunk by an F4F-4 Wildcat flown by Cdr Charles W. Brewster USN and a TBF Avenger flown by Lt R. W. Hayman USNR of VC-13 operating from the USS *Core*.

U274	*Launched*	*Commissioned*
	19 Sept 1942	7 Nov 1942
Type	Type VIIC	
CO	*Oberleutnant zur See* Günther Jordan (lost)	
Date of loss	23 October 1943	
Location	N Atlantic, SW of Iceland, 57°14'N 27°50'W	
Cause	Hedgehog	
Casualties	48	

Survivors	None
Salvaged	No

Notes *U224* was in contact with convoy ON.207 when she was spotted by Liberator 'Z' of No 224 Squadron flown by Sqn Ldr E.J.Wicht RAF. The Liberator was tasked to drop an urgently needed radar spare to HMS *Sunflower* of the B7 escort group before proceeding to the convoy. Homing in on a radar contact, Wicht came out of the cloud to find the U-boat two miles away. The Liberator fired six rockets but did not observe any damage and Wicht then circled since the destroyers *Duncan* and *Vidette* were coming up, having detached from the convoy. During Wicht's attack he had left his intercom switched into the radio telephone and his commentary was heard in all ships of ON.207's escort and acted as a tremendous encouragement.

Shortly after 1110 the U-boat dived and Wicht attacked again with two depth charges. He then dropped a flame float and circled the area until *Duncan* and the others were in sight. Wicht then set course for the convoy and left the Navy to finish the job. Gretton started a search based on the flame float heading towards the convoy and it was not long before he was in contact. *Duncan*'s first Hedgehog attack had no result, but the second produced three explosions followed by the appearance of what Gretton called 'gruesome evidence' of a 'kill' on the surface.

Sqn Ldr Edgar Wicht was a Swiss national serving with the RAF.

	Launched	*Commissioned*
U566	20 Feb 1941	17 Apr 1941
Class	Type VIIC	
CO	*Kapitänleutnant* Hans Hornkohl (survived)	
Date of loss	24 October 1941	
Location	Atlantic, NW of Cape Ortegal, 31°12'N 09°31'W	
Cause	Air attack	
Casualties	None (?)	
Survivors	49	
Salvaged	No	

Notes In October it was learned that at least five U-boats were destined for the Mediterranean from the west coast of France. Special air and sea patrols were instituted to prevent this transit and three of the supposed five were sunk. *U566* was the first, sunk by Wellington 'A' of No 179 Squadron RAF; the others were *U732* (q.v.) and *U340* (q.v.). A Spanish fishing vessel landed the survivors at Vigo, where they were interned.

	Launched	*Commissioned*
U420	12 Aug 1942	16 Dec 1942
Class	Type VIIC	
CO	*Oberleutnant zur See* Reese (lost)	
Date of loss	26 October 1943	
Location	Atlantic, NE of Newfoundland, 50°49'N 41°01'W	
Cause	Air attack	
Casualties	49	
Survivors	None	
Salvaged	No	

Notes Sunk by Liberator 'A' of No 10 Squadron RCAF.

	Launched	*Commissioned*
U220	16 Jan 1943	7 Mar 1943
Class	Type XB	
CO	*Oberleutnant zur See* Bruno Barber (lost)	
Date of loss	28 October 1943	
Location	North Atlantic, 48°53'N 33°30'W	
Cause	Air attack	
Casualties	56	
Survivors	None	
Salvaged	No	

Notes The escort carrier USS *Block Island* and air group VC-1 left Norfolk, Virginia, on 15 October bound for the North Atlantic to interdict a refuelling concentration reported behind the boats of *Gruppe Siegfried*. Numerous HF/DF fixes indicated the presence of several U-boats and on the 28th Lt Franklin M. Murray and Ensign Harold L. Hanshuh were flying 'N' from the carrier when they sighted two U-boats on the surface twenty miles away. Both boats appeared to be taken completely by surprise. Both Murray and Handshuh went for the nearest boat, *U220*, which was returning from a minelaying operation off Newfoundland, and Murray dropped two depth charges which exploded on either side of the conning tower. The U-boat slewed round 180 degrees and then sank by the bow.

The other boat sighted in this attack, *U256*, put up flak while Murray and Handshuh feinted to keep her on the surface until reinforcements arrived. However, none did, and *U256* dived and escaped despite Murray dropping a Fido.

U282	*Launched*	*Commissioned*
	8 Feb 1943	3 Mar 1943
Class	Type VIIC	
CO	*Oberleutnant zur See* Rudolf Müller (lost)	
Date of loss	29 October 1943	
Location	Atlantic, S of Greenland, 55°28'N 31°57'W	
Cause	Hedgehog	
Casualties	48	
Survivors	None	
Salvaged	No	

Notes EG.7 had been detached from convoy ON.208 to meet convoy HX.263. In the hope of catching any U-boats lurking astern of the convoy, the SO, Cdr P. Gretton in *Duncan*, swept down the wake of the convoy. Six hours after leaving ON.208 *Vidette* was in contact with a U-boat which was destroyed, after a long hunt, by a well-aimed Hedgehog attack by the corvette HMS *Sunflower*. On this occasion there was evidence, blown to the surface by the Hedgehog explosion, in such quantities to identify the boat as *U282*.

U306	*Launched*	*Commissioned*
	1942	21 Oct 1942
Class	Type VIIC	
CO	*Kapitänleutnant* Klaus von Trotha (lost)	
Date of loss	31 October 1943	
Location	Atlantic, NW of Cape Finisterre, 46°19'N 20°44'W	
Cause	Depth charge	
Casualties	51	
Survivors	None	
Salvaged	No	

Notes *U306* was shadowing convoys SL.138 and KMS.28 (which had merged) from a position off the convoys' starboard bow when she was spotted by the destroyer HMS *Whitehall* and corvette HMS *Geranium*, depth-charged and sunk.

U584	*Launched*	*Commissioned*
	26 Jun 1941	21 Aug 1941
Class	Type VIIC	
CO	*Kapitänleutnant* Joachim Deecke (lost)	
Date of loss	31 October 1943	
Location	Atlantic, NW of the Azores, 49°14'N 31°55'W	
Cause	Air attack	
Casualties	53	
Survivors	None	
Salvaged	No	

Notes Following the sinking of *U220* (q.v.), the USS *Card* and VC-9 arrived in the area. Lt (jg) Fowler obtained a radar contact and found *U91* and *U584* cruising on the surface. While Fowler shadowed to await reinforcements (the Americans having decided that U-boat fight-back tactics made attacks by single aircraft too risky), *U91* dived, leaving *U584* to face a force of three Avengers. Deecke decided to dive. As he did so Fowler and Lt (jg) Balliett delivered a Fido on either side of his boat. A few seconds later plumes of water broke the surface, indicating that both Fidos had hit, followed by large amounts of oil and debris.

U732	*Launched*	*Commissioned*
	25 Aug 1942	24 Oct 1942
Class	Type VIIC	
CO	*Oberleutnant zur See* K. P. Carlsen (survived)	
Date of loss	31 October 1943	
Location	Atlantic, W of Strait of Gibraltar, 35°54'N 05°52'W	
Cause	Depth charge	
Casualties	31	
Survivors	2 officers, 2 senior rates, 15 ratings	
Salvaged	No	

Notes At 1330 on 31 October the trawler *Imperialist* sighted a U-boat and attacked her with a ten-charge pattern. The U-boat surfaced in the middle of the boil and *Imperialist* opened fire on her with her 4in gun and 40mm Bofors, scoring at least two hits with the former and many with the latter. The U-boat then sank and another 28 depth charges followed her down. *Imperialist* considered the attack to have been successful, but in fact *U732* had bottomed in 100 fathoms and was being carried along by the current. Carlsen waited until the air in the boat was too foul to breathe and then surfaced, hoping that his assailant had gone away. In fact the destroyer *Douglas* was nearby and she completed the destruction.

U405	*Launched*	*Commissioned*
	4 Jun 1941	17 Sept 1941
Class	Type VIIC	
CO	*Korvettenkapitän* Rudolf Hopman (lost)	
Date of loss	1 November 1943	
Location	Atlantic, N of the Azores, 49°00'N 31°14'W	
Cause	Depth charge/ramming	
Casualties	49	
Survivors	None	
Salvaged	No	

Notes Following the sinking of *U584* the *Card* group was keen to sink the other U-boat, which they believed to be a tanker. The old four-stacker USS *Borie* (Lt Charles H. Hutchins USN) was sent out to look for her and on the evening of the 31st carried out an attack on *U256* which *Borie*'s commanding officer considered successful. In fact *U256* had got away.

Shortly after 0200 on the 1st *Borie* found another sonar contact. Hutchins ordered a standard pattern dropped but there was a mistake in the drill and every depth charge in the chutes went over the stern. However, this had the desired effect for *U405* surfaced astern and to port of the destroyer. While the Germans (looking a hirsute bunch, their long hair tied back with coloured scarves) tried to man their armament, quick and accurate gunfire from *Borie* blew the deck gun over the side while 20mm fire kept the crew away from the flak armament. *Borie* came in to ram but just at the last moment Hopman turned quickly to port just as a big wave lifted *Borie* up, so that she settled gently on *U405*'s forward casing. The two vessels remained locked together for nearly ten minutes, angled 10 degrees apart in heavy seas. *Borie*'s gunners (two 4in guns and three 20mm weapons were able to bear) wrought havoc on the U-boat's bridge and casing. One German was killed by a 5in sheath-knife thrown by Fireman 1st Class David Southwick, while another German was felled by an accurately hurled 4in cartridge case.

Eventually *Borie* broke away: the collision had done her more damage than *U405* and the forward engine room was flooding rapidly. *U405* tried to open the range with *Borie* following, but the U-boat then began to circle and with her tighter turning ability was able to evade another ramming. Hutchins now ordered the searchlight to be turned off, hoping that in the darkness the U-boat might try to break away. This is exactly what happened, and Hutchins was able to watch *U405* head off on the radar. When the moment was right he illuminated the submarine. This time Hopman decided to ram the destroyer and turned in to *Borie*'s starboard quarter. As he did so Hutchins had three depth charges fired with 30ft settings which fell in a perfect straddle around the conning tower. The explosions lifted the submarine bodily and she lay stopped in the water. *Borie* increased speed to open the range, firing all the while, and as she did so *U405*'s bow came out of the water and she sank. As *Borie* began the task of rescuing survivors she was attacked by another U-boat, and in manoeuvring to avoid the torpedo ran down the survivors in the water.

Borie's damage was such that she could not be salved, and she was scuttled at 0945 on 2 November by four depth charges dropped by an Avenger. None of her crew had been killed in the duel with *U405*, but three officers and 24 men drowned in the icy sea as they tried to reach *Barry* and *Goff*.

U340	*Launched*	*Commissioned*
	20 Aug 1942	16 Oct 1942
Class	Type VIIC	
CO	*Oberleutnant zur See* Hans-Joachim Klaus (survived)	
Date of loss	2 November 1943	
Location	Strait of Gibraltar, E of Ceuta, 35°49'N 05°14'W	
Cause	Depth charge	
Casualties	1	
Survivors	4 officers, 4 senior rates, 40 junior rates	
Salvaged	No	

Notes Sunk just inside the Mediterranean by HM Ships *Active*, *Witherington* and *Fleetwood* supported by Wellingtons 'R' and 'W' of No 179 Squadron RAF. The following morning *Fleetwood* recovered 48 survivors from Spanish fishing vessels. The Spanish government protested bitterly at the infringement of their territorial waters and the removal of the U-boat men from Spanish-flag ships. However, the British government replied that *Fleetwood*'s actions (recommended by her medical officer) were motivated by humanitarian concerns: many, if not most, of *U340*'s crew were in a very poor condition and needed dry clothing, hot drinks and the facilities of a hospital—none of which they were receiving on the fishing vessels. The fact that a U-boat crew was removed from circulation was an additional bonus.

U848	*Launched* 6 Oct 1942	*Commissioned* 10 Feb 1943
Class	Type IXD2	
CO	*Korvettenkapitän* Wilhelm Rollmann (lost)	
Date of loss	5 November 1943	
Location	Atlantic, SW of Ascension Island, 10°09'N 18°00'W	
Cause	Air attack	
Casualties	63	
Survivors	None	
Salvaged	No	

Notes HF/DF fixes plotted *U848*'s position as south-west of Ascension Island and aircraft were sent out to look for her. *U848* put up a stout fight and survived attacks throughout the day by four USN PB4Ys and two USAAF B-25s (which tried to bomb her from 4,000ft and, not surprisingly, missed) before blowing up just after 1600. Twenty survivors were counted in the water and the aircraft dropped three liferafts while signalling for a merchant ship to rescue them. However, the rescue did not take place and one by one the survivors died until only one was left, to be rescued by the USS *Marblehead* a month later.

U226	*Launched* 18 Jun 1942	*Commissioned* 1 Aug 1942
Class	Type VIIC	
CO	*Oberleutnant zur See* Albrecht Gange (lost)	
Date of loss	6 November 1943	
Location	N Atlantic, E of Cape Race, 44°49'N 41°13'W	
Cause	Depth charge	
Casualties	51	
Survivors	None	
Salvaged	No	

Notes On 6 November Capt F. J. Walker's Second Support Group was carrying out an A/S sweep east-south-east of Newfoundland when *Kite* sighted a U-boat at 0212 which was evidently lining up to attack the escort carrier *Tracker*. *Kite* put the U-boat down in a snap attack, then *Starling* held contact until dawn since Walker did not wish to risk a collision with the ships of the group manoeuvring in close company in the dark. At 0718 *Woodcock* began a creeping attack, and at 0733 underwater explosions were heard and wreckage, including a German torpedo, came to the surface.

U842	*Launched* 14 Nov 1942	*Commissioned* 1 Mar 1943
Class	Type IXC/40	
CO	*Kapitänleutnant* H. Heller (lost)	
Date of loss	6 November 1943	
Location	N Atlantic, 43°42'N 42°08'W	
Cause	Depth charge	
Casualties	56	
Survivors	None	
Salvaged	No	

Notes Some hours after the sinking of *U226*, the 2nd SG was in radar contact with another U-boat and proceeded towards the spot at best speed while air support from Newfoundland and aircraft from *Tracker* kept the U-boat down. *Wild Goose* obtained an asdic contact at 1347 and this contact was attacked by *Starling* at 1404. When this proved unsuccessful Walker directed *Wild Goose* in a creeping attack in which only ten of the 25 depth charges were fired. Incandescent with rage, Walker stamped on his cap and was about to send a blistering signal to *Wild Goose* when an underwater explosion brought human remains, wreckage, oil and part of a German torpedo to the surface. As Walker wrote in his Report of Proceedings, 'I would have staked my last penny that that attack was bum (and I should have lost my money).'

U707	*Launched* 18 Dec 1941	*Commissioned* 1 Jul 1942
Class	Type VIIC	
CO	*Oberleutnant zur See* Gretschel (lost)	
Date of loss	9 November 1943	
Location	Atlantic, NE of the Azores, 40°31'N 20°17'W	
Cause	Air attack	
Casualties	51	
Survivors	None	
Salvaged	No	

Notes *U707* was stalking convoy MKS.29A when she was attacked and sunk by Fortress 'J' of

No 220 Squadron RAF flying from the Azores. This was the first occasion on which aircraft based on the Azores (a possession of Britain's oldest ally, Portugal) had sunk a U-boat.

	Launched	*Commissioned*
U966	14 Jan 1943	4 Mar 1943
Class	Type VIIC	
CO	*Oberleutnant zur See* E. Wolf	
Date of loss	10 November 1943	
Location	Atlantic, NW of Cape Ortegal, 44°00'N 08°30'W	
Cause	Air attack/grounding	
Casualties	8	
Survivors	?	
Salvaged	No	

Notes *U966* was sighted at 0409 by Wellington 'B' of No 612 Squadron, flown by WO I. D. Gunn. The aircraft attacked, dropping six Mk XI depth charges, and exchanged gunfire with the submarine. *U966* sustained damage to her periscopes, motors, clutches and shafts. However the damage was restored sufficiently for the boat to dive. Wellington 'T' of No 407 Squadron was diverted to the position but was shot down by the U-boat. The bodies of the six crewmen were recovered, but since they were not brought ashore their ultimate fate is unknown. At 0859 *U966* was sighted by Liberator 'R' of VP-105 USN, which made two unsuccessful attacks. On each run the depth charges failed to release since the aircraft's bomb bay had been damaged by flak. Liberators 'E' of VP-103 and 'E' of VP-110 joined the fray, delivering depth-charge attacks at 1150 and 1315. Finally, at 1345 Liberator 'D' of No 311 (Czech) Squadron RAF, flown by Flt Sgt Zanta, attacked the submarine with rockets.

U966 was now badly damaged, with water in the engine room rising as far as the clutches, and was unable to dive. Wolf decided to scuttle the boat had head for neutral Spain. Accordingly *U966* was blown up by her crew in 53m of water, two miles off the Spanish coast south-east of Punta de la Estaca de Bares at about 1600. A depth charge from one of the aircraft which had lodged in a ballast tank was set off by the scuttling charges. Some of the crew swam ashore while others were picked up by Spanish fishing boats—and were photographed by Catalina 'P' of No 202 Squadron RAF. The five dead from *U966* were buried on 12 November in El Barquero.

The crew were accommodated in hotels in El Ferrol while the Spanish government debated their status. There was some question as to whether *U966*'s survivors were combatants who should be interned or shipwrecked mariners who should be released. The German government lobbied hard for the latter view but on 30 November the German government was notified that *U966*'s survivors were liable to internment. The Spanish claim, which was supported by three independent legal assessors, was that the submarine had entered Spanish waters in an undamaged state and had continued to engage her assailants from there, which precluded her crew from being treated as shipwrecked. The Germans protested but on 21 December the crew were placed in an internment camp. However, eight were smuggled across the border to occupied France with the tacit understanding of the Spanish Admiralty.

	Launched	*Commissioned*
U508	30 Jul 1941	20 Oct 1941
Class	Type IXC	
CO	?	
Date of loss	12 November 1943	
Location	Atlantic, N of Cape Ortegal, 46°00'N 07°40'W	
Cause	Air attack	
Casualties	57	
Survivors	None	
Salvaged	No	

Notes Sunk by Liberator 'C' of VB-103, flown by Lt (jg) R. B. Brownell USNR, 95 miles north of Cape Penas. On sighting the U-boat Brownell sent a flash report but nothing was heard thereafter. The next day a search of the area revealed two oil slicks five miles apart. It was assumed that, although the Liberator had been successful, she had fallen victim to the U-boat's flak.

	Launched	*Commissioned*
U280	4 Jan 1943	13 Feb 1943
Class	Type VIIC	
CO	*Kapitänleutnant* Walter Hungershausen (lost)	
Date of loss	16 November 1943	
Location	Atlantic, N of the Azores, 49°11'N 07°30'W	
Cause	Air attack	

Casualties 49
Survivors None
Salvaged No

Notes Sunk by Liberator 'M' of No 86 Squadron RAF flown by Fg Off J. H. Brookless RAAF. The aircraft was flying ahead of convoy HX.265 when a U-boat was sighted and attacked. The first attack was carried out through heavy flak which destroyed the port outer engine. The depth charges all overshot, so Brookless came round for a second run. This time the Liberator's nose gunner managed to suppress the flak and the depth charges only slightly overshot. After the explosions subsided the boat could seen sinking by the stern without any forward motion.

	Launched	*Commissioned*
U718	26 Mar 1943	25 Jun 1943

Class Type VIIC
CO *Oberleutnant zur See* Wieduwilt (lost)
Date of loss 18 November 1943
Location Baltic, N of Bornholm, 55°21'N 15°24'E
Cause Collision
Casualties 43
Survivors None
Salvaged No

Notes Sunk in a collision with *U476* during training exercises. The exact circumstances of the collision are unknown.

	Launched	*Commissioned*
U211	15 Jan 1942	7 Mar 1942

Class Type VIIC
CO *Kapitänleutnant* Karl Hause (lost)
Date of loss 19 November 1943
Location Atlantic, NE of the Azores, 40°15'N 19°18'W
Cause Air attack
Casualties 54
Survivors None
Salvaged No

Notes Sunk by Wellington 'F' of No 179 Squadron RAF, flown by Fg Off D. M. McRae DFC RCAF. A radar contact was reported and the aircraft, flying ahead of the combined SL.139/MKS.30 convoy, went to investigate. Since there was a moon, McRae decided not to use the Leigh Light in the hope of taking the U-boat by surprise. Four depth charges were dropped which fell either side of the submarine, and the rear gunner reported two bright blue flashes after the depth charges had exploded. No wreckage or oil was sighted.

	Launched	*Commissioned*
U536	21 Oct 1942	21 Jan 1943

Class Type IXC/40
CO ?
Date of loss 20 November 1943
Location Atlantic, NE of the Azores, 43°50'N 19°39'W
Cause Depth charge
Casualties 38
Survivors 3 officers, 14 junior rates
Salvaged No

Notes The first U-boat sinking by an RCN support group. EG5 was covering the passage of the combined convoy SL.139/MKS.30 to the UK from African ports. The group joined the convoy on 19 November and had no sooner taken up their positions when a number of U-boat contacts were reported. Shortly after 2130 the frigate *Nene* reported a radar contact and chased after it, engaging it with gunfire and forcing the submarine to dive, whereupon contact was lost. Contact was then regained and unsuccessful attacks were carried out with Hedgehog and depth charges before contact was lost for a second time. This U-boat was *U648*, but the subsequent square search by the corvettes *Snowberry* and *Calgary* found *U536*, which had heard the attack on *U648*. The sudden detection by *Snowberry* took them by surprise, as did the depth-charge attack which followed. *Nene* and *Snowberry* then carried out repeated depth-charge attacks on the target. However, *U536* remained at depths below 500ft, which reduced the accuracy of the attacks.

Eventually *Snowberry* dropped a flare to mark the target's position and stood by with engines stopped, passing ranges to *Nene* which then delivered a full pattern on top of the flare. The boil had barely subsided when *U536* surfaced on *Snowberry*'s starboard beam. *Snowberry* was first to open fire, followed by *Nene* and *Calgary*. Before long *U536*'s casing was a shambles and the order to cease fire was given. The boat sank by the stern at 0247.

The Admiralty's assessment gave the credit to *Nene*'s final attack. However, testimony from the survivors revealed that *Snowberry*'s first attack had damaged the trimming system and it had not been possible to make repairs. The decision to surface had already been taken and *U536* was on the way up when *Nene* delivered her attack.

U768	*Launched*	*Commissioned*
	22 Aug 1943	14 Oct 1943
Class	Type VIIC	
CO	*Oberleutnant zur See* Buttjer (lost)	
Date of loss	20 November 1943	
Location	Baltic, exact position unknown	
Cause	Collision	
Casualties	49	
Survivors	None	
Salvaged	No	

Notes Sunk in a collision with *U745*, the exact circumstances of which are unknown.

U538	*Launched*	*Commissioned*
	20 Nov 1942	10 Feb 1943
Class	Type IXC/40	
CO	*Kapitänleutnant* Johann Ebert Gossler (lost)	
Date of loss	21 November 1943	
Location	Atlantic, SW of Ireland, 45°40'N 19°35'W	
Cause	Depth charge	
Casualties	55	
Survivors	None	
Salvaged	No	

Notes The second 'kill' by a British DE. *U538* was sunk by HMS *Foley* and HMS *Crane* of SG7 during operations in support of convoy SL.139/MKS.30.

U648	*Launched*	*Commissioned*
	17 Sept 1942	12 Nov 1942
Class	Type VIIC	
CO	*Oberleutnant zur See* Peter Stahl (lost)	
Date of loss	23 November 1943	
Location	Atlantic, NE of the Azores, 42°40'N 20°37'W	
Cause	Depth charge	
Casualties	50	
Survivors	None	
Salvaged	No	

Notes Sunk in a depth-charge attack by the frigate HMS *Blackwood* of EG4 during operations in support of convoys KMS.30/OG.5

U600	*Launched*	*Commissioned*
	16 Oct 1941	11 Dec 1941
Class	Type VIIC	
CO	*Kapitänleutnant* Bernhard Zurmuhlin (lost)	
Date of loss	25 November 1943	
Location	Atlantic, NE of the Azores, 41°45'N 22°30'W	
Cause	Depth charge	
Casualties	54	
Survivors	None	
Salvaged	No	

Notes Sunk in a depth-charge attack by the frigates HMS *Blackwood* and *Bazely* of EG4 during operations in support of convoys KMS.30/OG.5

U849	*Launched*	*Commissioned*
	31 Oct 1942	11 Mar 1943
Class	Type IXD2	
CO	*Kapitänleutnant* Heinz-Otto Schultze (lost)	
Date of loss	25 November 1943	
Location	S Atlantic, W of the Congo estuary, 06°30'S 05°40'W	
Cause	Air attack	
Casualties	63	
Survivors	None	
Salvaged	No	

Notes US Navy Liberators of VB-107 based on Ascension Island had been searching for a U-boat reported off St Paul's Rocks by the USS *Memphis* on 17 November. This was *U849*, outward-bound for Penang. Two Liberators found her on 25 November (Thanksgiving Day) and broke through cloud cover to achieve complete surprise. Lt (jg) Marion Dawkins straddled the submarine with six depth charges dropped from 25ft, one of which bounced and struck the Liberator's tail-plane. As Dawkins circled to observe results he saw the crew abandon the submarine as she settled by the stern before exploding. Dawkins dropped a life raft for the survivors. However, they were never picked up.

U542	*Launched*	*Commissioned*
	19 Jan 1943	7 Apr 1943
Class	Type IXC/40	
CO	*Oberleutnant zur See* Christian Coester (lost)	
Date of loss	28 November 1943	
Location	Atlantic, N of Madeira, 39°03'N 16°25'W	
Cause	Air attack	
Casualties	56	
Survivors	None	
Salvaged	No	

Notes Sunk in an attack by Wellington 'H' of No 179 Squadron RAF flown by Flt Sgt D. Cornish DFM. Radar contact was made in very bad weather at 0511. When the aircraft was a quarter of a mile away the Leigh Light was switched on to reveal a U-boat which immediately put up a heavy flak barrage. Nevertheless, Cornish succeeded in dropping six depth charges, four to starboard and two to port. The U-boat appeared to stop after the attack and then sank.

U86	*Launched*	*Commissioned*
	16 May 1941	8 July 1941
Class	Type VIIB	
CO	*Kapitänleutnant* Walter Schug (lost)	
Date of loss	29 November 1943	
Location	N Atlantic, 39°33'N 19°01'W	
Cause	Air attack	
Casualties	50	
Survivors	None	
Salvaged	No	

Notes *Bogue*'s task group were covering convoy UGS.24 when ordered to break off to hunt down promising contacts east of Bermuda. On the afternoon of 29 November, while the destroyers *Dupont* and *Badger* were investigating sonar contacts, Lt (jg) Bernard H. Volm USN sighted *U86* on the surface, 50 miles west of the carrier. Since the boat made no attempt to dive, Volm was content to shadow until six more aircraft arrived and sank her in a coordinated attack.

U172	*Launched*	*Commissioned*
	5 Aug 1941	5 Nov 1941
Class	Type IXC	
CO	*Oberleutnant zur See* Hermann Hoffmann (survived)	
Date of loss	13 December 1943	
Location	Atlantic, W of Canary Islands, 26°29'N 24°58'W	
Cause	Air attack	
Casualties	13	
Survivors	4 officers, 14 senior rates, 28 junior rates	
Salvaged	No	

Notes *Bogue*'s group had covered convoy GUS.23 before detaching to look for a refuelling rendezvous west of the Canary Islands. On 12 December Lt (jg) E. C. Gaylord USN sighted a fully surfaced U-boat four miles away. This was *U172*, outward-bound for the Indian Ocean and looking for *U219* to fuel from. Gaylord carried out a Fido attack, but although he saw the telltale explosion the submarine had not been sunk. Three more aircraft and the destroyers *Badger* and *Dupont* came to help and circled the oil slick left by the submarine. Although sonobuoys had been dropped they remained ominously quiet. Briefly the submarine broached, but the aircraft were all out of position, and before they could line up *U172* had disappeared again.

The two destroyers were now on the scene and conducted a series of depth-charge and Hedgehog attacks but without success. At 2120 *U172* surfaced and tried to creep off but was detected on *Badger*'s radar. The destroyer followed, and when the range came down to 6,000yds illuminated the scene with starshell. Three rounds of 3in were fired and the U-boat replied with an acoustic torpedo before diving. The destroyers delivered two more depth-charge attacks, which did considerable damage to *U172*. The destroyers were recalled at 0600 on the 13th but later that morning one of *Bogue*'s aircraft sighted a moving oil slick and the destroyers *Clemson* and *Osmond Ingram* (joined by *Badger*, which was unwilling to relinquish 'her' U-boat) were ordered to investigate. These destroyers carried out four more attacks and, unable to take any more, Hoffmann brought *U172* to the surface, where she was strafed by aircraft and shelled by the destroyers. *Ingram*'s CO wanted to ram but was restrained by *Bogue*, mindful of what had happened to *Borie*. In any case it was clear that most of the U-boat's crew were going over the side. Some diehards, however, elected to man the deck gun and scored one hit on the *Ingram*, killing one sailor. But it was an unequal duel. After being raked with gunfire by all three destroyers, *U172* was rocked by a heavy explosion, sank and then exploded underwater, suggesting that Hoffmann had set the scuttling charges.

	Launched	*Commissioned*
U391	5 Mar 1943	24 Apr 1943

Class Type VIIC
CO *Oberleutnant zur See* Gert Dultgen (lost)
Date of loss 13 December 1943
Location Bay of Biscay, 45°45'N 09°38'W
Cause Air attack
Casualties 51
Survivors None
Salvaged No

Notes Sunk by Liberator 'B' of No 53 Squadron RAF, flown by Sqn Ldr G. Crawford. The aircraft was searching for a U-boat reported by 'R' of the same unit. Despite the ASV radar not working satisfactorily, the U-boat was found and illuminated with the Leigh Light. The U-boat replied with accurate flak with damaged the Liberator. Crawford considered that the Leigh Light was aiding the German gunners as much as him, so he switched it off and attacked from up-moon with six depth charges which fell in a good straddle. As the aircraft overflew the spot it was difficult to see any sign of wreckage but two bodies were noticed. The radar then registered a contact which lasted for a moment—suggestive of the U-boat's bow or stern rising to the vertical before making the final dive.

	Launched	*Commissioned*
U593	3 Sept 1941	3 Oct 1941

Class Type VIIC
CO *Kapitänleutnant* Gerd Kelbing (survived)
Date of loss 13 December 1943
Location Mediterranean, off Djidjelli, 37°58'N 05°58'E
Cause Scuttled
Casualties None
Survivors 45
Salvaged No

Notes At 0710 on 12 December *U593* torpedoed the British destroyer *Tynedale*. HMS *Holcombe* and USS *Niblack* began a search, aided by three Wellington aircraft of Nos 36 and 458 Squadrons. After several hours with no contact made, the size of the search area was enlarged and the number of aircraft involved doubled. However, Kelbing proved to be a determined opponent for at 1445 he fired a T5 at *Holcombe* and sank her. The hunt continued until the morning of 13 December, when a Wellington attacked the submarine but was driven off by flak. The search went on until 1408, when the destroyer USS *Wainwright* found the submarine on sonar and started a number of depth-charge attacks, supported by HMS *Calpe*. *U593* was finally blown to the surface, where she was abandoned.

	Launched	*Commissioned*
U73	27 July 1940	30 Sept 1940

Class Type VIIB
CO *Oberleutnant zur See* Horst Deckert (survived)
Date of loss 16 December 1943
Location Mediterranean, NW of Oran, 36°09'N 00°50'W
Cause Depth charge/gunfire
Casualties 16
Survivors 4 officers, 3 senior rates, 27 junior rates
Salvaged No

Notes On the afternoon of 16 December *U73* torpedoed the US merchant ship *John S. Copley* in convoy GUS.24. The destroyers *Niblack* and *Ludlow* were detached from the screen to search for the culprit, supported by two SOC floatplanes from the cruiser *Brooklyn* which was lying at Oran. At 1715 the destroyers *Wolsey*, *Trippe* and *Edison* took over the hunt and an hour later *Wolsey* had a firm sonar contact. The contact disappeared, but was then reacquired and attacked with depth charges. At 1937 *Wolsey* and *Trippe* reported a radar contact dead ahead at less than a mile. This was *U73* surfacing and hoping to make her escape under cover of darkness. It was to no avail. Pursued by the destroyers, *U73* eventually sank after being hit by a number of 5in shells. Her crew were rescued and taken to Oran which, by coincidence, was where the *John S. Copley* had been towed for repairs.

	Launched	*Commissioned*
U850	7 Dec 1942	17 Apr 1943

Class Type IXD2
CO *Fregattenkapitän* Ewerth (lost)

Date of loss	20 December 1943
Location	Atlantic, W of Madeira, 32°54'N 37°01'W
Cause	Air attack
Casualties	66
Survivors	None
Salvaged	No

Notes *U850* was heading for the Indian Ocean when she was spotted on the surface by an Avenger flown by Lt (jg) Wallace A. LaFleur of VC-19 flying from the carrier USS *Bogue*. LaFleur's first attack took the U-boat by surprise since no flak was returned, but the depth charges failed to release. On his second attack the depth charges fell short. Four more aircraft had been flown off by *Bogue* on receipt of LaFleur's contact report. However, *U850*'s gunners were intent on LaFleur's aircraft and were unaware of the approach of reinforcements until two Wildcats roared over in a strafing pass. A depth-charge attack by Ensign G. C. Goodwin caused the U-boat to slow and begin leaking oil. It was two Fidos dropped by LaFleur and Lt (jg) H. G. Bradshaw as *U850* began to dive which sealed the submarine's fate. One Fido struck near the stern on the starboard side while the other hit on the same side half way between the conning tower and the stern. The two explosions merged into one and *U850* sank stern first. *George E. Badger* and *DuPont* reached the scene later and recovered human remains, clothing, wooden wreckage and lifejackets.

U284

	Launched	*Commissioned*
	6 Mar 1943	14 Apr 1943
Class	Type VIIC	
CO	*Oberleutnant* Günther Scholtz (lost)	
Date of loss	21 December 1943	
Location	N Atlantic, 55°04'N 30°23'W	
Cause	Scuttling	
Casualties	None	
Survivors	49	
Salvaged	No	

Notes Damage (presumably flooding of the battery) in heavy seas on 16 December made it impossible for *U284* to return to France or continue her patrol. Accordingly, the crew was taken off and she was scuttled by *U629*.

U345

	Launched	*Commissioned*
	11 Mar 1943	4 May 1943
Class	Type VIIC	
CO	*Oberleutnant zur See* Ulrich Knackfuss (lost)	
Date of loss	13 December 1943	
Location	Baltic, Kiel	
Cause	Air attack	
Casualties	?	
Survivors	?	
Salvaged	No (see notes)	

Notes Damaged beyond repair in a daylight USAAF raid on Kiel. The boat paid off on 23 December 1943 and was selected for transfer to Britain following the German surrender but she was mined off Warnemünde on 27 December 1945 in position 54°15'N 12°00'E.

U645

	Launched	*Commissioned*
	3 Sept 1942	22 Oct 1942
Class	Type VIIC	
CO	*Oberleutnant zur See* Ferro (lost)	
Date of loss	24 December 1943	
Location	Atlantic, NE of the Azores, 45°20'N 21°40'W	
Cause	Depth charge	
Casualties	55	
Survivors	None	
Salvaged	No	

Notes *Card*'s group were returning to Horta in the Azores to fuel when they were detected by the *Luftwaffe*. As a result, BdU ordered *Gruppe Borkum* to head for the carrier's position. These messages were read by the Tenth Fleet, which informed Capt Isbell that ten U-boats were within 100 miles of his position. During the night of 23–24 December *Card*'s escorts pursued a number of contacts while the carrier herself narrowly missed being sunk by *U415*. The destroyer *Schenk* (Lt-Cdr Earl W. Logsdon USN) was pursuing one contact which fired a torpedo at her before diving. Logsdon dropped one nine-charge pattern which brought the submarine to the surface. As *Schenk* headed in, the submarine dived, so Logsdon ordered the dropping of a pattern set shallow. Two minutes after the last charge was dropped there was a deep rumbling explosion and a surge of oil on the surface.

1944

U426

	Launched	Commissioned
U426	6 Feb 1943	12 May 1943
Class	Type VIIC	
CO	*Kapitänleutnant* Christian Reich (lost)	
Date of loss	8 January 1944	
Location	Atlantic, NW of Cape Ortegal, 46°47'N 10°42'W	
Cause	Air attack	
Casualties	51	
Survivors	None	
Salvaged	No	

Notes Sunderland 'U' of No 10 Squadron RAAF was flying a Percussion T2 patrol when at 1154 a U-boat was sighted trimmed down some twelve miles on the starboard bow. As the aircraft turned to attack, the U-boat came to full buoyancy and opened fire, although the firing ceased when the Sunderland's front turret gunner opened up. On the first attack the depth-charge trolley failed to run out and the attack was aborted. Coming in for a second attack, the flying boat dropped six depth charges, straddling the stern. The boat then listed to starboard and appeared to sink by the stern. As the crew abandoned ship, the bows rose up in the air before disappearing in a large explosion. Some forty men were left in the water.

U757

	Launched	Commissioned
U757	14 Dec 1941	28 Feb 1942
Class	Type VIIC	
CO	*Kapitänleutnant* Deetz (lost)	
Date of loss	8 January 1944	
Location	Atlantic, SW of Cape Clear, 50°33'N 18°03'W	
Cause	Depth charge	
Casualties	49	
Survivors	None	
Salvaged	No	

Notes During the passage of convoy OS.64, *U757* was detected close to the outer screen. After eight attacks had been made by *Bayntun*, *Camrose*, *Snowberry* and *Edmunston*, the noise of tanks being blown was heard. The contact then faded and shortly afterwards an amount of wreckage came to the surface

---

U81

	Launched	Commissioned
U81	22 Feb 1941	26 Apr 1941
Class	Type VIIC	
CO	*Oberleutnant zur See* Johann Krieg	
Date of loss	9 January 1944	
Location	N Adriatic, Pola	
Cause	Air attack	
Casualties	2	
Survivors	44	
Salvaged	Raised on 22 April 1944, paid off and broken up	

Notes Sunk while alongside at Pola during a daylight raid by the USAAF.

UIT19

	Launched	Commissioned
UIT19	20 Mar 1943	26 July 1943
Class	Ex-Italian *Fluto* class	
CO	?	
Date of loss	9 January 1944	
Location	N Adriatic, Pola	
Cause	Air attack	
Casualties	?	
Survivors	?	
Salvaged	Raised 1944	

Notes An ex-Italian *Fluto* class submarine, taken over by the Germans on 9 September 1943 on the Italian Armistice. It is not known whether or not she was fully operational when she was sunk while alongside at Pola during a daylight raid by the USAAF. The wreck was taken in 1945 as a prize by the Yugoslavs, who commissioned her in 1949 as *Sava*. She finally paid off in 1971.

U231

	Launched	*Commissioned*
U231	1 Oct 1942	14 Nov 1942
Class	Type VIIC	
CO	*Kapitänleutnant* Wolfgang Wenzel (survived)	
Date of loss	13 January 1944	
Location	Atlantic, NW of the Azores, 44°15'N 20°38'W	
Cause	Air attack	
Casualties	7	
Survivors	5 officers, 13 senior rates, 25 junior rates	
Salvaged	No	

Notes Wellington 'L' of No 172 Squadron, flown by P Off W. N. Armstrong RCAF, was operating with EG6 when the crew sighted and attacked a fully surfaced U-boat. Armstrong attacked with three depth charges but the Wellington was damaged by flak and the rear gunner was seriously wounded, making it imperative that Armstrong return to Azores for medical assistance.

Nevertheless, *U231* was so badly damaged that Wenzel ordered her to be scuttled and the crew took to their dinghies. They were rescued the next day by the USS *Block Island*. Wenzel had attempted to shoot himself after *U231* had sunk: he survived the attempt and was rescued with the bullet lodged in the back of his neck.

U377

	Launched	*Commissioned*
U377	12 Aug 1941	2 Oct 1941
Class	Type VIIC	
CO	*Oberleutnant zur See* Gerhard Kluth (lost)	
Date of loss	c. 15 January 1944	
Location	Atlantic, N of the Azores	
Cause	?	
Casualties	52	
Survivors	None	
Salvaged	No	

Notes *U377* was most likely the victim of a T5 *Zaunkönig* acoustic torpedo which ran back on the firing submarine. The boat was engaged in operations against the US Navy TG.21.16 miles north of the Azores. On 14 January the US destroyers *Bulmer* and *Parrott*, supported by a Fortress of No 206 Squadron, attacked a U-boat and it is often thought that *U377* was the victim of these attacks. The real victim was *U382*, which managed to return to Wilhelmshaven though badly damaged.

Twenty-four hours after these attacks *U377* reported that that she had unsuccessfully attacked TG.21.16. Shortly after that a corrupt message was received by BdU (on the 'Diana' frequency used by U-boats on operations) to the effect that the originator had been hit by a torpedo and was sinking.

The signal was adjudged to have come from *U377*, which was never heard from again. This was unusual given that *U377* was in contact with a task group and could reasonably have been expected to send further reports. The fact that no claims for her sinking were made by TG.21.16 supports this theory. The most likely scenario for her loss that she fired a Gnat at an escort which then ran rogue and homed in on her own hull noises. Nevertheless, the possibility that the submarine was lost by accident resulting either from equipment failure or from drill failure cannot be discounted.

U972

	Launched	*Commissioned*
U972	22 Feb 1943	8 Apr 1943
Class	Type VIIC	
CO	*Oberleutnant zur See* Klaus-Dietrich König (lost)	
Date of loss	c. 15 January 1943	
Location	Atlantic, position unknown	
Cause	Unknown	
Casualties	49	
Survivors	None	
Salvaged	No	

Notes The possibility that *U972* was lost as a result of an accident arising from equipment or drill failure cannot be ruled out.

U544

	Launched	*Commissioned*
U544	17 Feb 1943	5 May 1943
Class	Type IXC/40	
CO	*Kapitänleutnant* Willi Mattke (lost)	
Date of loss	16 January 1944	
Location	Atlantic, NW of the Azores, 40°30'N 37°20'W	
Cause	Air attack	
Casualties	57	
Survivors	None	
Salvaged	No	

Notes Late in the afternoon of the 16th, Ensigns Bert J. Hudson and William M. McLane, flying from the escort carrier USS *Guadalcanal*, sighted *U544*, *U516* and *U129* at a fuelling rendezvous, the position of which had been signalled to the carrier. *U129* dived immediately but the other two boats were coupled together by fuelling hoses. Hudson attacked from the starboard beam, firing two rocket salvos in quick succession. When he was virtually on top of *U544* he dropped two depth charges and fired another two rockets which punctured the pressure hull, causing extensive damage. Following hard on his heels came McClane, again using rockets and depth charges together (a combination frowned on by CinCLant on account of the differing trajectories of the weapons). As *U516* dived to safety, *U544* sank by the stern, leaving twenty-plus survivors struggling in a rapidly spreading oil slick. Though *Guadalcanal* detached two of her DEs to search for the survivors, none was rescued.

	Launched	*Commissioned*
U305	25 Jul 1942	17 Sept 1942

Class Type VIIC
CO *Kapitänleutnant* Rudolf Bahr (lost)
Date of loss 17 January 1944
Location N Atlantic, SW of Cape Clear, 49°39'N 20°10'W
Cause Depth charge
Casualties 51
Survivors None
Salvaged No

Notes Sunk in a depth-charge attack by HM Ships *Wanderer* and *Geranium*.

	Launched	*Commissioned*
U641	6 Aug 1942	24 Sept 1942

Class Type VIIC
CO *Kapitänleutnant* Rendtel (lost)
Date of loss 19 January 1944
Location Atlantic, SW of Cape Clear, 50°25'N 18°49'W
Cause Depth charge
Casualties 50
Survivors None
Salvaged No

Notes Sunk in a Hedgehog attack by the corvette HMS *Violet* during the passage of convoy OS.65. *Violet*'s first attack was unsuccessful, but the second produced a number of explosions.

	Launched	*Commissioned*
U263	18 Mar 1942	6 May 1942

Class Type VIIC
CO *Kapitänleutnant* Kurt Nolke (lost)
Date of loss 20 January 1944
Location Bay of Biscay, off La Pallice, 46°10'N 01°14'W
Cause Mine
Casualties 51
Survivors None
Salvaged No

Notes Lost on an air-dropped mine laid during one of the RAF's 'Gardening' sorties.

	Launched	*Commissioned*
U271	29 Jul 1942	23 Sept 1942

Class Type VIIC
CO *Kapitänleutnant* Kurt Barleben (lost)
Date of loss 28 January 1944
Location N Atlantic, W of Limerick, 53°15'N 15°52'W
Cause Air attack
Casualties 51
Survivors None
Salvaged No

Notes Sunk in an attack by Liberator 'E' of VB-103 flown by Lt C. A. Enloe USN. The aircraft was flying in support of convoys SC.151 and ON.221 when a U-boat was sighted. Enloe attacked from out of the sun and dropped six depth charges. When the explosions subsided the U-boat could be seen stopped, settling by the stern and surrounded by air bubbles. The boat then sank stern first, leaving oil and more air bubbles on the surface.

	Launched	*Commissioned*
U571	4 Apr 1941	22 May 1941

Class Type VIIC
CO *Oberleutnant zur See* Lussow (lost)
Date of loss 28 January 1944
Location W of Ireland, SW of Blacksod Bay, 52°41'N 14°27'W
Cause Air attack
Casualties 52
Survivors None
Salvaged No

Notes Sunk in an air attack by Sunderland 'D' of No 461 Squadron RAAF flown by Flt Lt R. D. Lucas RAAF. A radar contact was followed by the visual sighting of a U-boat, which was attacked through a barrage of flak. After the second attack the U-boat exploded, leaving nothing but wreckage and a number of survivors in the water.

U314

	Launched	*Commissioned*
	17 Apr 1943	11 Jun 1943

Class: Type VIIC
CO: *Kapitänleutnant* Georg Wilhelm Basse (lost)
Date of loss: 30 January 1944
Location: Arctic, N of North Cape, 73°45'N 26°15'E
Cause: Depth charge
Casualties: 49
Survivors: None
Salvaged: No

Notes Sunk by the destroyers HMS *Whitehall* and *Meteor* during the passage of convoy JW.56B to the Kola Inlet.

U364

	Launched	*Commissioned*
	21 Jan 1943	3 May 1943

Class: Type VIIC
CO: *Oberleutnant zur See* Paul Heinrich Sass (lost)
Date of loss: 30 January 1944
Location: Bay of Biscay, 45°25'N 05°15'W
Cause: Air attack
Casualties: 49
Survivors: None
Salvaged: No

Notes Sunk in an attack by Wellington 'K' of No 172 Squadron RAF flown by Flt Sgt L. D. Richards. Although the attack on *U364* was successful, the aircraft was so severely damaged by flak that it crashed in the sea. The crew were either all killed on impact or died in their dinghy while awaiting rescue.

U592

	Launched	*Commissioned*
	20 Aug 1941	16 Oct 1941

Class: Type VIIC
CO: *Oberleutnant zur See* Jaschke (lost)
Date of loss: 31 January 1944
Location: Atlantic, W of Cape Clear, 50°20'N 17°29'W
Cause: Depth charge
Casualties: 49
Survivors: None
Salvaged: No

Notes The 2nd Support Group (Senior Officer Captain F. J. Walker RN) were operating southwest of Ireland with the escort carriers *Nairana* and *Activity* in response to intelligence that three groups of U-boats were deployed in the area through which convoys SL.47 and MKS.38 would be passing. Shortly after 1015 on 31 January the carriers turned into wind to launch their aircraft and at that moment *Wild Goose* picked up an asdic contact. Immediately speed was reduced (to avoid attracting a Gnat), while at the same time *Wild Goose* attacked in order to discourage the U-boat from making an attack on the carriers. After the first depth charges had been dropped *Magpie* carried out a Hedgehog attack which was unsuccessful. *Wild Goose* then directed *Starling* into an attack which was also unsuccessful, so Walker settled down to a long hunt.

Directed by *Wild Goose*, *Starling* dropped a full pattern of depth charges and just after the fourteenth charge had left the rails there was a massive double explosion. The first was the detonation of the depth charges set to explode at 700ft but the second was considerably greater and threw up a huge column of water not ten yards from *Starling*'s starboard quarter. Tons of water cascaded over the ship, but the depth-charge crews continued to launch the rest of the pattern. *Wild Goose* was just about to carry out a follow-up attack when the asdic reported hull banging noises and two more explosions. Oil, wood, clothes, papers (which identified the boat as *U592*) and human remains then came to surface and were collected by *Wild Goose*. The asdic team then listened as the echo faded while *U592* began her descent to the bottom some 2,500 fathoms below.

U854

	Launched	*Commissioned*
	5 Apr 1943	19 July 1943

Class: Type IXC/40
CO: *Kapitänleutnant* Weiher (lost)
Date of loss: 4 February 1944

Location	Baltic, N of Swinemünde, 54°44'N 14°16'E	
Cause	Mine	
Casualties	51	
Survivors	None	
Salvaged	Raised 18 November 1968 and broken up	

Notes Sunk by an Allied air-dropped mine.

	Launched	*Commissioned*
U177	1 Oct 1941	14 Mar 1942
Class	Type IXD2	
CO	*Korvettenkapitän* Heinz Bucholz (survived)	
Date of loss	6 February 1944	
Location	S Atlantic, W of Ascension Island, 10°35'S 23°15'W	
Cause	Air attack	
Casualties	50	
Survivors	2 officers, 10 senior rates, 2 junior rates	
Salvaged	No	

Notes Sunk in an attack by a Liberator of VB-107 flown by Lt (jg) C. I. Pinnell USN. The survivors were rescued by USS *Omaha*.

Under the command of *Korvettenkapitän* Robert Gysae, *U177* had been a very successful submarine. Bucholz was different character. His relentless drilling of the crew, with frequent punishments for mistakes, turned an efficient ship's company into a disaffected group of individuals. Good practice disintegrated, so that Pinnell's Liberator was able to appraoch to within less than a mile of *U177* before it was spotted (in good visibility). The attack took the U-boat by surprise and only those on the bridge and Bucholz, who was climbing up to the bridge when the alarm was given, survived.

	Launched	*Commissioned*
U762	21 Nov 1942	30 Jan 1943
Class	Type VIIC	
CO	*Oberleutnant zur See* Pietschmann (lost)	
Date of loss	8 February 1944	
Location	Atlantic, W of Cape Clear, 49°02'N 16°58'W	
Cause	Depth charge	
Casualties	51	
Survivors	None	
Salvaged	No	

Notes Sunk by ships of the Second Support Group. See the entry for *U734* below for details.

	Launched	*Commissioned*
U238	7 Jan 1943	20 Feb 1943
Class	Type VIIC	
CO	*Kapitänleutnant* Horst Hepp (lost)	
Date of loss	9 February 1944	
Location	Atlantic, SW of Cape Clear, 49°44'N 16°07'W	
Cause	Depth charge	
Casualties	50	
Survivors	None	
Salvaged	No	

Notes Sunk by ships of the 2nd Support Group. See the entry for *U734* below for details.

	Launched	*Commissioned*
U734	19 Sept 1942	5 Dec 1942
Class	Type VIIC	
CO	*Oberleutnant zur See* Blauert (lost)	
Date of loss	9 February 1944	
Location	Atlantic, 49 43'N 16 23'W	
Cause	Hedgehog	
Casualties	46	
Survivors	None	
Salvaged	No	

Notes During 8–9 February 1944 Walker's 2nd Support Group destroyed three U-boats (*U762*, *U238* and *U734*) in the space of fifteen hours. There were no survivors from any of the three boats and no clues gathered from the wreckage, so it is impossible to tell in what order they were lost. The details of the three sinkings are therefore presented here as a single narrative.

Following the loss of *U592* (q.v.), the carriers *Nairana* and *Activity* took position within convoy SL.47 to hide their presence from the Germans; decrypted signals showed that BdU was warning his U-boats about the presence of support groups in the area. This left Walker's 2nd SG operating independently, and during the night of 8–9 February, in conditions of poor visibility, *Wild Goose* sighted a U-boat on the surface about a mile away. *Wild Goose* immediately reduced speed and went bows-on to the U-boat. The U-boat dived but continued to approach *Wild Goose* after releasing an SBT, seemingly unaware of the sloop's presence. In fact the submarine passed down *Wild Goose*'s starboard side, so close that the 20mm Oerlikon gunner was able to empty a full drum at the head of the periscope.

Woodpecker now arrived to support *Wild Goose*, and both ships delivered an attack, during which *Woodpecker* dropped 22 depth charges. *Starling* then arrived on the scene and her asdic team could hear the sound of breaking-up noises, while through the light of a searchlight those on the bridge could see wreckage including tins, documents (which were picked up by *Woodpecker*'s seaboat for identification), clothing and human remains. 'Come over here and look at the mess you have made,' signalled Walker to *Woodpecker*.

Wild Goose then detected another U-boat by radar trying to break through the screen on the port side of the convoy while the previous attack was going on. The U-boat dived, releasing an SBT and firing a Gnat (which blew up at the end of its run) before settling down on a steady course. *Starling* arrived in support and directed *Wild Goose* in a creeping attack followed by a depth-charge pattern fired by eye on the position indicated by a flare dropped by *Wild Goose*. Some 25 minutes after the creeper breaking-up noises were heard. Another creeper was delivered, during which the U-boat fired a Gnat which detonated in *Starling*'s wake. The next attack was delivered while the U-boat was altering course, but it completed the job: there was a very heavy underwater explosion, followed by the usual debris coming to the surface.

Early in the morning of 9 February *Kite* was searching ahead of the convoy for a U-boat whose position had been fixed by HF/DF when she nearly collided with the submarine, which emerged from a fog bank less than half a mile away. Walker ordered *Magpie* to close *Kite* in support but could not proceed himself as *Starling* was dashing off in support of *Wild Goose*'s contact on the far side of the convoy. The U-boat dived as *Kite* engaged with her gun and dropped a single depth charge set shallow. Seconds later there was a tremendous explosion and *Kite* disappeared behind a column of water which rose higher than her masthead. It was feared that *Kite* had fallen victim to a Gnat fired by the U-boat. However, *Kite* reappeared—intact bar some badly bruised members of her crew on the upper deck. The U-boat had fired a Gnat on sighting the sloop but the prompt dropping of the depth charge had countered it. *Kite* now went on to the offensive, dropping three patterns at 30-minute intervals until *Magpie* arrived to launch a creeping attack. This was followed by another creeping attack, then a Hedgehog attack and two ten-charge patterns.

Asdic conditions were very bad with the U-boat contact continually fading. The U-boat's commander was extremely wily and his tactic of going slowly downwind and down-sea made it extremely difficult to hold the directing ship in position to control an attack. In what almost amounted to a state of exasperation, Walker ordered *Starling* to direct *Magpie* in a Hedgehog attack—a most unusual procedure. Nevertheless, the firing was followed by two sharp explosions, after which *Magpie* delivered a creeper, followed by *Starling* four minutes later. To everyone's surprise this makeshift attack produced all the grim detritus connected with a sunken U-boat. 'I was highly tickled by this hedge-hoggery', wrote Walker. 'Complicated instruments are normally deemed essential to score even occasional hits with this weapon; to get two bull's-eyes with someone else's Hedgehog 1,000 yards away is a ghastly fluke.' It had taken 252 depth charges and 48 Hedgehog bombs to sink this submarine.

The sinking of these three submarines represented a significant achievement for Walker and the officers and men under his command. The strain on the ships' companies during these attacks was enormous, thanks to the continual buffeting and shaking from depth-charge explosions and the never-ending fear of destruction by an acoustic torpedo.

	Launched	*Commissioned*
U545	3 Mar 1943	19 May 1943
Class	Type IXC/40	
CO	*Kapitänleutnant* Gert Mannesmann (survived)	
Date of loss	10 February 1944	
Location	Atlantic, W of the Hebrides, 58°17'N 13°22'W	
Cause	Air attack	
Casualties	1	
Survivors	48	
Salvaged	No	

Notes Flying from Limavady in Northern Ireland, Wellington 'O' of No 612 Squadron (P Off

M. Painter RAAF) obtained a radar contact at 2037 at a range of eight miles. Owing to bad weather the aircraft was some miles north of its intended track—which was very unfortunate for *U545*. The U-boat was clearly visible in the moonlight from one mile and four depth charges were dropped which landed in a perfect straddle. The radar contact was lost after the attack, but when the aircraft flew over the position the lights of men wearing their lifejackets could be seen in the water. The survivors were eventually picked up by *U714* and landed at St Nazaire.

Mannesmann subsequently commanded *U230* and *U2502* but was killed in an air raid on Hamburg in 1945.

U666	*Launched* 18 Jul 1942	*Commissioned* 26 Aug 1942
Class	Type VIIC	
CO	*Oberleutnant zur See* Wilberg (lost)	
Date of loss	10 February 1943	
Location	N Atlantic, 53°56'N 17°16'W	
Cause	Air attack	
Casualties	51	
Survivors	None	
Salvaged	No	

Notes Sunk by Swordfish 'A' from 842 NAS, HMS *Fencer*.

U283	*Launched* 17 Feb 1943	*Commissioned* 31 Mar 1943
Class	Type VIIC	
CO	*Oberleutnant zur See* Günther Ney (lost)	
Date of loss	11 February 1944	
Location	Atlantic, SW of Faeroe Islands, 60°43'N 12°50'W	
Cause	Air attack	
Casualties	49	
Survivors	None	
Salvaged	No	

Notes Wellington 'D' of No 407 Squadron RCAF, flown by Fg Off P.W. Heron, detected a submarine by radar dead ahead at a range of six miles. The submarine was visible when two miles away and the Leigh Light was switched on at 0410. A stick of six depth charges and a flame float were dropped from 60ft, and as the plumes subsided the rear gunner saw a dull red glow marking the submarine's position. Heron banked round to starboard towards the flame float for a second attack. The submarine was still on radar but not moving, then contact was lost as the submarine sank.

U283 had been attacked by 'N' of No 612 Squadron the previous day and had shot the aircraft down.

U424	*Launched* 28 Nov 1942	*Commissioned* 7 Apr 1943
Class	Type VIIC	
CO	*Oberleutnant zur See* Günther Lüders (lost)	
Date of loss	11 February 1944	
Location	N Atlantic, 50°00'N 18°14'W	
Cause	Depth charge	
Casualties	50	
Survivors	None	
Salvaged	No	

Notes After the dramatic events of 8–9 February Walker ordered *Woodpecker*, *Wild Goose* and *Magpie* to sweep back along the previous day's battlefields. In the middle watch (0000–0400) on the night of 11 February *Wild Goose* obtained an asdic contact despite the poor conditions with numerous fish echoes. The contact came at a time when the ships were altering course in succession from south to east, but *Wild Goose* attacked immediately. The U-boat manoeuvred constantly behind a screen of SBTs and neither *Woodpecker* nor *Wild Goose* could hold the target in continuous contact. Numerous attacks produced no result, and eventually both ships lost the target together. *Wild Goose* reacquired the target astern of her but it took a good deal of persuasion by the asdic team to force Weymss, *Wild Goose*'s CO, to attack. The contact improved as the ships ran in for the attack, and after the pattern had been dropped a series of underwater explosions was heard followed by the appearance of wreckage on the surface. On passing through the area that afternoon the ships steamed through a slick of oil six miles wide.

U738	*Launched* 12 Dec 1942	*Commissioned* 20 Feb 1943
Class	Type VIIC	
CO	*Oberleutnant zur See* Erich Hoffmann	

Date of loss	14 February 1944
Location	Baltic, off Gotenhafen (Gdynia), 54°31'N 18°33'E
Cause	Collision
Casualties	22
Survivors	?
Salvaged	Raised 3 March 1944 and subsequently broken up

Notes Sunk following a collision with the merchant ship SS *Erna*.

	Launched	*Commissioned*
UIT23	3 Dec 1939	3 Feb 1940
Class	Ex-Italian *Liuzzi* class	
CO	*Korvettenkapitän* Heinrich Schaffer	
Date of loss	14 February 1944	
Location	Strait of Malacca, 04°27'N 100°11'E	
Cause	Submarine attack	
Casualties	26	
Survivors	?	
Salvaged	No	

Notes The ex-Italian *Reginaldo Giuliani*, seized at Penang by the Germans on the Italian Armistice, was recommissioned as *UIT23* for cargo-carrying duties between Germany and the Far East. The boat was on her way back to Germany with a cargo of Malay tin—a strategically important material which was in very short supply in Germany—when she was sighted by HM Submarine *Tally-Ho* (Lt-Cdr L. W. A. Bennington DSO RN) on the surface dead ahead and proceeding at 14kts. Bennington altered course so that he was firing on a 90-degree track angle. As *Tally-Ho* answered the helm the U-boat disappeared into a bank of mist but reappeared some minutes later, whereupon Bennington fired three MkVIII** torpedoes before diving. One explosion was heard 2min 20sec after the firing of the third torpedo and the target's HE subsequently faded.

	Launched	*Commissioned*
U7	29 Jun 1935	18 Jul 1935
Class	Type IIB	
CO	*Oberleutnant zur See* Hans Schrenck (lost)	
Date of loss	18 February 1944	
Location	Baltic, W of Pillau, 54°25'N 19°50'E	
Cause	Accident	
Casualties	28	
Survivors	None	
Salvaged	No	

Notes Lost in a diving accident, the exact circumstances of which are unknown..

	Launched	*Commissioned*
U406	16 Jun 1941	22 Oct 1941
Class	Type VIIC	
CO	*Kapitänleutnant* Horst Dietrichs	
Date of loss	18 February 1944	
Location	Atlantic, SW of Cape Clear, 48°32'N 23°36'W	
Cause	Depth charge	
Casualties	12	
Survivors	4 officers, 11 senior rates, 26 junior rates	
Salvaged	No	

Notes The first of two kills within a 24-hour period by the frigate HMS *Spey*, SO's ship of the 10th Escort Group. Sweeping to starboard of convoy ONS.29, *Spey* obtained an asdic contact at 1523 at a range of 1,700yds. Contact was maintained until 'simultaneous echo' appeared on the main set, when ten depth charges set to 50ft and 140ft were dropped. The U-boat then surfaced in the middle of the pattern and was engaged with gunfire. *Spey* believed that one ten-charge pattern was not sufficient to sink the U-boat so she steamed across her bows to lay a shallow pattern all around her. In the event only half the pattern was dropped since it was evident that *U406*'s crew were abandoning the submarine.

	Launched	*Commissioned*
U386	19 Aug 1942	10 Oct 1942
Class	Type VIIC	
CO	*Oberleutnant zur* See Fritz Albrecht (survived)	
Date of loss	19 February 1944	
Location	Atlantic, 48°51'N 22°41'W	
Cause	Depth charge	
Casualties	33	
Survivors	2 officers, 16 junior rates	
Salvaged	No	

Notes Twenty-four hours later HMS *Spey* was en route to join convoy ON.224 when at 1426 another submarine was detected by asdic. *Spey* was fitted with the latest Type 147B asdic set which included a depth predictor and which showed the U-boat to be lurking at 350ft, and depth charges were set accordingly. After the first pattern the U-boat broke surface at a very steep angle. This boat, *U386*, had much more fight in her than *Spey*'s previous victim for not only was the frigate's fire returned but the U-boat made an attempt to escape on the surface. *Spey* closed and straddled the submarine with a shallow-set pattern, causing the boat to sink stern first.

U264	*Launched* 2 Apr 1942	*Commissioned* 22 May 1942
Class	Type VIIC	
CO	*Kapitänleutnant* Hartwig Looks (survived)	
Date of loss	19 February 1944	
Location	N Atlantic, 48°31'N 22°05'W	
Cause	Depth charge	
Casualties	None	
Survivors	6 officers, 9 senior rates, 36 junior rates	
Salvaged	No	

Notes This was the sixth U-boat to be sunk by Walker's 2nd Escort Group during its deployment in the Western Approaches in February 1944. *Woodpecker* detected the U-boat by asdic at 1016 and marked the spot with a flare while all ships slowed for fifteen minutes to allow any Gnats that had been fired to run their course. A long and persistent hunt followed until 1659, when the U-boat surfaced off *Starling*'s port quarter. During this period the U-boat had manoeuvred under cover of numerous SBTs, aided by poor asdic conditions. The ships exhausted their stocks of depth charges and at one stage Walker was reduced to looking over the side of *Starling*'s bridge as if he were searching for the submarine.

When the U-boat surfaced Walker ignored his standing orders about slowing, so as not to attract a Gnat, and presenting the smallest target to the U-boat. Instead he turned to ram at full speed while opening fire with every gun that could be brought to bear. Amid a hail of fire, *U264*'s crew abandoned the submarine after Looks had set the scuttling charges. Eventually the submarine sank stern first. Looks and his entire ship's company were picked up by *Starling*, *Wild Goose* and *Woodpecker*.

U264 was the first operational U-boat to be fitted with the snorkel underwater breathing device. The eleven members of her complement picked up by *Woodpecker* survived when that ship was torpedoed by *U256* on the same day.

The 2nd Escort Group returned to Liverpool on 25 February. Admiral Sir Max Horton, CinC Western Approaches, described their patrol as being 'One of the greatest cruises ... ever undertaken in this war by an Escort Group.' Walker was quick to give credit where it was due: 'The chief credit for this sock in the jaw for Dönitz should undoubtedly go to HMS *Wild Goose* [Lt-Cdr D. E. G. Wemyss DSC RN]. Of six kills, four were detected by *Wild Goose* and her action [in launching a snap attack on *U592*] saved *Nairana*.'

U257	*Launched* 19 Nov 1941	*Commissioned* 14 Jan 1942
Class	Type VIIC	
CO	*Kapitänleutnant* Heinz Rahe (lost)	
Date of loss	24 February 1944	
Location	Atlantic, N of the Azores, 47°19'N 26°00'W	
Cause	Depth charge	
Casualties	30	
Survivors	1 officer, 6 senior rates, 12 junior rates	
Salvaged	No	

Notes Sunk by HMCS *Weskesieu* while operating in support of convoy SC.153. This sinking was interesting because *Weskesieu*'s commanding officer was persuaded by his asdic team that the contact was genuine and so persisted with the hunt even though the Senior Officer of the 6th Escort Group was not convinced.

U713	*Launched* 23 Sept 1942	*Commissioned* 29 Dec 1942
Class	Type VIIC	
CO	*Oberleutnant zur See* Gosejakob	
Date of loss	24 February 1944	
Location	Arctic, NW of Lofoten Islands, 69°27'N 04°53'E	
Cause	Depth charge	
Casualties	36	
Survivors	?	
Salvaged	No	

Notes Sunk during the passage of convoy JW.57 to the Kola Inlet. The U-boat was detected on the surface by a Swordfish flying from HMS *Chaser* which called up the destroyer HMS *Keppel*. The latter sank the U-boat with depth charges.

U761	*Launched*	*Commissioned*
	26 Sept 1942	3 Dec 1942

Class Type VIIC
CO *Oberleutnant zur See* Horst Geider
Date of loss 24 February 1944
Location Strait of Gibraltar, 35°55'N 05°45'W
Cause Depth charge
Casualties Nine
Survivors ?
Salvaged No

Notes *U761* was sighted to the west of Gibraltar by Catalinas '14' and '15' of VP-63 which were equipped with MAD gear. HMS *Anthony* and *Wishart*, patrolling a mile away, saw the smoke float dropped by the Catalinas and joined the pursuit. Asdic contact was gained and after a hunt lasting about 40 minutes the aircraft were once again in contact. After a series of concerted attacks by the two ships, Catalina 'G' of No 202 Squadron and a Ventura of VB-127, the U-boat surfaced and exploded.

U601	*Launched*	*Commissioned*
	29 Oct 1941	18 Dec 1941

Class Type VIIC
CO *Oberleutnant zur See* Hansen
Date of loss 25 February 1944
Location Arctic, NW of Lofoten Islands, 70°26'N 12°40'E
Cause Air attack
Casualties 51
Survivors None
Salvaged No

Notes Catalina 'M' of No 210 Squadron, providing air cover to convoy JW.57, was flying at extreme range—750 miles—from its base at Sullom Voe in the Shetlands when it detected *U601* 250 miles north-west of the Lofoten Islands. Two depth charges were dropped: one landed off the starboard quarter while the other landed level with the conning tower on the port side. The U-boat sank in less than thirty seconds, leaving eight or ten men on the surface who were subsequently lost to sight in a snowstorm.

U91	*Launched*	*Commissioned*
	30 Nov 1941	28 Jan 1942

Class Type VIIC
CO *Kapitänleutnant* Heinz Hungershausen (survived)
Date of loss 26 February 1944
Location Atlantic, W of Cape Clear, 49°45'N 26°20'W
Cause Depth charge
Casualties 35
Survivors 3 officers, 2 senior rates, 11 junior rates
Salvaged No

Notes *U91* was detected by HMS *Gore*'s asdic at 2240 on 25 February and at 2302 was attacked and sent deep. Two creeping attacks by *Gore* and *Affleck* were made at 0041/26 and 0048/26. The Senior Officer, in HMS *Affleck*, was inclined to hold the contact till morning but the weather showed signs of deteriorating so he decided to proceed. *Affleck* and *Gore* each made two more attacks before the noise of a submarine's tanks being blown was heard. Shortly afterwards *Affleck* obtained a short-range radar contact. The U-boat was then sighted and, after a brief gun action, surrendered.

U851	*Launched*	*Commissioned*
	15 Jan 1943	21 May 1943

Class Type IXD2
CO *Korvettenkapitän* Hans Weingartner (lost)
Date of loss March 1944 (?)
Location Atlantic
Cause ?
Casualties 70
Survivors None
Salvaged No

Notes The possibility that the submarine was lost as a result of an accident arising from equipment or drill failure cannot be discounted.

U358	*Launched*	*Commissioned*
	21 Apr 1942	15 Aug 1942

Class Type VIIC

CO	*Kapitänleutnant* Rolf Manke (survived)
Date of loss	1 March 1944
Location	North Atlantic, 45°46'N 23°16'W
Cause	Gunfire/depth charge
Casualties	43
Survivors	1
Salvaged	No

Notes Contact had been made by HMS *Garlies* at 0507 on 29 February 1944 but the U-boat proved determined and cunning, constantly manoeuvring and changing depth throughout the 29th and most of 1 March with one or other of the frigates chasing her in contact most of the time. At 1920 on 1 March HMS *Gould* had just completed an attacking run and had lost contact with the U-boat which was off her port quarter. The next astern, HMS *Affleck*, had just acquired the contact when a sudden improvement in the echo was observed. The U-boat had come shallow and promptly torpedoed HMS *Gould*. In doing so her conning tower broke surface, and she was finished off by gunfire and depth charges by *Affleck*. Only one survivor was rescued as *Affleck* was rescuing *Gould*'s survivors and the other two frigates had had to depart to Gibraltar at 1505 to fuel. This was the longest recorded U-boat hunt, lasting over 38 hours, in which senior officers again resisted the temptation to disbelieve evidence offered by their asdic apparatus and were rewarded for their perseverance.

U709

	Launched	*Commissioned*
	14 Apr 1942	12 Aug 1942
Class	Type VIIC	
CO	*Oberleutnant* Rudolf Ites (lost)	
Date of loss	1 March 1944	
Location	Atlantic, N of the Azores, 49°10'N 26°00'W	
Cause	Depth charge	
Casualties	52	
Survivors	None	
Salvaged	No	

Notes On the evening of 29 February an TBF/FM-2 team from the USS *Block Island* sighted a periscope feather only twenty miles from the carrier. Contact was maintained by sonobuoys while the five escorts conducted sonar searches. Just after 2100 the DE *Bronstein* illuminated a U-boat on the surface—a very surprised *U709*, whose commanding officer had been concentrating on *Thomas* and *Bostwick* and was unaware that *Bronstein* had closed him. *U709* dived quickly, her descent hastened by a barrage of gunfire, two Hedgehog salvos from Bronstein and more Hedgehogs and depth charges from *Thomas* and *Bostwick*. The DEs began a 'hunt to exhaustion' which culminated on the morning of 1 March with a deep-set pattern from *Thomas*. Following the explosions, breaking-up noises were heard and wreckage appeared on the surface.

U603

	Launched	*Commissioned*
	16 Nov 1941	2 Jan 1942
Class	Type VIIC	
CO	*Kapitänleutnant* Joachim Bertelsmann (lost)	
Date of loss	1 March 1944	
Location	Atlantic, N of the Azores, 48°55'N 26°10'W	
Cause	Depth charge	
Casualties	51	
Survivors	None	
Salvaged	No	

Notes *U603* was moving in on *Block Island* while *U709* was being dealt with. Although *Bronstein* was a newly worked-up ship on her first deployment, her sonar operators picked up the noise of another U-boat despite the noises associated with the destruction of *U709*. Bronstein dropped several patterns of depth charges and was rewarded at 0122 on 1 March by a massive underwater explosion which shook the DE.

Lt Sheldon H. Kinney was later awarded the Legion of Merit for *Bronstein*'s role in the two sinkings.

U472

	Launched	*Commissioned*
	6 Mar 1943	26 May 1943
Class	Type VIIC	
CO	*Oberleutnant zur See Freiherr* von Forstner (survived)	
Date of loss	4 March 1944	
Location	Arctic, N of North Cape, 73°05'N 26°40'E	
Cause	Depth charge	
Casualties	22	
Survivors	27	
Salvaged	No	

Notes *U472* was sighted on the surface by Swordfish 'B' of 816 NAS embarked in HMS *Chaser* for the passage of convoy RA.57 from the Kola Inlet. The pilot, Sub-Lt P. J. Beresford RNVR, attacked and scored two hits with 'bombs' on the hull. The U-boat began to leak oil and her course became very erratic. Using an Aldis lamp, Beresford's observer, Sub-Lt Laing, called up the destroyer HMS *Onslaught* (Cdr the Hon. A Pleydell-Bouverie RN), which at once increased to full speed to close the position. When she was within range *Onslaught* opened fire with her 4.7in main armament but *U472* was already sinking. As the survivors clambered into their dinghies *Onslaught*'s crew rigged scrambling nets and lifelines. Last to leave was von Forstner, who unconcernedly climbed into his own personal dinghy. Despite the rescue work, only 27 of *U472*'s crew were plucked from the icy sea.

Forstner climbed over *Onslaught*'s rail unaided and defused a potentially hostile reception by a punctilious salute to the colours and to the destroyer's First Lieutenant. Two of *U472*'s crew later died and were buried at sea. Forstner accepted that *Onslaught* did not carry German colours and agreed that the two men should be buried beneath the White Ensign.

U366

	Launched	*Commissioned*
	16 Apr 1943	16 Jul 1943
Class	Type VIIC	
CO	*Oberleutnant zur See* Bruno Langenburg (lost)	
Date of loss	5 March 1944	
Location	Arctic, NW of North Cape, 72°10'N 14°45'E	
Cause	Air attack	
Casualties	50	
Survivors	None	
Salvaged	No	

Notes Sunk in a rocket attack by Swordfish 'F' of 816 NAS, flown by Sub-Lt Mason, from HMS *Chaser* during the passage of RA.57. The Swordfish sighted the U-boat 12 miles from the outer screen of the convoy at a range of six miles. The aircraft then climbed and manoeuvred so as to attack the U-boat from 90 degrees on her port side. At one mile Mason dived, firing his rockets when at 1,200ft. Three hits were observed aft of the conning tower. Two minutes later the U-boat's bows rose up and she sank stern first. Thirty survivors were seen floating in the water.

U973

	Launched	*Commissioned*
	10 Mar 1943	15 Apr 1943
Class	Type VIIC	
CO	*Oberleutnant zur See* Paepenmoller (lost)	
Date of loss	6 March 1944	
Location	Arctic, 70°04'N 05°48' E	
Cause	Air attack	
Casualties	49	
Survivors	2	
Salvaged	No	

Notes Sunk by Swordfish 'X' of 816 NAS from HMS *Chaser* during the passage of convoy RA.57. HF/DF indicated that this submarine was gaining bearing on the convoy, and when sighted by the Swordfish she was some fifteen miles ahead of the convoy. The Swordfish attacked, firing six rockets, of which one was seen to hit. White smoke was seen issuing from the place where the rocket had struck. The U-boat then began to weave an extremely erratic course before sinking bow first. Fifteen survivors were seen swimming in the water, only two of whom were later rescued by HMS *Boadicea*.

A common factor in the loss of *U472* and *U973* (apart from their both being sunk by rockets) was that they were outward-bound at the time of their loss and had considerable amounts of stores and provisions on board. The way that stores were crammed into every conceivable space made it extremely difficult for the crew to locate and plug the holes made by the RPs, with the result that both boats flooded very quickly.

U744

	Launched	*Commissioned*
	11 Mar 1943	5 Jun 1943
Class	Type VIIC	
CO	*Oberleutnant zur See* Heinz Blischke (lost)	
Date of loss	6 March 1944	
Location	Atlantic, 52°01'N 22°37'W	
Cause	Depth charge/scuttling	
Casualties	12	
Survivors	3 officers, 4 senior rates, 33 junior rates	
Salvaged	No	

Notes The destruction of *U744* was the culmination of one of the classic U-boat hunts of the Second World War. The C2 escort group—HMS *Icarus* and HMCS *Gatineau*, *Chaudière*, *Fennel*, *St Catherines* (SO: Cdr P.W. Burnett RN) and *Chilliwack*—were sweeping five miles ahead of convoy HX.280 on 4 March. U-boats were known to be in the area (*Icarus* had obtained HF/DF contacts), so it was no surprise when *Gatineau* obtained an asdic contact at 1000. From then until 1520 on 5 March ships of C2, joined by the Squid-equipped HMS *Kenilworth Castle* from the B7 group escorting the convoy, carried out an unrelenting series of twenty-four Hedgehog, depth charge and Squid attacks. *U744* proved a wily opponent by going deep, turning inside the escorts' turning circles and hiding in the disturbed water following each attack. By the afternoon of 5 March Burnett had expended every weapon in his armoury—over 291 depth charges—and there seemed no other option but to wait for the exhaustion of the U-boat. Inside the submarine the position was dire: the pressure hull was damaged and the engine base plates were fractured together with the cylinder blocks. Moreover, the crew were reaching the limits of their endurance. The submarine had been dived for over 24 hours and carbon dioxide levels were very high.

Finally Blischke decided to surface and at 1520Z the U-boat broached directly ahead of *Chilliwack*, which opened fire with every gun that would bear. However, fire was checked when it became apparent that *U744*'s crew were in no state to offer resistance. There then followed an unseemly race by the escorts to be the first to get a boat alongside the sinking submarine—a race that was eventually won by *Chilliwack*. However, the encounter was not without incident. The whalers from *Chilliwack* and *St Catherines* capsized in the heavy seas, leaving the task of rescuing friend and foe alike to a motor boat and whaler from *Chaudière* and to *Fennel*'s whaler. The thought of salvage was uppermost, but *U744* was clearly sinking in the rising seas so she was scuttled at 1830 on 6 March by a torpedo from *Icarus*.

U343

	Launched	*Commissioned*
	21 Dec 1942	18 Feb 1943
Class	Type VIIC	
CO	*Oberleutnant zur See* Wolfgang Rahn (lost)	
Date of loss	10 March 1944	
Location	Mediterranean, N of Bizerta, 38°07'N 09°41'E	
Cause	Depth charge	
Casualties	51	
Survivors	None	
Salvaged	No	

Notes Sunk in a depth-charge attack by the trawler HMS *Mull*.

U450

	Launched	*Commissioned*
	4 Jul 1942	12 Sept 1942
Class	Type VIIC	
CO	*Oberleutnant zur See* Boehme	
Date of loss	10 March 1944	
Location	Mediterranean, SE of Anzio, 41°11'N 12°27'E	
Cause	Depth charge	
Casualties	?	
Survivors	?	
Salvaged	No	

Notes Sunk in a depth-charge attack by HM Ships *Blankney*, *Exmoor*, *Blencathra* and *Brecon* and the USS *Madison*.

U625

	Launched	*Commissioned*
	15 Apr 1942	4 Jun 1942
Class	Type VIIC	
CO	*Oberleutnant zur See* Straub (lost)	
Date of loss	10 March 1944	
Location	Atlantic, W of Cape Clear, 52°35'N 20°19'W	
Cause	Air attack	
Casualties	53	
Survivors	None	
Salvaged	No	

Notes Sunk in an attack by Sunderland 'U' of No 422 Squadron RCAF (WO W. F. Morton RCAF). The aircraft was escorting convoy SC.154 when a U-boat was sighted at 1500. At the time of the sighting the aircraft was being flown by Flt Lt S. W. Butler RAF, who was on board since it was the crew's first operation. Butler attacked through flak to drop six depth charges which straddled the target. The U-boat dived, only to resurface three minutes later, its course slow and erratic. Even though the majority of the U-boat's crew abandoned the submarine and took to their dinghies (signalling 'Fine Bombing' to the Sunderland as they did so), they were not rescued.

	Launched	*Commissioned*
U845	22 Jan 1943	1 May 1943
Class	Type IXC/40	
CO	*Korvettenkapitän* Walter Weber (lost)	
Date of loss	10 March 1944	
Location	Atlantic, 48°20'N 20°33'W	
Cause	Depth charge/gunfire	
Casualties	10	
Survivors	45	
Salvaged	No	

Notes *U845* was trailing convoy SC.154 when she was spotted on the surface by the Canadian destroyer *St Laurent* (Cdr R. G. Stephen RCNR) and frigate *Owen Sound*, which were coming up to join the same convoy, having been detached to assist a straggling merchant ship. HF transmissions had been detected between the lagging ship and the convoy and the two ships were proceeding to investigate one of these when they sighted *U845*. The U-boat dived on being sighted and went deep, so deep that SBTs could not be fired. However Weber was hampered by the fact that he had just completed a long period submerged and had not been on the surface long enough to put a decent charge into the battery. Three depth-charge attacks were launched, followed by a Hedgehog attack and then a series of creeping attacks by *St Laurent* and the British destroyer *Forester*. All of this endeavour produced nothing in the way of a result, so Stephen resolved to wait until the moon rose and the frigate *Swansea* had joined in support.

As the three escorts were preparing to renew their attacks *U845* suddenly surfaced 400yds away and headed off at full speed (some estimate put her speed as 21kts, 3kts higher than rated) while opening fire with her flak armament. *St Laurent* headed off in pursuit, returning fire with radar-controlled gunnery from her forward 4in. *Forester* and *Swansea* followed, but it took them more time to work up to speed. Eventually *St Laurent*'s gunnery told and she surged past *U845*, firing every gun that would bear and dropping a pattern of shallow-set depth charges across the U-boat's track. By the time *St Laurent* turned it was all over and *Swansea* and *Forester* were picking up survivors. *U845*'s bridge and casing were a shambles, with Weber lying dead on the bridge. After the survivors had been picked up *U845* sank at 2348.

It had been a tremendous engagement, with *St Laurent* alone expending 119 rounds of 4in, 1,440 rounds of 20mm and some 1,500 rounds of other SA ammunition.

	Launched	*Commissioned*
U410	4 Oct 1941	23 Feb 1942
Class	Type VIIC	
CO	*Oberleutnant zur See* Fenski (survived)	
Date of loss	11 March 1944	
Location	Mediterranean, Toulon, 43°07'N 05°55'E	
Cause	Air attack	
Casualties	?	
Survivors	?	
Salvaged	No	

Notes Bombed and sunk while alongside at Toulon during a USAAF raid on the port.

	Launched	*Commissioned*
U380	15 Nov 1941	22 Dec 1941
Class	Type VIIC	
CO	*Kapitänleutnant* Albrecht Brandi (survived)	
Date of loss	11 March 1944	
Location	Mediterranean, Toulon, 43°07'N 05°55'E	
Cause	Air attack	
Casualties	1	
Survivors	?	
Salvaged	No	

Notes Bombed and sunk while alongside at Toulon during a USAAF raid on the port.

	Launched	*Commissioned*
UIT22	28 Oct 1939	?
Class	Ex-Italian *Liuzzi* class	
CO	*Oberleutnant zur See* Karl Wunderlich (lost)	
Date of loss	11 March 1944	
Location	S Atlantic, S of Cape of Good Hope, 41°28'S 17°40'E	
Cause	Air attack	
Casualties	43	
Survivors	None	

Salvaged No

Notes This submarine, the former Italian *Alpino Bagnoli*, had been taken over by the Germans at Bordeaux on 10 September 1943 for employment as a cargo-carrier between Europe and the Far East. It was while she was on her way out to the Far East that she was bombed and sunk by South African aircraft of No 226 and 279 Squadrons.

U575

	Launched	*Commissioned*
	30 Apr 1941	19 June 1941
Class	Type VIIC	
CO	*Oberleutnant zur See* Wolfgang Boehme (survived)	
Date of loss	13 March 1944	
Location	Atlantic, W of Cape Finisterre, 46°18'N 27°34'W	
Cause	Depth charge	
Casualties	18	
Survivors	5 officers, 10 senior rates, 22 junior rates	
Salvaged	No	

Notes *U575* was the second *Frontboot* to be fitted with a snorkel and had recently transmitted a lengthy signal about the latter's performance. It is possible that this signal was the cause of her undoing and that her location by *Bogue*'s aircraft was no accident.

It was while she was attempting to run on the surface during the night of 12–13 March that *U575* was located by *Bogue*'s radar-equipped aircraft (aided by HF/DF), which used sonobuoys to maintain contact until the DE *Haverfield* arrived on the morning of the 13th. As the hunt developed the frigate HMCS *Prince Rupert* was detached from escort group C3 which was covering convoy ON.227. She arrived to find *Bogue*'s aircraft circling along with Wellington 'B' of No 172 Squadron and Fortresses 'R' of No 206 and 'J' of No 220 Squadrons while *Haverfield* attacked. *Prince Rupert* then attacked with depth charges and Hedgehog before attempting to direct *Haverfield* in a creeper, but communications problems between ships of two navies not used to working together foiled the attempt. With the arrival of the DE *Hobson* a variation on the creeper was tried. *Haverfield* and *Prince Rupert* held *U575* in contact on either side at 1,200yds while *Hobson* went between to deliver the attack, and it was this attack which forced *U575* to the surface.

Few U-boats can have faced such a reception. She was engaged by all three ships with every gun that would bear, and one of *Bogue*'s Avengers from VC-95 attacked with rockets and cannon fire. Boehme sent BdU one last signal informing him of the situation before abandoning the submarine. The survivors were picked up by all three ships.

U653

	Launched	*Commissioned*
	31 Mar 1941	25 May 1941
Class	Type VIIC	
CO	*Oberleutnant zur See* Hans-Albrecht Kandlet (lost)	
Date of loss	15 March 1944	
Location	North Atlantic, 53°46'N 24°35'W	
Cause	Depth charge	
Casualties	51	
Survivors	None	
Salvaged	No	

Notes Walker's 2nd Support Group had just finished four days of intensive exercises with HMS *Vindex* when at 0115/15 the latter reported that her aircraft were in contact with a U-boat. HMS *Wren* closed the flare and marker dropped by the aircraft and was soon in contact, joined shortly afterwards by *Starling*, *Magpie* and *Wild Goose*. In contrast to some of Walker's earlier marathon hunts, *U653* was disposed of comparatively quickly. After *Starling*'s first ten-charge pattern, underwater explosions were heard and wreckage, including a headless German torpedo, appeared on the surface.

U392

	Launched	*Commissioned*
	10 Apr 1943	29 May 1943
Class	Type VIIC	
CO	*Oberleutnant zur See* Henning Schumann (lost)	
Date of loss	16 March 1944	
Location	Strait of Gibraltar, 35°54'N 05°45'W	
Cause	Depth charge	
Casualties	52	
Survivors	None	
Salvaged	No	

Notes Two PBY5s of VP-63 were carrying out MAD sweeps in the Strait of Gibraltar when one obtained a contact at 0853. Forty seven retro-bombs were dropped before the aircraft requested that the destroyer HMS *Vanoc* (which had been an interested spectator of events) attack. *Vanoc* found asdic conditions poor owing to currents and fish echoes and made an unsuccessful attack with Hedgehog. After this both *Vanoc* and the aircraft lost contact. EG1 then joined the action and *Affleck* attacked with Hedgehog. The attack produced three distinct explosions followed by breaking-up noises, and oil and wooden wreckage appeared on the surface. All ships were then shaken by a considerable underwater explosion, after which asdic contact faded.

U1013	*Launched* 19 Jan 1944	*Commissioned* 2 Mar 1944
Class	Type VIIC	
CO	*Oberleutnant zur See* Gerhard Lincke	
Date of loss	16 March 1944	
Location	Baltic, E of Rugen, 55°36'N 13°58'E	
Cause	Collision	
Casualties	25	
Survivors	2 officers, 24 ratings	
Salvaged	No	

Notes Sunk in a collision with *U286* during working-up exercises.

U28	*Launched* 14 Jul 1936	*Commissioned* 12 Sept 1936
Class	Type VII	
CO	*Oberleutnant zur See* Dietrich Sachse (lost)	
Date of loss	17 March 1944	
Location	Baltic, off Neustadt, 54° 07'N 10°50'E	
Cause	Accident	
Casualties	?	
Survivors	None	
Salvaged	Raised March 1944 and paid off 4 August 1944; details of subsequent disposal unknown	

Notes Lost in a diving accident, the exact circumstances of which are unknown.

U801	*Launched* 31 Oct 1942	*Commissioned* 24 Mar 1943
Class	Type IXC/40	
CO	*Kapitänleutnant* Hans-Joachim Brans (lost)	
Date of loss	17 March 1944	
Location	Atlantic, near Cape Verde Islands, 16°42'N 30°28'W	
Cause	Air attack	
Casualties	10	
Survivors	?	
Salvaged	No	

Notes On the morning of 15 March *U801* was detected on the escort carrier *Block Island*'s radar no more than eight miles away. However, haze caused by drifting dust from the Sahara prevented aircraft and ships from finding her, but the radar kept indicating that she was in the area. The next day, the 16th, Brans was conducting gunnery drills (a practice forbidden by BdU for boats on patrol) when two aircraft from *Block Island*'s VC-6 roared overhead in a strafing pass. The attack started a fire in ready-use AA ammunition and Brans submerged. Lt (jg) C.A. Wooddell dropped a Fido but to no effect. More Avengers were launched to relieve Wooddell and another Fido was dropped on noises reported by a sonobuoy.

During the night of 16/17 March Brans surfaced to report his plight to BdU. He had a number of wounded on board and needed fuel. A meeting with *U488* was arranged for the 20th.

At 0141 on the 17th *U801* was spotted by an Avenger heading west at 18kts. The submarine dived but surfaced again an hour later. Brans' determination to clear the area on the surface would cost him dear. At 0302 Lt (jg) Norman G. Dowty sighted *U801*'s periscope and dropped a Fido. There was no conclusive evidence of a hit but in fact the torpedo ruptured an external fuel tank and *U801* began to leave a large oil slick behind her. The slick was sighted when daylight came and a pattern of sonobuoys laid by Dowty and Lt (jg) Elefter confirmed that the submarine was still moving. Accordingly, the Avengers called up the destroyers *Corry* and *Bronstein*. At 0842 both destroyers were in sonar contact and over more than two hours launched eight attacks which turned the interior of *U801* into a shambles. Brans realised that his position was hopeless so he decided to surface and scuttle the boat.

As *U801* broke surface she was engaged by *Corry* and *Bronstein*. Brans and the *Obersteuermann* were killed as they emerged from the conning tower. The order to abandon *U801* had not been clearly given: most of the seamen in the fore ends only realised what was happening when they saw the telegraphists smashing the radio and cypher machine. The 1WO and 2WO simply leapt overboard, leaving the LI to get the crew out of the boat and over the side. Then the LI returned inside the boat to await the end, which came at 1124 when *U801* sank by the stern.

U1059	*Launched*	*Commissioned*
	12 Mar 1943	1 May 1943
Class	Type VIIF	
CO	*Oberleutnant zur See* Günther Leupold (survived)	
Date of loss	19 March 1943	
Location	Atlantic, SW of Cape Verde Islands, 13°10'N 33°44'W	
Cause	Air attack	
Casualties	47	
Survivors	8	
Salvaged	No	

Notes *U1059* was outward-bound for Penang with a cargo of torpedoes. Her commanding officer had been warned about the activities of US Navy escort carrier groups but nevertheless considered it safe enough to be able to order 'hands to bathe' on the morning of 19 March—an error of judgement which would cost him his command and his life. Some eighteen of the boat's company, including Leupold, were swimming when a TBM Avenger of VC-6 operating from USS *Block Island* and flown by Lt (jg) Norman T. Dowty and an FM-2 Wildcat flown by Lt (jg) William H. Cole roared out of the sky and attacked the submarine with machine guns. The aircrew had been looking for the Type XIV *U488* which sigint indicated was in the area but instead sighted the large *U1059* lying motionless on the surface.

After Cole had strafed the boat, Dowty attacked with two depth charges which fell astride the conning tower. The explosion lifted *U1059* out of the water and broke her back and she began to sink stern first with fires raging around the conning tower. Dowty came round for a second run and prepared to drop a Fido, but as he began to turn his aircraft suddenly ploughed into the water. Of the three crewmen only the gunner, Ensign Mark E. Fitzgerald, survived the crash. Fitzgerald managed to inflate his raft and was joined by three of *U1059*'s survivors (including Leupold) while another five of *U1059*'s crew clung to wreckage. At least seven others from the U-boat's crew abandoned the submarine but did so without lifejackets and either drowned or succumbed to sharks which were seen circling. Fitzgerald and the eight survivors from *U1059* were eventually rescued by the USS *Corry*.

Lt (jg) Norman T. Dowty was awarded a posthumous Navy Cross for this action.

U976	*Launched*	*Commissioned*
	25 Mar 1943	5 May 1943
Class	Type VIIC	
CO	*Oberleutnant zur See* Raimund Tiesler	
Date of loss	25 March 1944	
Location	Bay of Biscay, W of St Nazaire, 46°48'N 02°43'W	
Cause	Air attack	
Casualties	4	
Survivors	?	
Salvaged	No	

Notes Sunk by Mosquitos 'I' (Fg Off A. H. Hilliard) and 'L' (Fg Off D. J. Turner) of No 618 Squadron RAF. The aircraft sighted a U-boat off La Pallice escorted by a destroyer and two minesweepers. Turner made four and Hilliard one attack with the Tsetse gun. The 57mm shells punched through the thin pressure hull in the galley area and also into the battery, causing flooding. Chlorine gas began to fill the boat and she was abandoned. The survivors were rescued by the destroyer and minesweepers.

The two Mosquitos were trials aircraft equipped with the 57mm Tsetse gun. They were escorted by four Mosquitos of No 248 Squadron led by Flt Lt L. S. Dobson. However, wartime secrecy demanded that the ORB for No 248 Squadron make no mention of the two No 618 aircraft. Thus in most sources the loss of *U976* is credited to No 248 Squadron.

U961	*Launched*	*Commissioned*
	17 Dec 1942	4 Feb 1943
Class	Type VIIC	
CO	*Oberleutnant zur See* Klaus Fischer (lost)	
Date of loss	29 March 1944	
Location	Atlantic, N of Faeroe Islands, 64°31'N 03°19'W	

Cause	Depth charge
Casualties	49
Survivors	None
Salvaged	No

Notes HMS *Starling* was screening convoy JW.58 when at 2208 the asdic operator reported a contact at 1,900yds. *Starling* attacked first with two ten-charge patterns designed to keep the U-boat down and occupied while *Magpie* took station to execute a creeping attack. However, before *Magpie* could begin the attack breaking-up noises were heard, and at 2301 *Starling* was shaken by a very heavy underwater explosion. Shortly afterwards wreckage and oil came to the surface.

U961 was on passage to the Atlantic and may not even have been aware of 2EG's presence when she was attacked.

	Launched	*Commissioned*
U223	16 Apr 1942	6 Mar 1944
Class	Type VIIC	
CO	*Oberleutnant zur See* Peter Gerlach (lost)	
Date of loss	30 March 1944	
Location	Mediterranean, NE of Palermo, 38°54'N 14°18'E	
Cause	Depth charge	
Casualties	23	
Survivors	3 officers, 5 senior rates, 19 junior rates	
Salvaged	No	

Notes The destroyers *Laforey*, *Ulster* and *Tumult* were carrying out a routine A/S sweep when *Ulster* gained a firm asdic contact at 0450 on 29 March. The destroyers launched a series of depth-charge attacks until 1222, when *Ulster* was detached to Palermo having expended all her depth charges. Her place was taken by *Wilton*. At 1530 the destroyers *Hambledon* and *Blencathra* joined and the attacks continued. During the night the destroyers refrained from attacking and instead simply maintained contact, intending to resume the assault at daybreak. Maintaining contact was not easy: throughout the night the U-boat manoeuvred fast and evasively to either throw off her pursuers or break through the screen. At 0050 the sound of tanks being blown was heard, the U-boat surfaced and all ships opened fire. Almost simultaneously *Laforey* was hit by a torpedo and sank very quickly. In the confusion the U-boat tried to escape on the surface at 15kts—a futile exercise when pitted against two fleet destroyers and three escort destroyers. She finally sank by the stern at 0110, having been on the receiving end of 27 depth-charge and Hedgehog attacks.

	Launched	*Commissioned*
U355	5 Jul 1941	29 Oct 1941
Class	Type VIIC	
CO	*Korvettenkapitän* Günther La Baume (lost)	
Date of loss	1 April 1944	
Location	Arctic, W of North Cape, 72°49'N 30°41'W	
Cause	Air attack	
Casualties	52	
Survivors	None	
Salvaged	No	

Notes Sunk during the passage of convoy JW.58 to the Kola Inlet. *U355* was sighted on the surface by Avenger 'H' of 826 NAS embarked in HMS *Tracker*. The aircraft delivered a rocket attack which left the U-boat in a damaged state. The *coup de grâce* was administered by the destroyer HMS *Beagle*.

	Launched	*Commissioned*
U360	28 Jul 1942	12 Nov 1942
Class	Type VIIC	
CO	*Kapitänleutnant* Klaus Becker (lost)	
Date of loss	2 April 1944	
Location	Arctic, SW of Bear Island, 73°28'N 13°04'E	
Cause	Hedgehog	
Casualties	52	
Survivors	None	
Salvaged	No	

Notes During the night of 2/3 April HMS *Keppel* obtained an asdic contact while screening 25 miles from the convoy. A Hedgehog attack was launched and at least four explosions were heard; five minutes later there was a very violent underwater explosion. Oil and wreckage came to the surface. Among the wreckage recovered was a jar of coffee beans.

	Launched	*Commissioned*
U288	15 Apr 1943	26 Jun 1943
Class	Type VIIC	

CO	*Oberleutnant zur See* Willi Meyer (lost)
Date of loss	3 April 1944
Location	Arctic, N of North Cape, 73°44'N 13°04'E
Cause	Air attack
Casualties	49
Survivors	None
Salvaged	No

Notes Early on 3 April the last of the three U-boats sunk during the passage of JW.58 was sighted by the dawn air patrol. The U-boat's gunners were very alert and shot the sighting Swordfish down. However, the aircraft had summoned help and Swordfish 'C' of 819 NAS from *Activity* and Avengers 'G' and 'Y' of 826 NAS in *Tracker* were soon on the scene. Meyer seemed determined to fight it out on the surface and to eliminate the threat of rocket attack by keeping his stern towards the aircraft at all times (thereby presenting a much smaller target and allowing most of his flak armament to bear). After all three aircraft had made attacks, the U-boat sank horizontally before reappearing and sinking once again, leaving wreckage on the surface. The 2nd Support Group was quickly on the scene and found Meyer's cap with its distinctive white cover floating in the oil.

U302

	Launched	*Commissioned*
	25 Apr 1942	16 Jun 1942
Class	Type VIIC	
CO	*Kapitänleutnant* Herbert Sickel (lost)	
Date of loss	6 April 1944	
Location	Atlantic, NW of the Azores, 45°05'N 35°11'W	
Cause	Depth charge	
Casualties	51	
Survivors	None	
Salvaged	No	

Notes Sickel had made a very successful attack on convoy SC.156. He had penetrated the screen and sunk two merchant ships, the *Ruth 1* and the *South America*. Coming out of the convoy, he was detected by HMS *Swale*'s radar and forced to dive. Having shown himself so enterprising in attack, Sickel was curiously passive about the defence of his own boat. He made no attempt to fire an acoustic torpedo at *Swale*, nor did he use SBTs or employ any kind of evasive manoeuvring. Instead he dived to 450ft and remained at that depth on a steady course. HMS *Swale* made two Hedgehog attacks and on the second was rewarded with three explosions. Some minutes later there was a large, muffled underwater explosion.

U455

	Launched	*Commissioned*
	21 Jun 1941	21 Aug 1941
Class	Type VIIC	
CO	*Kapitänleutnant* Hans-Martin Scheibe (lost)	
Date of loss	6 April 1944	
Location	Mediterranean, off La Spezia, 44°04'N 09°51'E	
Cause	?	
Casualties	51	
Survivors	None	
Salvaged	No	

Notes Possibly lost in an Axis minefield off the port of La Spezia, but the the boat may have sunk by accident arising from mechanical or drill failure.

U856

	Launched	*Commissioned*
	11 May 1943	19 Aug 1943
Class	Type IXC/40	
CO	*Oberleutnant zur See* Dietrich Wittenberg (survived)	
Date of loss	7 April 1944	
Location	North Atlantic, S of Sable Island, 40°18'N 62°22'W	
Cause	Depth charge	
Casualties	27	
Survivors	3 officers, 6 senior rates, 19 junior rates	
Salvaged	No	

Notes Sunk in a depth-charge attack by the USS *Champlin* and *Huse*.

U2

	Launched	*Commissioned*
	1 Jul 1935	25 Jul 1935
Class	Type IIA	
CO	*Oberleutnant zur See* H. Frose (lost)	
Date of loss	8 April 1944	
Location	Baltic, W of Pillau, exact position unknown	
Cause	Collision	
Casualties	16	

Survivors 9
Salvaged Raised and paid off; details of final disposal unknown

Notes Sunk in a collision with the steam trawler *Hinrich Freese*, the exact circumstances of which are unknown.

U962

	Launched	*Commissioned*
	17 Dec 1942	11 Feb 1943

Class Type VIIC
CO *Oberleutnant zur See* Ernst Liesberg (lost)
Date of loss 8 April 1944
Location Atlantic, NE of the Azores, 45°43'N 19°57'W
Cause Depth charge
Casualties 50
Survivors None
Salvaged No

Notes Sunk in a depth-charge attack by HMS *Crane* and *Cygnet*.

U515

	Launched	*Commissioned*
	2 Dec 1941	21 Feb 1942

Class Type IXC
CO *Kapitänleutnant* Werner Henke (survived)
Date of loss 9 April 1944
Location Atlantic, N of Madeira, 34°35'N 19°18'W
Cause Air attack/depth charge/gunfire
Casualties 16
Survivors 43
Salvaged No

Notes *U515* had been sighted by one of *Guadalcanal*'s aircraft on the evening of 8 April but the sighting report had not been received in the carrier. Despite nightfall Capt Gallery decided to launch more aircraft in case the submarine was still in the area. His supposition was correct, for at 2330 a TBF Avenger sighted *U515* and delivered a surprise attack with depth charges before the U-boat dived. Henke was in a poor position since he had not been able to get a full charge on the battery and therefore could not manage a prolonged dive; accordingly, he surfaced when he felt the coast was clear. Shortly after 0640 on the 9th he was sighted again by a TBF and was straddled by depth charges in an accurate attack before he managed to submerge. The DEs *Pillsbury*, *Chatelain*, *Flaherty* and *Pope* now began to search the area and at 1030 *Pope* was in sonar contact. For the next four hours the four DEs delivered a succession of attacks. Henke's response was to go deep: the depleted state of his battery did not permit any high-speed evasive manoeuvring.

Inside *U515* the attacks had caused a good deal of damage. The after ends had to be sealed because of flooding and tanks forward had to be flooded to correct the stern-down angle. Now the boat aquired a bow-down angle and Henke knew he had no option but to surrender. As he did so the Americans lost sonar contact. Just as the four DEs were sorting themselves out into a scouting line *U515* broached only 75yds on *Chatelain*'s starboard quarter. *U515*'s crew tried to man their armament but were swept away by a fusillade from *Chatelain* and *Flaherty*.

Events now degenerated into a free-for-all. As *Guadalcanal*'s crew watched from the flight deck an Avenger and two Wildcats strafed the U-boat while *Flaherty* and *Chatelain* continued their barrage of gunfire. As an added diversion *Flaherty* fired a torpedo which took off after *Pillsbury* and had to be sunk by a Wildcat. Finally, at 1908 the U-boat was shaken by an explosion, her bow reared up and she sank.

Henke had sunk the British liner *Ceramic* in December 1942 and there had been but one survivor from her passengers (which included women and children) and crew. Capt Gallery told Henke that the British were very keen to lay their hands on him and that he could expect a hard time. Henke then signed a statement to the effect that he would be cooperative with US Naval Intelligence if Gallery undertook not to hand him over to the Royal Navy at Gibraltar. Although Henke subsequently repudiated the statement, it was circulated among *U515*'s crew with the result that many were unusually helpful.

U68

	Launched	*Commissioned*
	22 Nov 1940	11 Feb 1941

Class Type IXC
CO *Oberleutnant zur See* Albert Lauzemis (lost)
Date of loss 10 April 1944
Location Atlantic, NW of Madeira, 33°24'N 18°59'W
Cause Air attack

Casualties	56
Survivors	1
Salvaged	No

Notes In sinking *U515* the 'Can-Do' had stumbled on a U-boat fuelling rendezvous. *U488* was waiting to fuel *U129*, *U66*, *U637*, *U68* and the unlucky *U515*. *U214* reported to BdU that *Guadalcanal* was in the area and the rendezvous was changed. The change came too late for *U68*. She was sighted at dawn on the 10th by two Avengers and a Wildcat. The U-boat was caught by surprise and was hit by several rockets and then had two Mk 47 depth charges dropped just aft of the conning tower. A further strafing run by the Wildcat swept away the flak gunners and in the absence of any opposition the second Avenger delivered another rocket and depth-charge attack. At 0535 *U68* sank, leaving one rating floating in an oily scum.

U108

	Launched	Commissioned
U108	15 Jul 1940	22 Oct 1940
Class	Type IXB	
CO	?	
Date of loss	11 April 1944	
Location	Baltic, Stettin (Szcecin)	
Cause	Air attack	
Casualties	?	
Survivors	?	
Salvaged	Raised on 17 July 1944 and paid off; wreck scuttled there 24 April 1945	

Notes Sunk while alongside at Stettin in a bombing raid.

U448

	Launched	Commissioned
U448	6 May 1942	1 Aug 1942
Class	Type VIIC	
CO	*Oberleutnant zur See* Dauter (survived)	
Date of loss	14 April 1944	
Location	Atlantic, N of the Azores, 46°22'N 19°35'W	
Cause	Depth charge	
Casualties	9	
Survivors	5 officers, 4 senior rates, 33 junior rates	
Salvaged	No	

Notes EG9, comprising the Canadian frigates *Matane*, *Swansea* and *Stormont* and the corvette *Owen Sound*, sailed on 9 April for a patrol north of the Azores. The presence of a U-boat in their area was confirmed by HF/DF, and the escort carrier HMS *Biter* and the sloops of EG7 were sent to support. At 1218Z on the 14th *Swansea* obtained an asdic contact just two miles ahead of *Biter* and in view of the risk to the carrier (later confirmed by *U448*'s survivors) attacked immediately to put the U-boat down.

The U-boat went to a depth of 820ft and *Swansea*'s subsequent attacks using depth charges and Hedgehog were unsuccessful. Two creepers were then organised with HMS *Pelican* acting as the directing ship. The first at 1414Z was unsuccessful; the second at 1615Z, followed by a ten-charge pattern from *Pelican*, appeared equally unsuccessful but in fact did considerable damage. The seventh charge was a direct hit which blew a small hole in the pressure hull aft, wrecked the diesels and caused much other damage. Dauter had no choice but to surface. *U448* came up at 1625Z into a barrage of heavy fire from both ships, a number of her crew being killed while climbing out of the conning tower before fire was checked. The destruction of *U448* had taken over four hours and seen 56 depth charges expended.

U550

	Launched	Commissioned
U550	12 May 1943	28 Jul 1943
Class	Type IXC/40	
CO	*Kapitänleutnant* Hanert	
Date of loss	16 April 1944	
Location	N Atlantic, E of New York, 40°09'N 69°44'W	
Cause	Depth charge/gunfire/ramming	
Casualties	44	
Survivors	3 officers, 1 senior rate, 8 junior rates	
Salvaged	No	

Notes *U550* had just torpedoed a tanker, the *Pan Pennsylvania*, in convoy CU.21 and after a sonar search in appalling conditions contact had been made by the USS *Joyce*. The first attack was delivered at 0948 and this brought *U550* to the surface. There she was destroyed by gunfire from *Joyce*, *Peterson* and *Gandy* before being rammed by *Gandy*.

U342

	Launched	Commissioned
U342	10 Nov 1942	12 Jan 1943

Class — Type VIIC
CO — *Oberleutnant zur See* Albert Hossenfelder (lost)
Date of loss — 17 April 1944
Location — N Atlantic, SW of Iceland, 60°23'N 29°20'W
Cause — Air attack
Casualties — 51
Survivors — None
Salvaged — No

Notes Sunk in an attack by Canso 'S' of No 162 Squadron RCAF.

U986

	Launched	Commissioned
U986	20 May 1943	1 Jul 1943

Class — Type VIIC
CO — *Oberleutnant zur See* Ernst Kaiser (lost)
Date of loss — 17 April 1944
Location — N Atlantic, 50°09'N 12°51'W
Cause — Depth charge
Casualties — 50
Survivors — None
Salvaged — No

Notes Sunk by the USS *Swift* and *PC619*.

U974

	Launched	Commissioned
U974	11 Mar 1943	22 Apr 1943

Class — Type VIIC
CO — *Oberleutnant zur See* Heinz Wolff (lost)
Date of loss — 19 April 1944
Location — Norwegian Sea, off Stavanger, 59°08'N 05°23'E
Cause — Submarine attack
Casualties — 42
Survivors — 1 officer, 6 ratings
Salvaged — No

Notes The Norwegian submarine *Ula* (Lt-Cdr R. M. Sars RNorN)) was on anti-shipping patrol off Hangesund when the conning tower of a U-boat was sighted at a range of only 400yds. Despite the target altering course away from him at the moment of firing, Sars pressed on with the attack, firing four torpedoes and scoring a hit with the second. *Ula* had to endure some half-hearted depth-charging from the U-boat's escort before being able to make her escape.

UIT4

	Launched	Commissioned
UIT4	21 Oct 1943	–

Class — Italian *Romolo* class
CO — None appointed
Date of loss — 20 April 1944
Location — N Adriatic, Monfalcone
Cause — Air raid
Casualties — –
Survivors — –
Salvaged — Raised 31 May 1946 and broken up 1948

Notes The Italian *Romolo* class transport submarine *R7* was seized by the Germans while under construction at CRDA Monfalcone. She was bombed while incomplete alongside the fitting-out jetty.

UIT5

	Launched	Commissioned
UIT5	28 Dec 1943	–

Class — Italian *Romolo* class
CO — None appointed
Date of loss — 20 April 1944
Location — N Adriatic, Monfalcone
Cause — Air raid
Casualties — –
Survivors — –
Salvaged — Raised 3 June 1946 and broken up 1948

Notes The Italian *Romolo* class transport submarine *R8* was seized by the Germans while under construction at CRDA Monfalcone and was bombed while incomplete alongside the fitting-out jetty.

U311

	Launched	Commissioned
U311	1 Feb 1943	23 Mar 1943

Class — Type VII
CO — *Kapitänleutnant* Joachim Zander (lost)
Date of loss — 22 April 1944
Location — N Atlantic, 52°09'N 19°07'W
Cause — Depth charge
Casualties — 51
Survivors — None
Salvaged — No

Notes *U311* was once thought to have been the victim of an attack by Sunderland 'A' of No 423 Squadron but the boat involved in this attack was in fact *U672*, which survived and reported her ordeal to BdU. *U311*'s fate was subsequently given as 'unknown'. However, on the night of 22 April 1944 the Canadian EG9 was operating independently when *Matane* obtained an asdic contact. Visual confirmation was obtained some moments later when the swirl of a U-boat was seen together with the periscope. Fearing an immediate Gnat launch, *Matane* delivered a hasty depth-charge attack to put the U-boat down. *Matane* was low on fuel and was having difficulty in maintaining contact in the heavy seas, so was reinforced by *Swansea*. However, she too only managed to deliver one deep pattern before losing contact. The verdict of these two attacks was that the U-boat had got away, but research some forty years later revealed that *U311* never made another signal.

	Launched	*Commissioned*
U488	17 Oct 1942	1 Feb 1943
Class	Type XIV	
CO	*Oberleutnant zur See* Bruno Studt (lost)	
Date of loss	26 April 1944	
Location	Mid Atlantic, NW of Cape Verde Islands 17°54'N 38°	
Cause	Depth charge	
Casualties	64	
Survivors	None	
Salvaged	No	

Notes On the night of 19/20 April the carrier USS *Croatan* (Cdr J. P. W. Vest USN) picked up signals from *U66* which was asking for a fuelling rendezvous before heading home. BdU ordered *U66* to fuel from *U488*, unaware that *Croatan* and her escorts were also hastening to the area. On the night of the 25th an Avenger sighted *U66* in the moonlight but failed to maintain contact. Vest ordered a retiring search, which was rewarded at 0442 on the 26th when the DE *Frost* obtained a sonar contact. The DE *Inch* delivered two Hedgehog attacks but the sea was so calm that the turbulence lingered long after the attack, thwarting the use of sonar. The search continued into the early morning when, guided by oil coming to the surface, *Snowden*, *Frost* and *Barber* dropped several patterns of depth charges on a motionless target at 560ft. No debris appeared, but *U488* was considered to have been sunk in this attack and she was never heard from again.

	Launched	*Commissioned*
U803	1 Apr 1943	7 Sept 1943
Class	Type IXC/40	
CO	*Kapitänleutnant* Schimpf	
Date of loss	27 April 1944	
Location	Baltic, near Swinemünde, 53°55'N 14°17'E	
Cause	Mine	
Casualties	9	
Survivors	?	
Salvaged	Raised 9 August 1944 and paid off; details of ultimate fate unknown	

	Launched	*Commissioned*
U193	24 Aug 1942	10 Dec 1942
Class	Type IXC/40	
CO	*Oberleutnant zur See* Ulrich Abel (lost)	
Date of loss	28 April 1944	
Location	Bay of Biscay, W of Nantes, 45°38'N 09°43'W	
Cause	Air attack	
Casualties	59	
Survivors	None	
Salvaged	No	

Notes Wellington 'W' of No 612 Squadron, flown by Fg Off G. C. Punter RAAF, had already made one U-boat contact during the night of 27–28 April but it had been lost. At 0405 on the 28th a second contact was picked up. While homing in, Putter was told that the Leigh Light was not working so the navigator, after spotting first the wake and then the boat, illuminated it with tracer. Putter attacked from 50ft and after the aircraft passed over the U-boat the rear gunner saw the bows lift out of the water and the submarine roll over. Radar contact was then lost, but on over-flying the position the Wellington's crew noticed the lights of some ten men in the water.

There were few tears shed in *U-boot Führung* when Abel was reported lost. As 1WO of *U154*, he had made up in Nazi fervour for what he lacked in competence. On return from a patrol in the Caribbean in December 1943 he denounced the boat's CO, *Oberleutnant zur See* Oskar Kusch (a quiet, courageous man and a committed Catholic), to *FdU West* for lack of aggression and *'Wehrkraft Zerzetsung'* (literally, 'undermining military strength'). Despite a lack of evidence and the retraction of statements which

Abel had persuaded some of *U154*'s officers to make, the charge was found proven and Kusch was sentenced to be reduced to the ranks and to be shot. Despite appeals to Dönitz and Raeder, the sentence was carried out on 12 May 1944 at Kiel. The command of *U193* was Abel's reward—a prize he did not enjoy for long.

U421	*Launched* 24 Sept 1942	*Commissioned* 13 Jan 1943
Class	Type VIIC	
CO	*Oberleutnant zur See* Kolbus	
Date of loss	29 April 1944	
Location	Mediterranean, Toulon	
Cause	Air attack	
Casualties	–	
Survivors	–	
Salvaged	Final details of disposal of wreck unknown	

Notes Sunk while alongside at Toulon during a USAAF air raid.

U277	*Launched* 7 Nov 1942	*Commissioned* 21 Dec 1942
Class	Type VIIC	
CO	*Kapitänleutnant* Robert Lubsen (lost)	
Date of loss	1 May 1944	
Location	Arctic, SW of Bear Island, 73°24'N 15°42'E	
Cause	Air attack	
Casualties	50	
Survivors	None	
Salvaged	No	

Notes Sunk by Swordfish 'C' of 842 NAS embarked in HMS *Fencer* during the passage of convoy RA.58 from the Kola Inlet.

U674	*Launched* 8 May 1943	*Commissioned* 15 Jun 1943
Class	Type VIIC	
CO	*Oberleutnant zur See* Harald Muhs (lost)	
Date of loss	2 May 1944	
Location	Arctic, NE of Jan Mayen Island, 70°32'N 04°37'E	
Cause	Air attack	
Casualties	49	
Survivors	None	
Salvaged	No	

Notes The second U-boat sunk by a Swordfish of 842 NAS, on this occasion aircraft 'B', aboard HMS *Fencer* during the passage of RA.58. Three depth charges straddled abaft the conning tower and when the explosions had died away the boat could be seen sinking by the stern. She continued to do this until the bows were clear of the water. After the bows had sunk, air bubbles were seen bursting on the surface for some time.

U959	*Launched* 3 Dec 1942	*Commissioned* 21 Jan 1943
Class	Type VIIC	
CO	*Oberleutnant zur See* Friedrich Weitz (lost)	
Date of loss	2 May 1944	
Location	Arctic, NE of Iceland, 69°20'N 00°20'W	
Cause	Air attack	
Casualties	53	
Survivors	None	
Salvaged	No	

Notes Sunk by Swordfish 'K' of 842 NAS from *Fencer* during the passage of RA.58.

U852	*Launched* 28 Jan 1943	*Commissioned* 15 Jun 1943
Class	Type IXD2	
CO	*Kapitänleutnant* Heinz Eck (survived)	
Date of loss	2 May 1944	
Location	Indian Ocean, off the Somali coast, 50 miles S of Cape Guardafui, 09°32'N 50°59'E	
Cause	Air attack/grounding	
Casualties	7	
Survivors	59	
Salvaged	No	

Notes *U852* had been 'followed' by HF/DF fixes on her long voyage around the Cape of Good Hope. Once she came within the remit of East Africa Command, No 621 Squadron RAF began flying regular search patrols and on 1 May she was found by Wellington 'E', flown by Fg Off H.R. Mitchell. Mitchell's attack, which fractured the submarine's air induction valve making it impossible for her to dive, was the beginning of two days of attacks by Wellingtons of Nos 621 and 8 Squadrons. The *coup de grâce* was administered on 3 May by aircraft 'G' of No 8 Squadron, flown by Fg Off J. R. Forrester RCAF. The attack did such damage that Eck decided to run the boat aground and abandon her, after which scuttling charges were set which blew off her bow and stern. Written sources say that just the stern was destroyed, but photographs clearly show that both bow and stern were destroyed. A landing party from HMS *Falmouth* was put ashore to round up some of *U852*'s crew who had managed to make land.

After the war Eck, three of his officers and a Leading Seaman stood trial for the murder of survivors of the merchant ship *Peleus*, which had been sunk by *U852* in the South Atlantic on 13 March 1944. Eck's defence, that by shooting the survivors and shooting up the wreckage he was attempting to remove all trace's of his boat's passage, was rejected, as was the defence offered by the other four defendants that they were obeying orders. Eck, *Leutnant zur See* August Hoffmann (2WO) and *U852*'s medical officer, *Stabsarzt* Walter Weisspfennig, were sentenced to death and were executed by firing squad on Lüneburg Heath on 30 November 1945. The others received long terms of imprisonment, all of which were subsequently commuted. Eck was the only German U-boat commander to be tried and executed for war crimes.

U371	*Launched* 27 Jan 1941	*Commissioned* 15 Mar 1941
Class	Type VIIC	
CO	*Oberleutnant zur See* Horst-Arno Fenski (survived)	
Date of loss	4 May 1944	
Location	Mediterranean, Gulf of Bougie, 37°49'N 05°39'E	
Cause	Depth charge	
Casualties	4	
Survivors	5 officers, 8 senior rates, 36 junior rates	
Salvaged	No	

Notes During the night of 2/3 May a U-boat was detected approaching convoy GUS.9 on the surface. Fenski was charging his batteries while closing the convoy but he had overestimated the convoy's range and was much closer to the screen than he thought he was. He then dived and let the convoy pass over him, only to surface astern. As he began to close he was sighted by the destroyer *Menges*, which began to head towards him. Fenski dived but not before firing a T5, which struck *Menges* aft though did not sink her. *U371* was then attacked by the destroyers *Pride* and *Campbell*, which drove her towards the coast where she bottomed. These two American destroyers were reinforced by HMS *Blankney*, the USS *Sustain* and the French ships *L'Alcyon* and *Sénégalais*. Fenski remained on the bottom for 21 hours, until 0315 on the 4th, when he had to surface. On coming up he found himself surrounded. *Sénégalais* opened fire but in turn was hit by a T5 which Fenski fired just before abandoning the submarine.

U846	*Launched* 17 Feb 1943	*Commissioned* 29 May 1943
Class	Type IXC/40	
CO	*Oberleutnant zur See* Hashagen (lost)	
Date of loss	4 May 1944	
Location	Atlantic, N of Cape Ortegal, 46°04'N 09°20'W	
Cause	Air attack	
Casualties	57	
Survivors	None	
Salvaged	No	

Notes Sunk by Wellington 'M' of No 407 Squadron RCAF, flown by Flt Lt I. J. Bateman RCAF. After radar contact a fully surfaced U-boat was sighted. The moon was so bright that the Leigh Light was not required. Despite both guns in the Wellington's front turret jamming after one round, Bateman pressed on and dropped six depth charges. When the aircraft returned for a second pass there was no sign of the U-boat other than an oil slick forming on the water.

U473	*Launched* 17 Apr 1943	*Commissioned* 16 Jun 1943
Class	Type VIIC	
CO	*Kapitänleutnant* Heinz Sternberg	
Date of loss	6 May 1944	
Location	Atlantic, W of Cape Clear, 49°29'N 21°22'W	
Cause	Depth charge	
Casualties	23	
Survivors	30	
Salvaged	No	

Notes The Second Support Group was out looking for a weather-reporting U-boat when on 3 May *U473* torpedoed the USS *Donnell* only 200 miles from the group's position. An HF/DF bearing at 2319/3 put the U-boat only 30 miles away and Walker, guessing that she was going west, headed after her. Three days later *Wild Goose* hoisted the familiar black flag (indicating that she was in contact and attacking) and dropped a ten-charge pattern. For the next fifteen hours the group expended 345 depth charges, *Wren* 114 in five attacks, *Wild Goose* 107 in five attacks and *Starling* 124 charges in eight . The Monthly Anti Submarine Report for May 1944 recorded that the sloops had, to use a sporting analogy, 'Worked together like a first class three-quarter line'.

At 0014 on 6 May *U473* surfaced and headed off, being shot to pieces despite high-speed zigzagging. Walker wrote: 'At least one torpedo passed down *Wren*'s port side but the prudent *Herrenvolk* soon took to the water, leaving their boat circling to port at high speed.' Abandoned, *U473* headed straight for *Starling*, which had to take violent avoiding action. The U-boat's end was hastened by two explosions, probably scuttling charges. 'Cease firing. Gosh, what a lovely battle!' signalled an ecstatic Walker. This was the nineteenth U-boat he had destroyed.

	Launched	*Commissioned*
U66	10 Oct 1940	2 Jan 1941
Class	Type IXC	
CO	*Oberleutnant zur See* Gerhard Seehausen (lost)	
Date of loss	6 May 1944	
Location	Atlantic, W of Cape Verde Islands, 17°17'N 32°29'W	
Cause	Ramming/gunfire	
Casualties	24	
Survivors	36	
Salvaged	No	

Notes *U66* had been operating off the northwest coast of South America and was now low on fuel and had signalled BdU for a rendezvous with a Milch Cow or other boat with fuel to spare. All efforts to achieve such a rendezvous proved unsuccessful and *U66*'s crew were now suffering the effects of a long patrol in a sapping climate and poor rations. Meanwhile *Croatan* had been relieved by *Block Island* which, in response to HF/DF fixes, began a series of aerial searches.

Late in the evening of 1 May a TBM Avenger fitted for night work spotted *U66*'s wake and swirl where the boat had dived. Sonobuoys and a Fido were dropped, but the attack was unsuccessful. For the next few days *U66* was hunted intensively by ships and aircraft. Numerous attacks were made (including one where two Fidos dropped simultaneously ended up chasing each other) with the intention of hunting *U66* to exhaustion.

Inside the submarine conditions had reached the limits of human endurance. At 2122 on the night of 5–6 May *U66* surfaced only 5,000yds away from *Block Island*. The carrier turned away, sending the DE *Buckley* (Lt-Cdr Brent M. Abel USN) after the submarine. However, Seehausen dived when he realised where he had surfaced and *Buckley* was unable to make contact. Some hours later Lt (jg) Jimmie Sellars USNR, flying a TBM Avenger fitted for night operations (and armed with nothing more than a .45 calibre pistol), spotted *U66* on the surface only eighteen miles from the carrier.

Seehausen was making a desperate passage on the surface, using valuable fuel to put as much distance between him and his pursuers and to put a charge in the battery that would enable him to spend the next day dived. His look-outs were aware of Sellars' Avenger overhead, but Seehausen kept going, believing that if he made to dive the aircraft would attack. His concentration on the Avenger was to prove his undoing, for while Sellars remained in contact he was guiding in the DE *Buckley* racing up from the south. It was at about this time that Seehausen signalled BdU that he was being pursued, commenting that the area was more unhealthy than the Bay of Biscay.

At 0317 on 6 May *Buckley* sighted the submarine and turned to open her 'A' arcs and unmask her Foxer should *U66* let loose a Gnat. At the same time *U66* saw the DE and opened fire. *Buckley* closed the U-boat, smothering her with 3in and small-arms fire before turning to ram at 0329. *U66*'s crew began to swarm out of the submarine and up on to *Buckley*'s forecastle. In the dark and confusion the Americans thought they were being boarded (some of the Germans carried small arms) and a rough brawl ensued with everything and anything that could be used being employed to drive the Germans off the forecastle—including fists. *Buckley* then backed off, leaving a group of five armed German sailors on the forecastle who were swiftly disarmed and hustled below.

U66 then began to draw ahead, and as the DE drew alongside with every gun sweeping *U66*'s casing the submarine suddenly turned to port and struck *Buckley* by the after engine room, the bow driving down and under the DE's hull. For the second time a hail of small-arms fire ripped across the casing, supplemented by grenades. *U66* then fell astern, flames coming from the conning tower, before sinking, her end hastened by a final salvo from *Buckley*'s after 3in gun. Some moments later there was a heavy underwater explosion.

It had taken 105 rounds of 3in, 3,118 rounds of 40mm and 20mm, 390 rounds of small-arms fire and 'an unknown number of coffee cups and shell cases' to defeat *U66*. *Buckley* had been badly damaged in the action, but superb damage control enabled her to be patched up and she reached New York under her own power. Lt-Cdr Abel was awarded the Navy Cross for the action. Among the U-boat casualties were two British merchant seaman PoWs.

	Launched	*Commissioned*
U765	22 Apr 1943	19 Jun 1943
Class	Type VIIC	
CO	*Oberleutnant zur See* Werner Wendt (survived)	
Date of loss	6 May 1944	
Location	N Atlantic, 52°30'N 28°28'W	
Cause	Depth charge	
Casualties	37	
Survivors	8	
Salvaged	No	

Notes Although the sinking took place on 6 May, the hunt for *U765* could be said to have started five days earlier when HF/DF bearings of a weather-reporting U-boat were noted. The escort carrier *Vindex* and 5th Escort Group were ordered to search for her. A sighting report by Swordfish 'X' of 825 NAS in HMS *Vindex* caused the frigate *Keats* to be detached, and at about 0400/6 she was in radar contact. The U-boat dived and discharged a series of SBTs, which caused *Keats* to spend an hour in fruitless searching. At 0515 she was joined by *Bligh*, *Aylmer* and *Bickerton*, the last obtaining an asdic contact 2½ miles from where *Keats* was hunting. A Hedgehog attack was started but abandoned in favour of a creeping attack. This was so successful that as soon as the last charge had exploded the U-boat surfaced. While she was being engaged by gunfire, Swordfish 'V' from *Vindex* swooped down and delivered two more depth charges which blew her in half.

	Launched	*Commissioned*
U1234	7 Jan 1944	19 Apr 1944
Class	Type IXC/40	
CO	?	
Date of loss	14 May 1944	
Location	Baltic, harbour roads of Gotenhafen	
Cause	Collision	
Casualties	13	
Survivors	35	
Salvaged	Raised 17 October 1944 and returned to service	

Notes Collided with the tug *Anton*, the exact circumstances of this loss being unknown. The boat was finally scuttled on 5 May 1945 at Horup Haff; the wreck was broken up *in situ*.

	Launched	*Commissioned*
U731	25 Jul 1942	3 Oct 1942
Class	Type VIIC	
CO	*Oberleutnant zur See* Alexander *Graf* Keller (lost)	
Date of loss	15 May 1944	
Location	Mediterranean, N of Tangier, 35°54'N 05°45'W	
Cause	Depth charge	
Casualties	54	
Survivors	None	
Salvaged	No	

Notes Two MAD-fitted Catalinas of VP-63 obtained a contact and called up HM Ships *Blackfly*, *Aubretia* and *Kilmarnock*. The U-boat was detected near Cape Spartel and, following a successful Hedgehog attack by *Kilmarnock*, immense quantities of oil came to the surface.

	Launched	*Commissioned*
U240	18 Feb 1943	3 Apr 1943
Class	Type VIIC	
CO	*Oberleutnant zur See* Günther Link (lost)	
Date of loss	16 May 1944	

Location	Norwegian Sea, W of Trondheim, 63°05'N 03°10'E
Cause	Air attack
Casualties	50
Survivors	None
Salvaged	No

Notes Sunderland 'V' of No 300 (Norwegian) Squadron RAF, flown by Sub-Lt C. T. Johnsen, sighted a U-boat at 1720 at a range of three miles. In the first attack the depth charges hung up and the aircraft was damaged by flak, despite the U-boat being engaged by the front and rear gunners. During the second attack the front gunner, Quartermaster A. J. Johansen, was killed and two other members of the crew wounded. Despite being blinded by smoke pouring up from the front gunner's position, Johnsen pressed home the attack and released four depth charges, three of which exploded along the port side of the submarine. The bows were seen to rise up at an acute angle before the submarine sank stern first.

The flying boat reached Sullom Voe at 1918 despite the severe damage.

U616

	Launched	*Commissioned*
	8 Feb 1942	2 Apr 1942
Class	Type VIIC	
CO	*Oberleutnant zur See* Koitschka (survived)	
Date of loss	17 May 1944	
Location	Mediterranean, E of Cartagena, 36°46'N 00°42E	
Cause	Depth charge	
Casualties	None	
Survivors	53	
Salvaged	No	

Notes Following the torpedoing of two merchant ships from convoy GUS.39 on the night of 13–14 May, four destroyers (*Ellyson*, *Rodman*, *Hambleton* and *Emmons*) of the US Destroyer Squadron 10, commanded by Capt Adelbert F. Converse USN and with a communications team from No 500 Squadron RAF embarked, were detached to search for the offending U-boat. The ships left Oran on 14 May and rendezvoused with the destroyers *Hilary P. Jones* and *Macomb* and two DEs, *Gleaves* and *Nields*, of GUS.39's escort which were attacking a contact. Attacks continued until the morning of 15 May, when a large oil slick was reported on the surface. Searches continued for another two days until a Wellington of No 36 Squadron caught *U616* on the surface at 2226. The destroyers closed and at 2359 the USS *Macomb* illuminated the submarine with starshell. Sonar contact was made at 0014 and from then on attacks were continuous until 0807 on 17 May, when *U616* came to the surface and was abandoned by her crew.

The operation had been code-named 'Monstrous' and had lasted 72 hours from the first depth-charge attack. Of particular interest were the excellent communications between the ships and No 36 Squadron's aircraft.

U241

	Launched	*Commissioned*
	25 Jun 1943	24 Jul 1943
Class	Type VIIC	
CO	*Oberleutnant zur See* Arno Werr (lost)	
Date of loss	18 May 1944	
Location	Norwegian Sea, W of Trondheim, 63°36'N 03°10'E	
Cause	Air attack	
Casualties	51	
Survivors	None	
Salvaged	No	

Notes Catalina 'S' of No 210 Squadron, flown by Fg Off B. Bastable, sighted *U241* on the surface at a range of five to eight miles. Bastable went straight in and attacked with six depth charges, placing them perfectly across the submarine. A large oil slick began to form as the boat sank stern first. Many survivors were seen in the water.

U960

	Launched	*Commissioned*
	3 Dec 1942	28 Jan 1943
Class	Type VIIC	
CO	*Oberleutnant zur See* Günther Heinrich	
Date of loss	19 May 1944	
Location	Mediterranean, NW of Algiers, 37°35'N 01°39'E	
Cause	Depth charge	
Casualties	31	
Survivors	4 officers, 5 senior rates, 11 junior rates	
Salvaged	No	

Notes *U960* had just arrived in the Mediterranean from La Pallice when she was sighted on 17 May by an RAF aircraft. Four US destroyers of DesDiv 25 (*Woolsey*, *Ludlow*, *Niblack* and

Benson), under the command of Cdr Robert B. Ellis, were sent to investigate. Wellingtons of No 36 and Venturas of No 500 Squadron joined the search and made contact with the submarine at 2100. The search continued all night, throughout the 18th and into the night of the 18th–19th. At 0140 on the 19th radar contact was made ahead of *Niblack* and *Ludlow* and within an hour both destroyers were in sonar contact. Eleven depth-charge attacks followed, but the U-boat managed to break away for at 0609 she was sighted on the surface. *Woolsey* and *Benson*, joined by *Madison*, opened fire, and as they did so Wellington 'M' of No 36 Squadron roared in to deliver a depth-charge attack, miraculously escaping damage (or worse) from the destroyers' gunfire. The U-boat dived but was blown to the surface by a depth-charge attack by *Niblack* and was abandoned.

This hunt had lasted for 42 hours 18 minutes and the sinking of *U960* and the earlier loss of *U616* did much to dispel the criticism that American escorts lacked persistence when it came to hunting a U-boat.

U1015	*Launched* 7 Feb 1944	*Commissioned* 23 Mar 1944
Class	Type VIIC/41	
CO	*Oberleutnant zur See* Boos	
Date of loss	19 May 1944	
Location	Baltic, W of Pillau, 54°25'N 19°50'E	
Cause	Collision	
Casualties	36	
Survivors	?	
Salvaged	No	

Notes Sank following a collision with *U1014*, the exact circumstances of which are unknown.

U453	*Launched* 30 Apr 1941	*Commissioned* 26 Jun 1941
Class	Type VIIC	
CO	*Oberleutnant zur See* Dierk Luhrs (survived)	
Date of loss	21 May 1944	
Location	Mediterranean, NW of Cape Spartivento, 38°13'N 16°36'E	
Cause	Depth charge	
Casualties	1	
Survivors	5 officers, 16 senior rates, 29 junior rates	
Salvaged	No	

Notes At 1755 on 19 May convoy HA.43 was attacked by a U-boat. The initial hunt was carried out by the Italian co-belligerent ships *Urania*, *Danaide* and *Monzambano*, reinforced by HM Ships *Termagant*, *Tenacious* and *Liddesdale*. The three British ships reached the area at 1030/20 and commenced searching. Contact was made an hour later—twelve miles from where the Italian ships were still searching. Between 1250 and 2040 the destroyers made eleven attacks. After 2040 the SO decided merely to hold the contact until the next morning: asdic conditions were good and he knew that the U-boat would have to surface eventually for air. At 0024/21 the submarine surfaced and was destroyed by gunfire.

U476	*Launched* 5 Jun 1943	*Commissioned* 28 Jul 1943
Class	Type VIIC	
CO	*Oberleutnant zur See* Otto Niethmann (lost)	
Date of loss	24 May 1944	
Location	Arctic, SW of Lofoten Islands, 65°08'N 04°53'E	
Cause	Foundered following air attack	
Casualties	33	
Survivors	21	
Salvaged	No	

Notes At 0716 Catalina 'V' of No 210 Squadron, flown by Capt F.W.L. Maxwell SAAF, sighted a fully surfaced U-boat at a range of five miles. As the aircraft ran in it was met by a heavy flak barrage, but at least one of the six depth charges fell close alongside. The explosion seemed to blow the U-boat out of the water and round in a 360-degree turn before the submarine sank stern first. The boat reappeared briefly before sinking again, taking nearly ten minutes to do so. The view of the scene was then hidden by a snow squall.

U476 had been so badly damaged in this attack that she subsequently foundered. The survivors were picked up by *U990*.

U675	*Launched* 6 Jul 1943	*Commissioned* 14 Jul 1943
Class	Type VIIC	
CO	*Oberleutnant zur See* Karl-Heinz Sammler (lost)	

Date of loss	24 May 1943
Location	Norwegian Sea, NW of Stradtlandet, 62°27'N 03°04'E
Cause	Air attack
Casualties	51
Survivors	None
Salvaged	No

Notes Sunderland 'R' of No 4(C) OTU, flown by Fg Off T. P. Frizell RAAF, sighted a U-boat at 1349. Frizell attacked through the flak and dropped six depth charges from 20ft. After the explosions, the U-boat's bows rose to the vertical and began to sink. As they did so there was a further large explosion and the bows disappeared. A considerable number of air bubbles began to burst on the surface, followed by the appearance of bodies, wooden wreckage and oil.

	Launched	*Commissioned*
U990	16 Jun 1943	28 Jul 1943

Class	Type VIIC
CO	*Kapitänleutnant* Hubert Nordheimer (survived)
Date of loss	25 May 1944
Location	Norwegian Sea, NW of Trondheim, 65°05'N 07°28'E
Cause	Air attack
Casualties	20
Survivors	31
Salvaged	No

Notes Liberator 'S' of No 59 Squadron RAF sighted a U-boat at 0623. The pilot, Sqn Ldr B. Sisson, attacked under cover of a rain squall and dropped six depth charges. When the explosions subsided the submarine could be seen sinking amid a large oil slick. The survivors were rescued by *VP5901*.

	Launched	*Commissioned*
U292	17 Jul 1943	25 Aug 1943

Class	Type VIIC
CO	*Oberleutnant zur See* Werner Schmidt (lost)
Date of loss	27 May 1944
Location	Norwegian Sea, NE of Shetlands, 62°37'N 00°57'E
Cause	Air attack
Casualties	51
Survivors	None
Salvaged	No

Notes Liberator 'S' of No 59 Squadron, flown by Flt Lt V. Camacho RCAF, attacked a U-boat found on the surface with six depth charges. The rear gunner and starboard beam gunner saw the charges explode in a good straddle, followed by a bright yellow explosion from the U-boat. Her bows were then seen to rise before she sank on an even keel.

	Launched	*Commissioned*
U549	28 Apr 1943	14 Jul 1943

Class	Type IXC/40
CO	*Kapitänleutnant* Detlev Krankenhagen (lost)
Date of loss	29 May 1944
Location	Atlantic, SW of Madeira, 31°13'N 21°03'W
Cause	Depth charge
Casualties	57
Survivors	None
Salvaged	No

Notes *U549* had escaped an air attack by an Avenger from the USS *Block Island* on 28 May and another attack the next day. *Block Island*, escorted by four DEs, was running down the track of the target on the evening of 29 May when she was struck by three torpedoes fired in succession by *U549*, which had managed to slip inside the screen. While the carrier's crew proceeded with damage control measures, *U549*'s periscope was sighted by the destroyer *Eugene E. Elmore*, which carried out an unsuccessful attack. The U-boat's commander would not be deterred, for his next move was to fire a Gnat, which hit and wrecked the stern of the destroyer *Barr*. The decision had now been taken to abandon the carrier in view of the amount of avgas and munitions on board, and while the crew were going over the side another torpedo missed *Elmore*. Tactical command was now assumed by Cdr Henry Mullins USN in *Ahrens*, who ordered the two remaining escorts to hunt the submarine while he closed *Block Island* to take off the crew. While doing so he obtained a sonar contact and ordered *Elmore* to attack. She made three attacks with Hedgehog, and after the third two small explosions followed by a large blast and concluding with another 'heavy, crawling explosion' were heard.

Block Island was the only US carrier to be sunk in the Atlantic. Her aircraft had been involved in the sinking of seven U-boats.

U289

	Launched	Commissioned
	29 May 1943	10 Jul 1943

Class Type VIIC
CO *Kapitänleutnant* Alexander Hellwig (lost)
Date of loss 31 May 1944
Location Arctic, NE of Jan Mayen Island, 73°32'N 00°28'E
Cause Depth charge
Casualties 51
Survivors None
Salvaged No

Notes Sunk by the destroyer HMS *Milne.*

U477

	Launched	Commissioned
	3 Jul 1943	18 Aug 1943

Class Type VIIC
CO *Oberleutnant zur See* Karl Joachim Jenssen (lost)
Date of loss 3 June 1944
Location Norwegian Sea, NE of Shetlands, 63°59'N 01°37'E
Cause Air attack
Casualties 51
Survivors None
Salvaged No

Notes Operating from Wick, Canso 'T' of No 162 Squadron RCAF, flown by Flt Lt R. E. MacBridge RCAF, sighted a surfaced U-boat and attacked with six depth charges. The explosions appeared to lift the boat clear of the water. She then swung to port, stopped and sank, leaving five men in the water. An oil slick measuring one mile by 400yds then formed.

U505

	Launched	Commissioned
	24 May 1941	26 Aug 1941

Class Type IXC
CO *Oberleutnant zur See* Harald Lange (survived)
Date of loss 4 June 1944
Location Atlantic NW off Dakar, 21°30'N 19°20'W
Cause Air attack
Casualties 1
Survivors ?
Salvaged Yes

Notes *U505* had been operating without success off the west coast of Africa and at the end of May headed for home. Her progress was monitored by HF/DF and the *Guadalcanal*'s group was alerted to her presence. As Lange ran north his Naxos receiver warned that he was entering the area covered by the *Guadalcanal*'s air patrols. At the same time sonobuoys dropped by *Guadalcanal*'s aircraft registered faint contacts. In the event both sides almost blundered into one another. Just after 1100 on 4 June the DE *Chatelain* reported a firm sonar contact. At the same time Lange's hydrophone operator reported engine noises, so Lange took *U505* up to periscope depth for a look—to see three DEs bearing down on him with a carrier in the distance.

Chatelain attacked with Hedgehog and then a fourteen depth-charge pattern which did such damage to *U505* that Lange ordered her to the surface, where she was abandoned. There was some confusion as the Americans were unsure if the U-boat was being abandoned, but when it was clear the order was given to send away the boarding parties and *U505* was taken in tow.

The capture of *U505* sent morale in the little carrier sky-high. When the communiqué announcing the successful invasion of Europe was posted, one sailor commented, 'Boy! Look what Eisenhower had to do to top us!'

After tow to Port Royal Bay, Bermuda, the boat commissioned in the US Navy as the USS *Nemo* and used for evaluation. In 1954 *U505* was presented to the Museum of Science and Industry in Chicago, where she remains on display.

U987

	Launched	Commissioned
	2 Jun 1943	8 Jul 1943

Class Type VIIC
CO *Oberleutnant zur See* Hilmar Schreyer (lost)
Date of loss 5 June 1944
Location Arctic, W of Lofoten Islands, 68°091'N 05°08'E
Cause Submarine attack
Casualties 52
Survivors None
Salvaged No

Notes HM Submarine *Satyr* (Lt T. S. Weston RN) sighted a surfaced U-boat just after 0900. The U-boat was 4,500yds away on a course of 355. *Satyr* was on her port bow so turned to port and ran in fast for three minutes to gain a favourable firing position. When Weston came back to persicope depth he found that the U-boat had altered course to port. *Satyr* altered course to starboard and then at 0915, fearing that if the U-boat went to port again he would be out of range, Weston fired six torpedoes. Two of the torpedoes collided, alerting the U-boat to what was afoot, but it was too late. Two torpedoes struck the U-boat in the bow and under the conning tower. Weston saw the forward part of the target thrown into the air as if its back had been broken. After both halves of the submarine sank, breaking-up noises were audible aboard *Satyr*.

U955

	Launched	*Commissioned*
	13 Nov 1942	31 Dec 1942
Class	Type VIIC	
CO	*Oberleutnant zur See* Hans Baden (lost)	
Date of loss	7 June 1944	
Location	Bay of Biscay, 45°13'N 08°30'W	
Cause	Air attack	
Casualties	50	
Survivors	None	
Salvaged	No	

Notes *U955* had already been unsuccessfully attacked on 5 June; now a search had been established to find her. Sunderland 'S' of No 201 Squadron RAF, flown by Flt Lt L. Baveystock DFC DFM, obtained a radar contact which he illuminated with flares. However, the U-boat dived, so Baveystock began baiting tactics in the hope that it would surface again. At 0300 a contact was reported which, when illuminated with flares, proved to be the U-boat. Six depth charges were dropped, one of which seemed to explode directly under the boat. The 'blip' marking the U-boat then faded from the radar screen. Subsequent analysis showed that *U955* had been the victim of this attack.

U970

	Launched	*Commissioned*
	11 Feb 1943	25 Mar 1943
Class	Type VIIC	
CO	*Oberleutnant zur See* Heinrich Ketels (survived)	
Date of loss	8 June 1944	
Location	Bay of Biscay, 45°15'N 04°10'W	
Cause	Air attack	
Casualties	38	
Survivors	2 officers, 11 ratings	
Salvaged	No	

Notes Sunderland 'R' of No 228 Squadron, flown by Flt Lt C. G. Lancaster DFC, attacked a surfaced U-boat which had been found by the aircraft's radar and later illuminated with flares. The U-boat disappeared in the attack and Lancaster was unsure if his attack had been successful. However, the Germans knew just how successful the attack had been when their air–sea rescue service picked up the thirteen survivors later that morning.

U629

	Launched	*Commissioned*
	12 May 1942	2 Jul 1942
Class	Type VIIC	
CO	*Oberleutnant zur See* Hans-Helmut Bugs (lost)	
Date of loss	8 June 1944	
Location	English Channel, SW of Ushant, 48°27'N 05°47'W	
Cause	Air attack	
Casualties	51	
Survivors	None	
Salvaged	No	

Notes See entry for *U373* below.

U373

	Launched	*Commissioned*
	5 Apr 1941	22 May 1941
Class	Type VIIC	
CO	*Oberleutnant zur See* Detlev von Lehsten (lost)	
Date of loss	8 June 1944	
Location	English Channel, SW of Ushant, 48°10'N 05°31'W	
Cause	Air attack	
Casualties	Four	
Survivors	?	
Salvaged	No	

Notes At 0211 Liberator 'G' of No 224 Squadron RAF, flown by Flt Lt K. O. Moore RCAF, sighted a submarine which had first been located by radar. The Leigh Light was not needed as there was sufficient moonlight, and an attack was made in which six depth charges were dropped in a straddle, three landing on either side of the conning tower. The explosions seemed to lift the U-boat clear of the water and when Moore flew over the site oil and wreckage could be seen in the water. This marked the end of *U629*.

Less than half an hour later another radar contact was made and at 2½ miles' range was sighted and confirmed as a U-boat. Attacking from a height of 50ft, Moore dropped another six depth charges of which four fell to starboard and two to port. After the attack the U-boat could be seen listing to starboard and sinking by the stern. After the boat had sunk, three dinghies and a number of survivors were seen in the oily water. This was the end of *U373*. Her survivors were picked up by a VP boat.

It was a remarkable sortie by one aircraft. Two U-boats had been sunk in the space of less than thirty minutes, and the achievement was marked by the immediate award of a DSO and the US Silver Star to Moore.

U740

	Launched	*Commissioned*
U740	23 Dec 1942	27 Mar 1943

Class — Type VIIC
CO — *Kapitänleutnant* Günther Stark (lost)
Date of loss — 9 June 1944
Location — English Channel, SW of Isles of Scilly, 49°09'N 08°37'W
Cause — Air attack
Casualties — 51
Survivors — None
Salvaged — No

Notes Liberator 'F' of No 120 Squadron, flown by Flt Lt A. K. Sherwood, sighted the wake of a U-boat. It was about five to six miles away and the boat was diving. Sherwood dropped six depth charges ahead of the swirl and after the explosions oil was seen rising to the surface. A sonobuoy was dropped, and breaking-up noises were heard; the latter ceased roughly fifteen minutes after the attack.

U821

	Launched	*Commissioned*
U821	26 Jun 1943	11 Oct 1943

Class — Type VIIC
CO — *Oberleutnant zur See* Ulrich Knackfuss (lost)
Date of loss — 10 June 1944
Location — English Channel, N of Ushant, 48°31'N 05°11'W
Cause — Air attack
Casualties — 50
Survivors — 1
Salvaged — No

Notes Mosquitos 'T', 'S', 'V' and 'W' of No 248 Squadron, led by Flt Lt S. G. Nunn, were on patrol over the approaches to Brest with the intention of attacking any U-boats trying to break out. Flying at low level, the aircrews saw a U-boat break surface about 2½ miles ahead. The U-boat had evidently not seen the aircraft since they were flying at an altitude of only 30ft. Each Mosquito attacked in turn, and after a series of strafing runs the crew were seen abandoning the U-boat, which appeared to be sinking by the stern. Liberator 'K' of No 206 Squadron, flown by Flt Lt A. D. S. Saunders, came up in support and made two depth-charge attacks, the second of which was a perfect straddle. When the boil subsided the U-boat had disappeared.

The survivors were picked up by a VP boat which was spotted by six No 248 Squadron Mosquitos as it returned to Brest later that afternoon. As one of the aircraft overflew the launch it was fired on, sustained some damage and later crashed. The other five aircraft (two of which were armed with the 6pdr Tsetse gun) proceeded to blow the VP boat out of the water.

U980

	Launched	*Commissioned*
U980	15 Apr 1943	27 May 1943

Class — Type VIIC
CO — *Kapitänleutnant* Hermann Dahms (lost)
Date of loss — 11 June 1944
Location — North Sea, 63°07'N 00°26'E
Cause — Air attack
Casualties — 52
Survivors — None
Salvaged — No

Notes Canso 'B' of No 162 Squadron RCAF, flown by Fg Off L. Sherman, sighted a U-boat on the surface at 1515 hours and immediately attacked, dropping four depth charges. When the explosions subsided the U-boat was seen trailing oil, although it continued to engage the aircraft with flak until it was seen to sink at 1532 hours, leaving wreckage and about 35 men in the water.

The next day the same aircraft and crew were shot down while attacking a U-boat in 64°10'N 00°11'E.

U490

	Launched	*Commissioned*
U490	24 Dec 1942	27 Mar 1943

Class Type XIV
CO *Oberleutnant* Wilhelm Gerlach (survived)
Date of loss 11 June 1944
Location Atlantic, NW of the Azores, 42°48'N 40°08'W
Cause Depth charge/gunfire
Casualties None
Survivors 53
Salvaged No

Notes U490 was outward-bound to Penang and just after midnight during the night of 10/11 June she sent a brief weather report to BdU. This was her—like so many others'—undoing. HF/DF plotted the position of the transmission and three destroyers in TG.22.5 (the carrier *Croatan* and five DEs) were able to obtain ground wave bearings on the transmission.

On the morning of the 11th, midway between Flores and Flemish Cap, the DEs found *U490* and commenced their attacks. Gerlach went deep—his own account says 1,000ft—and prepared to wait it out. Back on the surface, Cdr Frank G. Gianbattista was annoyed that his attacks were having no effect although his sonar remained in contact with the U-boat. Eventually, at 2100, the DEs retired, noisily and at speed, before returning quietly and at slow speed to the contact position to wait for the submarine to come up as she surely must. At 2147 *U490* surfaced between *Frost* and *Snowden* and was immediately fired on. The game was quickly up. Gerlach signalled his intention to surrender before scuttling the boat, although the DEs kept up the fire until it was clear that *U490* was sinking.

U490 was the last of the ten Type XIV Milch Cow U-boats to be sunk. Allied code-breaking and DF skills had made the wireless communications so essential for their operations their Achilles' heel.

U715

	Launched	*Commissioned*
U715	14 Dec 1942	17 Mar 1943

Class Type VIIC
CO *Kapitänleutnant* Helmut Rottger (lost)
Date of loss 13 June 1944
Location NE of Faeroe Islands, 62°45'N 02°59'W
Cause Air attack
Casualties 51
Survivors None
Salvaged No

Notes *U715* was attacked by Canso 'T' of 162 Squadron RCAF flown by Wg Cdr C. St G.W. Chapman. A particular impressive piece of observation had picked out the 'feather' from a periscope and the aircraft attacked. The U-boat then surfaced, began to steer an erratic course and then began to settle by the bows. As the stern rose up the Canso flew over for a final observation and was damaged by flak fired by a last desperate member of *U715*'s crew.

The Canso was forced to ditch, and although a lifeboat and two Lindholme dinghies were dropped by a Liberator and a Warwick, by the time an air–sea rescue launch arrived one of the crew had died of exposure; two more died before they could reach hospital.

U860

	Launched	*Commissioned*
U860	23 Mar 1943	12 Aug 1943

Class Type IXD2
CO *Fregattenkapitän* Paul Buchel (survived)
Date of loss 15 June 1944
Location S Atlantic, S of St Helena, 25°27'S 05°30'W
Cause Air attack
Casualties 42
Survivors 2 officers, 5 senior rates, 13 junior rates
Salvaged No

Notes *U860* was northward-bound and her position had been consistently plotted from HF/DF fixes. Astride her route was TG.41.6, consisting of the CVE *Solomons* with the experienced VC-9 embarked and four DEs. At 1021 on 15 June *U860* was located and attacked by an Avenger flown by Ensign George E. Edwards. However, Edwards was shot down and it was not until 1722 that the submarine was sighted by Lt-Cdr Howard Avery, VC-9's CO. Three Wildcats and two Avengers were then flown off in support. The aircraft launched a series of cannon and rocket attacks on the submarine which inflicted considerable damage. The U-boat was seen to be on fire and leaking oil. For the *coup de grâce* Lt (jg) William F. Chamberlain flew in low to deliver a depth-charge attack. Unfortunately

Chamberlain was too low: his Avenger was engulfed in the explosion of the depth charges and crashed 500yds ahead of the U-boat. Chamberlain and his crew were recovered.

Meanwhile *U860*, devastated by repeated rocket attacks, had sunk, leaving 21 survivors in the water who were picked up by *Straub*.

U998	*Launched* 18 Aug 1943	*Commissioned* 7 Oct 1943
Class	Type VIIC	
CO	*Kapitänleutnant* Hans Fiedler (survived)	
Date of loss	16 June 1944	
Location	Norwegian Sea, NW of Bergen, 61°01'N 03°00'E	
Cause	Air attack/CTL	
Casualties	None	
Survivors	51	
Salvaged	Details of ultimate disposal unknown	

Notes Three Mosquito aircraft of No 333 (Norwegian) Squadron RAF were deployed on anti-U-boat operations and sighted a U-boat at 1904. Mosquito 'H', flown by Lt E. U. Johansen, broke through cloud to deliver a cannon and depth-charge attack which left the U-boat leaking oil and steering an erratic course before diving, leaving wooden wreckage on the water (probably pieces of the casing). The bows then reappeared, so Johansen delivered a second attack before the bows sank. It appeared as if the U-boat were lying on its side.

Johansen's claim of a 'kill' was accepted. In fact Fiedler managed to bring his badly damaged boat back to Bergen on 17 June, where she was surveyed. The verdict was that the damage was not worth repairing, so she was formally paid off on 27 June 1944. Thus Johansen's claim stands.

U423	*Launched* 7 Nov 1942	*Commissioned* 3 Mar 1943
Class	Type VIIC	
CO	*Oberleutnant zur See* Klaus Hacklander (lost)	
Date of loss	17 June 1944	
Location	North Sea, 63°06'N 02°05'E	
Cause	Air attack	
Casualties	53	
Survivors	None	
Salvaged	No	

Notes Catalina 'D' of No 333 (Norwegian) Squadron, flown by Lt C. F. Krafft, sighted a surfaced U-boat at 1603 and attacked with six depth charges. The attack was a perfect straddle and the U-boat sank in six minutes, leaving wreckage and forty survivors on the surface.

U123	*Launched* 2 Mar 1944	*Commissioned* –
Class	Type IXB	
CO	*Kapitänleutnant* Horst von Schroeter	
Date of loss	17 June 1944	
Location	Bay of Biscay, Lorient	
Cause	Scuttling	
Casualties	None	
Survivors	–	
Salvaged	Yes (see notes)	

Notes Despite being a relatively new boat, *U123* was paid off on 17 June 1944 because she needed spares for her battery which could not be supplied locally. Since there was no future for the large Type IX submarines in the inshore campaign being fought in the Channel, it was decided to pay her off and redistribute the crew. She was scuttled in August 1944 when Lorient was evacuated. Her crew, along with those of other boats paid off in the Biscay ports, were evacuated through France to Germany.

The boat was surveyed by the French on the liberation of Lorient and incorporated into the *Marine Nationale* as *Blaison*. She remained in service until 1957 and was then sold for breaking up.

U441	*Launched* 13 Dec 1941	*Commissioned* 21 Feb 1942
Class	Type VIIC (converted to *U Flak 1* 16 April 1943)	
CO	*Kapitänleutnant* Klaus Hartmann (lost)	
Date of loss	June 1944	
Location	?	
Cause	?	
Casualties	51	
Survivors	None	
Salvaged	No	

Notes This boat was thought to have been the victim of an attack by Wellington 'A' of No 304 (Polish) Squadron RAF, flown by Fl Lt L. Antoniewicz. However, the real victim of this attack may have been *U1191*. In the circumstances, the verdict 'Unknown' is the most apt for *U441*.

U767	*Launched*	*Commissioned*
	10 Jul 1943	11 Sept 1943
Class	Type VIIC	
CO	*Oberleutnant zur See* Walter Dankleff (lost)	
Date of loss	18 June 1944	
Location	English Channel, SW of Guernsey, 49°03'N 03°13'W	
Cause	Hedgehog/depth charge	
Casualties	48	
Survivors	1	
Salvaged	No	

Notes At 1005 a U-boat was located by D/F by the 14th Escort Group comprising HMS *Fame* (Senior Officer), *Hotspur*, *Inconstant*, *Icarus* and *Havelock*. Although the signal was weak, its position, between Lannion and St Malo, corresponded with the track of a U-boat making a passage along the coast, so the group proceeded at full speed to the area. At 1620 *Fame* was in asdic contact and attacked first with Hedgehog—she was rewarded with three explosions after 4½ seconds, followed by the appearance of a large bubble of oil—and then with depth charges. *Havelock* followed up with more depth charges. *Inconstant* was just running in for a Hedgehog attack when a man wearing Dräger apparatus appeared on the surface in an air bubble. He was quickly picked up by *Fame*. German shore batteries now began laying down an accurate fire on the ships. *Hotspur* was ordered to make smoke while the other ships withdrew, having delivered a number of attacks to make sure that the U-boat was 'dead'.

The sole survivor, who identified himself as coming from *U767*, said that the Hedgehog attack had struck the U-boat forward. He had been stationed aft had had simply been blown out of the boat in an air bubble. Cdr Currie, *Fame*'s CO, noted that 'His escape from 40 fathoms between attacks made him a rather precious commodity'.

U971	*Launched*	*Commissioned*
	22 Feb 1943	1 Apr 1943
Class	Type VIIC	
CO	*Oberleutnant zur See* Walter Zeplien (survived)	
Date of loss	24 June 1944	
Location	English Channel, NW of Ushant, 49°01N 05°35'W	
Cause	Depth charge	
Casualties	1	
Survivors	52	
Salvaged	No	

Notes *U971* was on her first patrol, having sailed from Norway on 8 June. By the time she reached her operating area in the Channel she had been repeatedly attacked by aircraft, with the result that all her flak armament was damaged and only two of her six torpedo tubes were working. Zeplien decided to head for Brest and repairs. On the afternoon of 24 June *U971* was attacked by Liberator 'O' of No 311 (Czech) Squadron, which summoned the Canadian destroyer *Haida* and HMS *Eskimo*. A number of depth-charge attacks were delivered, and at 1825 Zeplien decided to surface and scuttle the boat. The battery was flat, his torpedo tubes were damaged and the air in the boat was foul. The plan was explained to the crew while they finished off the last of boat's beer ration standing knee-deep in rising water in the control room. The ballast tanks were then blown with the last remaining air and *U971* shot to the surface in full view of the two destroyers. The crew poured out of the hatch in a hail of gunfire while the boat sank beneath them.

U1225	*Launched*	*Commissioned*
	21 Jul 1943	10 Nov 1943
Class	Type IXC/40	
CO	*Oberleutnant zur See* Ernst Sauerberg (lost)	
Date of loss	24 June 1944	
Location	Norwegian Sea, NW of Bergen, 63°00'N 00°50'W	
Cause	Air attack	
Casualties	56	
Survivors	None	
Salvaged	No	

Notes Canso 'P' of No 162 Squadron RCAF was returning to Wick from patrol after ten hours in the air when the pilot, Flt Lt D. Hornell RCAF, sighted a surfaced U-boat. As the Canso flew in, the U-boat responded with a barrage of flak which damaged the starboard engine, so much so that Hornell had great difficulty controlling the aircraft. Despite the damage Hornell succeeded in defeating a last-minute evasive turn by the U-boat and dropped four depth charges which fell in a straddle.

However the Canso was so badly damaged—by now the starboard engine had fallen off and the wing was on fire—that Hornell had to ditch. The crew of eight then spent 21 hours in their dinghy, four taking turns to sit in it while the other four clung to the sides. Later all eight crammed into the dinghy and huddled together for warmth. A Catalina of No 333 (Norwegian) Squadron sighted the men on the 25th and also about 35–40 survivors from the U-boat a couple of miles away. However, the German survivors gradually succumbed to cold and drowning as the day progressed. At 1100 on the 25th a Wellington aircraft dropped a lifeboat, but the men in the dinghy were too cold and exhausted to reach it. Finally at 1500 on the 25th the crew were picked up by an air–sea rescue launch. Two of the eight had died in the dinghy and Hornell died shortly after rescue.

For pressing on with his attack and for his courage and inspiring conduct while in the dinghy, Hornell was awarded a posthumous Victoria Cross. One DSO, two DFCs and two DFMs went to the surviving members of the crew.

U269	*Launched* 24 Jun 1942	*Commissioned* 19 Aug 1942

Class	Type VIIC
CO	*Oberleutnant Zur See* Georg Uhl (lost)
Date of loss	25 June 1944
Location	English Channel, SE of Start Point, 50°01N 02°59'W
Cause	Depth charge
Casualties	12
Survivors	4 officers, 9 senior rates, 26 junior rates
Salvaged	No

Notes Early in the morning of 25 June HMS *Bickerton* of EG5 made contact with *U269* to the south-east of Statrt Point and after a number of depth-charge attacks blew her to the surface, where she was abandoned.

U1191	*Launched* 6 Jul 1943	*Commissioned* 9 Sept 1943

Class	Type VIIC
CO	*Oberleutnant zur See* Peter Grau (lost)
Date of loss	25 June 1944
Location	English Channel, SE of Torquay, 50°13'N 03°38W
Cause	Depth charge
Casualties	50
Survivors	None
Salvaged	No

Notes After the sinking of *U269* EG5 continued their operations but at 1514 one of the group, HMS *Goodson*, was struck by a Gnat fired by *U984*. EG1 took over the task of hunting for the culprit while EG5 escorted their stricken consort back to port. EG1 began hunting to the west of the attack and at 2129 HMS *Balfour* obtained a contact by asdic. Unfortunately the boat was *U1191*. *Affleck* attacked with a Hedgehog, the target being at 175ft and the bombs exploding after nine seconds' sinking time. When *Affleck* ran in to deliver a depth-charge attack she found herself steaming through a growing oil slick. There was then some concern that EG1 might have been attacking the wreck of *U269*, but this was confirmed as being some three miles away. *Balfour* and *Affleck* then carried out a series of attacks which pounded 'their' wreck to destruction.

U317	*Launched* 1 Sept 1943	*Commissioned* 23 Oct 1943

Class	Type VIIC
CO	*Oberleutnant zur See* Peter Rahlff (lost)
Date of loss	26 June 1944
Location	Norwegian Sea, NE of Shetlands, 62°03'N 01°45'E
Cause	Air attack
Casualties	50
Survivors	None
Salvaged	No

Notes Consolidated Liberator 'N' of No 86 Squadron, flown by Flt Lt G.W. Parker RAF, made two attacks on a surfaced U-boat on 26 June. On the second run, three depth charges were dropped and these all fell alongside the starboard side of the submarine. The U-boat then rolled over to port and began to sink, and a large number of bodies were seen to be floating in a growing oil slick.

U719

	Launched	*Commissioned*
U719	28 Apr 1943	27 Jul 1943

Class Type VIIC
CO *Kapitänleutnant* Klaus-Dietrich Steffens (lost)
Date of loss 26 June 1944
Location Atlantic, NW of Bloody Foreland, 55°33'N 11°02'W
Cause Depth charge
Casualties 52
Survivors None
Salvaged No

Notes Early on 26 June a U-boat was reported 50 miles to the north-west of Blacksod Bay. After HMCS *St Thomas* had obtained an HF/DF bearing, HM Ships *Bulldog* and *Awe* were directed to search along the line of bearing. Within 2½ hours *Bulldog* was in asdic contact and made three Hedgehog attacks. Throughout the hunt the U-boat continued to manoeuvre evasively, making frequent changes of course and depth. However, the third Hedgehog attack produced a number of explosions, after which contact was lost and it was thought that the U-boat must have sunk in over 2,000ft of water. The ships remained in the vicinity and then at 1415, three hours after the attack, oil began to well up on the surface. At first it was little more than a trickle but by 1800 the slick covered an area of three square miles and was still welling up to the surface.

U988

	Launched	*Commissioned*
U988	3 Jun 1943	15 Jul 1943

Class Type VIIC
CO *Oberleutnant zur See* Erich Dobberstein (lost)
Date of loss June 1944
Location ?
Cause ?
Casualties 50
Survivors None
Salvaged No

Notes *U988* was previously thought to have been the victim of Liberator 'L' of No 224 Squadron RAF and HM Ships *Essington*, *Domett*, *Duckworth* and *Cooke*. However, recent research suggests that she may have been sunk by Wellington 'A' of No 304 (Polish) Squadron on 18 June. In the circumstances the verdict 'Unknown' seems the most appropriate.

U478

	Launched	*Commissioned*
U478	17 Jul 1943	8 Sept 1943

Class Type VIIC
CO *Oberleutnant zur See* Rudolf Rademacher (lost)
Date of loss 30 June 1944
Location Atlantic, NE of Faeroe Islands, 63°27'N 00°50'W
Cause Air attack
Casualties 52
Survivors None
Salvaged No

Notes *U478* was first sighted and reported by Canso 'A' of No 162 Squadron. The pilot, Flt Lt R. E. MacBride, had tried to attack but his depth charges would not release, so he homed in Liberator 'E' of No 86 Squadron (Fg Off N. E. Smith). The latter arrived at 2115 and attacked, blowing the U-boat's bows out of the water with six depth charges. The boat then sank stern first, leaving a number of survivors in two dinghies.

U543

	Launched	*Commissioned*
U543	3 Feb 1943	21 Apr 1943

Class Type IXC/40
CO *Kapitänleutnant* Hans-Jurgen Hellriegel (lost)
Date of loss 2 July 1944
Location Atlantic, SW of Tenerife, 25°34'N 21°36'W
Cause Fido
Casualties 58
Survivors None
Salvaged No

Notes HF/DF bearings had located *U543* around 26°N 20°W. Ensign Frederick L. Moore USN, flying a VC-58 Avenger from *Bogue*, found the U-boat on the evening of 2 July. He dropped two depth charges and then, as the U-boat dived, he dropped a Fido. He then laid a pattern of sonobuoys, but by the time they became active the Fido had struck the submarine and she was gone, leaving nothing but a large and expanding oil slick on the surface.

U154

	Launched	*Commissioned*
U154	21 Apr 1941	2 Aug 1941

Class Type IXC
CO *Oberleutnant zur See* Gerth Gemeiner (lost)

Date of loss	3 July 1944
Location	Atlantic, W of Madeira, 34°00'N 19°30'W
Cause	Depth charge
Casualties	57
Survivors	None
Salvaged	No

Notes *U154* was heading for the Cape Hatteras area when her wireless transmissions, interecepted by the Americans, placed her north-west of Madeira. TG.22.5, based around the carrier *Croatan*, put to sea to look for her. On the morning of 2 July the US destroyer *Inch* gained a sonar contact but then had to manouevre rapidly to avoid two Gnats fired at her. Joined now by *Frost*, the two destroyers started a systematic search and followed with a number of depth-charge attacks. After the fourth attack an underwater explosion separate from the depth charge detonations was heard, and this was followed by the appearance of oil and wreckage on the surface. The wreckage included human remains, German uniforms and splintered wood.

	Launched	*Commissioned*
U233	8 May 1943	22 Sept 1943
Class	Type XB	
CO	*Kapitänleutnant* Hans Steen (lost)	
Date of loss	5 July 1944	
Location	N Atlantic, E of Halifax, 4 2°16'N 59°49'W	
Cause	Ramming/depth charge/ gunfire	
Casualties	31	
Survivors	3 officers, 4 senior rates, 22 junior rates	
Salvaged	No	

Notes *U233* was en route to Halifax for a mine-laying operation when she was found first by a VC-12 aircraft from *Card* and then by the destroyer *Baker*. *Baker*'s depth-charge attack took *U233*, whose crew were busy with the daily torpedo maintenance routines, by surprise. She took water aft and began to sink. The LI could not restore the trim so Steen gave the order to surface. *U233* broached in full view of the destroyer *Thomas*, which opened fire on the submarine, as did the *Baker*. *Baker* also fired two torpedoes which, although they hit, failed to explode since they had not run a sufficient distance to arm. *Baker* laid a shallow depth-charge pattern around *U233* as *Thomas* came in to ram. The latter struck *U233* just aft of the conning tower, the impact breaking the submarine in half. Her bows rose into the air and she sank.

Steen, who had been wounded in the engagement, died the next day and was buried with full military honours.

	Launched	*Commissioned*
U390	23 Jan 1943	13 Mar 1943
Class	Type VIIC	
CO	*Oberleutnant zur See* Heinz Geizsler (lost)	
Date of loss	5 July 1944	
Location	English Channel, Seine Bay, 49°52'N 00°48'W	
Cause	Hedgehog	
Casualties	47	
Survivors	1 petty officer	
Salvaged	No	

Notes The destroyer HMS *Wanderer* and frigate HMS *Tavy* were escorting a northbound convoy off Pointe de Barfleur when they detected a U-boat. *Tavy* delivered the first Hedgehog attack, which probably mortally damaged the U-boat, for in the interval between the first and second attacks one petty officer came to the surface wearing Dräger apparatus. A further five Hedgehog attacks were made before the U-boat was considered to have been sunk. A total of thirty depth charges were then dropped on the stationary target to achieve her complete destruction.

	Launched	*Commissioned*
U586	10 Jul 1941	4 Sept 1941
Class	Type VIIC	
CO	*Oberleutnant zur See* Hans Gotz	
Date of loss	5 July 1944	
Location	Mediterranean, Toulon	
Cause	Air attack	
Casualties	?	
Survivors	?	
Salvaged	Wreck dismantled *in situ*	

Notes Sunk while alongside at Toulon during a daylight USAAF air raid.

	Launched	*Commissioned*
U642	6 Aug 1942	1 Oct 1942
Class	Type VIIC	

CO	*Kapitänleutnant* Herbert Brunning
Date of loss	5 July 1944
Location	Mediterranean, Toulon
Cause	Air attack/CTL
Casualties	?
Survivors	?
Salvaged	Wreck dismantled *in situ*

Notes Damaged while alongside at Toulon during a daylight USAAF air raid. The hull was subsequently surveyed and declared a constructive total loss. The boat was paid off on 12 July 1944.

U678	*Launched* 18 Sept 1943	*Commissioned* 25 Oct 1943
Class	Type VIIC	
CO	*Kapitänleutnant* Guido Hyronimus (lost)	
Date of loss	6 July 1944	
Location	English Channel, off Beachy Head, 50°32'N 00°23'W	
Cause	Depth charge	
Casualties	52	
Survivors	None	
Salvaged	No	

Notes The sinking of *U678* is a perfect example of the difficulties confronting Allied ASW forces hunting U-boats in the shallow, wreck-strewn waters of the English Channel. On the evening of 5 July EG11 were having a frustrating time pursuing numerous contacts, all of which turned out to be wrecks, when they responded to a signal from the British corvette *Statice* that she was in contact with a submerged U-boat. *Ottawa* and *Kootenay* were detached and both ships were in contact with the U-boat by 0940 the next morning. The target was assessed as bottomed in 225ft of water, but it was subsequently assessed as moving eastwards at 2kts, the same speed as the tide. At 1017Z *Ottawa* attacked with Hedgehog and was rewarded with one explosion. The target then changed direction and moved across the tidal stream. *Kootenay* delivered a depth-charge attack and *Statice* delivered a Hedgehog attack at 1123 which produced one hit, some oil and wooden wreckage. The U-boat now appeared to bottom, although motion and tidal noise suggested otherwise. Once these distractions had been eliminated, it was clear that the target never moved again. A further depth-charge attack by *Kootenay* at 1159Z produced more wreckage, including a number of German publications (including novels) and an object resembling a human lung.

However, the evidence was insufficient for a 'kill' to be claimed so the ships began the grisly business of blowing the wreck apart to release more evidence. Consequently, throughout the 6th and the night of the 6th–7th the ships continued to plaster the wreck with depth charges, Hedgehog and towed charges. The last was a refinement by *Ottawa*'s commanding officer, Capt J. D. Prentice RCN, and consisted of a depth charge towed behind the ship on a long wire fitted with a grappling hook. When the hook snagged an object the charge was fired. At 0649Z on the 7th *Statice* and *Kootenay* delivered another depth-charge attack which produced more oil and a German locker door. Although the evidence was no more conclusive than that of the day before, Prentice abandoned the hunt and returned to Portsmouth. In the subsequent analysis Commodore (D) Western Approaches commended Prentice for his persistence but commented that pursuing the hunt after 1200 on 6 July was over-zealous: 'it is inconceivable that a submarine should live to withstand two Hedgehog hits and the explosion of a 300lb Minol depth charge in contact with its hull...The necesssity for the pulverising of the dead hull is not clear.'

U243	*Launched* 2 Sept 1943	*Commissioned* 2 Oct 1943
Class	Type VIIC	
CO	*Kapitänleutnant* Hans Martens (lost)	
Date of loss	8 July 1944	
Location	Bay of Biscay, SW of Ushant, 47°06'N 06°40'W	
Cause	Air attack	
Casualties	12	
Survivors	2 officers, 2 senior rates, 34 junior rates	
Salvaged	No	

Notes Sunderland 'H' of No 10 Squadron RAAF, flown by Fg Off W. B. Tilley RAAF, sighted the U-boat at 1435 fully surfaced at a range of six miles. At two miles the U-boat opened fire on the Sunderland but the aircraft's front gunner, Flt Sgt L. E. Cooke, replied with such accuracy that the U-boat's flak crews were eliminated. Tilley dropped six depth charges which exploded in a perfect straddle around the stern. As the aircraft circled, the U-boat was seen lying dead in the water with a list to port. Just after 1500 the crew were seen launching dinghies and taking to the water. As the crew were going over the side their departure was hastened by attacks by another No 10 Squadron Sunderland and a B-24 of VP-105. All three aircraft saw the boat sink stern first, the bows rising to the vertical before sinking. Tilley overflew the site, dropping a dinghy and an emergency food pack to the men in the water, before heading for home.

The survivors of *U243*, including Martens who later died of a head wound received during the attack, were rescued by HMCS *Restigouche*.

U1222

	Launched	*Commissioned*
U1222	9 Jun 1943	1 Sept 1943
Class	Type IXC/40	
CO	*Kapitänleutnant* Hans Bielefeld (lost)	
Date of loss	11 July 1944	
Location	Bay of Biscay, W of La Rochelle	
Cause	Air attack	
Casualties	56	
Survivors	None	
Salvaged	No	

Notes Sunderland 'P' of No 201 Squadron was flown by Flt Lt B. F. Waters DFC RAF, an exceptionally experienced officer but who on this occasion was flying with a new and untested crew. The aircraft was flying a rectangular search pattern between 45° and 47°N with other No 19 Group aircraft when the Sgt J. B. Beck sighted the tell-tale head of a snorkel with the radar operator reporting the contact a few seconds later—a most impressive performance.

As the aircraft came in the U-boat dived, warned either by visual sighting of the aircraft or by a warning receiver on the snorkel mast. The dive was steep and the boat's stern came into view just as five depth charges were released (one of the six hung up), which fell in a straddle around the stern. When the explosions subsided, a large amount of wreckage was seen on the surface.

U415

	Launched	*Commissioned*
U415	9 May 1942	5 Aug 1942
Class	Type VIIC	
CO	*Oberleutnant zur See* Herbert Werner (survived)	
Date of loss	14 July 1944	
Location	Brest, France, 48°22'N 04°29'W	
Cause	Mine	
Casualties	2	
Survivors	47	
Salvaged	No	

Notes *U415* was one of the last operational U-boats working from the Biscay ports. On the morning of 14 July she put to sea for engine trials under the command of the Flotilla Engineer Officer since her CO had overslept. Just after clearing the U-boat pens she ran over an acoustic mine laid by the British which was activated by her diesels. Though rescue work was speedily effected, many of the crew sustained multiple fractures from the shock of the explosion.

Werner went on to command *U953*. He survived the war and wrote the best-selling *Iron Coffins*.

U319

	Launched	*Commissioned*
U319	16 Oct 1943	4 Dec 1943
Class	Type VIIC	
CO	*Oberleutnant zur See* Johann Clemens (lost)	
Date of loss	15 July 1944	
Location	Norwegian Sea, 57°40'N 05°00'E	
Cause	Air attack	
Casualties	50	
Survivors	None	
Salvaged	No	

Notes Presumed sunk by Liberator 'E' of No 206 Squadron RAF, flown by Fg Off D. W. Thynne. The aircraft failed to return from this sortie and it is presumed that she was shot down by the U-boat's flak. A large oil slick was sighted in the position given above by Liberator 'B' of No 206 Squadron on the same day. On 16 July the body of one of the Liberator's crew was picked up by an air–sea rescue launch.

U361

	Launched	*Commissioned*
U361	9 Sept 1942	18 Dec 1942
Class	Type VIIC	
CO	*Kapitänleutnant* Klaus Becker (lost)	
Date of loss	17 July 1944	
Location	Norwegian Sea, NW of Lofoten Islands, 68°36N 08°33'E	

Cause	Air attack
Casualties	52
Survivors	None
Salvaged	No

Notes At 2148 Liberator 'U' of No 86 Squadron, flown by P Off M. G. Mosely, caught *U361* on the surface. Mosely attacked with six depth charges which straddled the U-boat. Six men were seen in the water amid oil and wreckage after the submarine foundered.

U347

	Launched	Commissioned
	24 May 1943	7 Jul 1943
Class	Type VIIC	
CO	*Oberleutnant zur See* Johann de Buhr (lost)	
Date of loss	17 July 1944	
Location	Arctic, 68°35'N 06°00'E	
Cause	Air attack	
Casualties	49	
Survivors	None	
Salvaged	No	

Notes Eight minutes after the loss of *U361* and a few miles to the north, Catalina 'Y' of No 210 Squadron RAF, flown by Fg Off J.A. Cruikshank, sighted *U347*. During the run-in the depth charges refused to release so Cruikshank took the aircraft round again. The Catalina flew through a considerable amount of flak which killed the navigator and four members of the crew—including, eventually, Cruikshank. Nevertheless, Cruikshank pressed home the attack and dropped his depth charges in a perfect straddle which sank the U-boat. The second pilot, Flt Sgt J. Garnett, took over and brought the aircraft back to Sullom Voe.

Cruikshank had refused morphia for his wounds and now insisted on being taken back to the cockpit, where he and Garnett safely landed the badly damaged aircraft by running it up on the beach. Cruikshank had lost so much blood that he had to be given an emergency transfusion in the aircraft before being removed to hospital.

For his gallantry in carrying out the attack and then for refusing medication which would have prevented him from landing the aircraft, Cruikshank was awarded the Victoria Cross—the third to be awarded to a Coastal Command pilot.

U672

	Launched	Commissioned
	27 Feb 1943	6 Apr 1943
Class	Type VIIC	
CO	*Oberleutnant zur See* Ulf Lawaetz (survived)	
Date of loss	18 July 1944	
Location	English Channel, 32m off Start Point, 50°03'N 02°30'W	
Cause	Depth charge	
Casualties	None	
Survivors	4 officers, 4 senior rates, 38 junior rates	
Salvaged	No	

Notes *U672* had sailed from St Nazaire on 6 July and took nearly twelve days to grope her way through very aggressive anti-submarine patrols to a position off Start Point, which she reached on the 18th. There she was attacked and badly damaged in depth-charge attacks by the frigate HMS *Balfour* but managed to escape. However, the damage was so extensive that Lawaetz had no option but to abandon the boat on the night of 18–19 July and take to the dinghies. The survivors were spotted the next morning. Lawaetz was collected as a 'sample' by a Fleet Air Arm Walrus aircraft and the remainder were picked up by air–sea rescue launches.

U742

	Launched	Commissioned
	4 Feb 1943	1 May 1943
Class	Type VIIC	
CO	*Kapitänleutnant* Heinz Schwassmann (lost)	
Date of loss	18 July 1944	
Location	Norwegian Sea, W of Lofoten Islands, 68°24'N 09°51'E	
Cause	Air attack	
Casualties	52	
Survivors	None	
Salvaged	No	

Notes *U742* was sighted on the surface by Catalina 'Z' of No 210 Squadron, flown by Fg Off R.W. Vaughan. The U-boat's crew were alert and began firing at the Catalina, badly damaging the starboard engine. Nevertheless, Vaughan pressed on and saw the U-boat disappear following the explosions of his depth charges. About forty men were seen swimming in the water amid a large oil slick. Vaughan could not remain in the area as his aircraft was losing oil from the starboard engine (which had to be stopped) and fuel from the port wing. Although he managed to beach the Catalina at Heinkel Cape, he had flown the last 500 miles on one engine.

U212	*Launched*	*Commissioned*
	11 Mar 1942	25 Apr 1942

Class Type VIIC
CO *Kapitänleutnant* Helmut Vogler (lost)
Date of loss 21 July 1944
Location English Channel, SW of Beachy Head, 50°27'N 00°13'E
Cause Depth charge
Casualties 49
Survivors None
Salvaged No
Notes Sunk in a depth-charge attack by the frigates HMS *Curzon* and HMS *Ekins*. At the time the attack was not assessed as 'Known sunk', but after the war it was learned that *U212* had in fact gone down.

U1166	*Launched*	*Commissioned*
	28 Aug 1943	8 Dec 1943

Class Type VIIC/41
CO *Oberleutnant zur See* Sarto Ballert
Date of loss 28 July 1944
Location Baltic, Kiel Bay, Eckernförde
Cause Torpedo explosion
Casualties ?
Survivors ?
Salvaged Paid off 28 August 1944 and not recommissioned
Notes *U1166* was particpating in trials at the *Kriegsmarine*'s torpedo testing establishment in Eckernförde when she was damaged beyond repair in a torpedo explosion. The wreck was scuttled at Kiel on 3 May 1945.

U239	*Launched*	*Commissioned*
	28 Jan 1943	13 Mar 1943

Class Type VIIC
CO *Oberleutnant zur See* Ulrich Voge (survived)
Date of loss 23 July 1944
Location Baltic, Kiel
Cause Air attack
Casualties ?
Survivors ?
Salvaged No
Notes *U239* had never become an operational *Frontboot* and had been employed on training duties since her completion. However, this did not make her immune from the attentions of the RAF since she was damaged beyond repair in a bombing raid on the port of Kiel on 23 July 1943. The wreck was broken up in August 1944.

U1164	*Launched*	*Commissioned*
	3 Jul 1943	27 Oct 1943

Class Type VIIC/41
CO *Kapitänleutnant* Hans Wengel
Date of loss 24 July 1944
Location Baltic, Kiel
Cause Air attack
Casualties ?
Survivors ?
Salvaged No
Notes Sunk during an RAF bombing raid on the port of Kiel.

U214	*Launched*	*Commissioned*
	18 Sept 1941	1 Nov 1941

Class Type VIIC
CO *Oberleutnant zur See* Gerhard Conrad (lost)
Date of loss 26 July 1944
Location English Channel, off Start Point, 49°55'N 03°31'W
Cause Depth charge
Casualties 48
Survivors None
Salvaged No
Notes *U214* had been instructed to lay mines off Start Point but was detected by the frigate *Cooke* and depth-charged to destruction.

U2323	*Launched*	*Commissioned*
	?	?

Class Type XXIII
CO *Oberleutnant zur See* Walter Angermann
Date of loss 26 July 1944
Location Baltic, Kiel Bay, W of Moltentort, 54°23'N 10°11'E
Cause Mine
Casualties 2

Survivors	12
Salvaged	No

Notes The first of the Type XXIII coastal submarines to be lost. She was sunk when she ran over an Allied air-laid mine.

U872	*Launched* 20 Oct 1943	*Commissioned* 10 Feb 1944
Class	Type IXD2	
CO	*Kapitänleutnant* Grau	
Date of loss	29 July 1944	
Location	Baltic, Bremen	
Cause	Air attack	
Casualties	1	
Survivors	?	
Salvaged	No	

Notes Sunk in a USAAF bombing raid on Bremen. Paid off 10 August 1944.

U890	*Launched* 1944 (?)	*Commissioned* –
Class	Type IXC/40	
CO	None appointed	
Date of loss	29 July 1944	
Location	Baltic, Bremen	
Cause	Air attack	
Casualties	?	
Survivors	?	
Salvaged	No	

Notes Destroyed during a USAAF bombing raid on the city. Construction suspended and hull subsequently broken up.

U891	*Launched* 1944 (?)	*Commissioned* –
Class	Type IXC/40	
CO	None appointed	
Date of loss	29 July 1944	
Location	Baltic, Bremen	
Cause	Air attack	
Casualties	?	
Survivors	?	
Salvaged	No	

Notes Destroyed during a USAAF bombing raid on the city. Construction suspended and hull subsequently broken up.

U892	*Launched* 1944 (?)	*Commissioned* –
Class	Type IXC/40	
CO	None appointed	
Date of loss	29 July 1944	
Location	Baltic, Bremen	
Cause	Air attack	
Casualties	?	
Survivors	?	
Salvaged	No	

Notes Destroyed during a USAAF bombing raid on the city. Construction suspended and hull subsequently broken up.

U250	*Launched* 11 Nov 1943	*Commissioned* 12 Dec 1943
Class	Type VIIC	
CO	*Kapitänleutnant* Werner-Karl Schmidt (survived)	
Date of loss	30 July 1944	
Location	Baltic, Gulf of Finland, 60°29'N 28°28'E	
Cause	Depth charge	
Casualties	49	
Survivors	1 officer, 4 senior rates, 1 junior rate	
Salvaged	Yes	

Notes *U250* had sunk the Soviet patrol boat *MO-105* at 1240 on 30 July. This action had started a full-scale hunt for the submarine by Soviet patrol craft supported by aircraft. Soviet sources do not indicate how *U250* was detected by *MO-103* (Captain 2nd Rank A. P. Kolenko) but they reveal that the second pattern of depth charges breached the pressure hull around the engine room and water flooded into the submarine, causing the battery to release chlorine gas. Schmidt could do no more than bring the boat to the surface, where he and five others were able to escape before the boat sank beneath them.

The Soviet authorities, being sure of *U250*'s location, decided to send down divers to see what items of interest could be recovered from the wreck. However, it proved impossible to enter the wreck so the decision was taken to raise her. Salvage teams were summoned from the Black Sea Fleet (under the command of Captain 3rd Rank A.V. Razuvayev) and found the boat lying in 27m of water with a 14-degree list to starboard. The salvage operation was complicated by the fact that the Germans held one shore of the

Gulf of Finland and were able to lay down harassing artillery fire on the salvagers. As a result a large number of minesweepers were deployed to maintain a permanent smokescreen to hide the work. The divers, led by I. P. Fedorchenko, succeeded in placing two 8in wires under the submarine and secured them to two 200-ton pontoons. Despite bad weather, which meant that the number of pontoons involved had to be increased from two to four, *U250* was raised and placed in dock at Kronstadt on 15 September, where she was examined.

The intelligence gain was immense. Not only did the Soviets recover two of the T5 *Zaunkönig* acoustic torpedoes, together with two G7E standard electric torpedoes which were fitted with the FAT and LUT manoeuvring devices, but they also recovered the boat's Enigma cipher machine and a complete set of confidential and technical publications which, though waterlogged, could be restored. Details of the ultimate disposal of the hull are unknown.

	Launched	*Commissioned*
U333	14 Jun 1941	25 Aug 1941
Class	Type VIIC	
CO	*Kapitänleutnant* Hans Fiedler (lost)	
Date of loss	31 July 1944	
Location	English Channel, SW of Isles of Scilly, 49°39'N 07°28'W	
Cause	Depth charge	
Casualties	45	
Survivors	None	
Salvaged	No	

Notes Sunk by depth charges from HM Ships *Starling* and *Loch Killin*.

	Launched	*Commissioned*
U671	27 Feb 1943	3 Mar 1943
Class	Type VIIC	
CO	*Oberleutnant zur See* Wolfgang Hegewald (lost)	
Date of loss	5 August 1944	
Location	English Channel, 50°23'N 00°06'E	
Cause	Depth charge	
Casualties	47	
Survivors	2 officers, 4 ratings	
Salvaged	No	

Notes *U671* had been badly damaged during her previous patrol in the English Channel and had been forced to make for Boulogne. Since there were no U-boat repair facilities at that port, a party of technicians made the long and dangerous journey overland from St Nazaire to effect repairs. They suceeded sufficiently for *U671* to be declared fit for another patrol in the Channel.

However, on this occasion the U-boat was detected by the frigate HMS *Stayner*. The frigate was deploying for operations against German *S-boote* and thus her Hedgehog was not loaded. While the Hedgehog was readied *Stayner* made three attacks with depth charges. Hegewald had evaded these attacks by making last-minute alterations of course, depth and speed when his hydrophone operator reported that *Stayner* had steadied on her attacking run. However, *Stayner's* Hedgehog attack took him by surprise. *Stayner's* third depth-charge attack and Hedgehog attack had done *U671* some serious damage. Hegewald tried to surface and it was while the engineers were trying to raise the boat that *Wensleydale* (which had joined the hunt together with *Offa* and *Rowley*) delivered another three depth-charge attacks and a Hedgehog attack. After the Hedgehog attack *Wensleydale* sighted men in the water and rescued six of them. They identified themselves as coming from *U671* and that they had escaped from the submarine when all efforts to raise the boat had failed.

	Launched	*Commissioned*
U471	6 Mar 1943	5 May 1943
Class	Type VIIC	
CO	*Kapitänleutnant* Friedrich Kloevekorn	
Date of loss	6 August 1944	
Location	Mediterranean, Toulon	
Cause	Air attack	
Casualties	?	
Survivors	?	
Salvaged	Yes	

Notes *U471* was sunk in shallow water during a daylight raid on Toulon by the USAAF. The boat was raised by the French in 1945 and commissioned into the *Marine Nationale* as *Mille*. She was sold for breaking up in 1963.

U736

	Launched	*Commissioned*
U736	31 Oct 1942	16 Jan 1943

Class Type VIIC
CO *Oberleutnant zur See* Reinhard Reff (survived)
Date of loss 6 August 1944
Location Atlantic, W of St Nazaire, 47°19'N 04°16'W
Cause Squid
Casualties 28
Survivors 3 officers, 3 senior rates, 13 junior rates
Salvaged No

Notes *U736* was the first U-boat to be sunk using the Squid ahead-throwing weapon.

The frigate HMS *Loch Killin*, part of the 2nd Escort Group which was on patrol in the Bay of Biscay, sighted a periscope on her starboard bow and then 'heard' the U-boat passing down her starboard side. As the British vessel reduced speed she altered course under full starboard helm and, at a range of 600yds, obtained a firm asdic contact. The attack was conducted in such a short period that there was only just enough time to obtain one clear indication of the target's depth using the Type 147B before a pattern of six Squid charges was fired. Just before the pattern exploded, a Gnat was countermined on the frigate's port side, just abreast the pom-pom armament.

Just after the explosion of the Squid charges the U-boat broke surface, heading for *Loch Killin*'s port side. The frigate went full astern and then stopped, but the U-boat came to rest caught up on her port 'A' bracket. The U-boat's conning tower and flak armament were a mass of mangled wreckage and her crew seemed to want nothing more than to climb over on to *Loch Killin*'s quarterdeck and surrender. The U-boat then took on a steeper trim before sinking vertically by the stern. *Loch Killin* hastily cleared the position in case the U-boat exploded, but she did not and her shattered hull was eventually finished off by a twenty-charge pattern fired by *Starling*.

The U-boat's survivors were under the impression that they had been rammed by *Loch Killin*. So great was the explosion of the Squid pattern that although before the charges exploded *U736* was steering 90 degrees, when she was blown to the surface her bows were pointing 340 degrees.

U952

	Launched	*Commissioned*
U952	14 Oct 1942	10 Dec 1942

Class Type VIIC
CO *Kapitänleutnant* Oscar Curio
Date of loss 6 August 1944 (?)
Location Mediterranean, Toulon
Cause Air attack
Casualties ?
Survivors ?
Salvaged No

Notes *U952* was bombed and sunk during a USAAF daylight raid on Toulon.

U969

	Launched	*Commissioned*
U969	11 Feb 1943	24 Mar 1943

Class Type VIIC
CO *Oberleutnant zur See* Max Dobbert
Date of loss 6 August 1944
Location Mediterranean, Toulon.
Cause Air attack
Casualties ?
Survivors ?
Salvaged No

Notes *U969* was bombed and sunk during a USAAF daylight raid on Toulon.

U608

	Launched	*Commissioned*
U608	11 Dec 1941	5 Feb 1942

Class Type VIIC
CO *Oberleutnant zur See* Wolfgang Reisner (survived)
Date of loss 10 August 1944
Location Bay of Biscay, SW of St Nazaire, 46°30'N 03°08'W
Cause Air attack/depth charge
Casualties None
Survivors 51
Salvaged No

Notes Liberator 'C' of No 53 Squadron, flown by Wg Cdr R. 'Crasher' Gates AFC RAF, sighted a U-boat, submerged, slightly ahead of a mile-long oil slick. Gates dropped six depth charges and saw bubbles and more oil rising to the surface before heading off at 1503 to contact the 2nd Escort Group operating nearby. EG2 arrived but the SO, appreciating that the U-boat had bottomed, left *Wren* and *Loch Killin* to carry on the hunt while taking *Starling*, *Dominica* and *Loch Fada* off to pursue a more promising contact.

Eventually, at 2200, *Loch Killin* obtained a firm echo sounder trace which she attacked with depth charges. About six hours later *Wren* reported a radar contact on the surface which then disappeared. On investigating the area, *Wren* found Reisner and his crew in the water: damaged in the attack by the Liberator, *U608* had been further damaged by *Loch Killin*. Reisner concluded that the combination of the opposition on the surface and the damage to his boat had left him no option but to surface and scuttle.

U385	*Launched*	*Commissioned*
	8 Jul 1942	29 Aug 1942
Class	Type VIIC	
CO	*Oberleutnant zur See* Hans-Guido Valentiner (survived)	
Date of loss	11 August 1944	
Location	Bay of Biscay, W of La Rochelle, 46°16'N 02°45'W	
Cause	Air attack/depth charge	
Casualties	1	
Survivors	4 officers, 10 senior rates, 27 junior rates	
Salvaged	No	

Notes At 2057 *U385* broke surface about 9,000yds ahead of the ships of the 2nd Escort Group. She was engaged, and she then dived after giving a recognition signal. The ships searched the position but found nothing other than a mass of 'Non-Sub' contacts. Six hours later, at 0300/11, Sunderland 'P' of No 461 Squadron RAAF, flown by P Off Ivan Southall RAAF, attacked a surfaced U-boat with six depth charges. Although the U-boat continued to engage the aircraft with flak after the attack, she was seen lying dead in the water.

Southall now homed the ships of EG2 on to his position. The ships found that they were steering down the path of a very bright moon so they divided and passed either side of the markers dropped by the Sunderland until they were ten miles beyond them, then they reversed course and returned to the scene at 7kts. At 0630 the U-boat surfaced 3,000yds ahead of the ships and lay stopped bows-on. She was abandoned by her crew under fire from the ships of the group and sank some five minutes later.

Valentiner told his interrogators that it was the attack by the Sunderland which had done the most damage. The port hydroplane had been blown off, the starboard shaft jammed and the steering destroyed. The stern tube had also developed a bad leak which the pumps could not hold. The sinking of *U385* marked the end of a very successful deployment for the 2nd Escort Group: four U-boats (*U333*, *U736*, *U608* and *U385*) had been sunk in less than ten days and over 100 prisoners taken. It was a worthy memorial to Captain Walker.

U198	*Launched*	*Commissioned*
	15 Jun 1942	3 Nov 1942
Class	Type IXD2	
CO	*Oberleutnant zur See* Heusinger von Waldegg (lost)	
Date of loss	12 August 1944	
Location	Indian Ocean, NW of Seychelles 03°45'S 52°58'E	
Cause	Depth charge	
Casualties	66	
Survivors	None	
Salvaged	No	

Notes The only U-boat sunk by a hunter-killer group in the Indian Ocean. *U198* had sunk the *Empire City* on 5 August and the *Empire Day* on the 7th. The sinkings, together with von Waldegg's lengthy signals to BdU reporting the boat's operations, enabled the British to pin point the position to within 200 miles of 08°00'S 44°00'E. Force 66, consisting of the escort carriers *Shah* and *Begum*, seven frigates and two sloops, was ordered to search for the U-boat based on her 'furthest on' position. On 10 August she was sighted and attacked by one of *Shah*'s aircraft. Although the U-boat dived, the aircraft brought the sloops to the area. On the morning of the 12th the target was sighted and attacked by another of *Shah*'s aircraft. Once again the aircraft homed the frigates on to the contact and at 1323 the Indian sloop *Godavari* made asdic contact and held it until the other ships arrived. *Findhorn* then carried out a Hedgehog attack which caught the U-boat unawares for she took no avoiding action. Two hits were made and these were followed by one small and one larger underwater explosion. The SO was concerned that the U-boat was damaged and might try to surface and escape under cover of darkness. Consequently all ships formed a radar 'box' around the area, but nothing was sighted other than a large oil slick the next morning.

U981

	Launched	Commissioned
U981	29 Apr 1943	3 Jun 1943

Class Type VIIC
CO *Oberleutnant zur See* Günther Keller (survived)
Date of loss 12 August 1944
Location Bay of Biscay, off La Rochelle, 45°41'N 01°25'W
Cause Air attack
Casualties 12
Survivors 40
Salvaged No

Notes *U981* was approaching La Pallice when she was mined just before meeting her escort. While on the surface and waiting for assistance, she was then attacked by Halifax 'F' of No 502 Squadron using a 600lb anti-submarine bomb. The aircraft made two attacking runs despite intense flak put up by both *U981* and *U309*. However, the damage sustained in the original mining plus that inflicted by the Halifax was too great. Almost without warning *U981* started to sink as her crew tumbled up on to the casing and into their dinghies. The survivors were rescued by *U309*.

U547

	Launched	Commissioned
U547	3 Apr 1943	16 Jun 1943

Class Type IXC
CO *Oberleutnant zur See* Heinrich Niemeyer
Date of loss 13 August 1944
Location Bay of Biscay, Gironde estuary
Cause Mine
Casualties ?
Survivors ?
Salvaged See notes

Notes *U547* was damaged by mine off Pauillac, but the damage did not prevent the boat from making the return journey to Germany. However, she was paid off at Stettin on 31 December 1944. Details of the final disposal of the wreck are unknown.

U270

	Launched	Commissioned
U270	11 Jul 1942	5 Sept 1942

Class Type VIIC
CO *Oberleutnant zur See* Heinrich Schreiber (survived)
Date of loss 13 August 1944
Location Bay of Biscay, W of La Rochelle, 46°19'N 02°56'W
Cause Air attack
Casualties 10
Survivors 5 officers, 10 senior rates, 56 junior rates and passengers
Salvaged No

Notes *U270* was on passage from Lorient to La Pallice and was carrying base personnel who were being evacuated—hence her grossly overloaded state. She was sighted and attacked with six depth charges by Sunderland 'A' of No 461 Squadron RAAF, flown by Fg Off D. A. Little RAAF. The explosion of the depth charges fractured the pressure hull, causing massive flooding. Diving was out of the question, but Schreiber tried to keep going on the surface until the boat had to be abandoned.

U618

	Launched	Commissioned
U618	20 Feb 1942	16 Apr 1942

Class Type VIIC
CO *Oberleutnant zur See* Erich Faust (lost)
Date of loss 14/15 August 1944
Location Bay of Biscay, W of St Nazaire, 47°22'N 04°39'W
Cause Depth charge
Casualties 51
Survivors None
Salvaged No

Notes *U618* was surfacing when she was picked up by the radar of Liberator 'G' of No 53 Squadron at 2356. The pilot, Flt Lt G. Potier DFC, illuminated the U-boat with his Leigh Light, dropped six depth charges and observed an explosion and fire from aft of the U-boat's conning tower. After the attack the radar contact faded but no wreckage or oil could be seen by Potier or by a Wellington which had been homed in to the scene. Five hours after the attack EG3 arrived, having been alerted by the aircraft. HMS *Essington* obtained an asdic contact with a bottomed target, but her attacks produced nothing but oil. The ships of EG3 then carried out a series of massive depth-charge attacks which produced no wreckage but yielded a large amount of dense oil which continued to rise to the surface for some hours.

U741	*Launched* 4 Feb 1943	*Commissioned* 10 Apr 1943
Class	Type VIIC	
CO	*Oberleutnant zur See* Gerhard Palmgren (lost)	
Date of loss	15 August 1944	
Location	English Channel, 40m SE of St Catherine's Point, 50°02'N 00°36'W	
Cause	Depth charge	
Casualties	48	
Survivors	1 rating	
Salvaged	No	

Notes *U741* had just attacked convoy FTC.68 and had sought refuge on the bottom after firing. The corvette HMS *Orchis* soon made contact and carried out two attacks with depth charges. Her CO then changed to using his Hedgehog, and after the second attack there was a loud explosion which was followed by the appearance of large quantities of oil. While manouevring for a third attack two men were sighted on the surface, one of whom died before he could be picked up. The other was the sole survivor of *U741*.

U107	*Launched* 2 Jul 1940	*Commissioned* 8 Oct 1940
Class	Type IXB	
CO	*Leutnant zur See* Fritz (lost)	
Date of loss	18 August 1944	
Location	Bay of Biscay, W of La Rochelle	
Cause	Air attack	
Casualties	58	
Survivors	None	
Salvaged	No	

Notes Sunderland 'W' of 201 Squadron RAF, flown by Flt Lt L. Baveystock DFC DFM, was on patrol to prevent U-boats evacuating German personnel from Brest to Bordeaux. A periscope was sighted and six depth charges were dropped which landed in a perfect straddle. As the Sunderland banked for a second attack the crew saw wreckage and oil coming to the surface. Subsequently British warships were homed in and these collected a number of items including charts.

U621	*Launched* 29 Mar 1942	*Commissioned* 7 May 1942
Class	Type VIIC	
CO	*Oberleutnant zur See* Hermann Stuckmann (lost)	
Date of loss	18 August 1944	
Location	Bay of Biscay, 45°52'N 02°36'W	
Cause	Depth charge	
Casualties	54	
Survivors	None	
Salvaged	No	

Notes *Ottawa* (Cdr J. D. Prentice RCNR, Senior Officer) *Restigouche*, *Kootenay* and *Chaudière* of EG11 were deployed off the approaches to Rochefort when *Kootenay* reported a firm asdic contact at 0953. While *Chaudière* and *Restigouche* carried out square searches, *Ottawa* lined up for a Hedgehog attack. At this juncture the submarine tried to take some evasive action but it was too little and too late. One Hedgehog bomb exploded and an oil slick formed on the surface. Prentice considered the U-boat disabled when asdic showed the target bottomed on the seabed.

However, there was insufficient proof to claim that the U-boat had been sunk, so the wreck had to blown apart to produce the requisite evidence. Attacks continued with depth charges and Hedgehog until 1529, when an attack blew a fountain of bubbles to the surface. Prentice now considered the U-boat sunk and headed off, leaving *Chaudière* just in case the boat had just been damaged and came to the surface. She left to rejoin the group on the morning of the 19th after losing contact, but was ordered back to the spot by CinC Plymouth and there she remained throughout the day. As the wind rose, it drove the oil into a well defined slick. *Chaudière* was able to get a firm enough contact with the wreck to make two Hedgehog attacks at 1607 and 1609. These attacks produced some documents, wooden wreckage and more oil. A final attack produced a massive underwater explosion from the wreck but no additional evidence.

U129	*Launched* 28 Feb 1941	*Commissioned* 21 May 1941
Class	Type IXC	
CO	*Oberleutnant zur See* Richard von Harpe	
Date of loss	18 August 1944	
Location	Bay of Biscay, Lorient	
Cause	Scuttling	
Casualties	?	
Survivors	?	

Salvaged No

Notes On 18 August 1944 Hitler gave the order for the evacuation of the southern French ports of La Pallice and Bordeaux. Submarines lying at those ports and which could not make the journey to Norway were to be wrecked and scuttled. *U129* was surveyed, but it was found that she needed extensive repairs to her battery which could not be effected at Lorient. Accordingly she was wrecked and scuttled.

U967	*Launched* 28 Jan 1943	*Commissioned* 11 Mar 1943
Class	Type VIIC	
CO	*Oberleutnant zur See* Rorbach	
Date of loss	19 August 1944	
Location	Mediterranean, Toulon	
Cause	Scuttling	
Casualties	2	
Survivors	?	
Salvaged	No	

Notes *U967* was scuttled at Toulon after being thoroughly wrecked by her crew to prevent her falling into Allied hands.

U466	*Launched* 30 Mar 1942	*Commissioned* 17 Jun 1943
Class	Type VIIC	
CO	*Kapitänleutnant* Gerhard Thater	
Date of loss	19 August 1944	
Location	Mediterranean, Toulon	
Cause	Scuttling	
Casualties	?	
Survivors	?	
Salvaged	No	

Notes *U466* was scuttled at Toulon after being thoroughly wrecked by her crew in order to avoid capture.

U9	*Launched* 30 Jul 1935	*Commissioned* 21 Aug 1935
Class	Type IIB	
CO	*Oberleutnant zur See* Heinrich Klapdar	
Date of loss	20 August 1944	
Location	Black Sea, Constanza	
Cause	Air attack	
Casualties	?	
Survivors	?	
Salvaged	No	

Notes Bombed by Soviet aircraft while alongside at Constanza.

U178	*Launched* 28 Oct 1941	*Commissioned* 14 Feb 1942
Class	Type IXD2	
CO	*Kapitänleutnant* Wilhelm Spahr	
Date of loss	20 August 1944	
Location	Bay of Biscay, Bordeaux	
Cause	Scuttling	
Casualties	?	
Survivors	?	
Salvaged	No	

Notes *U178* was another of the boats abandoned in France following Hitler's decision to evacuate La Pallice and Bordeaux. Like *U129* she needed urgent repairs to her battery which could not be carried out by the local dockyard. Accordingly, the boat was wrecked by her crew and then scuttled at Bordeaux to avoid capture.

U188	*Launched* 31 Mar 1942	*Commissioned* 5 Aug 1942
Class	Type IXC/40	
CO	*Kapitänleutnant* Siegfried Ludden	
Date of loss	20 August 1944	
Location	Bay of Biscay, Bordeaux	
Cause	Scuttling	
Casualties	?	
Survivors	?	
Salvaged	No	

Notes *U188* was scuttled in the same circumstances as *U178* (q.v.).

U413	*Launched* 15 Jan 1942	*Commissioned* 3 Jun 1942
Class	Type VIIC	
CO	*Oberleutnant zur See* Dietrich Sachse (lost)	
Date of loss	20 August 1944	
Location	English Channel, 50°21'N 00°01'W	
Cause	Depth charge	
Casualties	45	
Survivors	1 officer	
Salvaged	No	

Notes Contact with a submerged U-boat was made by HMS *Vidette*, in company with HMS *Forester* and HMS *Wensleydale* on a routine A/S sweep. The ships attacked with depth charges and Hedgehog and after about 45 minutes one of the U-boat's crew, the engineer officer, came to the surface and was picked up. However, although the U-boat was giving off large amounts of oil she was still moving, so attacks were carried out for another hour, after which wooden wreckage, clothing and personal effects came to the surface together with more oil.

	Launched	*Commissioned*
U984	12 May 1943	17 Jun 1943

Class	Type VIIC
CO	*Oberleutnant zur See* Hans Sieder (lost)
Date of loss	20 August 1944
Location	Atlantic, W of Brest, 48°16'N 05°33'W
Cause	Depth charge
Casualties	45
Survivors	None
Salvaged	No

Notes *Ottawa*, *Chaudière* and *Kootenay* of EG11 were returning to Londonderry after the sinking of *U621* (q.v.), *Restigouche* having detached to Plymouth with defects, when *Ottawa* got a firm asdic contact at 1935. *Chaudière*, equipped with the superior 147B and Q asdic sets, used her last Hedgehog bombs but without result. She then resorted to depth charges in an attack that her commanding officer, Cdr C. P. Nixon RCN, claimed 'Must have burst a few more rivets'. However, *Ottawa* and *Chaudière* were low on fuel, while *Kootenay*'s main feed pump had sprung another leak. By 2300 it was too dark to see, so the hunt was abandoned. The Admiralty's assessment was that there was 'Insufficient evidence for the presence of a U-boat', a verdict hotly disputed by EG11. Post-war analysis confirmed that *Chaudière*'s depth-charge attack had sunk *U984*.

	Launched	*Commissioned*
U1229	22 Oct 1943	13 Jan 1944

Class	Type IXC
CO	*Kapitänleutnant* Arnim Zinke (lost)
Date of loss	20 August 1944
Location	Atlantic, SE of Newfoundland
Cause	Air attack
Casualties	17
Survivors	1 officer, 7 senior rates, 32 junior rates, 1 passenger (see notes)
Salvaged	No

Notes *U1229* was on her way to land Oskar Mantel on the coast of Maine when she was detected by radar-equipped TBM Avenger aircraft of VC-42 flying from the USS *Bogue*, which had been looking for *U802*. Although his boat was fitted with a snorkel, Zinke (later characterised as one of the more inept U-boat commanders) was determined to remain on the surface. At 1227 *U1229* was attacked with rockets and depth charges by Lt (jg) A. X. Brokas' Avenger. U1229 was badly damaged in the attack and Zinke finally decided to dive, although his boat was leaving a massive diesel slick on the surface. Brokas dropped sonobuoys and stayed airborne over the position to wait for reinforcements—two more TBMs and two FM-2s. The aircraft arrived an hour later and found a large U-shaped oil slick. One group of aircraft investigated the north-west end of the slick while the other aircraft looked at the other end, where at 1419 the dim shape of *U1229* could be seen coming to the surface.

U1229's batteries had been badly damaged by Brokas' attack and Zinke had tried, unsuccessfully, to raise the snorkel. He was now surfacing to try to repair the snorkel mast. The first attack by Avengers was aborted when the two planes realised that they were approaching each other head on and had to pull out sharply to avoid a collision, dropping their charges short. However, one of them returned to the attack with his rockets, seven of which struck home. Men could now been seen on the bridge and casing, donning lifejackets and breaking out the dinghies stowed in the casing. Following a further attack by an Avenger (one of whose charges hung up while the other failed to explode), *U1229* began to sink by the bow at 1440. Just after she disappeared beneath the sea a tremendous explosion was observed which showered the area with debris.

Oskar Mantel, self-styled spy and 'propaganda expert', who had been resident in Yorkville, New York, before the war, was turned over to the FBI along with $1,940 in twenty-dollar bills found in his possession. After the the war some of his

US relatives unsuccessfully sued *Bogue*'s Captain Vosseller for the return of the money, claiming that it belonged to Mantel's poverty-stricken mother in Germany.

	Launched	*Commissioned*
U230	10 Sept 1942	24 Oct 1942
Class	Type VIIC	
CO	*Oberleutnant zur See* Heinz-Eugen Eberbach	
Date of loss	21 August 1944	
Location	Mediterranean, Toulon	
Cause	Scuttling	
Casualties	?	
Survivors	?	
Salvaged	No	

Notes *U230* was blown up by her crew at Toulon to avoid capture.

	Launched	*Commissioned*
U180	10 Dec 1941	16 May 1942
Class	Type IXD1	
CO	*Oberleutnant zur See* Rolf Riesen (lost)	
Date of loss	22 August 1944	
Location	Bay of Biscay, off the Gironde estuary, 44°00'N 02°00'W	
Cause	Mine	
Casualties	56	
Survivors	None	
Salvaged	No	

Notes Mined west of Bordeaux.

	Launched	*Commissioned*
U354	6 Jan 1942	22 Apr 1942
Class	Type VIIC	
CO	*Kapitänleutnant* Hans-Jurgen Sthamer (lost)	
Date of loss	22 August 1944	
Location	Arctic, N of Murmansk, 72°49'N 30°41'E	
Cause	Air attack	
Casualties	51	
Survivors	None	
Salvaged	No	

Notes August 22 had started off in grand style for Sthamer and the crew of *U354*. Searching for convoy JW.59, Stahmer encountered a British carrier group engaged in Operation 'Goodwood', an air strike on the German battleship *Tirpitz*, and managed to sink the frigate *Bickerton* and cripple the carrier *Nabob*. The carrier's Avengers prevented him from finishing her off, so he set off on the surface in search of the convoy.

He found it, but was detected by the frigate *Mermaid* at 0351. The frigate took anti-Gnat precautions just in time, for Sthamer fired two Gnats, both of which exploded astern of the frigate. Asdic conditions were poor and *Mermaid*'s asdic team were having difficulty in holding the contact. Sthamer was not making their task any easier by evasive manouevring and by releasing SBTs. *Mermaid* was joined by the Squid-equipped frigate *Loch Dunvegan*, but this excellent weapon could not be used because the ships's asdic was broken. *Mermaid*'s third depth-charge attack brought oil to the surface—oil which would continue to appear for the next twelve hours and cover an area of five square miles.

The SO was concerned about the vulnerability of the two frigates—the convoy had by now moved on some distance—in the face of the air and surface threat. *Mermaid*'s CO, Lt-Cdr J. P. Mosse RN, was ordered to re-join the screen. Mosse, an ASW specialist, was reluctant to do so since he wanted more conclusive evidence of a kill. His protestations won him three extensions but eventually at 1418 he had to leave. He left the U-boat bottomed and gushing oil. Mosse's persistence earned him warm praise: 'A grand story of pertinacity . . . There is no moss on Mosse,' wrote Rear-Admiral Edelsten.

	Launched	*Commissioned*
U344	29 Jan 1943	26 Mar 1943
Class	Type VIIC	
CO	*Kapitänleutnant* Ulrich Pietsch (lost)	
Date of loss	22 August 1944	
Location	Arctic, NW of Bear Island, 74°54'N 15°26'E	
Cause	Air attack	
Casualties	50	
Survivors	None	
Salvaged	No	

Notes Swordfish 'C' of 825 NAS, flown by Lt (A) Gordon Bennett, was flying a routine A/S patrol when the U-boat was sighted on the surface three miles away and heading north-east. Bennett attacked from astern using his boost override to extract every last ounce of speed from the old 'Stringbag', and three Mk XII Torpex-filled depth charges were released from a height of 50ft as the U-boat dived. The first charge fell alongside the U-boat's starboard quarter and the second by the starboard side of the conning tower. The third was seen to hit the forward casing then roll forward and lodge firmly under the jumping wire. Ten seconds later, when the bows had reached 24ft, the charge went off. In contrast to the explosion of the first two depth charges, which had produced impressive columns of white water, the third explosion produced a burst of black smoke—indicative, perhaps, of the sympathetic detonation of some if not all of the U-boat's remaining torpedoes. The stern of the submarine rose to a steep angle before slipping down. One survivor was seen floating in the water waving frantically. The aircrew tried to drop an inflatable dinghy but as it was being released from the cockpit it inflated itself, fouled the tailplane and had to be shot away.

U445	*Launched* 1 Feb 1942	*Commissioned* 30 May 1942
Class	Type VIIC	
CO	*Oberleutnant zur See* Fischler *Graf* von Trenberg (lost)	
Date of loss	24 August 1944	
Location	Bay of Biscay, W of St Nazaire, 47°21'N 05°50'W	
Cause	Hedgehog/depth charge	
Casualties	52	
Survivors	None	
Salvaged	No	

Notes The 'Captain' class frigate HMS *Louis*, part of the 15th Escort Group, had just begun a patrol in a new area in the Bay of Biscay when she obtained an asdic contact. Three attacks were made using Hedgehog, the last of which was thought to have been lethal. However, it was not until after a depth-charge attack and another Hedgehog attack that oil was seen rising to the surface. It came up in great quantities, and when *Louis* returned to the spot twenty-four hours later it was still rising.

U445's other claim to a place in the history books is that on 7 December 1942 she fuelled from *U460* in area BD (mid-Atlantic) for three hours, both boats proceeding dived at a depth of 50m. Communication between the two boats was maintained by SST.

U18	*Launched* 6 Dec 1935	*Commissioned* 4 Jan 1936
Class	Type IIB	
CO	*Oberleutnant zur See* Karl Fiege	
Date of loss	25 August 1944	
Location	Black Sea, off Constanza, 44°12'N 28°41'E	
Cause	Scuttling	
Casualties	?	
Survivors	?	
Salvaged	No	

Notes *U18* was damaged in a Soviet air raid on Constanza. In the face of the inexorable advance of the Red Army, it was decided that she should be scuttled since she was not suffiently seaworthy to head for neutral Turkey and internment. The wreck was finally broken up in 1960.

U667	*Launched* 29 Aug 1942	*Commissioned* 20 Oct 1942
Class	Type VIIC	
CO	*Oberleutnant zur See* Werner Lange (lost)	
Date of loss	25 August 1944	
Location	Bay of Biscay, off La Pallice, 46°10'N 01°14'W	
Cause	?	
Casualties	45	
Survivors	None	
Salvaged	No	

Notes *U667* is presumed sunk by a mine laid by the RAF off the port of La Pallice.

UIT21	*Launched* 29 Jun 1935	*Commissioned* ?
Class	Italian *Pietro Calvi* class	
CO	*Oberleutnant zur See* Friedrich Steinfeldt	
Date of loss	25 August 1944	
Location	Bay of Biscay, Bordeaux	
Cause	Scuttling	
Casualties	?	
Survivors	?	
Salvaged	No	

Notes Launched as the Italian *Giuseppe Finzi* and taken over by the Germans on 9 September 1943 when the Italians signed the Armistice. The intention was use her as a cargo-carrying submarine, but manning problems meant that she was never so employed. She was scuttled at Bordeaux to prevent her capture.

U1000

	Launched	Commissioned
U1000	17 Sept 1943	4 Nov 1943
Class	Type VIIC/41	
CO	*Oberleutnant zur See* Willy Müller	
Date of loss	31 August 1944	
Location	Baltic, off Pilau, 54°41'N 19°49'E	
Cause	Mine	
Casualties	?	
Survivors	?	
Salvaged	?	

Notes *U1000* was damaged by a mine but managed to return to Pillau. There she was surveyed but found to be beyond repair. On 29 September 1944 she was paid off. The details of the ultimate disposal of the wreck are unknown.

U247

	Launched	Commissioned
U247	23 Sept 1943	23 Oct 1943
Class	Type VIIC	
CO	*Oberleutnant zur See* Gerhard Matschulat (lost)	
Date of loss	1 September 1944	
Location	English Channel, SW of Wolf Rock, 49°54'N 05°49'W	
Cause	Depth charge	
Casualties	52	
Survivors	None	
Salvaged	No	

Notes EG9 was patrolling the waters off Land's End when on 31 August it was ordered to move to the area off Trevose Head on the north coast of Cornwall in response to a aircraft radar report. At 1845Z, as the ships were passing Land's End, the frigate *St John* obtained a good contact 15 miles east of the Wolf Rock Light. *Monnow*, *Stormont* and *Meon* were ordered north to pursue the search ordered by CinC Plymouth, while *St John*, *Swansea* and *Port Colborne* remained to pursue the contact. Tide conditions made the contact difficult to hold, and after a number of depth-charge and Hedgehog attacks contact was lost just after 2300Z.

The group then set about sweeping across the likely path of the target, and at 0155Z *St John* regained contact three miles from the Wolf Rock on the bottom in 42 fathoms. The frigate then carried out two depth-charge attacks which produced oil and explosions from the target. The next day, after a search of the area which produced nothing, EG9 returned to the oil slick. *St John* obtained an echo sounder trace which showed that the U-boat was very heavily damaged. At 1407Z *St John* dropped five depth charges on the target, directed by her echo sounder. This attacked completely destroyed the U-boat. Documents (including a certificate celebrating *U247*'s 10 millionth engine revolution), clothing, equipment and internal fittings came to the surface which were sufficient to identify the boat.

U394

	Launched	Commissioned
U394	19 Jun 1943	7 Aug 1943
Class	Type VIIC	
CO	*Kapitänleutnant* Wolfgang Borger (lost)	
Date of loss	2 September 1944	
Location	Norwegian Sea, W of Lofoten Islands, 69°47'N 04°41'E	
Cause	Depth charge	
Casualties	50	
Survivors	None	
Salvaged	No	

Notes Sunk during the passage of convoy RA.59 from the Kola Inlet. Swordfish 'A' of 825 NAS sighted the U-boat and dropped a smoke marker. The frigates *Mermaid* and *Peacock* and destroyers *Whitehall* and *Keppel* were detached from the convoy to investigate. They reached the marker shortly after 0900 and delivered a series of depth-charge attacks. However, the U-boat was a wily customer and went deep, exploiting the density layers and making frequent alterations of speed and course.

By 1614 matters had to be decided, so a creeping attack was organised. Lt-Cdr John Mosse in HMS *Mermaid* recalled that 'All four ships reduced to a silent speed of 7 knots. *Peacock*, directing from astern, guided us like a ploughman with three horses. *Keppel* and *Whitehall* each fired 22 depth charges from their outboard throwers and rails while *Mermaid* dropped eighteen down the centre. Charges were set to make a sandwich explosion between 500 and 850 feet.' *Mermaid* and *Peacock* then made one more attack, dropping ten depth charges each. Asdic contact then faded as bubbles and oil together with wreckage and human remains came to the surface.

	Launched	*Commissioned*
U362	21 Oct 1942	4 Feb 1943

Class: Type VIIC
CO: *Kapitänleutnant* Ludwig Franz (lost)
Date of loss: 5 September 1944
Location: Arctic, Kara Sea
Cause: Depth charge
Casualties: 51
Survivors: None
Salvaged: No

Notes Depth-charged by the Soviet minesweeper *SC-116*. There is little information concerning the circumstances of this attack.

	Launched	*Commissioned*
U484	20 Nov 1943	19 Jan 1944

Class: Type VIIC
CO: *Korvettenkapitän* Wolf-Axel Schaeffer (lost)
Date of loss: 9 September 1944
Location: Atlantic, S of Hebrides, 55°46'N 11°41'W
Cause: Depth charge
Casualties: 52
Survivors: None
Salvaged: No

Notes Sunk by HMS *Portchester Castle* and *Helmsdale*, part of the close escort for convoy ONF.252. The sinking of *U484* is usually attributed to depth-charge attacks by HMCS *Dunver* and *Hespeler* of the MOEF. However, there was little or no evidence to suggest a 'kill', and the attack only rated the verdict 'promising' in the September 1944 Monthly Anti Submarine Report. In view of the circumstances surrounding the loss of *U743* (q.v.), it seems more likely that *U484* was the victim of the two British ships.

	Launched	*Commissioned*
U19	21 Dec 1935	16 Jan 1936

Class: Type IIB
CO: *Oberleutnant zur See* Willi Oldenburg (survived)
Date of loss: 10 September 1944
Location: Black Sea, off Ergeli on Turkish coast, 130m E of the Bosphorus
Cause: Scuttling
Casualties: ?
Survivors: ?
Salvaged: No

Notes After *U18* had been damaged the writing on the wall was painfully clear for the crews of the remaining German boats at Constanza, *U19*, *U20* and *U23*: they had a choice between scuttling their craft and then facing a precarious existence as naval infantry, with the added bonus of captivity in a Soviet prisoner-of-war camp, or they could opt for internment in Turkey. They took the latter choice, and after sinking their boat were interned at Beyschir, where they spent the rest of the war in a simple but not uncomfortable internment.

	Launched	*Commissioned*
U20	14 Jan 1936	1 Feb 1936

Class: Type IIB
CO: *Oberleutnant zur See* Karl Grafen
Date of loss: 10 September 1944
Location: Black Sea, off Ergeli on Turkish coast, 130m E of the Bosphorus
Cause: Scuttling
Casualties: ?
Survivors: ?
Salvaged: No

Notes See the entry for *U19* above.

	Launched	*Commissioned*
U23	28 Aug 1936	24 Sept 1936

Class: Type IIB
CO: *Oberleutnant zur See* Rolf Wahlen
Date of loss: 10 September 1944
Location: Black Sea, off Ergeli on Turkish coast, 130m E of the Bosphorus
Cause: Scuttling
Casualties: ?
Survivors: ?
Salvaged: No

Notes See the entry for *U19* above.

	Launched	*Commissioned*
U925	6 Nov 1943	30 Dec 1943

Class: Type VIIC

CO	*Oberleutnant zur See* Helmut Knoke (lost)
Date of loss	? September 1944
Location	N Atlantic, off Iceland
Cause	?
Casualties	51
Survivors	None
Salvaged	No

Notes *U925* departed for patrol on 24 August 1944 and was not heard from again. It is possible she was the victim of a drifting mine, but she may instead have been the victim of an accident resulting from material or drill failure.

U743	*Launched* 11 Mar 1943	*Commissioned* 15 May 1943
Class	Type VIIC	
CO	*Oberleutnant zur See* Helmut Kandzior (lost)	
Date of loss	Mid/late September 1944	
Location	North Atlantic, NW of Ireland, exact location unknown	
Cause	?	
Casualties	50	
Survivors	None	
Salvaged	No	

Notes The loss of *U743* is usually attributed to depth-charge attacks by HMS *Helmsdale* and *Portchester Castle* on 9 September. However, this verdict is open to question as *U743* was not ordered into this area until 11 September—two days after she had been supposedly been sunk. It is therefore appropriate to record the cause of *U743*'s loss as 'Unknown'. She may have been the victim of either a mine or an accident.

U855	*Launched* 17 Apr 1943	*Commissioned* 2 Aug 1943
Class	Type IXC/40	
CO	*Oberleutnant zur See* Prosper Ohlsen (lost)	
Date of loss	c.18 September 1944	
Location	Atlantic, 63°10'N 12°30'W	
Cause	Mine	
Casualties	56	
Survivors	None	
Salvaged	No	

Notes *U855* was returning home from a weather-reporting patrol when she was mined. She was originally assessed as having been sunk by Liberator 'A' of No 224 Squadron, but the victim of this attack was *U763*, which was damaged.

U407	*Launched* 16 Aug 1941	*Commissioned* 18 Dec 1941
Class	Type VIIC	
CO	*Oberleutnant zur See* Hans Kolbus (survived)	
Date of loss	19 September 1944	
Location	Mediterranean, S of Melos, 36°27'N 24°33'E	
Cause	Depth charge	
Casualties	5	
Survivors	3 officers, 6 senior rates, 38 junior rates	
Salvaged	No	

Notes At 1700 on 18 September the Polish destroyer ORP *Garland* sighted the characteristic 'gefuffle' of a U-boat's snorkel at a range of eight miles and was able to close to a range of 200yds before the U-boat dived. It is possible that the exhaust made periscope observation difficult and the noise of the diesel rendered the U-boat's passive hydrophones useless. *Garland* delivered one Hedgehog attack before contact was lost. The hunt was then joined by the destroyers *Troubridge*, *Terpsichore*, *Brecon* and *Zetland*. Depth-charge attacks were made by *Troubridge* at 1842 and 2235 and by *Terpsichore* at 2322. Contact was then held with the U-boat until 0438 the next morning, when, his air supplies exhausted, Kolbus surfaced and scuttled the boat. Among the five casualties were the 1WO and a war correspondent temporarily on board.

Under the command of *Oberleutnant zur See* Bruller, *U407* had sunk the P&O liner *Viceroy of India* on 11 November 1942.

U865	*Launched* 11 Jul 1943	*Commissioned* 25 Oct 1943
Class	Type IXC/40	
CO	*Oberleutnant zur See* Dietrich Stellmacher (lost)	
Date of loss	September 1944	
Location	Atlantic, SE of Iceland (?)	
Cause	?	
Casualties	59	
Survivors	None	

Salvaged	No

Notes *U865* sailed for patrol on 8 September. No Allied claim exists for her loss, and it is presumed that she was mined south-east of Iceland.

U867	*Launched* 24 Aug 1943	*Commissioned* 11 Dec 1943
Class	Type IXC/40	
CO	*Kapitän zur See* Arved von Muhlendahl (lost)	
Date of loss	19 September 1944	
Location	Norwegian Sea, NE of Shetlands, 62°15'N 01°50'E	
Cause	Air attack	
Casualties	61	
Survivors	None	
Salvaged	No	

Notes The U-boat was picked up on radar by Liberator 'Q' of No 224 Squadron RAF. Seven minutes after the contact the pilot, Flt Lt H. J. Rayner, sighted the boat fully surfaced on the aircraft's starboard beam. Flt Lt Rayner attacked through a heavy flak barrage and dropped six depth charges which overshot. Nevertheless, photographs taken during the attack show the crew throwing dinghies over the side as the depth charges are exploding. After the explosions had subsided the boat was seen stopped and then sank on an even keel. Around fifty men were seen in several dinghies floating in a patch of oil.

U867 had left Kristiansund on 12 September and had been attacked by a Liberator of No 248 Squadron. The attack by aircraft 'Q' compounded the damage and Muhlendahl scuttled the boat.

U859	*Launched* 2 Mar 1943	*Commissioned* 8 Jul 1943
Class	Type IXD2	
CO	*Kapitänleutnant* Johann Jebsen (lost)	
Date of loss	23 September 1944	
Location	Malacca Strait, off Penang, 05°46'N 100°04'E	
Cause	Submarine attack	
Casualties	47	
Survivors	18	
Salvaged	No	

Notes *U859* was about to enter the port of Penang at the conclusion of her first patrol in Eastern waters when she was spotted by the British submarine HMS *Trenchant* (Lt-Cdr A. R. Hezlet RN) which was on patrol off Penang for precisely that purpose. Hezlet fired three torpedoes from his stern tubes and recorded one hit. Hezlet then surfaced to rescue ten of the eighteen men swimming in the water. Another eight survivors were later rescued by a Japanese submarine.

U565	*Launched* 20 Feb 1941	*Commissioned* 10 Apr 1941
Class	Type VIIC	
CO	*Kapitänleutnant* Fritz Henning	
Date of loss	24 September 1944	
Location	Aegean, near Skaramanga, 37°57'N 23°40'E	
Cause	Air attack	
Casualties	5	
Survivors	?	
Salvaged	No	

Notes Badly damaged during a raid on Piraeus and Skaramanga by B-24 Liberators of the USAAF. The damage was so extensive that the boat was scuttled on 30 September 1944 with depth charges.

U596	*Launched* 17 Sept 1941	*Commissioned* 13 Nov 1941
Class	Type VIIC	
CO	*Oberleutnant zur See* Hubertus Korndorfer	
Date of loss	24 September 1944	
Location	Mediterranean, Salamis	
Cause	Air attack	
Casualties	1	
Survivors	?	
Salvaged	No	

Notes Destroyed during a raid on the port by B-24 Liberators of the USAAF.

U871	*Launched* 7 Sept 1943	*Commissioned* 15 Jan 1944
Class	Type IXD2	
CO	*Kapitänleutnant* Erwin Ganzer (lost)	
Date of loss	24 September 1944	
Location	Atlantic, NW of Azores	
Cause	Air attack	

Casualties	69
Survivors	None
Salvaged	No

Notes Fortress 'P' of No 220 Squadron RAF was investigating a U-boat sighting made by aircraft 'H' of the same unit. 'P', flown by Flt Lt A. F. Wallace, circled the position and at 1544 a periscope wake was spotted. Wallace attacked with three depth charges. The depth charges fell around the conning tower which was just breaking surface as the aircraft attacked. After the explosion of the depth charges, oil, wreckage and human remains were sighted on the surface.

U863	*Launched* 29 Jul 1943	*Commissioned* 3 Nov 1943
Class	Type IXD2	
CO	*Kapitänleutnant* Dietrich von der Esch (lost)	
Date of loss	29 September 1944	
Location	Atlantic, off Ascension Island, 10°45'S 25°30'W	
Cause	Air attack	
Casualties	69	
Survivors	None	
Salvaged	No	

Notes Sunk by a Liberator of VB-107.

U703	*Launched* 16 Jul 1941	*Commissioned* 16 Oct 1941
Class	Type VIIC	
CO	*Oberleutnant zur See* Joachim Brunner (lost)	
Date of loss	30 September 1944	
Location	Atlantic, SE of Iceland	
Cause	Mine	
Casualties	54	
Survivors	None	
Salvaged	No	

U921	*Launched* 3 Apr 1943	*Commissioned* 30 May 1943
Class	Type VIIC	
CO	*Oberleutnant zur See* Alfred Werner (lost)	
Date of loss	30 September 1944	
Location	Arctic, W of Bear Island, 72°32'N 12°55'E	
Cause	Air attack	
Casualties	50	
Survivors	None	
Salvaged	No	

Notes During the passage of convoy RA.60 from the Kola Inlet to the UK, Swordfish 'F' of 813 NAS was on routine A/S patrol from the escort carrier *Campania* when she sighted and attacked *U921*.

U1062	*Launched* 8 May 1943	*Commissioned* 19 Jun 1943
Class	Type VIIF	
CO	*Oberleutnant zur See* Karl Albrecht (lost)	
Date of loss	30 September 1944	
Location	Atlantic, SW of Cape Verde Islands, 11°36'N 34°44'W	
Cause	Air attack/depth charge	
Casualties	55	
Survivors	None	
Salvaged	No	

Notes *U1062* was nearing the end of her long voyage from Penang to Europe with a cargo of petroleum-based products. BdU had ordered her to rendezvous with *U219* west of the Cape Verde Islands and fuel the latter boat which was heading for Japan. Unfortunately, all this wireless chatter had come to the ears of Tenth Fleet HF/DF operators who guessed what was afoot. The escort carrier *Mission Bay* (with VC-36 embarked) and four destroyers, designated TG.22.1, were ordered to search for these boats, which intelligence believed were to meet on 28 September. TG.22.1 later joined with TG.41.7, consisting of the carrier *Tripoli* and four destroyers.

From the 28th onwards a number of contacts were attacked which proved either false or the outward-bound *U219*—which managed to shoot down one of *Tripoli*'s Avengers. On the 30th *Mission Bay*'s aircraft had been prosecuting several contacts and had dropped a number of Fidos, but to no visible effect. Three DEs were detached to search the position of the last airborne attack near 11°37'N 34°43'W. This point was within 15 miles of where the Tenth Fleet estimated the two boats would meet. At 1617 *Fessenden* obtained a firm sonar contact and closed to 600yds before definitely classifying it as a submarine. *Fessenden* then retired to 1,600yds to carry out a Hedgehog attack. Just fourteen seconds after the weapon was fired, four explosions were heard

320ft below the surface. Two minutes later, at 1632, *Fessenden* ran over the spot with a seventeen-charge pattern. This was unnecessary as the Hedgehog had already accounted for *U1062*.

The sinking of *U1062* was the last U-boat 'kill' made by the CVE groups in the Atlantic until April 1945.

U92	*Launched*	*Commissioned*
	10 Jan 1942	3 Mar 1942

Class Type VIIC
CO *Oberleutnant zur See* Wilhelm Brauel
Date of loss 4 October 1944
Location Norwegian Sea, Bergen
Cause Air attack
Casualties ?
Survivors ?
Salvaged ?

Notes On 4 October 1944 Nos 6 and 8 Groups, RAF Bomber Command, mounted a massive raid on the U-boat pens at Bergen. *U92* was so badly damaged that she was beyond repair. On 12 October 1944 she was paid off. There are no details concerning the disposal of the wreck.

U228	*Launched*	*Commissioned*
	30 Jul 1942	12 Sept 1942

Class Type VIIC
CO *Kapitänleutnant* Herbert Engel
Date of loss 4 October 1944
Location Norwegian Sea, Bergen
Cause Air attack
Casualties ?
Survivors ?
Salvaged No

Notes Sunk in the attack on the U-boat pens at Bergen on 4 October 1944 by Nos 6 and 8 Groups, RAF Bomber Command.

U437	*Launched*	*Commissioned*
	15 Jun 1941	25 Oct 1941

Class Type VIIC
CO *Kapitänleutnant* Hermann Lamby
Date of loss 4 October 1944
Location Norwegian Sea, Bergen
Cause Air attack
Casualties ?
Survivors ?
Salvaged ?

Notes During the RAF raid on the U-boat pens at Bergen *U437* was so badly damaged that she was beyond repair. Accordingly, she was paid off on 10 October 1944. No details are available concerning the disposal of the wreck.

U993	*Launched*	*Commissioned*
	5 Jul 1943	19 Aug 1943

Class Type VIIC
CO *Oberleutnant zur See* Karl-Heinz Steinmetz
Date of loss 4 October 1944
Location Norwegian Sea, Bergen
Cause Air attack
Casualties 4
Survivors ?
Salvaged No

Notes *U993* was the second of two U-boats to be sunk in the attack on the U-boat pens. Thus for the loss of one aircraft Bomber Command had sunk two U-boats and damaged another two beyond repair.

U168	*Launched*	*Commissioned*
	5 Mar 1942	10 Sept 1942

Class Type IXC
CO *Kapitänleutnant* Helmut Pich (survived)
Date of loss 6 October 1944
Location Java Sea, off Surabaya, 06°20'S 111°28'E
Cause Submarine attack
Casualties 23
Survivors 27
Salvaged No

Notes *U168* was on passage from Batavia to Surabaya, where she was to join *U537* and *U862* in operations off the Australian coast, when she was sighted by the Dutch submarine *Zwaardvisch* (Lt-Cdr H.A.W. Goosens RNethN). *Zwaardvisch* was well placed for an attack and eleven minutes after sighting the U-boat fired six torpedoes on a 95-degree track angle from a range of 900yds. One explosion was heard and Goosens raised the periscope to see the submarine sinking by the bows. Three officers, the 1WO, the medical officer and the LI, made escapes from the sinking submarine from a depth of 120ft without apparatus. Of the 27 rescued, Goosens retained the Commanding Officer, the 1WO, the LI and medical officer together with one wounded rating in *Zwaardvisch.* The remainder were consigned to a nearby fishing vessel and left to their own devices; they eventually got ashore in Java. The survivors told Goosens that three torpedoes had struck but that only one had exploded. They also gave him the very good news that the local Japanese air command did not start their anti-submarine patrols until after 1100!

The German U-boat command in the Far East became convinced that *U168*'s loss could be attributed to a lack of security on the part of her crew. Although they were supposed to sail in strict secrecy, a number of the crew had brought their Indonesian girlfriends back to the boat for a farewell party and the boat's loss was subsequently attributed to loose talk at that event. The truth is, of course, that *U168* had the misfortune to come into contact with an Allied submarine with a well-trained crew and an exceptionally competent commanding officer.

	Launched	*Commissioned*
U2331	22 Aug 1944	12 Sept 1944
Class	Type XXIII	
CO	*Oberleutnant zur See* Hans-Walter Pahl (lost)	
Date of loss	10 October 1944	
Location	Baltic, off Hela, 54°00'N 18°00'E	
Cause	Accident	
Casualties	16	
Survivors	None	
Salvaged	Yes	

Notes Lost in an accident during training, the exact circumstances of which are unclear. She was raised and taken to Gotenhafen, but no further details of her fate are available.

	Launched	*Commissioned*
U777	25 Mar 1944	9 May 1944
Class	Type VIIC	
CO	*Oberleutnant zur See* Ruperti	
Date of loss	15 October 1944	
Location	North Sea, Wilhelmshaven.	
Cause	Air attack	
Casualties	?	
Survivors	?	
Salvaged	No	

Notes Sunk during an RAF bombing raid on Wilhelmshaven.

	Launched	*Commissioned*
U1006	17 Nov 1943	11 Jan 1944
Class	Type VIIC/41	
CO	*Oberleutnant zur See* Horst Voigt (survived)	
Date of loss	16 October 1944	
Location	Atlantic, SW of Faeroe Islands, 60°59'N 04°49'W	
Cause	Depth charge	
Casualties	7	
Survivors	3 officers, 5 senior rates, 36 junior rates	
Salvaged	No	

Notes Operation 'SJ' involved EG6 and EG18 working with No 18 Group RAF to prevent U-boats getting out into the Atlantic from their Norwegian bases. The two escort groups were screened by Home Fleet destroyers and two CVEs since the operation required them to search well inshore in Norwegian coastal waters, right up to the approaches to Bergen. During the course of this operation the frigate HMCS *Annan* in EG6 attacked a contact which was subsequently assessed as being a whale. It was in fact *U1006*, which was badly damaged in the attack. After *Annan* had sped back to re-join EG 6 Voigt surfaced to take stock. The small silhouette of the U-boat would have gone unmissed had it not been for the very sharp Type 272 radar operator aboard HMS *Loch Achanalt*. *Annan* was sent back to investigate and, as she approached the scene, prudently streamed her CAT. This was just as well, for as she approached Voigt fired a T5 which exploded off the frigate's quarter. *Annan* illuminated the U-boat with rockets and opened fire. *U1006* fought back and her gunfire wounded eight of *Annan*'s crew. However, *U1006* could not hope to outfight *Annan* and sank after the frigate had dropped two depth charges which exploded under the submarine.

	Launched	*Commissioned*
U957	21 Nov 1942	7 Jan 1943
Class	Type VIIC	

CO	*Oberleutnant zur See* Gerd Schaar (survived)
Date of loss	19 October 1944
Location	Norwegian coastal waters, Vestfjord, 70°00'N 15°00'E
Cause	Collision/paid off
Casualties	?
Survivors	?
Salvaged	?

Notes *U957* was badly damaged in a collision with a merchant ship while proceeding down Vestfjord. She was surveyed but found to be beyond repair and paid off on 21 October 1944. The survivors were rescued by *U1060*. No details are available concerning the disposal of the wreck.

U985	*Launched*	*Commissioned*
	20 May 1943	24 Jun 1943
Class	Type VIIC	
CO	*Kapitänleutnant* Heinz Wolff	
Date of loss	22 October 1944	
Location	North Sea, 58°01'N 06°32'E	
Cause	Mine	
Casualties	?	
Survivors	?	
Salvaged	?	

Notes *U985* was badly damaged by a mine but managed to make the port of Kristiansund South. There she was surveyed and found to be beyond repair. On 15 November 1944 she was paid off. No details regarding the disposal of the wreck are available.

U673	*Launched*	*Commissioned*
	8 May 1943	18 May 1943
Class	Type VIIC	
CO	*Oberleutnant zur See* Gehrke	
Date of loss	24 October 1944	
Location	Norwegian Sea, off Stavanger, 59°20'N 05°53'E	
Cause	Collision	
Casualties	?	
Survivors	?	
Salvaged	No	

Notes *U673* sank after colliding with *U382*, the exact circumstances of the incident being unclear.

U1060	*Launched*	*Commissioned*
	8 Apr 1943	15 May 1943
Class	Type VIIF	
CO	*Oberleutnant zur See* Herbert Brammer (lost)	
Date of loss	27 October 1944	
Location	Norwegian coastal waters, between Narvik and Bergen, 65°24'N 12°00'E	
Cause	Air attack	
Casualties	61	
Survivors	13	
Salvaged	No	

Notes *U1060* was caught on the surface and damaged by a Firefly I of 1771 NAS flying from HMS *Implacable* during a routine anti-shipping strike. Damaged, *U1060* ran aground on the nearby island of Fleina. There she was found and attacked by Liberators 'Y' and 'H' of No 311 (Czech) Squadron RAF and Halifaxes 'D' and 'T' of No 502 Squadron RAF. After the attacks the U-boat was seen to have been blown over on to her side.

U1060 was carrying 28 survivors from *U957* in addition to her own ship's company.

U1226	*Launched*	*Commissioned*
	21 Aug 1943	24 Nov 1943
Class	Type IXC/40	
CO	*Oberleutnant zur See* August-Wilhelm Claussen (lost)	
Date of loss	? October 1944	
Location	Atlantic	
Cause	?	
Casualties	56	
Survivors	None	
Salvaged	No	

Notes *U1226* had sailed for patrol on 30 September. When she failed to answer signals she was declared missing on 29 October. It is possible that she was the victim of a mine, but she may have been the victim of an accident, possibly snorkel failure or battery explosion resulting from inadequate ventilation while snorkelling.

U537	*Launched*	*Commissioned*
	7 Nov 1942	27 Jan 1943
Class	Type IXC	
CO	*Kapitänleutnant* Peter Schrewe (lost)	

Date of loss 9 November 1944 (GMT)/10 November1944 (Zone time)
Location Java Sea, E of Surabaya, 07°13'S 115°17'E
Cause Submarine attack
Casualties 58
Survivors None
Salvaged No

Notes The USS *Flounder* (Cdr J. E. Stevens USN) had made the northward passage through the Lombok Strait and was dived when the OOW sighted through the periscope what he took to be the sail of a native craft. On further examination Stevens identified the target as a U-boat and the attack was begun. Just after 0800 four torpedoes were fired. At least two hits were observed and the U-boat disintegrated in a violent explosion.

	Launched	*Commissioned*
U771	26 Sept 1943	18 Nov 1943

Class Type VIIC
CO *Oberleutnant zur See* Helmuth Block (lost)
Date of loss 11 November 1944
Location Arctic, W of Tromsø, 69°17'N 16°28'W
Cause Submarine attack
Casualties 51
Survivors None
Salvaged No

Notes *U771* was returning from patrol when her conning tower was sighted by the British submarine HMS *Venturer* (Lt J. S. Launders RN). It took Launders just six minutes to set up his attack and fire four torpedoes.

This was the first of two U-boats sunk by *Venturer*—see the entry for *U864* sunk on 9 February 1945 for the second.

	Launched	*Commissioned*
U1200	12 Oct 1943	5 Jan 1944

Class Type VIIC
CO *Oberleutnant zur See* Hinrich Mangels (lost)
Date of loss 11 November 1944
Location Atlantic, 60m S of Cape Clear, 50°24'N 08°10'W
Cause Depth charge
Casualties 53
Survivors None
Salvaged No

Notes Early on 11 November EG30, consisting of HM Ships *Pevensey Castle* (SO), *Kenilworth Castle*, *Porchester Castle* and *Launceston Castle*, gained radar then asdic contact with a U-boat heading south-west at 2kts. A series of attacks brought up a quantity of wooden wreckage from the U-boat's casing together with some oil. EG4 joined on the 12th and both groups remained in contact with the wreck until the 14th, when oil was still rising to the surface.

	Launched	*Commissioned*
U322	18 Dec 1943	5 Feb 1944

Class Type VIIC/41
CO *Oberleutnant zur See* Gerhard Wysk (lost)
Date of loss 25 November 1944
Location Atlantic, N of Cape Wrath, 60°18'N 04°52'W
Cause Hedgehog
Casualties 52
Survivors None
Salvaged No

Notes *U322* was en route for the Atlantic when she was attacked and damaged by Sunderland 'G' of No 330 (Norwegian) Squadron RAF on 24 November. The aircraft directed HMS *Ascension* of EG5 to the area. After a short search *Ascension* gained asdic contact and destroyed the U-boat with her Hedgehog.

	Launched	*Commissioned*
U80	11 Feb 1941	8 Apr 1941

Class Type VIIC
CO *Oberleutnant zur See* Hans Keerl (lost)
Date of loss 28 November 1944
Location Baltic, Danzig Bay, 54°25'N 19°50'E
Cause Accident
Casualties 50
Survivors ?
Salvaged No

Notes Lost in a diving accident, the exact circumstances of which are unknown.

U196	*Launched* 24 Apr 1942	*Commissioned* 11 Nov 1942
Class	Type IXD2	
CO	*Oberleutnant zur See* Johannes Striegler (lost)	
Date of loss	c. 30 November 1944	
Location	Sunda Strait	
Cause	?	
Casualties	65	
Survivors	None	
Salvaged	No	

Notes Sunk through unknown cause, though an accident while diving or while trying the boat's newly fitted (and locally constructed) snorkel is a possibility.

U297	*Launched* 9 Oct 1943	*Commissioned* 17 Nov 1943
Class	Type VIIC/41	
CO	*Oberleutnant zur See* Wolfgang Aldegannan (lost)	
Date of loss	6 December 1944	
Location	Atlantic, NE of Cape Wrath, 58°44'N 04°29'W	
Cause	Depth charge	
Casualties	50	
Survivors	None	
Salvaged	No	

Notes On 6 December *U775* torpedoed the frigate *Bullen*. The hunt for the culprit turned up *U297* instead. HMS *Loch Insh* and *Goodall* carried out a series of attacks which brought wooden wreckage and oil to the surface. Aircraft were ordered to search the area. Later that afternoon Sunderland 'Y' of No 201 Squadron sighted white smoke and a periscope wake . In its first attack the depth charges hung up but in a second run the wake was straddled and afterwards a large slick of oil was sighted.

U775 survived the war and was sunk in Operation 'Deadlight'.

U387	*Launched* 1 Oct 1942	*Commissioned* 24 Nov 1942
Class	Type VIIC	
CO	*Kapitänleutnant* Rudolf Buchler (lost)	
Date of loss	9 December 1944	
Location	Arctic, off the Kola Inlet, 69°41'N 33°12'E	
Cause	Depth charge	
Casualties	51	
Survivors	None	
Salvaged	No	

Notes The number of U-boats gathered outside the Kola Inlet awaiting the sailing of the homeward-bound convoy RA.62 prompted the force commander, Rear-Admiral Roderick McGrigor, to sail the escorts a day early to clear the U-boats from the waters around the Kola Inlet. The escorts were supported by a division of four Soviet destroyers. The frigate *Bamborough Castle* obtained one contact and destroyed it with depth charges. Subsequent analysis showed that *U387* was the victim of this attack. However Soviet sources claimed that *U387* was rammed and sunk by the destroyer *Zhivuchi*. Interestingly enough, British observers saw no signs of damage to *Zhivuchi*'s bows—a testament to the strength of Soviet construction?

U416	*Launched* 9 May 1942	*Commissioned* 4 Nov 1942
Class	Type VIIC	
CO	*Oberleutnant zur See* Eberhard Reiger	
Date of loss	12 December 1944	
Location	Baltic, off Pillau, 54°58'N 19°33'E	
Cause	Collision	
Casualties	35	
Survivors	?	
Salvaged	No	

Notes Following her mine damage in April 1943, *U416* had recommissioned in October 1943 for service as a training submarine. On 12 December 1944 she sank after colliding with *M203*.

U479	*Launched* 14 Aug 1943	*Commissioned* 27 Oct 1943
Class	Type VIIC	
CO	*Oberleutnant zur See* Friedrich Sons (lost)	
Date of loss	12 December 1944	
Location	Baltic, Gulf of Finland	
Cause	Mine	
Casualties	51	
Survivors	None	
Salvaged	No	

U365	*Launched*	*Commissioned*
	9 Mar 1943	8 Jun 1943
Class	Type VIIC	
CO	*Oberleutnant zur See* Dieter Todenhagen (lost)	
Date of loss	13 December 1944	
Location	Arctic, NW of Lofoten Islands, 70°43'N 08°07'E	
Cause	Air attack	
Casualties	51	
Survivors	None	
Salvaged	No	

Notes Sunk during operations in support of convoy RA.62, homeward-bound from the Kola Inlet. *U365* was caught on the surface by Swordfish 'L' and 'Q' of 813 NAS flying from the escort carrier HMS *Campania.*

U400	*Launched*	*Commissioned*
	? Feb 1944	18 Mar 1944
Class	Type VIIC	
CO	*Kapitänleutnant* Horst Creutz (lost)	
Date of loss	17 December 1944	
Location	Atlantic, S of Queenstown, 51°16'N 08°05'W	
Cause	Depth charge	
Casualties	50	
Survivors	None	
Salvaged	No	

Notes Sunk in a depth-charge attack by the frigate HMS *Nyasaland* of EG18.

U1209	*Launched*	*Commissioned*
	9 Feb 1944	13 Apr 1944
Class	Type VIIC	
CO	*Oberleutnant zur See* Ewald Hulsenbeck (lost)	
Date of loss	18 December 1944	
Location	English Channel, off Wolf Rock, 49°55'N 05°48'W	
Cause	Grounding	
Casualties	9	
Survivors	1 officer, 6 senior rates, 35 junior rates	
Salvaged	No	

Notes *U1209* had been hunted by EG26 off Land's End. However, several promising contacts which were attacked by HMCS *Ribble* and *Montreal* were subsequently classified as wrecks. Shortly afterwards the group rescued the remains of the crew of *U1209*. The survivors said that the boat had grounded and had suffered sufficient damage to warrant her being abandoned. EG26 were quick to claim that it was their hunting which had caused the damage, but the Admiralty were having none of it.

After the grounding there was some debate among the Trinity House lighthouse keepers as to whether they were entitled to the usual awards commensurate with sinking a U-boat.

U737	*Launched*	*Commissioned*
	21 Nov 1942	30 Jan 1943
Class	Type VIIC	
CO	Oberleutnant zur See Friedrich-August Greus	
Date of loss	19 December 1944	
Location	Norwegian coastal waters, Vestfjord, 68°09'N 15°39'E	
Cause	Collision	
Casualties	31	
Survivors	?	
Salvaged	No	

Notes *U737* sank after colliding with the minesweeper *MRS25*.

U2342	*Launched*	*Commissioned*
	13 Oct 1944	1 Nov 1944
Class	Type XXIII	
CO	*Oberleutnant zur See* Schad von Mittelbiberach (lost)	
Date of loss	26 December 1944	
Location	Baltic, N of Swindemünde, 53°55'N 14°17'E	
Cause	Mine	
Casualties	7	
Survivors	7	
Salvaged	No	

U877	*Launched*	*Commissioned*
	10 Dec 1943	24 Mar 1944
Class	Type IXC/40	
CO	*Kapitänleutnant* Eberhard Findeisen (survived)	
Date of loss	27 December 1944	
Location	Atlantic, NW of the Azores	
Cause	Squid	
Casualties	None	

Survivors 5 officers, 4 senior rates, 46 ratings
Salvaged No

Notes *U877* had been deployed on weather-reporting duties south of Ireland in connection with the German Army's Ardennes offensive. Problems with her W/T meant that she was unable to transmit, so she was given discretion by BdU to operate at will. HMCS *St Thomas* of the C3 group detected the U-boat by pure luck. One Squid bomb was fired to keep the target dived while the frigate's asdic team set about a proper classification. The ASCO thought that the contact was fish but the SDI (Leading Seaman G. A. Elsey) considered it a submarine as it had doppler. *St Thomas*'s CO, Lt-Cdr L. P. Denny RCNR, was persuaded by his SDI (not the first time this had happened) that the target was a submarine and fired another Squid bomb at it. This exploded directly over *U877*'s stern, causing numerous leaks which could not be stopped. The boat had sunk to 1,200ft before Findeisen gave the order to surface. *St Thomas* and *Sea Cliff* opened fire on *U877* when she surfaced but ceased when it was clear that the U-boat was being abandoned.

U735

	Launched	Commissioned
	10 Oct 1942	28 Dec 1942

Class Type VIIC
CO *Oberleutnant zur See* Hans Joachim Borner (lost)
Date of loss 28 December 1944
Location Norway, Horten
Cause Air attack
Casualties 39
Survivors None
Salvaged No

Notes *U737* was sunk during an RAF bombing raid while alongside at Horten.

U772

	Launched	Commissioned
	31 Oct 1943	23 Dec 1943

Class Type VIIC
CO *Kapitänleutnant* Ewald Rademacher (lost)
Date of loss 30 December 1944
Location English Channel, off Portland Bill, 50°05'N 02°31'W
Cause Air attack
Casualties 48
Survivors None
Salvaged No

Notes *U772* was operating in the English Channel and had sunk three merchant ships while managing to remain undetected. On 29 December she attacked the coastal convoy TBC.1, sinking one merchant ship and damaging another. It was while withdrawing from this attack that the boat's periscope and snorkel were sighted by Wellington 'L' of No 407 Squadron RCAF. The aircraft attacked with six depth charges, having illuminated the U-boat's masts with the Leigh Light. On circling the scene the aircraft spotted no wreckage or oil, but there were no further ASV contacts either.

U906

	Launched	Commissioned
	28 Jun 1944	15 Jul 1944

Class Type VIIC
CO None appointed
Date of loss 31 December 1944
Location North Sea, Hamburg
Cause Air attack
Casualties ?
Survivors ?
Salvaged No

Notes Sunk at Hamburg during a large USAAF raid. Also sunk in the raid were *U908*, *U1011*, *U1012*, *U2530*, *U2532* and *U2537*, which were in various advanced stages of construction.

1945

U382

	Launched	Commissioned
U382	21 Mar 1942	25 Apr 1942

Class Type VIIC
CO *Oberleutnant zur See* Schimmel
Date of loss ? January 1945
Location North Sea, Wilhelmshaven
Cause Air attack
Casualties ?
Survivors ?
Salvaged Yes

Notes Sunk at Wilhelmshaven during an RAF bombing raid. Raised on 20 March 1945 and paid off. Not recommissioned and eventually scuttled on 8 May 1945.

U650

	Launched	Commissioned
U650	11 Oct 1942	26 Nov 1942

Class Type VIIC
CO *Oberleutnant zur See* Rudolf Zorn (lost)
Date of loss ? January 1945
Location Atlantic
Cause ?
Casualties 47
Survivors None
Salvaged No

Notes *U650* disappeared while en route for the southern Irish Sea. No Allied claim exists for her sinking and therefore her loss can be attributed either to a drifting mine or to an accident arising from drill or mechanical failure.

U1020

	Launched	Commissioned
U1020	22 Mar 1944	17 May 1944

Class Type VIIC/41
CO *Oberleutnant zur See* Otto Eberlein (lost)
Date of loss ? January 1945
Location North Sea, Moray Firth
Cause ?
Casualties 49
Survivors None
Salvaged No

Notes As did *U650*, *U1020* disappeared without trace. She had been ordered to patrol off Ronaldsay in the Orkneys to attack British carrier groups setting out from (or returning to) Scapa Flow on anti-shipping operations off the Norwegian coast. She patrolled the Pentland Firth until the end of December and, sighting nothing, moved south to what were hoped were the more productive waters of the Moray Firth. She then vanished. No Allied claim exists for her sinking, and therefore her loss can be attributed either to a drifting mine or to an accident arising from drill or material failure.

U679

	Launched	Commissioned
U679	20 Nov 1943	29 Nov 1943

Class Type VIIC
CO *Oberleutnant zur See* Eduard Aust (lost)
Date of loss 10 January 1945
Location Baltic, exact position unknown
Cause Depth charge
Casualties 51
Survivors None
Salvaged No

Notes *U679* was sunk by the Soviet submarine chaser *MO-124* but little further information is available concerning this attack.

U248

	Launched	Commissioned
U248	7 Oct 1943	6 Nov 1943

Class Type VIIC
CO *Oberleutnant zur See* Johann Loos (lost)
Date of loss 16 January 1945
Location Atlantic, N of the Azores, 47°43'N 26°37'W

Cause	Depth charge
Casualties	47
Survivors	None
Salvaged	No

Notes *U248* was on weather-reporting duties off the Azores and her daily W/T transmissions were of considerable importance in providing meteorological data for the German Army's Ardennes offensive. However her transmissions (and those of her fellow weather-reporters *U1053*, *U1232* and *U1230*, which began reporting after landing a spy on the coast of Maine) were being monitored by Tenth Fleet command. A group of four destroyers under the command of Cdr J. E. Bowling USNR in *Otter* was established (no carriers were available, being fully employed in aircraft ferry duties), and these ships searched unsuccessfully up until 10 January, when they returned to the Azores to fuel.

They sailed again on the 12th and at 0550 on the 16th three of the ships picked up HF transmissions from a submarine only ten miles away; eighty minutes later the ships were in sonar contact. *Varian* acted as 'control' ship while *Hayter* and *Otter* delivered a succession of depth-charge and Hedgehog attacks. The U-boat manoeuvred skilfully at 500ft but at 1012 a boil of water on the surface indicated that she was coming up. *Otter* delivered the final attack as the U-boat broke surface. The submarine sank very quickly and there was no time for any of the crew to escape. Afterwards a scum of diesel, wreckage and human remains spread across the surface. Sufficient evidence, including an official song publication, was recovered to identify the boat as *U248*.

	Launched	*Commissioned*
U482	25 Sept 1943	1 Dec 1943
Class	Type VIIC	
CO	*Kapitänleutnant Graf* von Matuschka (lost)	
Date of loss	16 January 1945	
Location	North Channel, NW of Machrihanish, 55°30'N 05°53'W	
Cause	Depth charge	
Casualties	48	
Survivors	None	
Salvaged	No	

Notes *U482* had been operating in the North Channel area since 1 December 1944 with seeming immunity from counter-attack. She had crippled the escort carrier *Thane* with a torpedo and damaged a Norwegian tanker in the approaches to the Clyde. It was while withdrawing from patrol in this area that she ran into the 22nd Escort Group (HM Ships *Amethyst*, *Hart*, *Peacock*, *Starling* and *Loch Craggie*) and was destroyed by depth charges.

	Launched	*Commissioned*
U2523	25 Oct 1944	26 Nov 1944
Class	Type XXI	
CO	*Kapitänleutnant* Hans-Heinrich Ketels	
Date of loss	17 January 1945	
Location	North Sea, Hamburg	
Cause	Air attack	
Casualties	?	
Survivors	?	
Salvaged	No	

Notes Bombed in an Allied air raid on the port of Hamburg.

	Launched	*Commissioned*
U1199	12 Oct 1943	23 Dec 1943
Class	Type VIIC	
CO	*Kapitänleutnant* Rolf Nollmann (lost)	
Date of loss	21 January 1945	
Location	English Channel, W of Land's End, 49°57'N 05°42'W	
Cause	Depth charge	
Casualties	46	
Survivors	1 rating	
Salvaged	No	

Notes *U1199* had torpedoed the freighter *George Hawley* in convoy TBC.43 when she was attacked by the corvette HMS *Mignonette* and destroyer HMS *Icarus* which was detached from EG14. *U1199* was hiding on the bottom but repeated attacks by *Mignonette* and *Icarus* destroyed the boat. Oil and wreckage came to the surface together with one survivor, *Obersteuermann* Klausen. Klausen had made an escape from the conning tower wearing Dräger apparatus from a depth of 240ft. At that depth the pressure on his body was well over 100psi and it was nothing short of miraculous that he did not burst his lungs on the way up. Klausen's escape remains the deepest escape conducted from an actual submarine casualty. Greater depths have been achieved since, but these escapes have been carried out by qualified instructors under strictly controlled conditions.

U763	*Launched* 16 Jan 1943	*Commissioned* 13 Mar 1943

Class Type VIIC
CO *Oberleutnant zur See* Karl-Heinz Schroter
Date of loss 24 January 1945
Location Baltic, Königsberg
Cause Air attack
Casualties ?
Survivors ?
Salvaged ?

Notes Sunk during a Soviet air raid on the port of Königsberg. No details are available regarding the ultimate disposal of the wreck.

U1051	*Launched* 3 Feb 1944	*Commissioned* 4 Mar 1944

Class Type VIIC
CO *Oberleutnant zur See* Heinrich von Holleben (lost)
Date of loss 26 January 1945
Location Irish Sea, 53°39'N 05°23'W
Cause Ramming/depth charge
Casualties 52
Survivors None
Salvaged No

Notes On 26 January *U1172* torpedoed and damaged the frigate HMS *Manners*. EG4 and EG5 closed and, acting on information from *Manners*, began searching. The boat they found, however, was *U1051*. HMS *Bentinck* obtained an asdic contact and attacked with depth charges. HMS *Calder* and *Aylmer* joined the hunt and one hit from a Hedgehog was obtained. The U-boat then surfaced at 1604 with her conning tower completely wrecked. After being fired on by all three ships, she was rammed by *Aylmer* and sunk. A great quantity of wreckage was left on the surface but there were no survivors.

U1172	*Launched* 3 Dec 1943	*Commissioned* 20 Apr 1944

Class Type VIIC/41
CO *Oberleutnant zur See* Jurgen Kuhlmann (lost)
Date of loss 27 January 1945
Location Irish Sea, St George's Channel, 52°24'N 05°42'W
Cause Depth charge
Casualties 52
Salvaged No

Notes *U1172* did not survive long to enjoy her success. At noon on 27 January convoy HX.332 was attacked by *U825*. EG5 was deployed to look for the U-boat and at 1955 HMS *Keats* was in asdic contact in a position 20 miles south-west of the attack. After a number of depth-charge attacks by *Keats* and *Bligh* a considerable amount of wreckage and oil rose to the surface.

U3520	*Launched* 23 Nov 1944	*Commissioned* 23 Dec 1944

Class Type XXI
CO *Oberleutnant zur See* Sarto Ballert (lost)
Date of loss 31 January 1945
Location Baltic, Kiel Bay, off Eckernförde, 54°28'N 10°12'E
Cause Mine
Casualties 80
Survivors None
Salvaged No

U1279	*Launched* 3 May 1944	*Commissioned* 5 May 1944

Class Type VIIC/41
CO *Oberleutnant zur See* Hans Falke (lost)
Date of loss 3 February 1945
Location NW of Shetlands, 61°21'N 02°00'W
Cause Squid
Casualties 48
Survivors None
Salvaged No

Notes In early February there were indications that a number of U-boats might be using the Shetlands–Faeroes Channel as a transit route to the Atlantic. Accordingly, the 10th Escort Group sailed from Londonderry to patrol the area. Early on the 3rd the frigate HMS *Bayntun* gained an asdic contact which was unsuccessfully attacked with Hedgehog by *Braithwaite* and *Bayntun*. However, it was a single Squid firing by HMS *Loch Eck* which brought much oil and wreckage (including the air bottle of a German torpedo) to the surface.

	Launched	*Commissioned*
U745	16 Apr 1943	19 Jun 1943
Class	Type VIIC	
CO	*Kapitänleutnant* Wilhelm von Trotha (lost)	
Date of loss	? February 1945	
Location	Baltic	
Cause	Unknown	
Casualties	48	
Survivors	None	
Salvaged	No	

Notes *U745* disappeared while on patrol in the Gulf of Finland. She may have been the victim of a mine. On the other hand, the possibility that she was lost as a result of an accident arising from mechanical or drill failure cannot be ruled out.

	Launched	*Commissioned*
U1014	30 Jan 1944	14 Mar 1944
Class	Type VIIC/41	
CO	*Oberleutnant zur See* Wolgang Glaser (lost)	
Date of loss	4 February 1945	
Location	NW of Ireland, off Lough Foyle, 55°17'N 06°44'W	
Cause	Depth charge	
Casualties	48	
Survivors	None	
Salvaged	No	

Notes HMS *Loch Scavaig* of EG23 was engaged in working-up excercises off Lough Foyle when asdic contact was made with an object lying on the bottom. She was joined by the other ships in her group (*Nyasaland* and *Papua*) and carried out a series of attacks which resulted in a considerable amount of wreckage, including clothing and German documents, coming to the surface.

	Launched	*Commissioned*
U923	7 Aug 1943	4 Oct 1943
Class	Type VIIC	
CO	*Oberleutnant zur See* Heinz Frommer (lost)	
Date of loss	9 February 1945	
Location	Baltic	
Cause	Mine	
Casualties	48	
Survivors	None	
Salvaged	Yes	

Notes Raised in January 1953 and broken up.

	Launched	*Commissioned*
U864	12 Aug 1943	15 Dec 1943
Class	Type IXD	
CO	*Korvettenkapitän* Ralf-Reimar Wolfram (lost)	
Date of loss	9 February 1945	
Location	Norwegian Sea, W of Bergen, 60°46'N 04°35'E	
Cause	Submarine attack	
Casualties	73	
Survivors	None	
Salvaged	No	

Notes This was the second submarine sunk by *Venturer* under the command of Lt Jimmy Launders, but this action was unusual in that both submarines were dived at the time.

Venturer was on patrol off Fejeosen (now known as Fedje), the most frequently used entrance to Bergen when, shortly after 0932, she detected faint noises on her Type 129 hydrophone. While the noise steadily increased, its source was confirmed as being a submarine at 1050 and the OOW sighted a periscope on the HE bearing. The submarine was not snorkelling as the tell-tale 'gefuffle' of the exhaust was missing, so the boat must have been running some item of noisy equipment such as a compressor. At 1122 *Venturer*'s First Lieutenant sighted both the other submarine's periscopes (or possibly one periscope and the HF W/T mast, since Wolfram would have been anxious to make contact with his shore base to notify his presence and prevent attack by friendly forces). The masts were kept up for quite some time and their use was subsequently described by *Venturer*'s flotilla commander as 'shockingly careless'. From the information provided by asdic and periscope observation, Launders concluded that he was broad on the target's starboard bow. For the next hour Launders used his very primitive Type 129 asdic to produce a plot of the target's course, and at 1212, when reasonably sure that the plot was correct, fired four Mk VIII** torpedoes in a 'hosepipe' salvo. The range on firing was reckoned to be 2,000yds, but, judging from the time it took the first torpedo to hit, it was probably more like

3,000yds. One explosion was heard on the right bearing after 2min 12sec ruuning time. Two more explosions were heard after five minutes, indicating that the torpedoes had detonated on the seabed. Two minutes after the first explosion asdic reported breaking-up noises and the ominous sound of rushing water. *U864*'s bulkheads were designed to survive a surface collision—but they could not survive pressure at depth.

Launders took *Venturer* to the scene to conduct an inspection through his periscope. There was an extensive slick of diesel, a considerable amount of wooden wreckage, probably from the U-boat's casing, and a large metal canister which may have been one of the upper deck lockers used for carrying dinghies or lifejackets but may have been the container for a Focke Achgelis tethered autogyro used for reconniassance purposes.

U989	*Launched* 16 Jun 1943	*Commissioned* 22 Jul 1943
Class	Type VIIC	
CO	*Kapitänleutnant* Roidler von Roithberg (lost)	
Date of loss	14 February 1945	
Location	N of Shetlands, 61°36'N 01°35'W	
Cause	Squid	
Casualties	46	
Survivors	2	
Salvaged	No	

Notes After the sinking of *U1279* EG10 refuelled at Scapa and then returned to the Shetlands–Faeroes gap. On the afternoon of the14th *Bayntun* had a firm asdic contact and all ships in the group made a number of attacks using Squid and Hedgehog. It was not until *Loch Dunvegan* had carried out three Squid attacks that wreckage started coming to the surface as well as two survivors, one of whom was von Roithberg. Both men died shortly after being rescued, probably as a result of escaping from deep without proper apparatus or training, but they did confirm the identity of the boat as being *U989*.

U1053	*Launched* 17 Jan 1944	*Commissioned* 12 Feb 1944
Class	Type VIIC	
CO	*Oberleutnant zur See* Helmut Lange (lost)	
Date of loss	15 February 1945	
Location	Norwegian coastal waters, off Bergen, 60°22'N 05°10'E	
Cause	Accident	
Casualties	44	
Survivors	?	
Salvaged	No	

Notes Sunk off Bergen during a diving accident, the exact circumstances of which are unknown.

U309	*Launched* 14 Dec 1942	*Commissioned* 27 Jan 1943
Class	Type VIIC	
CO	*Oberleutnant zur See* Herbert Loder (lost)	
Date of loss	16 February 1945	
Location	North Sea, Moray Firth, 58°09'N 02°23'W	
Cause	Depth charge	
Casualties	47	
Survivors	None	
Salvaged	No	

Notes EG9 was escorting convoy WN.74 into the Moray Firth when the frigate *St John* reported an asdic contact. The contact had no doppler so was stationary, but a fix taken with QH did not match with any known wreck. The contact was therefore assessed as being a U-boat hiding on the bottom. An attack with five depth charges produced some light oil on the surface. The second and third attacks were with Hedgehog and were unsuccessful. The fourth attack, with depth charges, produced a mass of wreckage including charts, signal books and quantities of cork insulation. The wreck was unsuccessfully attacked again on the 17th in the hope of releasing a body. *St John* was awarded a 'probable', and after the war this was confirmed when *U309* was adjudged the victim of this attack.

U425	*Launched* 19 Dec 1942	*Commissioned* 21 Apr 1943
Class	Type VIIC	
CO	*Kapitänleutnant* Heinz Bentzien (lost)	
Date of loss	17 February 1945	
Location	Arctic, off the Kola Inlet, 69°39'N 33°50'E	
Cause	Depth charge	
Casualties	48	

Survivors	1
Salvaged	No

Notes On the day before convoy RA.64 was to sail from the Kola Inlet, every available escort was ordered to sea to clear the approaches to the Inlet. HMS *Alnwick Castle* and *Lark* detected *U425* during these routine sweeps and destroyed her with depth charges. The attacks blew the submarine to the surface. On surfacing, the submarine, much to the British ships' surprise, gave the Russian recognition signal currently in force! One man escaped before she sank.

	Launched	*Commissioned*
U1273	10 Jan 1944	16 Feb 1944
Class	Type VIIC/41	
CO	*Kapitänleutnant* Helmut Knollmann (lost)	
Date of loss	17 February 1945	
Location	Norwegian coastal waters, Oslo Fjord, off Horton	
Cause	Mine	
Casualties	43	
Survivors	None	
Salvaged	No	

	Launched	*Commissioned*
U1278	15 Apr 1944	31 May 1944
Class	Type VIIC/41	
CO	*Kapitänleutnant* Erich Müller-Bethke (lost)	
Date of loss	17 February 1945	
Location	N of Shetlands, 61°32'N 01°36'W	
Cause	Hedgehog	
Casualties	48	
Survivors	None	
Salvaged	No	

Notes After the sinking of *U989* EG10 remained in the Shetland–Faeroes passage despite heavy weather. On the evening of the 17th *Bayntun* reported that she was in contact with a submarine—for the third time in the Group's operations. On this occasion *Bayntun* was able to complete what she had begun and destroyed *U1278* in a Hedgehog attack. Large quantities of oil came to the surface, together with a rubber dinghy and an inflated rubber ball covered with green canvas.

	Launched	*Commissioned*
U2344	24 Oct 1944	10 Nov 1944
Class	Type XXIII	
CO	*Oberleutnant zur See* Hermann Ellerlage (survived)	
Date of loss	18 February 1945	
Location	Baltic, off Heiligenhaven, 54°06'N 11°48'E	
Cause	Collision	
Casualties	7	
Survivors	7	
Salvaged	Yes	

Notes Sunk following a collision with *U2336*, the exact circumstances of which are unknown. The wreck was raised in June 1956 and broken up at Rostock in 1958.

	Launched	*Commissioned*
U676	6 Jul 1943	6 Aug 1943
Class	Type VIIC (configured as experimental flak boat and employed as AA escort to Baltic convoys August–October 1944)	
CO	*Kapitänleutnant* Werner Sass (lost)	
Date of loss	19 February 1945	
Location	Baltic, Gulf of Finland, exact position unknown	
Cause	Mine	
Casualties	57	
Survivors	None	
Salvaged	No	

Notes Mined in a Soviet-laid field.

	Launched	*Commissioned*
U300	23 Nov 1943	29 Dec 1943
Class	Type VIIC	
CO	*Oberleutnant zur See* Fritz Hein (lost)	
Date of loss	22 February 1945	
Location	Atlantic, off Cape St Vincent, 36°29'N 08°20'W	
Cause	Depth charge	
Casualties	8	
Survivors	3 officers, 4 senior rates, 34 junior rates	
Salvaged	No	

Notes *U300* had been operating off Iceland before Hein asked to be allowed to shift his patrol to the Gibraltar area. After making a landfall off Cape St Vincent, Hein was told that a convoy was expected. On 17 February he attacked UGS.2 and torpedoed two ships, the *Regent Lion* and the *Michael J. Stone*. Two days later *U300* was attacked by HMS *Evadne* and was badly damaged, the depth charges causing numerous leaks in the bow and fracturing an oil tank. Hein evaded the attack and made for Tangier Bay. There extemporary repairs were made, the holes in the bow, which had been temporarily plugged with wooden bungs and bacon fat, being sealed by welding. Repairs completed, Hein proceeded to a spot between Cadiz and Cape St Vincent and lay on the bottom to await developments. On 22 February Hein came to snorkel depth for routine W/T reception and sighted a convoy of LSTs. He fired one Gnat at an escort and missed, but when he saw another escort turn towards him he gave the order to surface and abandon ship. The survivors were picked up by HM Ships *Recruit* and *Pincher*.

U480	*Launched* 14 Aug 1943	*Commissioned* 6 Oct 1943
Class	Type VIIC	
CO	*Oberleutnant zur See* Hans Joachim Forster (lost)	
Date of loss	24 February 1945	
Location	English Channel, SW of Land's End, 49°55'N 06°08'W	
Cause	Depth charge	
Casualties	48	
Survivors	None	
Salvaged	No	

Notes While returning from the Channel *U480* attacked convoy BTC.78 and sank the *Oriskany*. Retribution was swift, for she was hunted by 3EG and destroyed by HMS *Duckworth* and *Rowley* after a six-hour hunt. Sufficient wreckage was recovered for a 'kill' to be claimed.

U927	*Launched* 3 May 1944	*Commissioned* 27 Jun 1944
Class	Type VIIC	
CO	*Kapitänleutnant* Jurgen Ebert (lost)	
Date of loss	24 February 1945	
Location	English Channel, SE of Falmouth, 49°54'N 04°45'W	
Cause	Air attack	
Casualties	47	
Survivors	None	
Salvaged	No	

Notes Warwick 'K' of No 179 Squadron, flown by Flt Lt A. G. Brownsill, obtained a radar contact which was subsequently illuminated with Leigh Light. There, revealed in the glare of the light, was a snorkel protruding some four or five feet out of the water. The aircraft dropped six depth charges which landed in a perfect straddle, three on each side of the boat. The aircraft returned to the spot, the Leigh Light was switched on and oil and wreckage were seen on the surface. After the explosions a large oil slick was observed in the moonlight.

U3007	*Launched* 4 Sept 1944	*Commissioned* 22 Oct 1944
Class	Type XXI	
CO	*Kapitänleutnant* Helmut Manseck	
Date of loss	24 February 1945	
Location	Baltic, Bremen	
Cause	Air attack	
Casualties	?	
Survivors	?	
Salvaged	No	

Notes Destroyed in a USAAF bombing raid on Bremen.

U1018	*Launched* 1 Mar 1944	*Commissioned* 25 Apr 1944
Class	Type VIIC/41	
CO	*Kapitänleutnant* Walter Burmeister (lost)	
Date of loss	27 February 1945	
Location	English Channel, SW of The Lizard, 49°56'N 05°20'W	
Cause	Depth charge	
Casualties	51	
Survivors	1 officer, 1 rating	
Salvaged	No	

Notes HMS *Loch Fada* detected the U-boat by asdic and after a number of attacks two survivors were rescued who confirmed the identity of the boat.

U327	*Launched* 27 Feb 1944	*Commissioned* 18 Jul 1944
Class	Type VIIC/41	
CO	*Kapitänleutnant* Hans Lemcke (lost)	
Date of loss	27 February 1945	
Location	English Channel, 49°46'N 05°47'W	
Cause	Depth charge	
Casualties	46	
Survivors	None	
Salvaged	No	

Notes *U327* was sighted by a Liberator of VP-112 twelve miles south of the Wolf Rock, snorkelling and leaking oil, and the aircraft lost no time in homing in the 2nd Escort Group. An attack carried out in the dark by *Labuan* produced a strong smell of diesel and what appeared to be an oil drum. EG2 then returned to Plymouth, believing the attack successful. Higher authority disagreed, and the next day the Group was sent back to give the wreck a pounding until satisfactory evidence of a 'kill' (i.e., human remains) was recovered. This action led to a good deal of discontent on the lower decks of the ships involved. An 'oil drum' was recovered and proved to be a pressure-tight container holding a dinghy. Further attacks were carried out, yielding woodwork and correspondence of German origin.

U869	*Launched* 5 Oct 1943	*Commissioned* 26 Jan 1944
Class	Type IXC	
CO	*Kapitänleutnant* Helmuth Neuerberg (lost)	
Date of loss	28 February 1945	
Location	Mediterranean, off Casablanca, 34°30'N 08°13'W	
Cause	Depth charge	
Casualties	56	
Survivors	None	
Salvaged	No	

Notes Sunk in a depth-charge attack by the US destroyer *Fowler* and the French submarine-chaser *L'Indiscret* after the U-boat had attempted an attack on convoy GUS.74.

U1208	*Launched* 13 Jan 1944	*Commissioned* 6 Apr 1944
Class	Type VIIC	
CO	*Korvettenkapitän* Georg Hagene (lost)	
Date of loss	? March 1945	
Location	English Channel	
Cause	?	
Casualties	49	
Survivors	None	
Salvaged	No	

Notes Sunk by unknown cause in the English Channel. Mine, snorkel failure or battery explosion are the most likely causes for the loss. *U1208*'s demise was previously attributed to an attack by HMS *Amethyst* on 20 February 1945.

U296	*Launched* 25 Sept 1943	*Commissioned* 3 Nov 1943
Class	Type VIIC	
CO	*Oberleutnant zur See* Karl Rasch (lost)	
Date of loss	March 1945	
Location	Irish Sea, North Channel, off Inishtrahull	
Cause	?	
Casualties	46	
Survivors	None	
Salvaged	No	

Notes *U296* disappeared in the first half of March 1945. Her loss has previously and incorrectly been attributed to an attack by Liberator 'M' of No 120 Squadron. She may have fallen victim to a mine or been the victim of an accident arising from mechanical or drill failure.

U3519	*Launched* 23 Nov 1944	*Commissioned* 15 Dec 1944
Class	Type XXI	
CO	*Kapitänleutnant* Richard von Harpe (lost)	
Date of loss	2 March 1945	
Location	Baltic, off Warnemünde, 54°11'N 12°05'E	
Cause	Mine	
Casualties	65	
Survivors	None	
Salvaged	No	

U3036	*Launched* 27 Jan 1945	*Commissioned* 6 Feb 1945
Class	Type XXI	

CO	None appointed
Date of loss	3 March 1945
Location	Baltic, Bremen
Cause	Air attack
Casualties	?
Survivors	?
Salvaged	No

Notes Destroyed in a raid on Bremen by B-17 bombers of the US Eighth Air Force.

	Launched	*Commissioned*
U3508	? Nov 1944	?
Class	Type XXI	
CO	*Kapitänleutnant* Detlev von Lehsten	
Date of loss	4 March 1945	
Location	North Sea, Wilhelmshaven	
Cause	Air attack	
Casualties	?	
Survivors	?	
Salvaged	No	

Notes Sunk at Wilhelmshaven during an attack by B-24 aircraft of the US Eighth Air Force.

	Launched	*Commissioned*
U1302	4 Apr 1944	25 May 1944
Class	Type VIIC/41	
CO	*Kapitänleutnant* Wolfgang Herwartz (lost)	
Date of loss	7 March 1945	
Location	Irish Sea, Cardigan Bay, 52°19'N 05°23'W	
Cause	Depth charge	
Casualties	49	
Survivors	None	
Salvaged	No	

Notes *U1302* had been operating in St George's Channel with some success: on 28 February she sank the *Soreldoc* and the *Norfolk Coast* and on 2 March the *King Edgar* and the *Novasli*. These attacks brought several escort groups out looking for her, but Herwartz was undaunted and remained in the area for another five days. However, on the night of 7 March he ran into the Canadian EG25. The frigate *La Hulloise* obtained a suspicious radar contact followed by an asdic contact which was classified as 'Submarine'. It took the ship's command a few minutes to appreciate that radar and asdic contacts were one and the same. *La Hulloise* had expended all her depth charges so her CO, Lt-Cdr John Brock RCNVR, decided to maintain asdic contact while calling up reinforcements. *Strathadam* and *Thetford Mines* were quickly on the scene. In almost perfect conditions—calm seas and excellent visibility—*Strathadam* made a Hedgehog attack which produced one hit followed by an underwater flash and the appearance of a large air bubble. Moments later the U-boat broached before sinking, leaving wreckage but no survivors. Subsequent attacks produced oil, books, clothing and personal effects. During the attack the SO of EG18, who was senior to the SO of EG25 and who was aware that the latter were in contact with a U-boat, tried to take over the attack and was politely but firmly warned off!

	Launched	*Commissioned*
U275	8 Oct 1942	25 Nov 1942
Class	Type VIIC	
CO	*Oberleutnant zur See* Helmut Wehrkamp (lost)	
Date of loss	10 March 1945	
Location	English Channel, SW of Beachy Head, 50°36'N 00°04'E	
Cause	Mine	
Casualties	48	
Survivors	None	
Salvaged	No	

Notes *U275* had come up-Channel from St Nazaire and had sunk the *Lornaston* in convoy ONA.289 on the 8th—and reported the sinking to BdU, the signal being received by the *xB-Dienst*. Two days later Wehrkamp was still in the area and strayed into the deep minefield laid off Beachy Head.

	Launched	*Commissioned*
U681	18 Jan 1944	3 Feb 1944
Class	Type VIIC	
CO	*Oberleutnant zur See* Werner Gebauer (survived)	
Date of loss	11 March 1945	
Location	English Channel, 49°53'N 06°31'W	
Cause	Grounding/air attack	
Casualties	11	
Survivors	3 officers, 5 senior rates, 30 junior rates	
Salvaged	No	

Notes *U681* ran aground while attempting to enter St Mary's roads in the Isles of Scilly and sustained damage to her hull and propellers. An excess pressure was set up in an inner fuel tank and oil poured into the control room. Soon the men in the control room were splashing around in two or three feet of diesel fuel from a ruptured tank. Nevertheless Gebauer managed to extricate his boat and surfaced. The boat could not dive, so Gebauer headed off at best speed towards Eire and internment. He might have succeeded had he not been spotted by Liberator 'N' of VP-103. The pilot, Lt R. N. Field USN, made two attacking runs and dropped eight depth charges on the second. The shock of the explosions started more leaks and Gebauer decided to abandon the submarine. The crew piled out and into the dinghies while demolition charges were set and the main vents opened. Shortly after disppearing beneath the waves, there was a violent explosion marking *U681*'s end.

U682

	Launched	*Commissioned*
	7 Mar 1944	17 Apr 1944
Class	Type VIIC	
CO	*Oberleutnant zur See* Thienemann (?)	
Date of loss	11 March 1945	
Location	North Sea, Hamburg	
Cause	Air attack	
Casualties	?	
Survivors	?	
Salvaged	No	

Notes Destroyed in a raid by Nos 1, 6 (RCAF) and 8 Groups RAF Bomber Command on the Blohm und Voss shipyard.

U2515

	Launched	*Commissioned*
	22 Sept 1944	19 Dec 1944
Class	Type XXI	
CO	*Kapitänleutnant* Rolf Bolchers	
Date of loss	11 March 1945	
Location	North Sea, Hamburg	
Cause	Air attack	
Casualties	?	
Survivors	?	
Salvaged	No	

Notes Sunk in No 3 Dock, Hamburg, while under repair during a daylight raid by the US Eighth Air Force.

U260

	Launched	*Commissioned*
	9 Feb 1942	14 Mar 1943
Class	Type VIIC	
CO	*Oberleutnant zur See* Klaus Becker (survived)	
Date of loss	12 March 1945	
Location	St George's Channel, off Galley Head, 51°15'N 09°05'W	
Cause	Mine	
Casualties	None	
Survivors	49	
Salvaged	No	

Notes *U260* had left Norway on 21 February and was conducting operations in St George's Channel. While proceeding dived the boat was damaged by the explosion of a mine in the deep minefield CF2(A), which had been recently laid off the Fastnet by HMS *Apollo*. The field consisted of 156 Mk XVII mines laid at alternating depths of 220 and 230ft. Becker and his crew succeeded in keeping their boat afloat for another two days but on the 14th he abandoned and scuttled the submarine just inside Irish territorial waters. Becker and his crew then paddled ashore in their dinghies and landed near Galley Head, where they requested internment from a surprised *Gardai*.

The sinking of *U260* had some interesting consequences. Becker informed BdU via the German minister in Dublin, Eduard Hempel, of the circumstances surrounding the loss of his boat. This information confirmed reports from *Abwehr* agents in the UK (the agent involved here was, in fact, the double agent Tate) about British minelaying operations in coastal waters and caused the Germans to withdraw their boats from these waters.

U683

	Launched	*Commissioned*
	7 Mar 1944	30 May 1944
Class	Type VIIC	
CO	*Kapitänleutnant* Günther Keller (lost)	
Date of loss	12 March 1945	
Location	English Channel, off Land's End, 49°52'N 06°31'W	
Cause	Depth charge	
Casualties	49	
Survivors	None	
Salvaged	No	

Notes Sunk by HMS *Wild Goose* and *Loch Ruthven* while proceeding down the English Channel.

U714	*Launched*	*Commissioned*
	12 Nov 1942	10 Feb 1943
Class	Type VIIC	
CO	*Kapitänleutnant* Hans-Joachim Schwebke (lost)	
Date of loss	14 March 1945	
Location	North Sea, off W coast of Scotland, 55°57'N 01°57'W	
Cause	Depth charge	
Casualties	50	
Survivors	None	
Salvaged	No	

Notes On 10 March *U714* had sunk the *Nordhav II* in convoy FS.56. The newly commissioned and worked-up South African frigate *Natal* was ordered to carry out a square search and after twenty minutes reported an asdic contact which was classified as 'Submarine'. After an attack with Squid a large amount of oil came to the surface together with a large cylinder. In a second attack more oil came to the surface. Contact was then lost. Three days later EG17 worked over the area, found the target lying on the bottom and depth-charged it to destruction, after which a considerable amount of wreckage came to the surface.

Natal's asdic team had only worked together for four days in a land trainer. Their achievement in sinking *U714* was described by the Official Historian thus: 'Sent her to the bottom with a promptitude which would have done credit to a much more experienced crew.'

U367	*Launched*	*Commissioned*
	11 Jun 1943	27 Aug 1943
Class	Type VIIC	
CVO	*Oberleutnant zur See* Hasso Stegemann (lost)	
Date of loss	15 March 1945	
Location	Baltic, off Danzig, 54°25'N 19°50'E	
Cause	Mine	
Casualties	43	
Survivors	None	
Salvaged	No	

U866	*Launched*	*Commissioned*
	29 Sept 1944	9 Nov 1944
Class	Type IXC	
CO	*Oberleutnant zur See* Peter Rogowsky (lost)	
Date of loss	18 March 1945	
Location	Atlantic, SE of Sable Island	
Cause	Hedgehog	
Casualties	55	
Survivors	None	
Salvaged	No	

Notes *U866* was one of three U-boats heading westwards across the Atlantic to operate in Canadian waters. En route Rogowsky's injudicious use of the wireless brought his boat's presence to the attention of the Canadians, who deployed EG16 and EG27, together with TG.22.14 (a force of USCG-manned DEs comprising *Pride*, *Menges*, *Moseley* and *Lowe*), to search for her. *U866* had been damaged in an air raid while under construction at Bremen, was less than seaworthy and had problems with the snorkel. The ships, operating under Canadian control and supported by the RCAF, began retiring searches along *U866*'s estmated line of advance from 6 March.

On 16 March the two groups were redeployed on other tasks, but, by coincidence, at 1019Z on the 16th the USS *Lowe* made contact with *U866* a few miles south-west of Sable Island. Rogowsky attempted to avoid *Lowe*'s first unsuccessful Hedgehog attack by hiding on the bottom—a futile tactic given that the sea bed here was smooth and sandy, making for almost ideal sonar conditions.

Lowe's second attack resulted in two explosions followed by a surge of wreckage and oil to the surface. However, the commander of TG.22.14 was not satisfied and ordered *Menges* to join *Lowe* in a series of attacks designed to break up the wreck and release sufficient evidence to claim a 'kill'. Sixty-five depth charges were dropped on the wreck until a massive underwater explosion was recorded at 1623Z. Further attacks were carried out on the 17th, more wreckage was recovered and the commander of TG 22.14 was finally satisfied.

U905	*Launched*	*Commissioned*
	20 Nov 1943	8 Mar 1943
Class	Type VIIC	

CO	*Oberleutnant zur See* Bernhard Schwarting (lost)
Date of loss	20 March 1945
Location	Atlantic, N of Cape Wrath, 59°42'N 04°55'W
Cause	Air attack
Casualties	45
Survivors	None
Salvaged	No

Notes Sunk in an attack by Liberator 'B' of No 86 Squadron.

U1003

	Launched	Commissioned
	27 Oct 1943	9 Dec 1943

Class	Type VIIC/41
CO	*Oberleutnant zur See* Werner Struebing (survived)
Date of loss	22 March 1945
Location	Atlantic, N of Lough Foyle, 55°25'N 06°53'W
Cause	Collision/scuttling
Casualties	18
Survivors	31
Salvaged	No

Notes This was the last U-boat to be sunk by the RCN in the Second World War. EG20 were en route from Londonderry to Loch Alsh for work-up. At about 2350Z the port look-out in HMCS *New Glasgow* reported the noise of a low-flying aircraft. However, no aircraft was seen and, eventually, the changing direction of the noise drew the look-out's attention downward. There he saw the periscope and snorkel of a U-boat, both masts wreathed in yellow fumes, closing from about 75yds away. There was barely time to order 'Action stations' before the U-boat struck the frigate below the bridge.

The U-boat was *U1003*. The Tunis set operator had obtained a contact but had not reported it, and the collision with *New Glasgow* came as a complete surprise. Both Struebing and the LI gave conflicting orders which resulted in *U1003* hitting the bottom very violently at 60m. EG26, supported by EG25 and C4, launched a series of attacks but were never in contact with *U1003* and an hour after the collision Struebing began to head west at slow speed out of the North Channel. At dawn on the 22nd he surfaced and surveyed the shambles on the bridge. The fairing and rails were buckled and both periscopes were wrecked together with snorkel mast. Radar and search receivers had been torn away and one of the 20mm guns had been wrenched from its mounting. A jury warning receiver was rigged and the boat ventilated, but half an hour after surfacing warning signals forced Struebing to dive.

The dive revealed that the upper hatch was no longer watertight. Although the conning tower was allowed to flood, water poured into the control room through a voicepipe. Throughout the 22nd *U1003* remained on the bottom as the air grew steadily foul. Finally Struebing surfaced and decided to head for the Irish Free State and internment. However, on surfacing strong radar impulses were noted and he decided to take to the liferafts and scuttle the boat. At 0825Z on the 23rd the survivors were picked up by HMCS *Thetford Mines*. Struebing unsuccessfully tried to pass himself off as an ordinary watchkeeping officer by the name of Striezel. Two of his crew died aboard *Thetford Mines* and were buried at sea.

U399

	Launched	Commissioned
	? Dec 1943	22 Jan 1944

Class	Type VIIC
CO	*Oberleutnant zur See* Heinz Buhse (lost)
Date of loss	26 March 1945
Location	English Channel, SW of The Lizard, 49°56'N 05°22'W
Cause	Hedgehog
Casualties	46
Survivors	1
Salvaged	No

Notes Buhse had successfully attacked the coastal convoy BTC.108 and sunk the 362-ton *Coastal Pacific*. Had he known that EG3 were trailing the convoy he might have been more circumspect. The frigates came up quickly and it was not long before the veteran *Duckworth* was in contact and delivered a Hedgehog attack. After the explosion of the warhead, a large air bubble containing two men, one of whom was alive, burst on the surface of the water, bringing up the grim evidence of a successful attack. The Group then carried out 'tin opener' attacks which produced satisfactory evidence of the sinking.

U722

	Launched	Commissioned
	18 Sept 1943	15 Dec 1943

Class	Type VIIC

CO	*Oberleutnant zur See* Hans-Heinrich Reimers (lost)
Date of loss	27 March 1945
Location	The Minches, ENE of Butt of Lewis, 57°09'N 06°55'W
Cause	Depth charge
Casualties	43
Survivors	None
Salvaged	No

Notes Sunk in a depth-charge attack by the frigates HMS *Fitzroy*, *Redmill* and *Byron* of EG21. A contact that was orignally assessed as being very dubious was confirmed when the 147B set showed the target as being at a depth of 266ft where the water depth was 396ft. A series of attacks forced the target to the bottom and released suffiient evidence for a 'kill' to be claimed.

	Launched	*Commissioned*
U965	14 Jan 1943	25 Feb 1943

Class	Type VIIC
CO	*Oberleutnant zur See* Günther Unverzagt (lost)
Date of loss	27 March 1945
Location	Atlantic, W of Cape Wrath, 58°34'N 05°46'W
Cause	Depth charge
Casualties	51
Survivors	None
Salvaged	No

Notes Sunk in a depth-charge attack by the frigate HMS *Conn* of EG21. *Conn* detected the U-boat on asdic and delivered a number of attacks which, however, failed to release suffient evidence to claim a 'kill' since the U-boat's remains had settled into deep mud. A few days later 'tin opener' attacks were carried out by HMS *Escapade*, releasing evidence that the boat had been destroyed.

	Launched	*Commissioned*
U246	7 Dec 1943	11 Jan 1944

Class	Type VIIC
CO	*Kapitänleutnant* Ernst Raabe (lost)
Date of loss	March 1945
Location	Irish Sea, St George's Channel, 53°42'N 04°53'W
Cause	?
Casualties	48
Survivors	None
Salvaged	No

Notes Wreckage brought up from a contact attacked by HM Ships *Hesperus* and *Havelock* assisted by Sunderland 'H' of No 201 Squadron on 30 April 1945 was conclusively identified as coming from *U246*. However, since *U246* was due to leave patrol in early April, she must have been dead on the bottom when found and attacked by the two destroyers and the Sunderland. In the absence of any other attack to account for *U246*, her loss must be attributed to an accident—most likely snorkel failure or battery explosion resulting from inadequate ventilation while charging.

Whether the loss of *U246* can be attributed to an attack by HMS *Duckworth* on 29 March in 49°58'N 05°25'W has yet to be determined.

	Launched	*Commissioned*
U1106	26 May 1944	5 Jul 1944

Class	Type VIIC
CO	*Oberleutnant zur See* Erwin Bartke (lost)
Date of loss	29 March 1945
Location	N of Shetlands, 61°46'N 02°16'W
Cause	Air attack
Casualties	49
Survivors	None
Salvaged	No

Notes Liberator 'O' of No 224 Squadron, flown by Flt Lt M. A. Graham, was on a routine anti-submarine patrol when a wake was sighted at a range of three miles. As the aircraft closed, the distinctive head and 'gefuffle' of a snorkel were noticed. After the first depth-charge attack, the submarine's stern was visible for a moment before sinking again. The aircraft laid a pattern of sonobuoys from which the sounds of banging and machinery noises could be heard. There was also an intermittent propeller beat, but this was drowned out by the noises.

U1106 had left Kiel on 23 March on her first patrol and it was adjudged that she was the victim of this attack.

	Launched	*Commissioned*
U72	22 Nov 1940	4 Jan 1941

Class	Type VIIC
CO	?

Date of loss 30 March 1945
Location Baltic, Bremen
Cause Air attack
Casualties ?
Survivors ?
Salvaged No
Notes *U72* was damaged beyond repair in a raid by B-17 bombers of the US Eighth Air Force on Bremen. The boat was scuttled on 2 May 1945.

	Launched	*Commissioned*
U96	1 Aug 1940	14 Sept 1940

Class Type VIIC
CO *Oberleutnant zur See* Robert Rix
Date of loss 30 March 1945
Location North Sea, Wilhelmshaven
Cause Air attack
Casualties ?
Survivors ?
Salvaged No
Notes Sunk in a raid by B-24 bombers of the US Eighth Air Force on Wilhemshaven.

	Launched	*Commissioned*
U329	–	–

Class Type VIIC
CO None appointed
Date of loss 30 March 1945
Location Baltic, Bremen
Cause Air attack
Casualties –
Survivors –
Salvaged No
Notes *U329* had been damaged in a raid on Bremen in September 1943 and her construction had been suspended. Her incomplete hull was finally destroyed in a raid by US Eighth Air Force B-17 bombers. A Ministry of Supply survey team inspecting the docks at Bremen after the war could find no trace of her hull.

	Launched	*Commissioned*
U348	25 Jun 1943	10 Aug 1943

Class Type VIIC
CO *Oberleutnant zur See* Hans Norbert Schunk (?)
Date of loss 30 March 1945
Location North Sea, Hamburg
Cause Air attack
Casualties 2
Survivors ?
Salvaged No
Notes Destroyed in a raid by Nos 1, 6 (RCAF) and 8 Groups RAF Bomber Command on the Blohm und Voss shipyard.

	Launched	*Commissioned*
U350	17 Aug 1943	7 Oct 1943

Class Type VIIC
CO *Oberleutnant zur See* Erich Niesten
Date of loss 30 March 1945
Location North Sea, Hamburg
Cause Air attack
Casualties ?
Survivors ?
Salvaged No
Notes Destroyed in a raid by Nos 1, 6 (RCAF) and 8 Groups RAF Bomber Command on the Blohm und Voss shipyard.

	Launched	*Commissioned*
U429	30 Mar 1943	14 Jul 1943

Class Type VIIC
CO *Oberleutnant zur See* Kutkatt
Date of loss 30 March 1945
Location North Sea, Wilhelmshaven
Cause Air attack
Casualties ?
Survivors ?
Salvaged No
Notes Sunk in an attack on Wilhelmshaven by B-24 bombers of the US Eighth Air Force.

	Launched	*Commissioned*
U430	22 Apr 1943	4 Aug 1943

Class Type VIIC
CO *Oberleutnant zur See* Ulrich Hammer
Date of loss 30 March 1945
Location Baltic, Bremen
Cause Air attack
Casualties ?
Survivors ?
Salvaged No
Notes Sunk during a raid on Bremen by B-17 bombers of the US Eighth Air Force.

U870

	Launched	*Commissioned*
U870	29 Oct 1943	3 Feb 1944
Class	Type IXC/40	
CO	*Korvettenkapitän* Ernst Hechler	
Date of loss	30 March 1945	
Location	Baltic, Bremen	
Cause	Air attack	
Casualties	?	
Survivors	?	
Salvaged	No	

Notes Sunk during a raid on Bremen by B-17s of the US Eighth Air Force.

U884

	Launched	*Commissioned*
U884	17 May 1944	–
Class	Type IXD2	
CO	None appointed	
Date of loss	30 March 1945	
Location	Baltic, Bremen	
Cause	Air attack	
Casualties	?	
Survivors	?	
Salvaged	No	

Notes Sunk during a raid on Bremen by Eighth Air Force B-17s. Construction was incomplete at the time of the boat's loss.

U886

	Launched	*Commissioned*
U886	–	–
Class	Type IXD2	
CO	None appointed	
Date of loss	30 March 1945	
Location	Baltic, Bremen	
Cause	Air attack	
Casualties	–	
Survivors	–	
Salvaged	No	

Notes This boat was just a hulk, construction having been suspended on 30 September 1944.

U1021

	Launched	*Commissioned*
U1021	13 Apr 1944	25 May 1944
Class	Type VIIC/41	
CO	*Oberleutnant zur See* Willi Holpert (lost)	
Date of loss	30 March 1945	
Location	North Atlantic, 58°19'N 05°31'W	
Cause	Depth charge	
Casualties	43	
Survivors	None	
Salvaged	No	

Notes Sunk in depth-charge attacks by the frigate HMS *Rupert* of EG21. *Rupert* detected *U1021* as she moved in to attack convoy EN.83. The attacks resulted in a violent underwater explosion, after which oil and wreckage, which included personal effects, came to the surface.

U1167

	Launched	*Commissioned*
U1167	28 Jun 1943	29 Dec 1943
Class	Type VIIC/41	
CO	*Oberleutnant zur See* Karl-Hermann Bordtfeldt	
Date of loss	30 March 1945	
Location	North Sea, Hamburg	
Cause	Air attack	
Casualties	1	
Survivors	?	
Salvaged	No	

Notes Sunk in a bombing raid on Hamburg by B-17 aircraft of the Eighth Air Force.

U2340

	Launched	*Commissioned*
U2340	28 Sept 1944	16 Oct 1944
Class	Type XXIII	
CO	*Oberleutnant zur See* Emil Klusmeier	
Date of loss	30 March 1945	
Location	North Sea, Hamburg	
Cause	Air attack	
Casualties	?	
Survivors	?	
Salvaged	No	

Notes Sunk in a bombing raid on Hamburg by B-17 aircraft of the Eighth Air Force.

U3042

	Launched	*Commissioned*
U3042	–	–
Class	Type XXI	
CO	None appointed	
Date of loss	30 March 1945	
Location	Baltic, Bremen	
Cause	Air attack	
Casualties	None	
Survivors	None	

Salvaged	No

Notes Destroyed in a raid on Bremen by B-17 bombers of the Eighth Air Force.

U3043

	Launched	*Commissioned*
U3043	–	–
Class	Type XXI	
CO	None appointed	
Date of loss	30 March 1945	
Location	Baltic, Bremen	
Cause	Air attack	
Casualties	None	
Survivors	None	
Salvaged	No	

Notes Destroyed in a raid on Bremen by Eighth Air Force B-17 bombers.

U747

	Launched	*Commissioned*
U747	13 May 1943	17 Jul 1943
Class	Type VIIC	
CO	*Oberleutnant zur See* Günther Zahnow	
Date of loss	1 April 1945	
Location	North Sea, Hamburg	
Cause	Air attack	
Casualties	?	
Survivors	?	
Salvaged	No	

Notes Sunk at Hamburg during a bombing raid by the US Eighth Air Force.

U321

	Launched	*Commissioned*
U321	27 Nov 1943	20 Jan 1944
Class	Type VIIC	
CO	*Oberleutnant zur See* Fritz Behrends (lost)	
Date of loss	2 April 1945	
Location	SW of Cape Clear, 50°00'N 12°57'W	
Cause	Air attack	
Casualties	58	
Survivors	None	
Salvaged	No	

Notes Sunk in an attack by Wellington 'Y' of No 304 (Polish) Squadron RAF, flown by WO R. Marczak. Investigating a radar contact, the navigator sighted a snorkel and periscope one mile ahead. *U321* must have been keeping a watch for aircraft for the masts dipped very soon after the Wellington's crew had sighted them. Nevertheless, Marczak dropped six depth charges, aiming by eye. Though no oil or wreckage were sighted, *U321* was subsequently adjudged the victim of this attack.

U1221

	Launched	*Commissioned*
U1221	2 May 1943	11 Aug 1943
Class	Type IXC	
CO	*Oberleutnant zur See* Paul Ackermann	
Date of loss	3 April 1945	
Location	Baltic, Kiel Bay	
Cause	Air attack	
Casualties	7	
Survivors	?	
Salvaged	No	

Notes Bombed and sunk while secured to Buoy A7 in Kiel Bay.

U1276

	Launched	*Commissioned*
U1276	25 Feb 1944	6 Apr 1944
Class	Type VIIC/41	
CO	*Oberleutnant zur See* Karl-Heinz Wendt (lost)	
Date of loss	3 April 1945	
Location	North Atlantic, 51°48'N 07°07'W	
Cause	Depth charge	
Casualties	49	
Survivors	None	
Salvaged	No	

Notes Sunk in a joint attack by HMS *Amethyst* and Liberator 'U' of No 224 Squadron RAF.

U2542

	Launched	*Commissioned*
U2542	22 Jan 1945	–
Class	Type XXI	
CO	*Oberleutnant zur See* Otto Hubschen	
Date of loss	3 April 1945	
Location	Baltic, Kiel	
Cause	Air attack	
Casualties	?	
Survivors	?	
Salvaged	No	

Notes Destroyed while under construction at Kiel in a raid by the US Eighth Air Force.

U3505

	Launched	Commissioned
U3505	? Sept 1944	–

Class Type XXI
CO *Oberleutnant zur See* Horst Willner
Date of loss 3 April 1945
Location Baltic, Kiel
Cause Air attack
Casualties ?
Survivors ?
Salvaged No
Notes Destroyed while under construction at Kiel in a raid by the Eighth Air Force.

U237

	Launched	Commissioned
U237	17 Dec 1942	30 Jan 1943

Class Type VIIC
CO *Kapitänleutnant* Karl Heinz Menard
Date of loss 4 April 1945
Location Baltic, Kiel
Cause Air attack
Casualties ?
Survivors ?
Salvaged No
Notes Destroyed while under construction at Kiel in a raid by the Eighth Air Force. *U237* had already been sunk once before at Kiel, during a USAAF raid on 14 May 1943. She had been refloated on 8 October 1943.

U749

	Launched	Commissioned
U749	10 Jun 1943	14 Aug 1943

Class Type VIIC
CO *Oberleutnant zur See* Heuchen
Date of loss 4 April 1945
Location Baltic, Kiel
Cause Air attack
Casualties ?
Survivors ?
Salvaged No
Notes Destroyed while at Kiel in a raid by the US Eighth Air Force.

U3003

	Launched	Commissioned
U3003	18 July 1944	–

Class Type XXI
CO *Oberleutnant zur See* Ludo Kregelin
Date of loss 4 April 1945
Location Baltic, Kiel
Cause Air attack
Casualties ?
Survivors ?
Salvaged No
Notes Destroyed while under construction at Kiel in a raid by the US Eighth Air Force.

U1055

	Launched	Commissioned
U1055	9 Mar 1944	8 Apr 1944

Class Type VIIC
CO *Oberleutnant zur See* Rolf Meyer (lost)
Date of loss 5 April 1945 or later
Location ?
Cause ?
Casualties 49
Survivors None
Salvaged No
Notes *U1055* sailed for patrol on 5 April 1945. She was originally thought to have been sunk by aircraft 'R' of VP-63 but this attack is now assessed as having been made on *U1107*. There is no Allied claim to account for *U1055*'s loss. She may have been the victim of a mine, an accident arising from mechanical or drill failure, or a battery explosion resulting from inadequate battery ventilation while snorkelling.

U242

	Launched	Commissioned
U242	20 Jul 1943	14 Aug 1943

Class Type VIIC
CO *Oberleutnant zur See* Heinrich Riedel (lost)
Date of loss 5 April 1945
Location Irish Sea, St George's Channel, 52°03'N 05°53'W
Cause Mine
Casualties 44
Survivors None
Salvaged No
Notes HMS *Willow* observed an explosion from within a British (?) minefield and later observed oil and some wreckage from a U-boat's interior on the surface. After the war the assessors decided, on rather weak evidence, that the victim of this explosion was *U1169*. However, this boat had been ordered into the English Channel and not the Irish Sea. Previously the loss of *U242* had

been attributed to an attack by HM Ships *Hesperus* and *Havelock* assisted by Sunderland 'H' of No 10 Squadron RAAF on 30 April 1945.

U677	*Launched* 18 Sept 1943	*Commissioned* 20 Sept 1943
Class	Type VIIC	
CO	*Oberleutnant zur See* Gerhard Ady	
Date of loss	5 April 1945	
Location	North Sea, Hamburg	
Cause	Air attack	
Casualties	?	
Survivors	?	
Salvaged	No	

Notes Destroyed in the Finkenwerder Bunker in Hamburg during an RAF bombing raid.

U1169	*Launched* 2 Oct 1943	*Commissioned* 9 Feb 1944
Class	Type VIIC/41	
CO	*Oberleutnant zur See* Heinz Goldbeck (lost)	
Date of loss	? April 1945	
Location	English Channel, exact location unknown	
Cause	?	
Casualties	?	
Survivors	None	
Salvaged	No	

Notes *U1169* had been ordered into the English Channel and later disappeared. It may have been that she was the victim of a mine, but the possibility that she was lost as a result of an accident arising from mechanical or drill failure cannot be discounted.

U1195	*Launched* 2 Sept 1943	*Commissioned* 4 Nov 1943
Class	Type VIIC/41	
CO	*Kapitänleutnant* Ernst Cordes (lost)	
Date of loss	6 April 1945	
Location	English Channel, 50°33'N 00°55'W	
Cause	Hedgehog	
Casualties	31	
Survivors	2 officers, 5 senior rates, 11 junior rates	
Salvaged	No	

Notes On 6 April *U1195* torpedoed and sank the 12,000-ton transport *Cuba* from convoy VWP.17. The convoy was escorted by the rump of EG9 comprising HMCS *Nene*, HMCS *Monnow* and HMS *Loch Alvie*, backed up by the British destroyer HMS *Watchman* (SO) and the French *L'Escarmouche*. After screening the convoy into Portsmouth *Watchman* and *Monnow* swept back to look for the culprit. *Monnow* was in asdic contact first but *Watchman*'s CO ordered her to stand clear while he carried out a Hedgehog attack. This display of RN superiority did not sit well with *Monnow*'s crew. The Hedgehog attack brought up oil and wreckage but the attack was assesssed as having been on a bottomed wreck, so *Watchman* merely buoyed the position and headed off. It came as some surprise when, an hour later, *L'Escarmouche* reported picking men up from the water who were clustered around the dan buoy, one man actually clinging to it.

The Hedgehog had hit *U1195* forward, causing severe flooding, and she settled in 96ft of water with a list of over 40 degrees. There were two groups of survivors, eight in the control room and eleven in the after ends. The control room group made a relatively straightforward escape through the conning tower, but the escape of the remaining eleven was something of an ordeal. The acute angle at which the boat was lying meant that instead of being able to ascend directly up through the escape trunks, the eleven survivors gathered in the after ends under the 1WO had to scramble up them at a steep angle. There were not enough Dräger sets to go around, the air was foul with chlorine and the compartment had to be flooded almost up to the deckhead (such terms are relative, with the boat lying at such a steep angle) in order to equalise the pressure. The first man to leave panicked and drowned in the trunk. It took three men to drag him back. The remainder began to panic (and no wonder), but the 1WO literally seized each man in turn and thrust him up though the trunk and out. Eventually he was the last to leave.

U857	*Launched* 23 May 1943	*Commissioned* 16 Sept 1943
Class	Type IXC/40	
CO	*Kapitänleutnant* Rudolf Premauer (lost)	
Date of loss	7 April 1945	

Location E coast of USA, off Cape Cod
Cause Depth charge
Casualties 59
Survivors None
Salvaged No

Notes *U857* had moved into the Gulf of Maine in late March and had damaged a tanker on 5 April. Within a few hours of thus announcing her presence a hunting group formed of two frigates and two DEs under the command of Cdr Ralph R. Curry USCG was out looking for her. *U857* tried to evade her pursuers by bottoming off Cape Cod but was located and dispatched in a series of Hedgehog attacks early in the morning of 7 April by USS *Gustafson*.

	Launched	*Commissioned*
U2509	27 Aug 1944	21 Sept 1944

Class Type XXI
CO *Kapitänleutnant* Rudolf Schendel
Date of loss 8 April 1945
Location North Sea, Hamburg
Cause Air attack
Casualties –
Survivors –
Salvaged No

Notes Bombed and sunk at Hamburg during an RAF bombing raid.

	Launched	*Commissioned*
U2514	17 Sept 1944	17 Oct 1944

Class Type XXI
CO *Kapitänleutnant* Rolf Bilger Wahlen
Date of loss 8 April 1945
Location North Sea, Hamburg
Cause Air attack
Casualties ?
Survivors ?
Salvaged No

Notes Bombed and sunk at Hamburg during an RAF bombing raid.

	Launched	*Commissioned*
U2516	27 Sept 1944	24 Oct 1944

Class Type XXI
CO *Oberleutnant zur See* Fritz Kallipke (survived)
Date of loss 8 April 1945
Location North Sea, Hamburg
Cause Air attack
Casualties ?
Survivors ?
Salvaged No

Notes Bombed and sunk at Hamburg during an RAF bombing raid.

	Launched	*Commissioned*
U2550	?	–

Class Type XXI
CO None appointed
Date of loss 8 April 1945
Location North Sea, Hamburg
Cause Air attack
Casualties None
Survivors –
Salvaged No

Notes Bombed and damaged beyond repair while under assembly during an Allied air raid while under construction in Hamburg. The hull was eventually broken up.

	Launched	*Commissioned*
U774	23 Dec 1943	17 Feb 1944

Class Type VIIC
CO *Kapitänleutnant* Sausmikat (lost)
Date of loss 8 April 1945
Location Atlantic, SW of Cape Clear, 49°58'N 11°51'W
Cause Depth charge
Casualties 44
Survivors None
Salvaged No

Notes Sunk by the frigates HMS *Calder* and *Bentinck*.

	Launched	*Commissioned*
U1001	6 Oct 1943	8 Nov 1943

Class Type VIIC/41
CO *Kapitänleutnant* Ernst-Ulrich Blaudow (lost)
Date of loss 8 April 1945
Location North Atlantic, 49°19'N 10°23'W
Cause Depth charge
Casualties 45
Survivors None
Salvaged No

Notes Sunk by the frigates HMS *Fitzroy* and *Byron*.

U3512	*Launched* 11 Oct 1944	*Commissioned* 27 Nov 1944
Class	Type XXI	
CO	None appointed	
Date of loss	8 April 1945	
Location	Baltic, Kiel	
Cause	Air attack	
Casualties	?	
Survivors	?	
Salvaged	No	

Notes Bombed and sunk during an Allied air raid on Kiel. The wreck was broken up *in situ*.

U982	*Launched* 29 Apr 1943	*Commissioned* 10 Jun 1943
Class	Type VIIC	
CO	*Oberleutnant zur See* Kurt Hartmann	
Date of loss	9 April 1945	
Location	North Sea, Hamburg	
Cause	Air attack	
Casualties	?	
Survivors	?	
Salvaged	No	

Notes Sunk at Hamburg during a bombing raid by the US Eighth Air Force.

U4708	*Launched* 26 Mar 1945	*Commissioned* –
Class	Type XXIII	
CO	None appointed	
Date of loss	9 April 1945	
Location	Baltic, Kiel	
Cause	Air attack	
Casualties	None	
Survivors	None	
Salvaged	No	

Notes Sunk while fitting out alongside the Germaniawerft Wharf at Kiel.

U804	*Launched* 1 Apr 1943	*Commissioned* 1 Dec 1943
Class	Type IXC	
CO	*Oberleutnant zur See* Herbert Meyer (lost)	
Date of loss	9 April 1945	
Location	Baltic, Little Belt, 57°58'N 11°15'E	
Cause	Air attack	
Casualties	55	
Survivors	None	
Salvaged	No	

Notes See the entry for *U1065* below for details of the fate of this boat.

U1065	*Launched* 3 Aug 1944	*Commissioned* 23 Sept 1944
Class	Type VII/41	
CO	*Oberleutnant zur See* Johann Panitz (lost)	
Date of loss	9 April 1945	
Location	Kattegat, 57°48'N 11°15'E	
Cause	Air attack	
Casualties	45	
Survivors	None	
Salvaged	No	

Notes The Banff Strike Wing, consisting of 34 Mosquito aircraft of Nos 143, 235 and 248 Squadrons, led by Sqn Ldr H. H. Gunnis DFC, was on an anti-U-boat patrol in the Skaggerak when two U-boats were seen on the surface. Mosquitos from Nos 143 and 235 Squadrons made strafing attacks with rockets, cannon and machine guns while the aircraft from No 248 orbited. One of the U-boats sank, leaving oil and wreckage on the surface. The other sank by the stern before exploding with such violence that four of the Mosquitos were damaged (three of them having to head for internment in Sweden), while a camera-fitted Mosquito from the RAF Film Unit was so badly damaged that it crashed into the sea.

U843	*Launched* 15 Dec 1943	*Commissioned* 24 Mar 1943
Class	Type IXC	
CO	*Kapitänleutnant* Oskar Herwartz (lost)	
Date of loss	9 April 1945	
Location	Baltic, Little Belt, 57°58'N 11°15'E	
Cause	Air attack	
Casualties	44	
Survivors	None	
Salvaged	Yes	

Notes Mosquito 'A' of No 235 Squadron, flown by Fg Off A. J. Randell, sighted *U843* on the surface not far from where *U804* and *U1065* were receiving the full attention of the Banff Wing. Randell made one pass with rockets and cannon and then attacked from the other side with cannon. After the attacks the submarine was seen lying stopped on the surface, wreathed in smoke.

The wreck was raised on 22 August 1958 and broken up at Gothenburg in Sweden.

U1131	*Launched* ? Jan 1944	*Commissioned* 9 Apr 1944
Class	Type VIIC	
CO	*Oberleutnant zur See* Günther Fiebig	
Date of loss	9 April 1945	
Location	North Sea, Hamburg	
Cause	Air attack	
Casualties	?	
Survivors	?	
Salvaged	No	

Notes Bombed and sunk at Hamburg-Finkenwerder during an RAF bombing raid.

U878	*Launched* 6 Jan 1944	*Commissioned* 14 Apr 1944
Class	Type IXC/40	
CO	*Kapitänleutnant* Hans Rodig (lost)	
Date of loss	10 April 1945	
Location	Atlantic, W of St Nazaire, 47°35'N 10°33'W	
Cause	Depth charge	
Casualties	51	
Survivors	None	
Salvaged	No	

Notes Sunk by HMS *Vanquisher* and HMS *Tintagel Castle*, part of the escort for convoy ONA.265.

U2547	*Launched* 9 Mar 1945	*Commissioned* –
Class	Type XXI	
CO	None appointed	
Date of loss	11 April 1945	
Location	North Sea, Hamburg	
Cause	Air attack	
Casualties	?	
Survivors	?	
Salvaged	No	

Notes Sunk while fitting out during an Allied air raid on Hamburg.

U486	*Launched* 12 Feb 1944	*Commissioned* 22 Mar 1944
Class	Type VIIC	
CO	*Oberleutnant zur See* Gerhard Meyer (lost)	
Date of loss	12 April 1945	
Location	Norwegian waters, NW of Bergen, 60°44'N 04°39'E	
Cause	Submarine attack	
Casualties	48	
Survivors	None	
Salvaged	No	

Notes *U486* surfaced at 0749 on 12 April 1945 near the island of Hellisøy. She had been making a submerged passage while snorkelling and Meyer evidently thought it safe enough to surface. HM Submarine *Tapir* (Lt J. C. Roxburgh RN) had been alerted by the HE of the U-boat's noisy diesels, and it was easy for Roxburgh to make a snap attack when the U-boat surfaced only 3,000yds away. Roxburgh ordered eight torpedoes fired at 0753, although in the end only six went on their way, and two minutes later one hit was seen. German observers on the island of Hellisøy were left in no doubt of what had happened when one of Tapir's MkVIII** torpedoes with its 750lb Torpex warhead ran on to the rocks and exploded 200yds from the lighthouse!

U1024	*Launched* 3 May 1944	*Commissioned* 28 Jun 1944
Class	Type VIIC	
CO	*Kapitänleutnant* Hans-Joachim Gutteck (lost)	
Date of loss	13 April 1945	
Location	Irish Sea, 53°39'N 05°03'W	
Cause	Sank while under tow after being captured	
Casualties	8	
Survivors	1 officer, 5 senior rates, 31 junior rates	
Salvaged	No	

Notes *U1024* had sunk a ship from each of convoys HX.346 and SC.171 in the Irish Sea on 7 and 12 December respectively. She evaded immediate detection but late on the evening of the 12th was detected by HMS *Loch Glendhu* of EG8. Although the frigate's 147B set was not working, a Squid pattern was fired at 2042 and three minutes later a U-boat broke surface. All ships in the group opened fire and HMS *Loch Achray* moved in to drop a pattern of depth charges. Gutteck was one of the first out of the conning tower and was wounded in the hand, after which he shot himself. Fire was checked when it was realised that the U-boat was being abandoned. Boarding parties went over and secured the boat, which was taken in tow by HMS *Loch More*. However, the weather deteriorated during the night and in thick fog—which reduced visibility to as little as 50ft—the tow parted and the U-boat sank.

U235	*Launched* 4 Nov 1942	*Commissioned* 19 Dec 1942
Class	Type VIIC	
CO	*Oberleutnant zur See* Friedrich Huisgen (lost)	
Date of loss	14 April 1945	
Location	Kattegat, 57°44'N 10°39'E	
Cause	Depth charge (own side)	
Casualties	45	
Survivors	None	
Salvaged	No	

Notes *U235* was heading north to Norway in company with *U1272*. Both boats snorkelled during the day since the RAF held total air superiority. Also in the area was a German convoy consisting of the ferry *Preussen* escorted by the torpedo boat *T17* and a number of smaller vessels. *U1272* was leading *U235* when they crossed the path of the convoy. *U1272*'s commander, *Oberleutnant zur See* Schatteburg, realised the potential for disaster so lowered his snorkel and went deep. However, the wake left by the snorkel was spotted by look-outs in *Preussen*, who reported it to *T17* as a torpedo track. *T17* increased speed and ran down the track while preparing to drop a depth charge pattern. As she did so *U235* surfaced in front of her but then dived quickly. *T17* ran over the spot and dropped a full pattern of depth charges. Some minutes later oil and wreckage came to the surface, but any elation on the part of *T17*'s crew was abruptly stilled when they saw that among the wreckage were bodies wearing familiar grey U-boat leathers.

There was a brief enquiry into the submarine's loss and it was found that the U-boats had not been warned about the convoy (and *vice versa*), and that the convoy had been warned that a British submarine was active in the area. Perhaps when Huisgen saw *T17* coming towards him he surfaced to identify himself, then suddenly changed his mind realising that a collision was imminent. We shall never know.

U1206	*Launched* 30 Dec 1943	*Commissioned* 16 Mar 1944
Class	Type VIIC	
CO	*Kapitänleutnant* Karl-Adolf Schlitt (survived)	
Date of loss	14 April 1945	
Location	North Sea, off Peterhead, 57°21'N 01°39'W	
Cause	Accident	
Casualties	4	
Survivors	4 officers, 6 senior rates, 36 junior rates	
Salvaged	No	

Notes *U1206* grounded off Buchan Ness and sustained such damage to her hull that Schlitt could not continue the patrol. He scuttled his boat and the survivors were picked up by HMS *Nodzu*.

U103	*Launched* 12 Apr 1940	*Commissioned* 5 Jul 1940
Class	Type IXB	
CO	*Oberleutnant zur See* Schunk	
Date of loss	15 April 1945	
Location	Baltic, port of Kiel	
Cause	Air attack	
Casualties	1	
Survivors	?	
Salvaged	No	

Notes Bombed during an Allied air raid on Kiel.

U285	*Launched* 3 Apr 1943	*Commissioned* 15 May 194
Class	Type VIIC	
CO	*Oberleutnant zur See* Konrad Bornhaupt (lost)	
Date of loss	15 April 1945	
Location	Atlantic, SW of Ireland, 50°13'N 03°52'W	

Cause Depth charge
Casualties 44
Survivors None
Salvaged No
Notes Sunk in a depth-charge attack by the frigates HMS *Grindall* and *Keats*.

	Launched	*Commissioned*
U1063	8 Jun 1944	8 Jul 1944

Class Type VII/41
CO *Kapitänleutnant* Karl-Heinz Stephan (lost)
Date of loss 16 April 1945
Location English Channel, off Start Point, 50°08'N 03°52'W
Cause Squid
Casualties 29
Survivors 1 officer, 2 senior rates, 14 junior rates
Salvaged No
Notes EG17, consisting of *Loch Killin*, *Cranstoun* and *Burges*, were trailing a convoy when *Loch Killin* obtained an asdic contact in very difficult conditions with a mass of 'Non-Subs' making the ASCO's job extremely arduous. Three Squid attacks were made before the U-boat surfaced on *Loch Killin*'s port quarter, where she was sunk by depth charges and gunfire.

	Launched	*Commissioned*
U1235	25 Jan 1944	17 May 1944

Class Type IXC
CO *Oberleutnant zur See* Fritz Barcsh (lost)
Date of loss 16 April 1945
Location North Atlantic
Cause Depth charge
Casualties 57
Survivors None
Salvaged No
Notes *U1235* was the first of a number of U-boats to be sunk during Operation 'Teardrop', carried out by USN CVE hunter-killer groups in the North Atlantic in April 1945. The agent from *U1229* (q.v.) and those landed in Maine by *U1203* had been captured by the FBI and had told of a forthcoming attack on the US East Coast using V1 rockets fired from U-boats. This threat was taken seriously and on 10 December 1944 Mayor Firoello LaGuardia warned New Yorkers about the possibility of a missile attack on their city. In response to this threat Operation 'Teardrop' was launched—a massive activation of US coastal defences to combat any missile attack from the sea. However, the core of 'Teardrop' was the unannounced deployment of two large carrier forces, each composed of one CVE and 20-plus DEs.

US concern about German intentions was heightened by the departure of a group of seven U-boats from Norway with orders to operate off the eastern US seaboard. When added to intelligence about 'launching rails' observed on the casings of various U-boats in Norway and the fact that one of the boats heading west was commanded by *Kapitänleutnant* Fritz Steinhoff, who while in command of *U511* had taken part in submered rocket-firing trials off Peenemünde, then stories from a captured spy suddenly acquired very real substance. In fact German intentions were more mundane—merely to operate in the Western Atlantic, where opposition was thought to be weaker, and to draw off some of the escort groups in British waters which were making life so difficult for the U-boats operating there.

Fortunately HF/DF and decrypted German signals enabled the Tenth Fleet to monitor the westward passage of *Gruppe Seawolf* so that Capt John R. Rushenberger's Northern Barrier Force, centred on the CVEs *Mission Bay* and *Croatan*, could position itself appropriately. Late at night on 15 April the USS *Stanton* acquired a radar contact in thick fog. She closed the contact and when 1,000yds off illuminated it with a searchlight. From the bridge a wake and the dim shape of a U-boat could be seen. It was *U1235*, which had surfaced since it was too rough to snorkel. While *Croatan* manoeuvred out of the way, *Stanton*, now joined by *Frost*, carried out a Hedgehog attack. Six minutes later both ships were shaken by an explosion so violent that those in *Stanton* thought they had been torpedoed. The fog was now so thick that neither *Frost* nor *Stanton* could see each other, so their movements were coordinated by *Croatan*. *Stanton*'s third attack produced another tremendous explosion at 0033—even *Croatan*, some twelve miles away, was shaken. The explosion was followed by the appearance of a large and spreading slick of diesel.

In light of the fact that there were no survivors from *U1235* and the fact that *U880* was sunk less than an hour later (also with no survivors), it is possible that the details of the sinking of these two craft are interchangeable.

U880	*Launched* 10 Feb 1944	*Commissioned* 11 May 1944
Class	Type IXC	
CO	*Oberleutnant zur See* Gerhard Schotzau (lost)	
Date of loss	16 April 1945	
Location	N Atlantic, 520m E of Flemish Cap, 47°53'N 30°26'W	
Cause	Depth charge	
Casualties	53	
Survivors	None	
Salvaged	No	

Notes Scarcely forty minutes after the sinking of *U1235*, *Frost* was in radar contact with another U-boat which was trying to escape on the surface, presumably having heard (and felt) the barrage which marked the end of *U1235*. The fog was now so thick that at 1,450yds *Frost*'s starshell failed to illuminate the target. At 650yds the searchlight was switched on and the U-boat sighted. The seas were too heavy for *Frost* to alter course or bring all her guns to bear, but as the U-boat dived *Frost* and *Stanton* followed her down with Hedgehog attacks. The two DEs remained in contact and at 0404 on 16 April there was a violent underwater explosion—as violent as that which had marked the end of *U1235*—followed by the spread of a diesel slick.

In view of the fact that there were no survivors from *U880* or *U1235* and the fact that the two boats were sunk close together without leaving any survivors or identifiable wreckage, the details of the sinking of these two craft may be interchangeable.

U78	*Launched* 7 Dec 1940	*Commissioned* 15 Feb 1941
Class	Type VIIC	
CO	*Oberleutnant zur See* Horst Hubsch	
Date of loss	16 April 1945	
Location	Baltic, Pillau	
Cause	Shore artillery	
Casualties	?	
Survivors	?	
Salvaged	No	

Notes *U78* was never fully operational, but spent her entire service as a generating plant or a training submarine. She was shelled and sunk by Soviet field artillery as the Germans evacuated Pillau. *U78* was one of only two submarines to be sunk by shore-based artillery during the Second World War (the other was the USS *Herring*, sunk on 1 June 1944 off Japan).

U1274	*Launched* 25 Jan 1944	*Commissioned* 1 Mar 1944
Class	Type VIIC/41	
CO	*Oberleutnant zur See* Hans-Hermann Fitting (lost)	
Date of loss	16 April 1945	
Location	North Sea, 6m E of Sunderland, 55°36'N 01°24'W	
Cause	Depth charge	
Casualties	44	
Survivors	None	
Salvaged	No	

Notes *U1274* had attacked and sunk the tanker *Athelduke* in convoy FS.1784 The old destroyer HMS *Viceroy* (launched in 1918) counter-attacked but saw no result for her efforts, although asdic indicated that the target was stopped and on the bottom. Eight days later she returned to the spot and, finding the target still there, delivered a series of attacks which brought much wreckage to the surface. In one of the liferaft canisters *Viceroy*'s crew found six cases of brandy, which were taken as a positive indication of the U-boat's destruction.

U251	*Launched* 14 Aug 1941	*Commissioned* 20 Sept 1941
Class	Type VIIC	
CO	*Oberleutnant zur See* Franz Sack	
Date of loss	19 April 1945	
Location	Kattegat, SE of Anhalt, 56°37'N 11°51'E	
Cause	Air attack	
Casualties	39	
Survivors	?	
Salvaged	No	

Notes A force of 22 Mosquito aircraft of Nos 143, 235, 248 and 333 Squadrons, led by Wg Cdr A. H. Simmonds, was flying an A/S sweep when three U-boats were sighted at 1631 astern of an 'M' class minesweeper. *U2502* and *U2335* dived and escaped, though not before receiving some damage. However, *U251* was overwhelmed by rocket and cannon fire and sank.

	Launched	*Commissioned*
U879	11 Jan 1944	19 Apr 1944

Class	Type IXC
CO	*Kapitänleutnant* Erwin Manchen (lost)
Date of loss	19 April 1945
Location	Atlantic, 150m SSE of Halifax, 42°19'N 61°45'W
Cause	Hedgehog
Casualties	52
Survivors	None
Salvaged	No

Notes USS *Buckley* attacked a sonar contact with Hedgehog. After the detonation a number of smaller explosions were seen, after which oil, wreckage and human remains came to the surface.

	Launched	*Commissioned*
U636	25 Jun 1942	20 Aug 1942

Class	Type VIIC
CO	*Oberleutnant zur See* Eberhard Schendel (lost)
Date of loss	21 April 1945
Location	Atlantic, NW of Bloody Foreland, 55°50'N 10°31'W
Cause	Depth charge
Casualties	42
Survivors	None
Salvaged	No

Notes Sunk by the frigates of EG4 (HMS *Bentinck* SO). HMS *Drury* and *Bazely* carried out attacks which brought oil, wreckage and human flesh to the surface.

	Launched	*Commissioned*
U518	11 Feb 1942	25 Apr 1942

Class	Type IXC
CO	*Oberleutnant zur See* Hans Offermann (lost)
Date of loss	22 April 1945
Location	Atlantic, NW of the Azores
Cause	Hedgehog
Casualties	56
Survivors	None
Salvaged	No

Notes The third U-boat to be sunk in Operation 'Teardrop', *U518* was detected on the sonar of the DE USS *Carter*, which directed *Neal A. Scott* in a creeping attack before attacking with Hedgehog at 2309. One explosion, followed by several large underwater detonations, marked the end of *U518*.

	Launched	*Commissioned*
U183	9 Jan 1942	1 Apr 1942

Class	Type IXC
CO	*Kapitänleutnant* Fritz Schneewind (lost)
Date of loss	23 April 1945
Location	Java Sea
Cause	Submarine attack
Casualties	54
Survivors	None
Salvaged	No

Notes Torpedoed and sunk by the American submarine USS *Besugo*.

	Launched	*Commissioned*
U396	27 Aug 1943	16 Oct 1943

Class	Type VIIC
CO	*Kapitänleutnant* Hilmar Siemon (lost)
Date of loss	23 April 1945
Location	Atlantic, SW of Shetlands, approx. 59°29'N 05°22'W
Cause	?
Casualties	45
Survivors	None
Salvaged	No

Notes *U396* was attacked by Liberator 'V' of No 86 Squadron RAF, flown by Flt Lt J.T. Lawrence, but without positive result.. However, she was not heard from again so might have been the victim of this attack or have suffered an accident, possibly diving too deep, while avoiding the aircraft.

	Launched	*Commissioned*
UIT1	12 July 1944	?

Class	Italian *Romolo* class cargo-carrying submarine
CO	None appointed

Date of loss	24 April 1945
Location	Mediterranean, La Spezia
Cause	Scuttling
Casualties	?
Survivors	?
Salvaged	No

Notes The former Italian *R10*, taken over by the Germans when Italy signed the Armistice. She was scuttled near the East Mole at La Spezia and her remains were broken up in 1946.

U546

	Launched	*Commissioned*
U546	17 Mar 1943	2 Jun 1943
Class	Type IXC	
CO	*Kapitänleutnant* Paul Heinz Just (survived)	
Date of loss	24 April 1945	
Location	N Atlantic	
Cause	Depth charge	
Casualties	25	
Survivors	47	
Salvaged	No	

Notes This was the fourth boat of *Gruppe Seawolf* to be sunk during 'Teardrop'. The violent end of the three boats sunk to date indicated that they might have been carrying more than just torpedoes. However, only the capture of survivors from one of these boats would confirm or deny whether a missile attack was imminent. The Americans' chance came with the sinking of *U546* on 24 April. At daybreak on that day *U546* sighted an escort carrier (which was *Bogue*, of the Southern Barrier Force) being screened by DEs of Escort Division 4. *Kapitänleutnant* Just was so intent on attacking the carrier that he attempted a penetration of the screen at periscope depth, only to be detected by *Frederick C Davis*. Just saw the DE turn towards him and fired a single T5 acoustic torpedo in a snap attack. The torpedo struck *Davis* amidships and she sank very quickly with the loss of 126 of her 192 crew.

The DEs now began a classic hunt using every attack method known to them. Just proved a wily opponent, going deep, using thermal layers and making constant alterations of course and speed while firing SBTs. After the quarry had been under attack for over ten hours, a Hedgehog attack by the USS *Flaherty* caused massive damage forward and Just had no option but to surface. On the surface *U546* was engaged by virtually the entire Divison before sinking. Despite having recently lost one of their number, the DEs spared no effort to rescue the 33 exhausted survivors of *U546*, whose ordeal had been 'heard' by *U805* which was creeping away as quietly as possible to the north.

Just (who had transferred to the *Kriegsmarine* from the *Luftwaffe* and had flown in the Polish Campaign and the Battle of Britain) and his officers were questioned aboard *Bogue*, where they had been transferred from the various DEs, but gave nothing away other than that which they were required to do by the Geneva Convention. However, on being landed on 27 April at Argentia in Newfoundland, eight of the crew, including Just, were placed in solitary confinement and treated as military prisoners rather than PoWs. They were then subjected to a rigorous exercise routine and repeated beatings in order to extract information on the V1 strike (which the unfortunate U-boat men knew nothing about). This treatment continued despite the fact that the USS *Varian* had recovered a diary from a *U546* survivor which showed that the boat was armed with nothing more than the usual mix of torpedoes. *Varian*'s CO, Lt-Cdr Leonard A. Myhre, was invited to witness one of Just's 'exercise' sessions and protested bitterly at what he saw. Possibly on account of this protest, the men were flown to Fort Hunt near Mount Vernon, where the 'exercise' and beatings resumed. This treatment only ceased after VE-Day when Just agreed to write a full account of *U546*'s operational history.

UIT2

	Launched	*Commissioned*
UIT2	6 Aug 1943	–
Class	Italian *Romolo* class	
CO	None appointed	
Date of loss	24 April 1945	
Location	Mediterranean, Genoa	
Cause	Scuttled	
Casualties	–	
Survivors	–	
Salvaged	Yes	

Notes Taken over by Germany on 9 September 1943. Fitting-out commenced on 13 September 1943 for service as a transport submarine between Europe and the Far East. However, the boat was scuttled on the German evacuation of Genoa. The wreck was raised in 1946, stricken in 1947 and used as floating oil tank *GR522*. Details of its final fate are unknown.

UIT3

	Launched	Commissioned
UIT3	29 Sept 1942	–
Class	Italian *Romolo* class	
CO	None appointed	
Date of loss	24 April 1945	
Location	Mediterranean, La Spezia	
Cause	Scuttled	
Casualties	–	
Survivors	–	
Salvaged	Yes	

Notes Taken over by Germany on 9 September 1943. Fitting out commenced on 13 September 1943 for service as a transport submarine between Europe and the Far East but the boat was scuttled near the East Mole on the German evacuation of La Spezia. Raised in 1946, the wreck was stricken in 1947 and used as floating oil tank *GR523*. Details of the boat's final fate are unknown.

U326

	Launched	Commissioned
U326	22 Apr 1944	6 Jun 1944
Class	Type VIIC	
CO	*Oberleutnant zur See* Peter Matthes (lost)	
Date of loss	25 April 1945	
Location	Atlantic, SW of Ushant, 48°12'N 05°42'W	
Cause	Air attack	
Casualties	44	
Survivors	None	
Salvaged	No	

Notes Sunk in an attack by Liberator 'K' of VP-103, flown by Lt Dwight D. Nott USNR. Nott attacked a snorkel sighted south-west of the Brest peninsula. As the explosion of the depth charges subsided, the snorkel mast was seen to jump out of the water (symptomatic of the mast snapping at its join with the hull: such a failure would cause massive flooding). Later one body was seen floating in the sea.

U56

	Launched	Commissioned
U56	3 Sept 1938	26 Nov 1938
Class	Type IIC	
CO	*Oberleutnant zur See* Sauerbeier	
Date of loss	28 April 1945	
Location	Baltic, Kiel, 54°19'N 10°10'E	
Cause	Air attack	
Casualties	?	
Survivors	?	
Salvaged	No	

Notes Sunk during a British air raid on Kiel.

U1223

	Launched	Commissioned
U1223	10 Jun 1943	6 Oct 1943
Class	Type IXC	
CO	*Oberleutnant zur See* Kneip (?)	
Date of loss	28 April 1945	
Location	Baltic, off Weser estuary	
Cause	Air attack	
Casualties	7	
Survivors	?	
Salvaged	No	

Notes Sunk in a British air raid.

U307

	Launched	Commissioned
U307	30 Sept 1942	18 Nov 1942
Class	Type VIIC	
CO	*Oberleutnant zur See* Erich Krueger (survived)	
Date of loss	29 April 1945	
Location	Arctic off the Kola Inlet, 69°26'N 33°39'E	
Cause	Depth charge	
Casualties	37	
Survivors	2 officers, 12 ratings	
Salvaged	No	

Notes *U307* was one of a pack of U-boats gathered off the Kola Inlet to await the sailing of convoy RA.66. Frigates of the 19th Escort Group and corvettes of the 7th Escort Group had been sailed in advance of the convoy to clear the U-boats from the approaches to the Inlet. *U307* was depth-charged by HMS *Loch Insh* of EG19.

U286

	Launched	Commissioned
U286	21 Apr 1943	5 Jun 1943
Class	Type VIIC	
CO	*Oberleutnant zur See* Willi Dietrich (lost)	
Date of loss	29 April 1945	
Location	Arctic, off the Kola Inlet, 69°29'N 33°37'E	
Cause	Depth charge	
Casualties	51	
Survivors	None	

Salvaged No

Notes Before the sailing of convoy RA.66 frigates and corvettes of the 19th and 7th Escort Groups sailed to clear a number of U-boats which were reported to be lying off the Kola Inlet. *U286* was detected by the frigates *Anguilla*, *Cotton* and *Loch Shin* and destroyed in concerted depth-charge attacks.

U1017

	Launched	*Commissioned*
	1 Mar 1944	13 Apr 1944

Class Type VIIC/41
CO *Oberleutnant zur See* Werner Riecken (lost)
Date of loss 29 April 1945
Location N Atlantic, 56°04'N 11°06'W
Cause Air attack
Casualties 34
Survivors None
Salvaged No

Notes Liberator 'Q' of No 120 Squadron, flown by Fg Off H. J. Oliver, sighted a snorkel wake off Malin Head at a range of three miles. When the aircraft was two miles away smoke could be seen and the Liberator attacked with four depth charges together with a sonobuoy. The aircrew recorded long and drawn-out breaking-up noises.

U325

	Launched	*Commissioned*
	25 Mar 1944	6 May 1944

Class Type VIIC
CO *Oberleutnant zur See* Erwin Dohrn (lost)
Date of loss ? April 1945
Location English Channel, Land's End area (?)
Cause ?
Casualties 50
Survivors None
Salvaged No

Notes *U325* had been ordered into the English Channel and then disappeared. There is no Allied claim to account for her loss, and she may have been the victim of a mine, an accident arising from mechanical or drill failure or a battery explosion resulting from inadequate battery ventilation while snorkelling.

U1107

	Launched	*Commissioned*
	30 Jun 1944	8 Aug 1944

Class Type VIIC/41
CO *Kapitänleutnant* Fritz Pahrdun (lost)
Date of loss 30 April 1945
Location Atlantic, W of Ushant, 48°00'N 06°30'W
Cause Fido
Casualties 36
Survivors ?
Salvaged No

Notes Sunk in an attack by US Navy Catalina 'R' of VP-63 flown by Lt F. G. Lake. The aircraft was flying a MAD Rover patrol but made a visual sighting of a prominent white wake caused by a snorkel at two miles at 1808. When three-quarters of a mile away, the snorkel mast could be clearly seen. As the aircraft flew over the mast the MAD apparatus registered a strong signal and 24 retro-bombs were dropped. Air bubbles, oil and wreckage subsequently rose to the surface.

The aircraft remained on the scene until 1830 and then dropped a pattern of sonobuoys, but no engine or motor sounds were recorded. The aircraft homed a nearby Escort Group on to the scene. Their asdics confirmed that the target was lying dead on the bottom and, using a 'thief', collected diesel oil samples from the water.

U548

	Launched	*Commissioned*
	14 Apr 1943	30 Jun 1943

Class Type IXC/40
CO *Oberleutnant zur See* Erich Kempel (lost)
Date of loss 30 April 1945
Location Atlantic, E of Cape Hatteras, 36°34'N 74°00'W
Cause Depth charge
Casualties 58
Survivors None
Salvaged No

Notes After the sinking of the freighter *Belgian Airman* on 14 April the US Navy instituted a massive search for the culprit. The submarine headed north, sinking another ship off the Delaware Capes on the 18th and a third south of Cape Henry on the 23rd. However, on 27 April the boat was sighted by the alert look-outs of a merchant ship, and with a definite position to work to the hunters were swiftly on the scene. On the night of 29–30 April the boat was detected by the DE *Natchez*, part of the escort for convoy KN.382. *Natchez* drove off the submarine with a scare barrage and called up a group of six DEs under the command of Capt G. A. Parkinson USNR which began a series of creeping attacks. Pfeffer was a wily opponent and used every manoeuvre open to him—sudden changes of course, speed and depth, reversing into his own wake and firing SBTs. Finally, at 0445 on the 30th, the DEs *Coffman* and *Thomas* delivered a creeping attack which resulted in underwater explosions and wreckage being brought to the surface.

	Launched	*Commissioned*
U398	? Nov 1943	18 Dec 1943
Class	Type VIIC	
CO	*Oberleutnant zur See* Wilhelm Cranz (lost)	
Date of loss	? May 1945	
Location	North Sea	
Cause	?	
Casualties	43	
Survivors	None	
Salvaged	No	

Notes *U398* disappeared while on patrol in the North Sea. There is no Allied claim to account for her loss. She may have been the victim of a mine (the most likely explanation), an accident arising from mechanical or drill failure or a battery explosion resulting from inadequate battery ventilation while snorkelling.

	Launched	*Commissioned*
U1007	8 Dec 1943	18 Jan 1944
Class	Type VIIC/41	
CO	*Kapitänleutnant* Ernst von Witzendorf (survived)	
Date of loss	2 May 1945	
Location	Baltic, off Lübeck, 53°54'N 11°28'E	
Cause	Air attack	
Casualties	1	
Survivors	48	
Salvaged	Yes	

Notes Sunk with cannon and rocket fire by Typhoon aircraft of No 245 Squadron. Five pairs of rockets were fired, which struck the U-boat in the stern, blowing a large hole in the pressure hull. Witzendorf managed to beach the boat so that he and his crew could get ashore. The wreck was raised and broken up in June 1946.

	Launched	*Commissioned*
U2359	23 Dec 1944	16 Feb (?) 1945
Class	Type XXIII	
CO	*Oberleutnant zur See* G Bischoff	
Date of loss	2 May 1945	
Location	Kattegat	
Cause	Air attack	
Casualties	12	
Survivors	2	
Salvaged	No	

Notes Thirty-five Mosquito aircraft of the Banff Wing (Nos 143, 248, 235, 333 and 404 Squadrons, with Mustang fighter escort), led by Sqn Ldr A. G. Deck RAF, were flying an anti-U-boat patrol in the Kattegat when they sighted two Type XXIII boats on the surface escorted by a minesweeper. The first boat was attacked and badly damaged by rocket fire. The second boat, *U2359*, was attacked by two 'Mossies' of No 143 Squadron and sustained at least two rocket hits. Aircraft from No 235 Squadron also attacked with rockets, scoring at least eight and possibly as many as sixteen hits. The submarine was then seen to sink, leaving oil, wreckage and survivors on the surface.

	Launched	*Commissioned*
U2503	29 Jun 1944	1 Aug 1944
Class	Type XXI	
CO	*Kapitänleutnant* Karljung Wachter (lost)	
Date of loss	3 May 1945	
Location	Baltic, N of Fyn Islands, 55°37'N 10°00'E	
Cause	Air attack/scuttling	
Casualties	13	
Survivors	?	
Salvaged	No	

Notes Sunk by a Beaufighter strike wing consisting of thirteen aircraft from No 236 Squadron and seventeen from No 254 Squadron, led by Wg Cdr E. P. Hutton DFC. At 1720 *U2503* was attacked by five of No 236's aircraft with rockets and six of No 254's with cannon. The boat caught fire and burned fiercely before exploding, leaving survivors in the water. In fact one rocket went straight through the conning tower hatch and exploded in the control room. Out of control, the boat ran aground and was abandoned.

U1210

	Launched	*Commissioned*
	9 Feb 1944	22 Apr 1944

Class Type VIIC
CO *Kapitänleutnant* Paul Grabert
Date of loss 3 May 1945
Location Kiel, Eckernförde Bay, 54°28'N 09°34'E
Cause Air attack
Casualties ?
Survivors ?
Salvaged No
Notes See entry for *U3032*.

U2540

	Launched	*Commissioned*
	13 Jan 1945	24 Feb 1945

Class Type XXI
CO *Oberleutnant zur See* Rudolf Schulz
Date of loss 3 May 1945
Location Great Belt, off Flensburg
Cause Air attack/scuttling
Casualties None
Survivors 57
Salvaged Yes
Notes See entry for *U3032*. The boat was raised in 1947 and recommissioned into the *Bundesmarine* as *Wilhelm Bauer* on 1 September 1960. She served as an experimental vessel first with a naval crew and then, after a virtual reconstruction, with a civilian crew for Trials Command 71. She was finally paid off on 15 March 1982 and is now preserved as a museum vessel in Bremen.

U3030

	Launched	*Commissioned*
	31 Dec 1944	14 Feb 1945

Class Type XXI
CO *Oberleutnant zur See* Reinhard Luttmann
Date of loss 3 May 1945
Location Baltic, E of Frederica, 55°30'N 10°00'E
Cause Air attack
Casualties ?
Survivors ?
Salvaged No
Notes See entry for *U3032*.

U3032

	Launched	*Commissioned*
	10 Jan 1945	12 Feb 1945

Class Type XXI
CO *Oberleutnant zur See* Horst Sievogt
Date of loss 3 May 1945
Location Baltic E of Frederica, 55°30'N 10°00'E
Cause Air attack
Casualties ?
Survivors ?
Salvaged No
Notes At the same time as the Strike Wings of No 16 Group were operating in and around the Kattegat, Typhoon aircraft of Nos 175, 184 and 245 Squadrons swept through the Kiel Bay/Eckernförde/Lübeck area and claimed three U-boats sunk and two damaged. *U1210*, *U2540*, *U3030* and *U3032* were victims of these attacks.

U2524

	Launched	*Commissioned*
	30 Oct 1944	9 Jan 1945

Class Type XXI
CO *Kapitänleutnant* Ernst von Witzendorf
Date of loss 3 May 1945
Location Baltic, E of Samsø
Cause Air attack
Casualties 2
Survivors ?
Salvaged No
Notes Thirteen Beaufighters of No 236 Squadron and seventeen from No 254 Squadron, led by Wg Cdr E. P. Hutton DFC, were on an anti-shipping strike escorted by Mustang fighters of Nos 65 and 118 Squadrons. *U2524* was sighted on the surface at 1720 and attacked by five Beaufighters of No 236 with rockets and by six from No 254 with cannon. The boat was left burning fiercely on the surface before she exploded. A number of survivors and a good deal of wreckage were left in the water.

U3028

	Launched	*Commissioned*
	22 Dec 1944	27 Jan 1945

Class Type XXI

CO	*Kapitänleutnant* Erwin Christopherson (lost)
Date of loss	3 May 1945
Location	Great Belt, exact location unknown
Cause	Air attack
Casualties	57
Survivors	None
Salvaged	No

Notes Sunk in an air attack by RAF aircraft. The exact circumstances of the loss are unknown.

U711

	Launched	*Commissioned*
U711	25 Jun 1942	26 Sept 1942
Class	Type VIIC	
CO	*Oberleutnant zur See* Wilhelm Lange	
Date of loss	4 May 1945	
Location	Arctic, off Harstad, 68°43'N 16°35'E	
Cause	Air attack	
Casualties	32	
Survivors	None	
Salvaged	No	

Notes *U711* was lying alongside the depot ship *Black Watch* at Harstad in Norway when she was sunk by Avenger/Wildcat teams of 846, 853 and 882 NAS operating from the escort carriers *Queen*, *Searcher* and *Trumpeter*. The carriers were on a sweep off Norway to destroy the bases and depot ships of the German Arctic U-boat Flotilla. *Black Watch* was their target and *U711* was a bonus. This was the last sinking of a U-boat by the Fleet Air Arm.

U236

	Launched	*Commissioned*
U236	24 Nov 1942	9 Jan 1943
Class	Type VIIC (non-operational: fitted out as repair boat)	
CO	*Oberleutnant zur See* Herbert Munn	
Date of loss	4 May 1945	
Location	Baltic, N of Fyn Islands, 54°37'N 10°03'E	
Cause	Air attack/scuttling	
Casualties	?	
Survivors	?	
Salvaged	No	

Notes See entry for *U2338* for details of this boat's loss.

U393

	Launched	*Commissioned*
U393	15 May 1943	3 Jul 1943
Class	Type VIIC	
CO	*Oberleutnant zur See* Friedrich Herrle	
Date of loss	4 May 1945	
Location	Baltic, N of Fyn Islands, 55°37'N 10°00'E	
Cause	Air attack	
Casualties	2	
Survivors	?	
Salvaged	No	

Notes See entry for *U2338* for details of this boat's loss.

U2338

	Launched	*Commissioned*
U2338	18 Sept 1944	9 Oct 1944
Class	Type XXIII	
CO	*Oberleutnant zur See* Karl Kaiser	
Date of loss	4 May 1945	
Location	Baltic N of Fyn Islands, 55°34'N 09°49'E	
Cause	Air attack	
Casualties	12	
Survivors	2	
Salvaged	Yes	

Notes *U236*, *U393* and *U2338* were caught on the surface by a Beaufighter Strike Wing made up of twelve aircraft of No 236 Squadron and ten from No 254 Squadron. All three U-boats were subjected to repeated cannon and rocket attacks and were sunk. Fortunately they were sunk so close to land that the majority of their crews survived. The wreck of *U2338* was raised in 1952 and broken up.

U534

	Launched	*Commissioned*
U534	23 Sept 1942	23 Dec 1942
Class	Type IXC/40	
CO	*Kapitänleutnant* Herbert Nollau (survived)	
Date of loss	5 May 1945	
Location	Kattegat, N of Helsingør, 56°39N 11°48'E	
Cause	Air attack	
Casualties	2	
Survivors	50	
Salvaged	Yes (see notes)	

Notes *U534* had spent most of her operational life on weather-reporting duties. Her last voyage was to take urgently needed spare parts and supplies to the U-boat flotillas concentrating in Norwegian ports. She, in company with two other boats, was attacked by Liberator 'E' of No 547 Squadron, which was shot down. Liberator 'G' of No 86 Squadron, flown by WO J. D. Nicol, then made two attack runs through fierce flak and dropped a total of ten depth charges. The submarine was afterwards seen sinking by the stern, leaving men, wreckage and oil on the water.

The wreck was raised by a Danish consortium in August 1993 amid considerable press speculation that the boat contained bullion, works of art and documentation which was was being shipped to Norway in preparation for the establishment of a 'National Redoubt'. However when the boat was opened up she was found to contain nothing more than an above average quantity of spare parts and tinned food and a large supply of condoms. At the time of writing (February 1997) plans exist to display the submarine permanently in Birkenhead.

U579	*Launched* 28 May 1941	*Commissioned* 17 Jul 1941
Class	Type VIIC	
CO	*Oberleutnant zur See* Hans-Dietrich Schwarzenburg (lost)	
Date of loss	5 May 1945	
Location	Baltic, Little Belt, 56°11'N 11°08'E	
Cause	Air attack	
Casualties	24	
Survivors	25	
Salvaged	No	

Notes *U579* had been severely damaged in a dockyard fire on 9 October 1941 and had been paid off. However, in May 1942 she was recommissioned, initially for training duties but eventually as a *Frontboot*. Liberator 'K' of No 547 Squadron, flown by Fg Off A. Bruneau RCAF, attacked and sank *U579*. After the depth charges had exploded the rear gunner reported that the U-boat had broken in half and sunk, leaving a mass of wreckage on the surface.

The boat was originally assessed as having been sunk by Liberator 'T' of No 224 Squadron, but this attack was made on *U1008*, which was damaged.

U2367	*Launched* 23 Feb 1945	*Commissioned* 17 Mar 1945
Class	Type XXIII	
CO	*Leutnant zur See* Heinz Schroder	
Date of loss	5 May 1945	
Location	Baltic, Great Belt, 55°00'N 11°00'E	
Cause	Collision	
Casualties	?	
Survivors	?	
Salvaged	Yes (see notes)	

Notes *U2367* sank following a collision with an unidentified U-boat. She was raised in 1956 and recommissioned in the *Bundesmarine* as *Hecht*. Non-operational, she was used as a systems and weapons trials submarine for the new Type 206 U-boats. She was sold for breaking up in 1969.

U2365	*Launched* 26 Jan 1945	*Commissioned* 2 Feb 1945
Class	Type XXIII	
CO	*Oberleutnant zur See* Fritz-Otto Korfmann	
Date of loss	5 May 1945	
Location	Kattegat, 50°51'N 11°49'E	
Cause	Air attack	
Casualties	None	
Survivors	14	
Salvaged	Yes (see notes)	

Notes *U2365* was damaged in an attack by Liberator 'S' of No 224 Squadron, flown by Flt Lt J. C. Downey DFC, so much so that Korfmann had to scuttle the boat. She was raised in 1956, renamed *Hai* and used for weapons and systems trials for the Type 206 submarines. She foundered with the loss of nineteen of her crew in bad weather on 14 September 1966.

U2521	*Launched* 18 Oct 1944	*Commissioned* 31 Dec 1944
Class	Type XXI	
CO	*Oberleutnant zur See* Joachim Methner (lost)	
Date of loss	5 May 1945	
Location	Baltic, SE of Aarhus	
Cause	Air attack	
Casualties	11	
Survivors	46	
Salvaged	No	

Notes Sunk in an air attack by aircraft 'K' of No 547 Squadron RAF

U3523	*Launched*	*Commissioned*
	14 Dec 1944	29 Jan 1945

Class Type XXI
CO *Oberleutnant zur See* Werner 'Willy' Müller (lost)
Date of loss 6 May 1945
Location Baltic, SE of Aarhus, 56°06'N 11°08'E
Cause Air attack
Casualties 57
Survivors 8
Salvaged No

Notes Sunk in an air attack by Liberator 'G' of No 86 Squadron RAF. The aircraft, flown by Flt Lt T. H. Goldie DFC made an attack on a periscope and snorkel mast. The explosion of six depth charges blew the U-boat to the surface, where her conning tower was seen by the aircrew. Debris was thrown into the air and much wreckage and oil was left on the water.

U853	*Launched*	*Commissioned*
	11 Mar 1943	25 Jun 1943

Class Type IXC/40
CO *Oberleutnant zur See* Helmut Fromsdorf (lost)
Date of loss 6 May 1945
Location W Atlantic, off Long Island
Cause Hedgehog
Casualties 55
Survivors None
Salvaged No

Notes At 1740 on 5 May 1945 the collier *Black Prince* was torpedoed and sunk off Nantucket. A subsequent sighting of the U-boat by the SS *Kamen* enabled the Commander Eastern Sea Frontier to put together a scratch 'hunter-killer' group. One hour and forty minutes after the sinking of the *Black Prince* Lt-Cdr L. B. Tollaksen in the USS *Moberly* was on the scene and assumed tactical command of the DEs *Atherton* and *Amick*. Within fifteen minutes *Atherton* was in sonar contact and delivered a series of depth-charge and Hedgehog attacks. However, the shallow water made it difficult to tell if the detonations were the Hedgehogs hitting the U-boat or striking the sea bed. The target remained stopped and on the bottom, and after one attack at 2337 oil was seen coming to the surface. The pounding of the bottomed wreck continued all night and resumed on 6 May. At noon sufficient evidence had been recovered, including Fromsdorf's cap with its white cover and the chart table, to say with certainty that the submarine was dead. Subsequent examination of the wreck by divers confirmed this claim, and the identity of the boat.

U881	*Launched*	*Commissioned*
	4 Mar 1944	27 Aug 1944

Class Type IXC/40
CO *Kapitänleutnant* Dr Heinz Frische (lost)
Date of loss 6 May 1945
Location Atlantic, SE of Cape Race, 43°18'N 47°44'W
Cause Depth charge
Casualties 53
Survivors None
Salvaged No

Notes Depth-charged by the USS *Farquar* shortly after the sinking of *U853*. *U881* was the last U-boat to be sunk by the US Navy during the Second World War.

U1008	*Launched*	*Commissioned*
	8 Dec 1943	1 Feb 1944

Class Type VIIC/41
CO *Oberleutnant zur See* Hans Gressner (survived)
Date of loss 6 May 1945
Location Skagerrak, 56°22'N 11°10'E
Cause Air attack/scuttling
Casualties None
Survivors 49
Salvaged No

Notes *U1008* was seriously damaged in an attack by Liberator 'K' of No 86 Squadron RAF. The damage was such that Gressner decided to scuttle her.

U2534	*Launched*	*Commissioned*
	11 Dec 1944	17 Jan 1945

Class Type XXI
CO *Kapitänleutnant* Ulrich Drews (lost)
Date of loss 6 May 1945

Location	Baltic, Kattegat, 57°08'N 11°52'E	
Cause	Air attack	
Casualties	1	
Survivors	56	
Salvaged	No	

Notes Sunk in an attack by Liberator 'K' of No 86 Squadron RAF.

	Launched	*Commissioned*
U320	6 Nov 1943	30 Dec 1943
Class	Type VIIC/41	
CO	*Oberleutnant zur See* Heinz Emmerich (survived)	
Date of loss	7 May 1945	
Location	Norwegian Sea, W of Bergen, 61°32'N 01°53'E	
Cause	Air attack	
Casualties	None	
Survivors	50	
Salvaged	No	

Notes The last U-boat to be sunk by direct action during the Second World War. *U320* was dived when she was attacked at 0445 by Catalina 'X' of No 210 Squadron, flown by Flt Lt K. M. Murray, who had spotted her periscope and snorkel. Four depth charges were dropped, after which oil was seen on the surface. A pattern of sonobuoys was dropped which recorded hammering noises as if the crew were trying to effect repairs. At 1410 hammering noises were still audible, but since the Catalina had reached PLE it had to depart. Two days later Emmerich brought his battered boat to the surface off the Norwegian coast, where he scuttled her.

	Launched	*Commissioned*
U3503	27 Sept 1944	9 Sept 1944
Class	Type XXI	
CO	*Oberleutnant zur See* Hugo Deiring	
Date of loss	8 May 1945	
Location	Baltic, off Gothenburg	
Cause	Air attack/scuttling	
Casualties	?	
Survivors	?	
Salvaged	Yes	

Notes On 6 May *U3503* was attacked and damaged by Liberator 'K' of No 86 Squadron. The submarine sustained such damage that she was incapable of carrying on with her voyage and, uncertain of the situation in Germany (that is, whether or not the Red Army would be in Kiel), Deiring scuttled the boat on the 8th and he and his crew sought internment in Sweden. The wreck was raised in 1946 and broken up.

	Launched	*Commissioned*
U2538	6 Jan 1945	16 Feb 1945
Class	Type XXI	
CO	*Oberleutnant zur See* Heinrich Klapdor (survived)	
Date of loss	9 May 1945	
Location	Off Marstal, SW of Aerö Island, 54°34'N 10°16'E	
Cause	Mine	
Casualties	?	
Survivors	?	
Salvaged	No	

Notes Despite the damage, Klapdor managed to drive the boat ashore, where she was abandoned. The wreck was broken up *in situ* in 1975.

At 2301 on 8 May 1945 the surrender of all German sea, land and air forces came into effect. The document had been signed at the headquarters of General Dwight D. Eisenhower. U-boats at sea were to surrender themselves to the nearest Allied forces and fly a large black flag for ease of recognition. Plans existed for the scuttling of U-boats in port in the event of a capitulation. The code-word for this operation was 'Regenbogen' (Rainbow). In the event the scuttling or destruction of submarines in port or under construction was specifically prohibited by the terms of the surrender.

However, many U-boat commanders could not simply hand their boats over without some last gesture. They argued that the non-destruction clauses of the surrender had been agreed to by Admiral Dönitz under duress (which was correct, up to a point) and therefore they were not bound by the decision. As *Korvettenkapitän* Peter 'Ali' Cremer, the successful commander of *U333* and commander of the new Type XXI *U2519*, said when asked for instructions by his 1WO, 'Ali Cremer does not show a white flag and does not surrender his boat—so scuttle it!' Dönitz had to show outward disapproval, but he privately supported his commanders' decision. Accordingly

218 boats were wrecked or scuttled on the surrender.

Some commanders were more resourceful. *Kapitänleutnant* Ehrenreich Stever scuttled *U1277* three miles north of Leixoes on the Portuguese coast and opted for internment to avoid surrender. *Oberleutnant zur See* Otto Wermuth took *U530* to Argentina, where she arrived on 10 July, to be joined by *U977* (*Oberleutnant zur See* Heinz Schaeffer) which arrived on 25 August. The remaining 154 boats in German and Norwegian ports were surrendered. A small number of these were retained for trials or as war booty, but the majority were sunk in Operation 'Deadlight' (December 1945–January 1946), a mass scuttling of U-boats in deep water to the north of Northern Ireland.

Glossary

ACI Atlantic Convoy Instructions.
ACNS Assistant Chief of the Naval Staff.
A/S Anti-Submarine.
ASCO Anti-Submarine Control Officer. The officer in a British or Canadian ship responsible for the working of the ship's anti-submarine weapons and equipment and the provision of the appropriate tactical advice to the command.
Asdic British term for underwater acoustic detection equipment coined during the First World War. The US equivalent was sonar. In this book 'asdic' is used in its Anglo-Canadian context and 'sonar' in reference to the US Navy.
ASV Air to Surface Vessel (radar).
ASW Anti-Submarine Warfare.
B group British escort group of MOEF (q.v.).
BdU *Befehlshaber der U-boote* = Commander-in-Chief U-boats. This was the appointment held by Karl Dönitz from October 1939 when he was promoted Rear-Admiral.
Bold See SBT.
BT Bathythermography.
C group Canadian group of MOEF (q.v.).
CAT Canadian anti-acoustic torpedo gear.
CinC Commander-in-Chief.
CMB Coastal Motor Boat.
Creeping (attack) Anti-U-boat tactic designed to confuse the U-boat about the direction from which the attack was coming. Because depth charges had to be dropped over the stern, U-boats learned to recognise the moment when the attacking ship had steadied on the final run in and then conduct violent alterations of course and depth. In the creeping attack one ship maintained constant asdic contact with the U-boat, while another, directed by the first and proceeding at dead slow and with her asdic switched off, ran over the U-boat and delivered the attack.
CVE Escort or auxiliary aircraft carrier.
Depth charge The principle anti-submarine weapon in both world wars. It comprised a cylinder filled with explosive (TNT, later replaced by Torpex) and fitted with a hydrostatic fuse so that the weapon would explode at a preset depth. Depth charges were dropped over the stern or they could be fired to port or starboard from depth-charge throwers. Lightweight depth charges were developed for use by aircraft.
DF Direction-finding.
DFC Distinguished Flying Cross. A British aircrew decoration.
Dräger (apparatus) Escape gear issued to U-boat crews. Could also be used as a respirator.
DSO Distinguished Service Order. A British decoration given to unit commanders for significant achievements in battle. In the early stages of the war the commanding officer of a ship or submarine sinking a U-boat could expect a DSO for the achievement. Later in the war, when U-boat sinkings were more common, the Admiralty was not so generous.
EG Escort group.
FdU *Führer der U-boote* = Senior Officer U-boats. This was the appointment held by Karl Dönitz before his promotion to flag rank in October 1939. It could also be used in a local context; for example, *FdU Mittelmeer* = Senior Officer U-boats Mediterranean.
Fido US-designed acoustic torpedo dropped by aircraft against submarines. For security reasons the weapon was known as the Mk XXIV Mine.
Fg Off Flying Officer.
Foxer British and American anti-acoustic torpedo gear.
Gefuffle Term used to describe the water disturbance produced by the exhaust of a snorkelling submarine.
Gnat British/American term for the German Navy acoustic torpedo. In German terminol-

ogy this torpedo was referred to as a T5 or *Zaunkönig*.
HE Hydrophone effect: listening using an asdic set in the passive mode.
Hedgehog British-designed weapon fitted in British and US escorts. The weapon fired ahead of the ship and thus asdic contact was not lost as in a depth-charge attack when the attacking ship had to pass over the target before dropping the charges. Hedgehog bombs were fitted with contact fuses: an explosion meant a hit and thus results were easy to assess. A smaller version of Hedgehog, known as Mousetrap, was fitted in small USN A/S craft.
HF/DF High-frequency direction-finding.
Leigh Light An 80 million-candlepower light fitted in RAF Coastal Command aircraft (the US variant built on the British pattern was the L7) and used to illuminate a submarine on the surface once the first contact (by eye or radar) had been made.
HX Code for fast eastbound Atlantic convoy.
KL Kapitänleutnant = German naval rank equvalent to Lieutenant-Commander.
LI *Leutnant Ingenieur*, the engineer officer in a German U-boat. Unlike his counterpart in the Royal and US Navies, the LI played a central role in the working of the submarine. He was responsible for ballasting and depth-keeping, as well as all aspects of the boat's machinery, and he was stationed in the control room.
MAC Merchant aircraft carrier.
MAD Magnetic Anomaly Detector. The apparatus used for the detection of submarines from an aircraft using variations in the earth's magnetic field created by the submarine.
MF/DF Medium-frequency direction-finding.
ML Motor launch.
MOEF Mid Ocean Escort Force.
NAS Naval Air Squadron.
NEF Newfoundland Escort Force.
Non Sub Term used to classify an asdic contact that was not a submarine. It could be a wreck, a shoal of fish or a whale. In the English Channel it was estimated that there was one 'Non Sub' every one and a half miles.
OIC Operational Intelligence Centre.
ON Code for fast westbound Atlantic convoy.
ONS Code for slow westbound Atlantic convoy.
OTU Operational Training Unit.
Pillenwerfer 'Pill Thrower' tube through which Bold canisters were ejected.
PLE Prudent limit of endurance.
PNM Pipe Noise Maker.
PO Petty Officer (RN).
P Off Pilot Officer (RAF).
Obersteuermann German naval rating of warrant rank who carried out the duties of navigating officer in a U-boat. There is no equivalent rank in the Royal or US Navies
RAAF Royal Australian Air Force.
RAN Royal Australian Navy.
RAF Royal Air Force.
RCAF Royal Candian Air Force.
RCN Royal Canadian Navy.
RCNR Royal Canadian Navy Reserve.
RCNVR Royal Canadian Navy Volunteer Reserve.
RDF Radio Direction Finding (British term for radar).
Retro-bomb Anti-submarine weapon designed for use with MAD. The accurate position of a submarine detected by MAD could only be determined when the aircraft was directly overhead. Conventional air-dropped weapons, if launched at this point, would have the forward velocity of the aircraft and thus fall some way ahead of the target. The retro-bomb was given reverse velocity, by means of a rocket, equal to that of the forward velocity of the aircraft.
RN Royal Navy.
RNZAF Royal New Zealand Air Force.
RP Rocket projectile.
SA Small arms.
Salmon Joint naval and air hunt to exhaustion for a U-boat.
SBT Submarine Bubble Target. Known by the Germans as Bold, these were canisters containing 370gm of a compound of calcium and zinc which when released into water produced hydrogen bubbles. A bold canister could operate for as long as 25 minutes, giving an echo similar to that of a U-boat.
SC Code for slow eastbound Atlantic convoy.
Snorkel (German *Schnorchel*) A mast containing air induction and exhaust pipes which allowed a U-boat to use diesel engines when dived.
S*KL Seekriegsleitung* = German Naval High Command.
SO Senior Officer.

SOE Senior Officer of the Escort.
Sonobuoy A passive hydrophone dropped by an aircraft to radio information back to the aircraft. When the buoy hit the water it deployed a hydrophone dangling on 21ft of cable while at the same time activating a wireless transmitter so that any sounds picked up by the hydrophone would be relayed to the aircraft.
Sqn Ldr Squadron Leader (RAF).
Squid British designed three-barrelled ahead-throwing weapon fitted in British and American escorts.
SST Underwater acoustic telephone.
Supermarina Italian Naval High Command.
TG Task Group.
Thief Device for taking oil samples from the water.
'Tin Opener' Depth-charge attack designed to open up the hull of a stopped and bottomed U-boat, allowing the release of evidence, preferably human remains, which would confirm that the boat had been sunk.
TU Task Unit.
Tunis German radar warning receiver.
USCG United States Coast Guard.
USN United States Navy.
VLR Very long range (aircraft).
WAC Western Approaches Command.
Wg Cdr Wing Commander (RAF).
WO (German) *Wachoffizier* = Watch Officer. Term used for commissioned officers in a U-boat excluding the commanding officer and the LI. The first WO (1WO) was responsible for the torpedo armament while the second WO (2WO) was responsible for the flak armament. (British) Warrant Officer (RAF).
xB-Dienst The signals intelligence service of the German Navy.

Bibliography

1914–1918 Period: Official Works Unpublished

Admiralty: *Chronological List of German U-Boats Sunk in the First World War 1914–1918*
Technical History Section Admiralty. A collection of fifty monographs of which the most valuable are:
TH 1: *Submarine v. Submarine*
TH 4: *Aircraft v. Submarine. Submarine Campaign 1918*
TH 7: *The Anti-Submarine Division of the Naval Staff*
TH 40: *Anti-Submarine Development and Experiments Prior to December 1916*
Naval Staff Studies:
Anti-Submarine Division Monthly Reports, May 1917–November 1918
RNAS Anti Submarine Reports, June 1917–March 1918, continued in *Air Division Naval Air Operations Monthly Reports*, April–October 1918

1914–1918 Period: Official Works Published

Corbett, Sir Julian S., and Newbolt, Sir Henry, *History of the Great War: Naval Operations*, 5 vols (London: Longman, 1920–1931)
Fayle, C. E., *History of the Great War: Seaborne Trade*, 3 vols (London: Murray, 1920–1924)
Spindler, Admiral Arno, *Der Krieg zur See 1914-1918: Der Handelskrieg mit U-booten*, 5 vols (Berlin: Mittler, 1932–1966)

1914–1918 Period: Secondary Sources

* *Indicates that the book is of additional relevance for the 1939–1945 period*

Admiralty, *German Warships of World War One* (London: Greenhill Books, 1992)
Aichelburg, W., *Die Unterseeboote Österreich-Ungarns*, 2 vols (Graz: Akademische Druck u Verlagsanstalt, 1981)
Bacon, Admiral Sir Reginald, *The Dover Patrol*, 2 vols (London: Hutchinson, 1919)
Belknap, R. R., *The Yankee Mining Squadron* (Annapolis: 1920)
Bywater, H., *Their Secret Purposes* (London: 1932)
Campbell, G., *My Mystery Ships* (London: Hodder & Stoughton, 1928)
Chatterton, E. K., *Beating the U-Boats* (London: 1943)
Dönitz K., *10 Jahre und 20 Tage* (Frankfurt: Athenaum, 1958) *
Dorling, T., *Swept Channels* (London: 1935)
Edwards, K., *We Dive at Dawn* (London: Rich & Cowan, 1939)
Gayer, A., *Die deutschen U-boote in ihrer Kriegführung 1914–1918* (Berlin: Mittler, 1930)
Gibson, R. H., and Prendergast, M., *The German Submarine War 1914–1918* (London: Constable, 1931)

Grant, R. M., 'Known Sunk: German Warship Losses 1914–1918', USNI *Proceedings*, vol, 64 (1938), pp. 66–77
———, *U-Boat Intelligence 1914–1918* (London: Putnam, 1969)
———, *U-Boats Destroyed* (London: Putnam, 1964)
Gray, E., *Few Survived: A History of Submarine Disasters* (London: Leo Cooper, 1986) *
Gröner, E., *German Warships*, vol, 2 (London: Conway Maritime Press) *
Hackmann, W., *Seek and Strike: Sonar, Anti-Submarine Warfare and the Royal Navy 1914–1954* (London: HMSO, 1984) *
Hashagen, Ernst, *The Log of a U-Boat Commander* (London: Putnam, 1931)
Hoy H. C., *40 OB, or How the War was Won* (London: 1932)
James, Admiral Sir William, *The Codebreakers of Room 40* (New York: 1956)
Keyes, Admiral Sir Roger, *Naval Memoirs. Vol. 2: From Scapa Flow to the Dover Straits* (New York: 1935)
Padfield, P., *Dönitz, The Last Führer* (London: Gollancz, 1984) *
Price, A., *Aircraft vs Submarine* (London: William Kimber, 1973) *
Sokol, H. H., *Österreich Ungarns Seekrieg 1914–1918*, 2 vols (Graz: Akademische Druck u Verlagsanstalt, 1967)
Tarrant, V. E., *The U-Boat Offensive 1914–1945* (London: Arms & Armour Press, 1989) *
Terraine, J., *Business in Great Waters: The U-Boat Wars 1916–1945* (London: Leo Cooper, 1989) *
Thetford, O., *British Naval Aircraft since 1912* (London: Putnam, 1977) *

1939–1945 Period: Primary Sources

Public Record Office, London:
Relevant Reports of Proceedings of HM Ships and Submarines together with appropriate RAF Squadron Operational Record Books
Admiralty: Anti-Submarine Warfare Division, *Monthly Anti-Submarine Reports*, September 1939–December 1945
Admiralty: *Monthly Intelligence Reports 1939–1945* and *Weekly Intelligence Reports 1939–1945*
Admiralty: Naval Staff, Operations Division, *Daily Summary of Naval Events*

Naval Historical Branch, Ministry of Defence, London:
U-Boat Loss Assessements
BdU War Diary

Naval Historical Center, Washington DC:
US Navy, *Anti Submarine Bulletin, 'Yellow Peril'*, June 1943–May 1945
German U-Boats from which Prisoners were taken during Hostilities by British and American Forces, nd, GNR Box T-76

1939–1945 Period: Official Histories and Monographs

Admiralty: Naval Staff History of the Second World War, *Submarines Vol. 2: Operations in the Mediterranean* (London, 1955)
———, *Submarines Vol. 3: Operations in Far Eastern Waters* (London 1956)
———, *Battle Summary No 22: Arctic Convoys 1941–1945* (CB 3305[4]) (London: 1954)
———, *Submarines Vol. 1: Operations in Home, Northern and Atlantic Waters* (London: 1953)
Admiralty, *German, Italian and Japanese U-Boat Casualties during the War* (London: HMSO, 1946)
———, *Preliminary Narrative of the War at Sea* (BR 1738), 6 vols (London: 1944 onwards)

Hessler, G., *The U-Boat War in the Atlantic* (London: HMSO, 1989)
Hinsley, F. H., Thomas E. E., et al, *British Intelligence in the Second World War: Its Influence on Strategy and Operation* (London: HMSO, 1979–1988)
Law Reports of Trials of War Criminals, vol 1., *The Peleus Case* (London: HMSO, 1947)
Roskill S.W., *The War at Sea 1939–1945*, 4 vols (London: HMSO, 1954–1961)
Schull, J., *The Far Distant Ships* (Ottawa: Ministry of National Defence, 1961)
Sternhall, C. M., and Thorndike, A. M., *Antisubmarine Warfare in World War Two* (Operational Evaluation Group Report No 51) (Washington: 1946)

1939–1945 Period: Secondary Sources

Adams T. A., and Lees, D. J. *Register of Type VII U-Boats* (World Ship Society, 1991)
Barnett, C., *Engage the Enemy More Closely: The Royal Navy in the Second World War* (London: Hodder & Stoughton, 1991)
Beesely, P., *Very Special Intelligence* (London: Hamish Hamilton, 1977)
Burn, A., *The Fighting Captain* (London: Leo Cooper 1993)
Chalmers, W. S., *Max Horton and Western Approaches* (London: Hodder & Stoughton, 1954)
Compton-Hall, R., *Submarine vs Submarine: The Tactics and Technology of Underwater Confrontation* (London: Grubb Street, 1988)
———, *The Underwater War 1939–1945* (Poole: Blandford Press, 1982)
Compton-Hall, R., and Moore, J. E., *Submarine Warfare Today and Tomorrow* (London: Michael Joseph, 1983)
Cremer, P., *U-Boat Commander: A Periscope View of the Battle of the Atlantic* (Oxford: Bodley Head, 1984)
Farago, Ladislas, *The Tenth Fleet* (New York: Obolensky, 1962)
Franks, N., *Conflict over the Bay* (London: 1986)
———, *Search, Find and Kill: The RAF's U-Boat Successes in WW2* (London: Grubb Street, 1995)
Gallery, D.V., *Clear the Decks!* (New York: Warner, 1951)
———, *Twenty Million Tons Under the Sea* (Chicago: Regnery, 1956)
Geise, O., and Wise, J. E., *Shooting the War: Memoirs of a WW2 U-Boat Officer* (Annapolis: US Naval Institute, 1994)
Goulter, Christina, 'The Forgotten Offensive: Royal Air Force Coastal Command's Anti-Shipping Offensive, 1940–1945', unpublished PhD thesis (University of London, 1993)
Gretton, Vice-Admiral Sir Peter, *Convoy Escort Commander* (London: Cassell, 1964)
———, *Crisis Convoy* (London: Peter Davies, 1974)
Hague, A., and Ruegg, R., *Convoys to Russia, 1941–1945* (World Ship Society, 1992)
Hinsley, F. H., and Stripp, A., *Codebreakers: The Inside Story of Bletchley Park* (Oxford: OUP, 1993)
Howse, D., *Radar at Sea*, 3 vols (London: Macmillan/Naval Radar Trust, 1993)
Johnson, B., *The Secret War* (London: BBC Books, 1978)
Jones, G., *Submarine vs U-Boat* (London: William Kimber, 1986)
Kahn, D., *Seizing the Enigma* (Boston: Houghton Mifflin, 1991)
Kemp, P., *Friend or Foe: Friendly Fire at Sea 1939–1945* (London: Leo Cooper, 1994)
———, *The T Class Submarine* (London: Arms & Armour Press, 1990)
Lewin, R., *Ultra Goes to War* (London: Hutchinson, 1978)
Macintyre, D., *U-Boat Killer* (London: Weidenfeld and Nicolson, 1958)
Mallmann Showell J. P., *U-Boat Command and the Battle of the Atlantic* (London: Conway Maritime Press, 1989)
Middlebrook, M., *Convoy: The Battle for SC.122 and HX.229* (London: Allen Lane, 1976)
Milner, M., *North Atlantic Run: The Royal Canadian Navy and the Battle for the Convoys* (Annapolis: Naval Insititute Press, 1985)
———, *The U-Boat Hunters* (Annapolis: Naval Institute Press, 1994)

Morison, S. E., *History of US Naval Operations in World War II; The Atlantic Battle Won, May 1943–May 1945* (Boston: Little, Brown, 1990)
Morsier, P. de., *Les Corvettes de France Libre* (Paris: Ed. France-Empire, 1972)
Padfield, P., *War Beneath the Sea* (London: John Murray, 1995)
Poolman, K., *HMS Vindex* (London: William Kimber, 1983)
Robertson, T., *The Golden Horseshoe* (London: Evans Bros, 1955)
———, *Walker RN* (London: Evans Bros, 1956)
Rohwer J., *Axis Submarine Successes 1939–1945* (Annapolis: Naval Institute Press, 1983)
———, *The Critical Convoy Battles of March 1943* (London: Ian Allen, 1977)
Rohwer J., and Hummelchen, G., *Chronology of the War at Sea* (London: Greenhill Books, 1992)
Roscoe, T., *United States Submarine Operations in World War II* (Annapolis: Naval Institute Press, 1988)
Roskill, S.W., *The Secret Capture: The Story of U110* (London: Collins, 1959)
Rossler, E., *The U-Boat: The Evolution and Technical History of German Submarines* (London: Arms & Armour Press, 1981)
Runyan T., and Copes, J. M., (eds), *To Die Gallantly: The Battle of the Atlantic* (San Francisco: Boulder Press, 1994)
Sainsbury, A., and Shrubb, R., *The Royal Navy Day by Day* (Centaur Press, 1979)
Schaeffer, H., *U-Boat 977* (London: William Kimber, 1952)
Schoenfeld, M., *Stalking the U-Boat: USAAF Offensive Anti-Submarine Operations in WW2* (Washington: Smithsonian, 1995)
Shelford, W. O., *Subsunk: The Story of Submarine Escape* (London: Harrap, 1960)
Simpson G.W. G., *Periscope View* (London: Macmillan, 1972)
Stern, R., *Type VII U-Boats* (London: Arms & Armour Press, 1991)
Syrett, D., *The Defeat of the German U-Boats* (Columbia: University of South Carolina Press, 1994)
Tarrant, V. E., *The Last Year of the Kriegsmarine* (London: Arms & Armour Press, 1994)
Thompson, J., *The Imperial War Museum Book of the War at Sea* (London: Sidgwick & Jackson, 1996)
Watts, A., *The U-Boat Hunters* (London: Macdonald & Jane's, 1976)
Wemyss, D. E. G., *Relentless Pursuit* (London: William Kimber, 1955)
Whinney, R., *The U-Boat Peril* (London: Blandford, 1987)
Wingate J., *The Fighting Tenth* (London: Leo Cooper, 1991)
Winton, J., *The Forgotten Fleet* (London: Michael Joseph, 1969)
———, *Ultra at Sea* (London: Leo Cooper, 1988)
Woodman, R., *Arctic Convoys* (London: John Murray, 1993)
Y'Blood, W.T., *Hunter Killer: US Escort Carriers in the Battle of the Atlantic* (Annapolis: Naval Institute Press, 1983)
Young, E., *One of Our Submarines* (London: Hart Davis, 1953)

Index of U-Boats

First World War, 1914–1918

Second World War, 1939–1945

Index of U-Boat Commanders

First World War, 1914–1918

Second World War, 1939–1945

General Index